Francis Mulhern

NLB

The Moment of 'Scrutiny'

NLB, 7 Carlisle Street, London W1

Typeset in Monotype Spectrum
and printed by
Western Printing Services Ltd, Bristol

Bound at Kemp Hall Bindery, Oxford

ISBN 86091 007 5

Contents

Preface

On April 14, 1978, F. R. Leavis died, and one of the longest and most controversial intellectual careers in England this century came to a close. It might be anticipated, then, that the nineteen-eighties will see a period of 'definitive' study, in which the man and the work will be chronicled, expounded and assessed with all the dispassionate thoroughness that the English academic mind can bring to bear on the objects of its attention. Yet there is good reason to doubt whether such a period is indeed ahead, whether the apparently natural laws that regulate academic impulse will hold good in this case. For above all others in modern English cultural history, the name of Leavis evoked asperity, dissension and bitter conflict – evoked and recharged them wherever it was mentioned. More than this, it symbolized antagonisms that invest the professional constitution of English-literary academic life at its deepest, least accessible levels. Many academic writers have defended Leavis's views; many more have reiterated them, wittingly or not, in countless variations; and still more have criticized him, on a scale of dissent ranging from journalistic aside to full-scale assault. But even the best products of the last category have been no more than partial; and none, in any category, could credibly claim to be a systematic reconstitution and assessment of Leavis's aesthetics, literary criticism and cultural analysis. There is no compelling reason why this well-established pattern should now be modified. It is scarcely to be expected that the fact of individual mortality will neutralize a presence which, formidable from the first, became controversial, notorious, then scandalous, and finally mythic.

Writers on the Left have been markedly more attentive than their liberal and conservative counterparts. Recognizing in Leavis's work a cultural argument of great weight and influence, expounded in an emphatically anti-Marxist spirit, they have produced critiques and counter-arguments of lasting value. Yet even here, nothing like a clear, comprehensive and authoritative position has been reached. If some theorists have engaged seriously and tenaciously with Leavis's ideas, others have assimilated them, sometimes quite defiantly, into their own work; and, among younger writers, his work is usually figured in the past perfect, to be inspected, if considered at all, from the far side of a theoretical gulf and, at all events, not a central issue today. This attitude is understandable but perilous. It may be logically unexceptionable to assume that contemporary Marxist literary and cultural theory shares no common substance with the ideological formation often known as 'Leavisism', but it is historically evasive and may, in the worst outcome, prove self-defeating. For what is forsworn, in this argument, is not merely a certain historiographical field, but an adequate understanding of the cultural present – of the dynamic forces that govern the circumstances of even the most radically 'alien' forms of Marxist theoretical work in England today. If 'Leavisism' still constitutes a 'problem' for the dominant culture, how can it have ceased to disturb the vulnerable, minoritarian exponents of Marxism? What is in question, now as much as in the far-off thirties, is a cultural *struggle*, to which the composed, self-sustaining practices of peaceful methodological competition will sooner or later prove fundamentally inadequate.

The case is still more paradoxical than these considerations suggest. For one of the main symptoms of the deficiencies in the discussion to date is precisely a persistent emphasis on the individual figure of F. R. Leavis. There are of course good reasons for the prominence accorded to him; but it must be recognized that this emphasis is *per se* a misconstruction of the problem of 'Leavisism'. It was not merely by force of personal intransigence and literary-critical rigorism that Leavis so disturbed the dominant literary culture of his time; and it was not merely by force of intellectual character and critical productivity that he became a pervasive influence among English literary intellectuals, teachers and journalists alike. The power of disturbance so often ascribed to his person was in reality that of a whole cultural current, and of the instrument that sustained and directed it: the quarterly journal of which Leavis was the chief editor for most of its two decades of existence. The true measure of the problem is that, twenty-five years after its closure and fifteen after its triumphant reissue, there exists not a single systematic examination of *Scrutiny*.

The present study is an attempt to begin such an examination. It sets out some elements of a critique of 'Leavisism' in combination with an effort to identify and explain the efficacy of one component of contemporary English culture. Historical in form, the book aims to analyse the conditions in which the journal came into being, the elaboration and modifications of its discourse over its life-time, the objective functions that it performed in the culture of mid-century England – and so, to define and assess what is called here the 'moment' of *Scrutiny*.

It will doubtless be noticed that the book lacks a systematic theoretical and methodological preamble of the kind that is now widely expected in Marxist studies. This was largely a matter of necessity. Few precedents exist for the study of a journal as such; it would quite evidently have been inadequate to construct a schema, by derivation and specification, from the existing conceptual resources of historical materialism; and it would just as evidently have been illegitimate to elicit one by induction from the investigation of a single case. However, the study was consciously carried out as a substantive exercise within historical materialism, and, given what has already been said, there is one central assumption that should be indicated here. The constant attempt in research and composition was to understand the journal in its material specificity: not as a serially published 'big book' but as a practice that unfolded in time, constituting a history that was specific to itself and at the same time bound to the other histories that made up mid-century English history as a whole; not as the 'expression' of a master-subject (Leavis) but as a play of many voices, within the ideological formation of which *Scrutiny* was the organizer and bearer. The main object of the book's three central parts, in short, is to trace the working of a discourse and its mutations in the successive politico-cultural conjunctures of its career.

Apart from these theoretical and methodological considerations (which are as much a matter for discussion as the substantive theses of the book) other, particular absences will be noted. The form of the study – monographic and historical – entailed the consequence that none of the issues raised by *Scrutiny* could be posed and pursued as if in 'independent' sub-discussions. The analyses of its aesthetics and literary criticism are manifestly incomplete; the wide range of questions now being debated among socialist teachers in England is scarcely echoed in the chapters on education; and the politically and culturally crucial problem of British Marxism in the thirties figures here *only* as it was perceived by *Scrutiny* itself. Another omission that should be mentioned is the music criticism of W. H. Mellers. One of the journal's most prolific contributors and for a time part of its editorial team, Mellers has received less recognition than any of his associates for his role in *Scrutiny*. If his writings on music have been mentioned only in passing here, it was for practical reasons of space and already over-strained authorial competence.

Finally, I have to thank those whose encouragement, help and co-operation alone brought the book to completion.

The doctoral research in which it originated was supervised from 1974 to 1977 by Professor Frank Kermode of King's College, Cambridge, and, during its final year, by Dr John Harvey of Emmanuel College. I am grateful to them both.

The Electors of the Robert Gardiner Memorial Scholarship, by their generosity, made it possible for me to continue full-time research in 1976–77.

Copyright material from *Scrutiny: A Quarterly Review* (reissued in Twenty Volumes with Index and a 'Retrospect' by F. R. Leavis) is reproduced here by permission of the Cambridge University Press.

I am grateful also to R. G. Cox, Boris Ford, L. C. Knights, the late F. R. Leavis, and Q. D. Leavis, who kindly agreed to talk to me about *Scrutiny*; and to D. W. Harding, Norman Podhoretz, Richard Poirier and Denys Thompson, with whom I had valuable correspondence.

It remains now to thank the friends and colleagues whose support, too extensive and too often demonstrated to be recalled with any acceptable degree of accuracy, was vital throughout. I mention only those who read my manuscripts in whole or in part: Perry Anderson, Anthony Barnett, Robin Blackburn, Quintin Hoare, Franco Moretti, Clara Mulhern, Bernard Sharratt and Alan Wall. Their guidance was indispensable to me; if, in spite of their painstaking criticism and advice, any errors of fact or interpretation persist, I alone can be held responsible.

One

The
Formation of 'Scrutiny'

Antonio Gramsci once remarked that to write the history of a political party was, in effect, 'to write the general history of a country from a monographic viewpoint'.[1] The same is true, in principle, of even the most marginal cultural movement. And when the case is that of *Scrutiny*, which, over a period of twenty years, was the practical instrument of a cultural 'party' that aspired 'to make a difference in history',[2] the practical implications of Gramsci's methodological rule become especially difficult to evade. It is insufficient, then, simply to record that *Scrutiny* came into being in Cambridge, in the spring of 1932. This curt statement of fact does no more than pose the essential questions. Why there? Why then? Why thus?

F. R. Leavis always emphasized the role of the Cambridge milieu in the formation of the journal. Only there, he declared, 'could the idea of *Scrutiny* have taken shape.... It was...a product, the triumphant justifying achievement, of the English Tripos.'[3] However, to make this claim was merely to reformulate the problem of *Scrutiny*'s genesis. What were the specific local conditions that favoured its emergence, and how are these, in their turn, to be explained?

'It was...in March 1917, while the German armies were falling back to the Hindenberg Line, while Russia was tottering into Revolution and America preparing for war, that at Cambridge members of the Senate met to debate the formation of an English Tripos separate

1. 'The Modern Prince', *Prison Notebooks*, Quintin Hoare and Geoffrey Nowell Smith (ed.), London 1971, p. 151.

2. F. R. Leavis, *'Scrutiny': A Retrospect*, Cambridge 1963, p. 1.

3. Ibid., p. 1. 'Tripos' is the name traditionally given in Cambridge to any course of studies leading to a first ('Bachelor's') degree.

from Modern Languages.'[4] The calculated bathos of this formulation does not negate its essential insight. For if its author, F. L. Lucas, was obdurately hostile to all that was distinctive in the Cambridge English School, he seems nevertheless to have sensed the pressures that shaped it. In order to explain the novel character of the new Tripos, it will be necessary to explore the conditions of its birth: the complex historical situation evoked in that brief inventory of 'great events'. The sketch that follows is neither comprehensive nor drawn to scale: for reasons of space, a few observations must serve here to highlight the conditions that favoured the new departure in English studies at Cambridge after the First World War.

I

The crisis that dogged inter-war Britain was not, in any strict sense, the result of August 1914 and its aftermath. By that date, its main elements – international political and economic rivalries, mounting working-class disaffection, the cultural shocks of scientific development and of iconoclastic movements in thought and art – were already familiar presences. But in the exceptional conditions of wartime these antagonisms fused in a highly unstable compound that the formalities of victory did little to neutralize.

By 1918, Britain had lost its command of the world market.[5] The manufacturing industries that had guaranteed its supremacy for a century were now in decline, outstripped by their more efficient and innovative competitors in the United States and elsewhere. After 150 years of almost uninterrupted growth, the British economy began to falter, and in the regions where the old export industries were sited, endemic mass unemployment set in. The roots of this predicament lay in the technical and organizational obsolescence of British industry, and in a certain tendency to introversion and retreat which had for some considerable time been the hallmark of British capital

4. F. L. Lucas, 'English Literature', Harold Wright (ed.), *University Studies: Cambridge 1933*, p. 259. The author was at this time a Fellow of King's College and University Lecturer in English Literature.

5. The following pages are based mainly on E. J. Hobsbawm, *Industry and Empire*, London 1969; Charles Loch Mowat, *Britain Between The Wars 1918–1940*, London 1968; Sidney Pollard, *The Development of the British Economy 1914–1967*, London 1969.

movements.[6] Moreover, the substantial modernization and expansion that did occur in the post-war period, in other, newer sectors of the economy, were governed by the same conditioned reflex. After the War, the State was more efficiently organized, spent more, employed more personnel, and intervened more widely and directly in economic and social life than ever before;[7] and partly under its aegis, there commenced an effort to reshape the technological and organizational bases of British industry. The main features of this belated attempt to emulate the German and US innovations of the previous century were: the concentration of capital into large trusts and monopolies; the systematic application of science to production; the extension of the division of labour, the mechanization of the labour process and the introduction of 'scientific management'; and the cultivation of a 'mass market' for the cheaper, standardized goods so produced.[8] The progress of these developments was halting and uneven. The concentration of capital, although rapid and thorough, was motivated less by any concerted strategy of modernization than by the desire to maintain price-levels in conditions of depression. The intensive development of the home market in consumer goods, although undoubtedly successful, was another expression of the old habit of evading competition wherever possible, in favour of less vigorously contested markets. The real difference between deliberately undertaken industrial renovation and this spiritless and improvised retreat into the future is illustrated by the fate of applied-scientific pursuits in this period. Despite the widespread popular vogue for scientific ideas, the exhortations of government agencies and commissions and the founding of bodies like the National Institute of Industrial Psychology, Britain continued to lag behind Germany and the USA in scientific research and development.[9] No adequate educational provision was made for a strategy of technological advance: throughout the Twenties, while Arts subjects gained steadily in popularity among university entrants (accounting for more than half the total by the end of the decade), the numbers studying pure sciences grew only slightly and those in technological and applied-scientific disciplines

6. Hobsbawm, p. 146.

7. Mowat, pp. 13–14, 42, 43f.

8. Hobsbawm, p. 172f; Pollard, ch. 3.

9. Pollard, pp. 94–96; Hobsbawm, p. 217f; Robert Thomson, *The Pelican History of Psychology*, London 1968, pp. 354–7.

declined, both absolutely and as a proportion of the whole.[10] Inept, costly and irresolute, Britain's post-war industrial modernization was, in terms that will become familiar in the course of this study, less a 'drive' than an aimless 'drift'.[11]

This combination of planless growth and unchecked decline was further complicated by the political dislocation that resulted from the destruction of Liberalism as a major force. By the turn of the century, the Liberal Party was visibly losing political coherence. The joint pressures of competition overseas and working-class militancy at home dictated measures that contravened every principle of *laissez-faire*.[12] Harried on one flank by Conservative demands for protectionist policies and challenged on the other by the growing political power of Labour, Asquith opted for an ineffectual amalgam of traditional economic liberalism and social reform. To no avail: after four years that saw constitutional crisis, mutiny and the prospect of revolt in Ireland, violent feminist agitation and industrial struggles of titanic force, the War came, and, nine months later, the fall of the last Liberal government in British history.[13] The liberal reformism of the Lloyd George coalition did not prove a durable substitute. Britain's participation in the war of intervention in Russia and the government's harsh reaction to the post-war strike wave both served to alienate a working class eager for material betterment and stirred by the example of the October Revolution. Its new allegiance was expressed in the rapid growth of electoral support for the Labour Party and sealed by the formation of the first Labour Government in 1923.

With the rise of Labour, the traditional two-party system passed into crisis. For although the Liberals could no longer hope to rule, the party that now supplanted them as the main opposition to Conserva-

10. Between 1919–20 and 1929–30, the numbers studying Arts rose from 11,000 (32%) to 24,000 (53%), approximately. The corresponding figures for Pure Sciences were 6,214 (18%) and 7,538 (17%), and for Technological and Applied Sciences, 5,300 (15%) and 4,152 (9%). By 1937, Arts had fallen to 47%, while the Pure and Applied Sciences rose slightly.

11. Pollard, p. 93.

12. Hobsbawm, p. 237f.

13. George Dangerfield, *The Strange Death of Liberal England*, London 1936, passim.

tism was not yet strong enough to govern alone; throughout the inter-war period, only the Conservative Party was ever capable of mustering an independent parliamentary majority. Outside, meanwhile, Parliament itself, as a mode of representative government, was being challenged by the newly founded Communist Party which, despite its numerical weakness, won considerable influence in the trades unions and among constituency activists, especially in the wake of the General Strike.[14] The economic and political storms of the following decade drove the parliamentary parties still further into confusion. The internal dissensions provoked by the formation of the National Government left the Liberals weaker than ever. Labour, already sapped and torn by the crisis of 1931, was shaken further by inner-party disputes over foreign policy and by the emergence of strong forces on its Left, grouped around the standard of anti-fascism. As the European political crisis worsened, the Conservative leadership sank deeper into indecision and passivity. Thus, the inter-war period was one of almost continuous political crisis, determined variously by domestic and international conditions. With the collapse of the Liberal Party and the rise of Labour, the British political order passed into a crisis that was to last for nearly thirty years, until its recomposition in the election of 1945.

The condition of British society in the 1920s was, then, one of crisis, defined at the economic level by a complex unity of innovation and decay, and politically, by a related dislocation of the inherited political order. Within the national culture, the effects of this crisis were pervasive. The economic and social developments of the period led directly to the transformation, or effective creation, of modern Britain's most powerful cultural media, and, at the same time, undermined the habits and assumptions of the established humanistic culture, casting it into confusion and self-doubt.

Among the first fruits of the union of technological innovation, the new 'mass market' and the interventionist State was the British Broadcasting Corporation. Founded in 1922 and granted a monopoly some

14. See Michael Woodhouse and Brian Pearce, *Essays on the History of Communism in Britain*, London 1975; also Mowat, pp. 5–46.

years later, the BBC combined with the burgeoning electronics industries to create, within the space of two decades, the British equivalent
of America's 'public information and entertainment' market (between
1922 and 1938, the number of licensed wireless sets increased from
36,000 to almost nine million).[15] The prompt government initiative
that secured the development of a national broadcasting service was
not repeated in the other major sector of 'mass entertainment', the
cinema. By the end of the War, Hollywood's dominion in the feature-
film industry was virtually beyond dispute, especially in Britain, whose
multiplying body of cinema-goers seldom saw films from any other
source. The infinitely smaller British industry resisted, with some
small success, but when a viable indigenous cinema finally emerged,
at the end of the Twenties, it was in the marginal area of documentary
film, inspired by US example and produced by and for the State.[16]

If, then, British cinema bore a strong resemblance to its tardy and
increasingly heteronomous parent economy, the newspaper industry
manifestly did not. Here, modernization was effected with energy and
efficiency.[17] As Raymond Williams has shown, the 'Northcliffe revolution' was not primarily carried out at the level of journalistic
'style' or 'standards': the literary character of the popular press had
evolved half a century before the founding of the *Daily Mail*, in the
period when the Sunday newspaper became established. The success
of the *Mail* and its later rivals was based rather on the formula that
the London *Times* had exploited in the early nineteenth century:
technical modernity, economic stability and a popular political stance.
The effects of this supremely successful 'revolution' were not confined
to the newspaper industry itself. Two in particular were of general
cultural importance.

The first was the qualitatively new role of advertising, both as an
instrument in the fierce and prolonged struggle to increase circulation and as the new financial basis of newspaper publishing. The
consolidation of the mass-circulation press gravely weakened the

15. Pollard, p. 139.

16. Mowat, p. 246. See also Alan Lovell, 'The Documentary Film Movement:
John Grierson,' in Lovell and Jim Hillier, *Studies in Documentary*, London 1972,
pp. 9–61.

17. The development of the reading public and of the popular Press are analysed
in detail in Williams, *The Long Revolution*, London 1965, pp. 177–94 and 195–236
respectively.

periodical press, whose audiences, limited by price and specialization, were too small to make advertising investment worthwhile. Together with the diffusion of us cinema and the advent of other transatlantic habits of recreation and consumption, advertising was also one of the main forms of that important post-war cultural phenomenon known as 'Americanization'.

Secondly, the spectacular expansion of the Press and related activities brought about a large increase in the numbers employed in them: whereas in 1891, according to the Census of that year, there were fewer than 6,000 'authors, editors and journalists' in England and Wales, the 1931 total in that category (by now expanded to include 'publicists') was approximately 19,000.[18] Striking in itself, this development belonged to a long and complex process whose result, already visible in the 1920s, was an irreversible alteration in the social and cultural character of the British intelligentsia. Historically, Britain's intellectuals had been a small and compact group, linked from birth by myriad ties of kinship and formed in the socially and culturally homogeneous milieu of England's public schools and older universities.[19] The political and ideological controversies of later Victorian England did no grave or lasting damage to this remarkably cohesive bloc, but from that time onwards, changes of a less dramatic character began gradually to erode the foundations of its cultural monopoly. The relative decline of the public schools and Oxbridge within an expanding educational system, the amelioration of the educational prospects of lower-middle-class children, the growth and diversification of State activity, the expansion of whole sectors of cultural production and the creation of new ones (publicity and the cinema, for instance) together induced the formation of an intellectual stratum which, although still dominated by the old Victorian bloc, was necessarily of a different character. By the early 1930s, the national intelligentsia was more numerous, more disparate in social

18. Between 1907 and 1935, output of 'paper, printing and publishing' rose by 162·6% – or, at six times the rate of clothing, and more than three times that of iron and steel (Pollard, p. 97).

19. The classic discussion of nineteenth-century British intellectuals is Noël Annan, 'The Intellectual Aristocracy,' J. H. Plumb (ed.), *Studies in Social History*, London 1955. For the pre-history of this Victorian stratum, see J. D. Hexter, 'The Education of the Aristocracy in the Renaissance,' *Reappraisals in History*, London 1961, pp. 45–70; and Hugh Kearney, *Scholars and Gentlemen: Universities and Society in Pre-Industrial Britain 1500–1700*, London 1970.

origin and occupational composition, and culturally less homogeneous than ever before.[20]

What, meanwhile, was the situation of the 'traditional' culture incarnated in academic specialisms and long-established forms of artistic practice? In order to answer this question, it will be necessary first of all to consider – briefly and selectively – the character and fate of the Victorian intellectual achievement.

Among the greatest intellectual syntheses of the nineteenth century was the sociology of Herbert Spencer. According to this theory, human society developed 'naturally', as part of a cosmic evolutionary process whose governing tendencies were differentiation and integration. These tendencies, whose specifically social modalities were the increasing division of labour and an expanding system of harmonious free exchange, would bear mankind inevitably towards perfection. Spencer's influence, in Britain and the USA, was profound but short-lived. For the cogency of his Lamarckian ultra-liberalism was entirely dependent on the vitality of the political and economic conceptions whose consummate expression it was, and with them, it passed into eclipse, so suddenly and totally that by the time of its completion, in the 1890s, Spencer's *Principles of Sociology* had lost both confidence and currency. The final volume, which betrayed its author's deepening pessimism, was received by the sociological community as an historical document, worthy of remembrance but without contemporary point.[21]

20. Between 1870 and 1934, the number of full-time elementary teachers in England and Wales increased from just under 14,000 to approximately 170,000. In the latter year, the numbers employed in public and grant-aided secondary schools reached 23,000 (from the 1909 level of nearly 9,500). Between 1925–6 and 1938–9, the number of full-time university staff grew by 31% to a total of nearly 4,000. In 1891, there were 5,771 authors, editors and journalists etc. in a population of 29m; in 1911, 13,786 out of 36m; in 1931, 19,037 out of just less than 40m (this represents a rate of growth six times that of the population). Sources: Censuses and official abstract of statistics.

According to Mowat (p. 207) the proportion of secondary-school leavers entering university increased from 4·6% in 1921–4 to 6·4% in 1931–4, when they constituted one third of all entrants. Between 1925–6 and the late 1930s, Oxbridge's share of the student population fell from 33% (compared with London's 27% and Manchester's 6%) to 20% approximately (the latter figure is Hobsbawm's).

21. See Göran Therborn, *Science, Class and Society*, London 1976, pp. 152–3 and 227–32.

The fate of the second major synthesis of this epoch was in many respects similar. Like Spencer's sociology, the neo-Idealist philosophy of T. H. Green was for several decades dominant in its own field and enjoyed massive cultural prestige, only to suffer precipitate and irreversible decline. Whereas the Spencerian system had been, in essentials, an idealized reflection of the political and economic order of mid-nineteenth century England, Green's more commanding synthesis was an attempt to confront and resolve the twin crises of Victorian culture: the erosion of traditional Christian belief and custom by the advances of the historical sciences of nature, and the contradiction within Liberal ideology between the received principle of individual freedom and the manifest need for legislated social reform.[22] It is pertinent here to consider Green's views in relation to those of a contemporary who was, in a sense, his ideological rival: Matthew Arnold. Both men acknowledged the force of the cumulative scientific critique of Christianity and the futility of the restorationist ambitions of High Church intellectuals. They agreed too that the only practical course was to devise a surrogate of comparable synoptic and normative power; and that the State, which both perceived as an organ that transcended the divergent interests of civil society, should henceforward assume a pre-eminent role in the moral leadership of society. However, Green rejected Arnold's claim that poetry could effectually succeed religion as the source of morality: immersed in ordinary language and thus in common sense, it could never be sufficiently critical.[23] His own more audacious solution was to refound Christianity as an 'undogmatic theology', on the basis of an idealist metaphysics proofed against further empirical erosion;

22. Melvin Richter, *The Politics of Conscience: T. H. Green and His Age*, London 1964, passim.
23. Ibid., 166–7, 172, 351. Arnold's major statement was *Culture and Anarchy*; see also 'The Literary Influence of Academies' from the *First Series* of *Essays in Criticism*, and from the *Second*, 'The Study of Poetry', where the preamble states: 'The future of poetry is immense, because in poetry, where it is worthy of its high destinies, our race, as time goes on, will find an ever surer and surer stay. There is not a creed which is not shaken, not an accredited dogma which is not shown to be questionable, not a received tradition which does not threaten to dissolve. Our religion has materialized itself in the fact, in the supposed fact; it has attached its emotion to the fact, and now the fact is failing it. But for poetry the idea is everything; the rest is a world of illusion, of divine illusion. Poetry attaches its emotion to the idea; the idea *is* the fact. The strongest part of our religion today is its unconscious poetry.'

and at the same time, to redirect it towards an ethics of citizenship and reform, thus replenishing the ideological stocks of Liberalism. The philosophical system that resulted was elegant and comprehensive. Green's conception of history as the unfolding of objective Reason was both a vindication of the liberal Idea of Progress and a covert theodicy; and in postulating the *telos* of 'the common good', in which individual right and civic duty were ultimately to achieve identity, he eluded the constraints of classical liberalism without in any way departing from its constitutive terms. Moreover, his neo-Hegelianism notwithstanding, Green suffused his thought with the intense moralism of his evangelical background: few philosophies can ever have combined so unquestioning a belief in inevitable progress with so exacting a sense of moral obligation.

Green's work was a bold attempt to recast the existing elements of a disintegrating cultural order into a form appropriate to altered political and social conditions, and its influence, from the 1880s onwards, was correspondingly great: in the universities, where by the turn of the century neo-Idealism had relegated Utilitarianism to second place; and in politics, where Green's influence extended to such diverse figures as Asquith, Toynbee, Tawney and Beveridge.[24] Yet, by the end of the War, neo-Idealism was evidently a movement of the past. The forces that combined to defeat it were diverse and unequal in their effect. Professional opposition to Green began just after the turn of the century in Cambridge, which, despite the presence of idealist thinkers like McTaggart and Ward, had remained a relatively secure bastion of utilitarian and empiricist thought.[25] This critique, initiated by Russell and Moore and continued by the analytical school inspired by them, could hardly have been more destructive, in intention or effect. By the 1920s, analytical philosophy had so completely overrun the positions of Green and his disciples, and so thoroughly discredited the type of philosophical project that it represented, that Britain's Idealist episode, scarcely deserving of anything

24. See, for instance, David Bell, 'Philosophy,' C. B. Cox and A. E. Dyson (ed.), *The Twentieth-Century Mind*, vol. 1, 1900–1918, Oxford 1972, pp. 182–3; and A. T. Quiller-Couch, *Memories and Opinions: An Unfinished Autobiography*, Cambridge 1944, p. 73, 77.

25. See G. E. Moore, 'Sidgwick and the Old Ethics,' *Cambridge Review*, November 20, 1902; and also Anon., 'Principia Ethica,' *Cambridge Review*, December 3, 1903, a review of Moore's major work of the same title.

like serious explanation, became an occasion for knowing irony. 'The speculative philosophies of the past,' wrote one Cambridge philosopher in the early thirties, 'seem to me to have been hybrids, bred out of Science by Poetry, and to be, like all hybrids, sterile.'[26]

It is unlikely, however, that the rout of neo-Idealism was simply the consequence of intellectual developments in philosophy, or, as some have argued, of changes in its institutional structure.[27] For some time at least, Cambridge remained exceptional within British philosophy, and, besides, Green's audience was by no means a narrowly professional one. The preconditions of that swift and crushing philosophical assault lay in the altered state of the culture as a whole. The Germanophobia that pervaded England from the late nineteenth century onwards, marring the reception of at least one neo-Idealist treatise – Bosanquet's *Philosophical Theory of the State* – was a noteworthy though not decisive circumstance.[28] The decline of religious belief among intellectuals in the post-war period was another. But the waning of Green's cultural influence was induced above all by the obsolescence of the politics and ideology on which it rested. In the aftermath of the First World War, his confident progressivism seemed merely smug and self-deluding; and with the rise of Labour, liberal reformism, its policies and philosophies alike, was condemned to permanent marginality. Although elements of Green's teaching were preserved, in Fabian thought and in the work of individuals like Grierson and Tawney, the comprehensive scope and appeal that were the essence of the neo-Idealist project were lost.

Spencer had no successors, and Green's line soon perished. The type of social investigation practised by Booth, Rowntree and the Webbs was intensely empirical in its methods, and eschewed social theory in favour of the immediate problems of state policy.[29] In its new mode, philosophy learned a similar modesty, confining itself to the analysis

26. R. B. Braithwaite, 'Philosophy,' in Wright, p. 31.

27. Gilbert Ryle's contention that the victory of analytic philosophy was the predictable consequence of the laicization and professionalization of philosophy not only overlooks Green's vigorous struggle to professionalize Oxford philosophy, but fails to account for the fact that in other countries – France, for example – analogous developments did not have comparable results. See his introduction to A. J. Ayer *et al.*, *The Revolution in Philosophy*, London 1956, pp. 1–11.

28. R. F. Atkinson, 'British Philosophy,' Cox and Dyson, vol. 2, 1918–1945, pp. 127–8.

29. Therborn, p. 230f.

and clarification of the given conceptual universe.[30] Both disciplines withdrew into a technicism that minimized their role in the general culture of England between the wars.

The period that saw the eclipse of Spencer and Green also witnessed the rise of new, radically different discourses on man and society: psychology and, rather later, Marxism.[31] After forty years of relatively slow progress, experimental psychology entered a phase of accelerated development. The techniques that had been devised to assist the war effort were now brought to bear on social relations in general, and new bodies like the National Institute of Industrial Psychology were founded for this purpose. The advance of applied psychology was, moreover, accompanied by an unprecedented level of theoretical debate, in which the recently translated works of Freud and his followers were so prominent that, as one historian of the discipline has observed, 'psychology' in the inter-war period became almost coterminous with 'psychoanalysis'.[32] Within the profession, the most notable result of the debate was the development of a flourishing child psychology. Within British culture generally, its resonance was universal. Auden, Caudwell, Lawrence, Empson and Richards are just a few of the more prominent intellectuals of the period whose writings exhibit, or at any rate profess, a debt to Freud or similar thinkers.[33] The immense cultural impact of psychoanalysis at the time was registered by the *Times Literary Supplement* in a note on the occasion of Freud's death: 'What is truly astonishing is the rapidity with which the Freudism [sic] doctrine spread. It was not until 1913 that it reached England: in twenty-six years an idea which is not intrinsically literary has permeated our literature. In fiction, in biography and in criticism it can be said to have reached saturation point. Even those who refused to accept completely the tenets of psychoanalysis with its dream symbols became infected by its terminology, and so were inevitably subjugated by some of its implications.'[34] The images of pestilence that haunt this retrospect have

30. Braithwaite, pp. 3, 30–31.
31. Atkinson, p. 142.
32. Thomson, pp. 174–89, 345f; see also Mowat, pp. 213–4.
33. See also two memoirs of the period: Christopher Isherwood, *Lions and Shadows*, London 1938; and Alick West, *One Man in His Time*, London 1969.
34. *Times Literary Supplement*, September 30, 1939, p. 563.

more to do with its author's ideological distress than with objective reality. But they do suggest the symptomatic nature of the inter-war vogue for psychoanalysis, and a possible explanation of its eclecticism and transience. The widespread popularity of psychological ideas was at least partly a compensatory reaction to the loss of the synoptic discourses of later Victorian England; the specific importance of psychoanalysis was that, especially as represented in Jung and the later Freud, it was the only point at which psychology – intrinsically weak as a source of social theory – seemed at all capable of generating a comprehensive world-view.

Marxism enjoyed no comparable esteem in the twenties. After an initial bout of enthusiasm for the October Revolution, intellectual interest in the Soviet Union waned. The political and theoretical weakness of the British Communist Party meant that the cultural impact of Marxist theory was slight. The General Strike drew a wide variety of responses from the literary intelligentsia, and caused a certain quickening of interest in revolutionary ideas, but in all, there were few auguries of the cultural prominence that Marxism was to attain only a few years later, in the wake of the Depression and the victory of fascism in Germany.[35]

In English literature, the first post-war decade marked an unsettled interregnum. The modernist movement had been strong enough to undermine but not to demolish the inherited literary order, and by the early 1920s its main energies had been dissipated. London was no longer an important international centre of avant-garde culture, and the most innovative English-language exponents of modernism now worked abroad. The aesthetic insurgency and political radicalism – of both Left and Right – that distinguished the modernist movements of France, Germany, Russia and Italy were for the most part unknown in the literary culture of post-war England. In the work of T. S. Eliot, aesthetic innovation was combined with a sedentary conservatism that became deeper and more overt in the *Criterion*, which he edited from 1922 onwards. Despite their evident modernist inflection, the

35. George Orwell, 'Inside the Whale,' *Collected Essays, Journalism and Letters*, vol. 1, London 1970, pp. 540–78; D. S. Mirsky, *The Intelligentsia of Great Britain*, London 1935, p. 31; Adrian Mellor, Chris Pawling and Colin Sparks, 'Writers and the General Strike,' a special supplement to Margaret Morris, *The General Strike*, London 1976, pp. 338–57.

novels of Virginia Woolf exhibited a fundamental continuity with the English literary past. England's indigenous literary modernism was, as one critic has observed, a temperate affair, a literature 'lit by lights from modernism', but still 'rooted in familiar, national, provincial experience, rather than in arcane worlds of its own making'.[36] This peculiar mode of literary development was defined and consecrated in Eliot's declaration that 'traditionality' was at once the warrant and the highest goal of poetic innovation.

Nevertheless, and in spite of early successes, literary modernism won acceptance only after a long and often bitter struggle, whose symbolic stake was the reputation of the author of *The Waste Land* and *The Sacred Wood*. Eliot had astutely flanked his poetry with a body of literary criticism that challenged the settled procedures and valuations on which the reigning poetic orthodoxy was founded. The distinctive themes of this criticism – the elevation of seventeenth-century poetry and demotion of the standard luminaries of the nineteenth, the attack on critical 'impressionism' and expressly 'classical' stress on 'traditionality' and 'impersonality' in poetry – were, if anything, more provoking than the poetry that they were designed to commend. Before long, the resistance of the old guard, led by such figures as Hugh Walpole and J. C. Squire, dwindled into merely irritating mockery; and the new generation of poets that emerged at the end of the twenties confirmed Eliot's pre-eminent role in contemporary poetry. But within literary criticism, especially its university sector, opposition was more sustained, persisting in some cases for decades. The rise of 'the moderns' in English literature was expressed not so much in a flurry of aesthetic manifestoes as in a struggle for a new critical canon.

These issues, and the larger cultural questions implicit in them, were at first debated mainly in the metropolitan reviews – in the *London Mercury*, home of Georgianism and good fellowship, in Middleton Murry's *Adelphi* and the antithetically 'classicist' *Criterion*, and in *The Calendar of Modern Letters*.[37] It was in the last of these that the cultural disturbances of the twenties were most sharply registered and most

---

36. Malcolm Bradbury, *The Social Context of Modern English Literature*, Oxford 1971, p. 20f.

37. For a general survey, see John Gross, *The Rise and Fall of the Man of Letters*, London 1973, ch. 9.

vigorously explored. Compared with, say, the *Criterion* or *Scrutiny*, *The Calendar* was rather miscellaneous in character. Much of its space was devoted to poetry and fiction, contributed by a wide assortment of authors (among others, Lawrence, Blunden, Graves and Coppard, the Americans Tate, Crowe Ransom and Crane, and from Europe, Pirandello, Chekhov and Babel). Literary criticism was practised in several modes, including reviewing, the celebrated 'Scrutinies' of hallowed reputations (Masefield, Bennett, Wells and Barrie, for example), studies of a quasi-theoretical nature (notably C. H. Rickword's essays on fiction) and more expansive treatments of general cultural themes. In its political coverage, the journal ranged eclectically from Wyndham Lewis's animadversions on Communism, through the liberalism of E. M. Forster, to Douglas Garman's enthusiastic review of Trotsky's *Where Is Britain Going?* However, the short life of *The Calendar* (March 1925–July 1927) amounted to more than the sum of its moments.[38] For although they lacked a common analysis or programme, the editors and their closest associates were nonetheless united by certain shared apprehensions. The obsessive theme of the journal was the disruption of cultural life brought about by the spread of scientific thought and the consequent dissolution of religious belief. 'We have a host of theories,' wrote Edwin Muir, '... but among them no ruling theory; a mass of enlightenment, but no faith in enlightenment; a number of ideals of society, but no hope that they will be realized. The world has changed around us, but we are not conscious of having changed it; and the future is still more uncertain than the present.'[39] In essay after essay, *The Calendar*'s inner circle dwelt on the effects of this generalized cultural disorder on the production and criticism of poetry. Starved of new practitioners by the more prestigious sciences, and intellectually debarred from many of its customary resorts by the new knowledge that they disseminated, poetry was forced to subsist in the unwonted modes of comedy, intellectualism and negativity.[40] Meanwhile, in the absence of an

38. For the reminiscences of its main editor, see Alan Young and Michael Schmidt, 'A Conversation with Edgell Rickword,' *Poetry Nation* I (1973), pp. 73–89.

39. 'The Present State of Poetry,' II, 11 (January '26), p. 328.

40. See, for example, Douglas Garman, 'Audience,' II, 7 (September '25); E[dgell] R[ickword], 'The Recreation of Poetry: the Use of "Negative" Emotion,' I, 3 (May '25), pp. 236–41; idem, 'The Returning Hero,' I, 6 (August '25), pp. 472–4; and also Muir, 'The Present State of Poetry'.

authoritative value-system, the properly 'classical' discipline of criticism had lapsed into a subjectivism that was especially flagrant in the writings of its irresponsible and aesthetically reactionary academic exponents.[41] Despite individual qualifications and variations of emphasis, the editorial circle tended to agree that the resolution of this literary crisis depended ultimately on the resolution of the larger cultural crisis that had precipitated it, and that a rigorous and committed practice of literary criticism, although indispensable, was not in itself sufficient to rejuvenate contemporary poetry. However, this estimate of the cultural situation was constantly shadowed by promptings of another kind, whose import for the cultural morphology of mid-century Britain was to be immeasurably greater. The pages of *The Calendar* are marked, from first to last, by the presence of a temptation, never yielded to but never decisively repressed, to put an end to the 'intellectual misery' brought on by 'the death of dogma' and the provisional incapacity of its successors, by establishing literature as the new repository of moral values and, therewith, literary criticism as the privileged arbiter of social thought.[42]

This ambition was not new. It had taken mature and programmatic shape fully half a century earlier, in the writings of Matthew Arnold. However, the coeval system of neo-Idealism proved stronger and more efficacious, and for the duration of Green's ascendancy, Arnold's project survived only as an idea, active in the work of individuals, but never finding that social anchorage in a stratum of 'disinterested' intellectuals, without which the passage from aspiration to action was inconceivable. But in the generalized crisis of the Victorian order that set in after the First World War, its prospects were suddenly transformed. Disorganized socially by the enlargement and diversification of the intelligentsia, and ideologically by the collapse of the pre-war intellectual universe, British culture entered a phase of open com-

41. See Garman; Rickword, 'Criticism as "a Charming Parasite",' (rev. F. L. Lucas, *Authors Dead and Living*), III, 1 (April '26); Bertram Higgins, 'Euthanasia: Or the Future of Criticism,' III, 2 (July '26), pp. 151–4.

42. It is not possible to trace this in adequate detail here, but see the review's inaugural statement, I, 1 (March '25); C. H. Rickword, rev. Elizabeth A. Drew, *The Modern Novel*, III, 2 (July '26), and 'A Note on Fiction,' III, 3 (October '26); Bertram Higgins, 'Art and Knowledge,' IV, 1 (April '27).'

petition whose eventual outcome was already discernible in the career of *The Calendar of Modern Letters*. In the unique cultural conjuncture of the 1920s, the two preconditions of a successful revival of the Arnoldian project began to converge.[43]

II

The upshot of these literary controversies was doubly improbable, given *The Calendar*'s anti-academic strictures. For it was in a university setting – and then in the eminently traditional setting of Cambridge – that the discrete intellectual forces of the post-war generation were finally concentrated, producing a 'critical revolution' that, within twenty years, transformed the academic study of literature and raised it to a new prominence within the national culture. What were the conditions of this sudden, localized release of creative energy, in an academic world that remained, overall, conservative and reclusive? With its stronger scientific traditions and more impressive record of hospitality to intellectual innovation, Cambridge offered a more favourable climate than, say, Oxford.[44] But the crucial circumstance was the timing of the decision to introduce a new English course. Planned in the last years of the War and inaugurated shortly after the Armistice, the new school was much more vulnerable than its older counterparts in Oxford, London and elsewhere to the manifold stresses of the post-1918 era; so much so that it can be said, without hyperbole, to have been distinctively the product of the cultural contradictions of the time.[45] It is not possible here to recount the

43. The phrase 'the Arnoldian project' does not imply conscious or systematic adherence to the letter of Arnold's writings, in whole or in part. It refers only to his belief in the cultural paramountcy of poetry, and to the ideal of a 'disinterested' intelligentsia.

44. The distinction Oxford/Cambridge has undoubtedly been over-polarized, and indeed mythologized, on many occasions; nevertheless, it is well-grounded in cultural-historical fact. For some materials on the two institutions, see Kearney, *passim*; Richter, *passim*; Noël Annan, *Leslie Stephen*, London 1951, p. 130f; George Santayana, *Soliloquies in England and Other Soliloquies*, London 1922, pp. 43–5. See also M. C. Bradbrook, 'I. A. Richards at Cambridge,' Reuben Brower, Helen Vendler and John Hollander (ed.), *I. A. Richards: Essays in His Honor*, New York 1973, p. 63; Q. D. Leavis, 'Leslie Stephen: Cambridge Critic,' *Scrutiny* VII, 4 (March '39), pp. 404–15; and 'The Discipline of Letters,' *Scrutiny* XII, 1 (Winter '43), pp. 12–26.

45. For Oxford and London at this time, see Stephen Potter, *The Muse in Chains*,

early history of the school in detail, or to dwell for long on its most prominent personages.[46] The following paragraphs are no more than an outline of its salient features.

The reform of English studies at Cambridge was, to a large extent, motivated and made possible by the circumstances of wartime. Hector Chadwick, the Professor of Anglo-Saxon, foresaw that peace would bring a new generation of students, more numerous, more mature in years and experience, and with needs and expectations that the constricting routines of the existing syllabus could not begin to meet.[47] The prevailing emphasis on philological and antiquarian topics was, in his estimation, doubly unsatisfactory: it obstructed the development of modern English as the humane discipline *par excellence*, and threatened ultimately to compromise the legitimate specialist aims of philology itself.[48] For both reasons, Tripos reform was now imperative. Chadwick's proposals effectively inverted the priorities of the old regime: Anglo-Saxon literature and philology were to be relegated to optional status, in a syllabus that was overwhelmingly modern and literary in orientation.[49] Interests and capacities that had

---

London 1937. See also Geoffrey Grigson, *The Crest on the Silver*, London 1950, pp. 97–98, 113f; and C. Day Lewis, *The Buried Day*, London 1960, ch. 8. It is obviously inadequate to base any generalization about the national state of academic English studies on the Oxford-Cambridge-London triangle. Unfortunately the 'civic' universities are much less well chronicled than these three. It should be recorded that the influence of the more advanced 'civic' sector played a role in the Cambridge reform.

46. Much of this history remains opaque. The main source, E. M. W. Tillyard, *The Muse Unchained*, London 1958, is avowedly 'not a history but a one-sided picture', an 'attempt to blend fact and gossip', and is deliberately unforthcoming about certain incidents germane to this discussion. The short memoirs that have now begun to appear, as one after another of the main actors are honoured with *festschriften*, help somewhat, but they are often allusive and impressionistic. See Bradbrook, 'I. A. Richards at Cambridge,' pp. 61–72; and from the same volume, ' "How It Strikes a Contemporary": The Impact of I. A. Richards' Literary Criticism in Cambridge, England,' pp. 45–59; William Empson, 'The Hammer's Ring,' pp. 73–83. See also, Basil Willey, *Cambridge and Other Memories 1920–53*, London 1968; Bradbrook, 'The Ambiguity of William Empson,' and Kathleen Raine, 'Extracts From Unpublished Memoirs,' both in Roma Gill (ed.), *William Empson: The Man and His Work*, London 1974; F. R. Leavis, *English Literature in Our Time and The University*, London 1969, pp. 1–35; J. Bronowski, 'Recollections of Humphrey Jennings,' *The Twentieth Century*, CLXV, 983 (January '59), pp. 45–50.

47. Tillyard, pp. 58–9. For Chadwick, see ibid., p. 41f; 'A Pupil' [Q. D. Leavis], 'Puofessor Chadwick and English Studies,' *Scrutiny* XIV, 3 (Spring '47), pp. 204–8.

48 Tillyard, p. 41f.   49. See ibid., p. 56, for the text of the agreed syllabus.

formerly been deemed the natural property of any cultivated individual were now to become the staple of an academic discipline. Resistance to the scheme was, inevitably, stubborn and widespread: on the Modern and Medieval Languages Board, where the interests of philology were jealously guarded by the German scholars, Breul and Braunholtz; in the university generally, where the power and prestige of classical and medieval scholarship were very great; and among English academics, in Cambridge and elsewhere, who at this time were more often than not classically trained.[50] Indeed, the successful passage of the reform owed less to the intrinsic strength of its advocates than to the temporary indisposition of its main opponents. In Cambridge as in other English universities, the chauvinism of the war years found academic expression in a patriotic distrust of German thought and scholarship. The quintessentially 'Teutonic' discipline of philology fell into disrepute – for a time at least – and Breul and Braunholtz, already compromised by their national origins, were silenced.[51] The reformers' progress was further facilitated by the complaisance of Sir Arthur Quiller-Couch (then King Edward VII Professor of English) who, fortified in his amateur's impatience of technical scholarship by a patriotic aversion from *Anglistik*, was content to accept Chadwick's proposals without demur.[52] Thus, an opposition that might well have prevailed in less exceptional circumstances was successfully circumvented, and in March 1917 the reform was passed.

The scope of the new course in 'English Literature, Life and Thought' was further widened by the impromptu institutional arrangements to which its founders were compelled to resort. Chadwick was aware that the existing complement was too small to cope with the imminent increase in student numbers and that it was, moreover, largely unsympathetic to the reformed syllabus.[53] Accordingly, he decided to recruit new personnel elsewhere. None of the trio to whom he entrusted the course had any specialist competence in English studies: Mansfield Forbes, his earliest and most inspirational

---

50. Ibid., p. 64f. Raleigh, then Professor at Oxford, was shown the proposals and expressed his disapproval of them. The English Association made a last-minute attempt to block the passage of the reform (Tillyard, pp. 55, 62).

51. Tillyard, pp. 35, 61.

52. Tillyard, pp. 49–51. For Quiller-Couch's chauvinism, see Gross, p. 206.

53. Tillyard, p. 64f.

ally, was a historian; E. M. W. Tillyard had read Classics; and I. A. Richards had been trained in Mental and Moral Sciences. The young 'freelances' whom they in turn enlisted as teachers and examiners were similarly diverse in intellectual background (the English Tripos did not begin to become academically self-sustaining until after 1923, and it was not until the end of the decade that the first group of students trained exclusively in English passed out).[54] The result of these makeshift provisions was a significant devolution of power and initiative. With Chadwick's blessing and Quiller-Couch's acquiescence, Forbes, Richards and Tillyard assumed effective command, and introduced a permissive, text-centred course that gave free rein to the diverse interests and skills of its personnel.[55] These informal, improvised conditions were not constitutive of the distinctive intellectual character of the early English school, but they did leave it peculiarly exposed to the general crisis whose outbreak marked the hour of its birth. In the unstructured, indefinitely bounded space opened up by the Tripos reform, the contradictory social and cultural forces of the twenties met and mingled freely, giving rise to a debate of unprecedented breadth and vigour.

After 1918, the traditionally homogeneous culture of Cambridge began, slowly and unevenly, to disintegrate. The political and ideological traumas of the War and its turbulent aftermath were borne directly into the university by the returning ex-servicemen. At the same time, the sociological profile of the institution began to be re-drawn by the middle-class students who, assisted by state or university scholarships, now began to enrol in increasing numbers. Thus, the ideological and social diversification of the national intelligentsia reproduced itself in miniature in the composition of the post-war student generation.

The intellectual cross-currents thus generated flowed strongly in every reach of the university, but in the new school of English, where no stable institutional apparatus existed to stem or channel them,

54. 'Freelances', or 'recognized lecturers', were teachers of 'inferior' rank whose only source of remuneration was the fees paid by the students who attended their courses (Tillyard, pp. 33–4).
55. Tillyard, pp. 81–3.

their power was especially great. The young freelances who taught for the Tripos, and the students who took it, were estranged from their seniors by a triple barrier. They were divided most deeply by the War. The main luminaries of English studies, in Cambridge and elsewhere, were all Victorians by personal formation. Saintsbury had resigned from his chair in Edinburgh in 1915, at the age of seventy. Bradley, six years his junior, had been in semi-retirement since 1905. Quiller-Couch's professorship was in effect a second career, begun in 1912 at the age of forty-nine, after some twenty years devoted to Liberal journalism and belles lettres. (Chadwick was forty-four at the outbreak of war.) Of the generation who actually implemented the Tripos reform, some had actually taken part in the War, Tillyard and Richards entering the army after graduation, while F. R. Leavis interrupted his studies to serve as a medical orderly at the front. The eldest of this generation – Tillyard and Forbes – were aged thirty in 1919, the youngest – Leavis and Basil Willey – twenty-four and twenty-two respectively; still further removed from the long-lived eminences of their discipline, the students who would eventually press 'the critical revolution' towards completion – William Empson, L. C. Knights, Q. D. Roth – were then just entering their teens. Furthermore, a significant number of these post-war levies were drawn from social classes that until recently had generally been excluded from the upper levels of the political and cultural order – petit and lower bourgeois students whose only access to Cambridge was through the fiercely competitive grammar-school and scholarship systems. Bradley, immensely successful in his own career, had come from a distinguished connection that included F. H. Bradley, the follower of Green, and G. G. Bradley, successively Head of Marlborough, Master of University College, Oxford, and Dean of Westminster. Quiller-Couch had been knighted in 1910 for his services to literature and Liberalism, and – it is said – owed his Cambridge appointment to the direct intervention of Lloyd George. The circumstances of their posterity, if not in any sense impoverished, were considerably more modest. Richards's father was a works manager in Cheshire, Willey's a North London electrical engineer. Leavis was the son of a musical instruments dealer from Cambridge, and Q. D. Roth, the daughter of a draper and hosier from Edmonton, on the northern fringes of London. Finally, the freelances and their immediate successors were

B

also, for the institutional reasons already mentioned, heterogeneous in academic formation (Saintsbury, Bradley, Quiller-Couch and Chadwick were all former classicists, as were the majority of English-literary academics of their vintage). As such, they were spontaneously more open than the old generation to developments in other disciplines and in the culture at large, and eager to test their possible utility in the uncertain conditions of their own lives and intellectual work.[56]

The frictions generated by these discrepancies of historical experience and social and occupational status were seldom made explicit, but their covert role in subverting the ideal of the scholar-gentleman – in the area where its mystique was strongest – was nonetheless crucial. The intimate liaison of social privilege, political conservatism and cultural obscurantism incarnated in this ideal was apparent to some at least of the early participants in the English school, as one of their number was later to testify: 'To look with Veblen's eyes at this "mode of life" . . . is at least to make one point – that its social standards and its conventional literary and cultural values are only different aspects of the same mentality. To threaten its security in any way, by casting aspersions against the genuineness of a literary idol like Landor or Milton or by suggesting that the social structure needs revision, is to get the same reaction. . . . This "mode of life" has a vested interest in the profession of letters identical with its economic interests. A life devoted to the humanities means not following a vocation but taking up the genteelest profit-making pursuit, one which confers a high caste on its members; literary appreciation must obey the same laws

56. George Saintsbury died in 1933, A. C. Bradley in 1935, Quiller-Couch in 1944 and Chadwick in 1947. Empson, Knights and Roth were born in 1906. (Sources: the *Dictionary of National Biography, Who's Who, The Cambridge University List of Members, 1976*, the Registrar General's Office.) For the background to Quiller-Couch's appointment, see Tillyard, p. 39. Quiller-Couch himself foresaw the cultural effects of the War: see his elegaic 'To the Front from the Backs,' *Cambridge Review* February 24, 1915. The editors of the anthology in which this piece appears describe it as 'a suitable epitaph' for a Cambridge culture that was not to survive 'the coup de grâce' of the War (Eric Homberger, William Janeway and Simon Schama ed., *The Cambridge Mind: Ninety Years of "The Cambridge Review" 1879–1969*, London 1970, pp. 15–17). The observations above concern the 'humane' culture of post-war Cambridge; a complementary account of the scientific culture of the time is now available in Gary Werskey, *The Visible College: A Collective Biography of British Scientists and Socialists of the 1930s*, London 1978.

as other expressions of social superiority. The Discipline of Letters is seen to be simply the rules of the academic English club.'[57] In this milieu, the notion of 'literary taste' was in no sense metaphorical: belles lettres was little more than a privileged mode of consumption. In their aversions too, the scholar-gentlemen were guided by deeper allegiances. As the same author observed, the resistance to Eliot's poetry came from the same quarter as the attempts to break the General Strike; the anti-modernist offensive was only one tactic in the defence of a whole social order. This caustic analysis was verified *a contrario* by the outcome of the Tripos reform. In the eyes of a generation excluded by social origin, occupational standing or historical experience from its comforts and certitudes, the intellectual authority of 'the academic English club' was virtually nil.

The literary criticism that now began to take shape was utterly distinct from the leisurely and expansive connoisseurism personified by Saintsbury and Quiller-Couch, in method, temper and preoccupation. Whatever their individual differences, its exponents typically prized analytic and judicial rigour, drew freely on the resources of other disciplines and laid strong emphasis on the reciprocal relations between literature and its social and cultural context, especially in the contemporary period. It was in the early writings of I. A. Richards that these motifs were first assembled. Under the influence of Moore's analytic philosophy, which he had absorbed as a student, Richards embarked on a critique of the bellelettristic subjectivism that held sway in literary criticism.[58] His *Principles of Literary Criticism* – conceived as a course of lectures for the Tripos and published in book form in 1924 – employed a 'scientific' conceptual scheme derived from utilitarian psychology to construct a general theory of literature, from which he thought to deduce new and more rigorous norms of interpretation and judgment. He supplemented these theoretical analyses some years later with *Practical Criticism*, a manual in which

57. Q. D. Leavis, 'The Discipline of Letters,' p. 18f. Her subject in this essay was the career of G. S. Gordon, who was Merton Professor at Oxford, but her strictures were clearly intended to have more general application. Mrs Leavis confirmed this in an interview given to me in March 1976.

58. Tillyard, p. 88f; *Principles of Literary Criticism*, London 1967, ch. 1.

he reported the findings of his celebrated inquiry into the reading capacities of his students and discussed their educational implications.[59] Richards's aesthetic and educational researches were inspired by a general interpretation of the contemporary cultural situation, which he summarized in *Science and Poetry*. The themes of this short exposition were recognizably those of *The Calendar*. The accelerated tempo of historical change, and in particular the advances of the sciences, had invalidated every received conception of the universe and man's place within it. Scientific discovery had effected an irreversible 'neutralization of nature', thereby disrupting the religious and magical world-views on which the delicate equipoise of the human psyche had always rested, but had not furnished any new affective orientation to succeed them.[60] The profound maladjustment that resulted was the prime cause of 'the modern crisis' and, especially, of the contemporary disablement of poetry. However, where *The Calendar*'s critics saw an 'age of transition' from which a re-stabilized culture, based now on science, would eventually emerge, Richards discerned the end of an entire epoch, and the approach of perils that only a conscious reorganization of the cultural order could avert.[61] Reiterating the binary theory of language first enunciated in *Principles*, he argued that, as cognitive discourses, the sciences were necessarily devoid of affective power, and that far from ensuring a new psychological equilibrium, their final victory was liable to cause 'a mental chaos such as man has never experienced'.[62] Richards's solution was to take the path that *The Calendar* had glimpsed but never taken. It was necessary now, he argued, to cast off the lingering vestiges of the old philosophies and religions, and to turn for existential 'assurance' to a discourse that equalled them in affective power without renewing their hopeless claim to literal truth. The sciences would henceforth rule alone in the domain of knowledge, but in order to maintain the psychological coherence of existence, men and women 'would be thrown back, as Matthew Arnold foresaw, upon

59. London 1929.

60. *Science and Poetry*, Psyche Miniatures 1, London 1926, p. 43f. This series was published in conjunction with the Cambridge quarterly *Psyche*, edited by C. K. Ogden from 1920 onwards. By 1926, its contributors included Russell, McDougall and Richards; Malinowski and Rivers; John B. Watson and Morris Ginsberg.

61. Ibid., ch. 1.

62. Ibid., pp. 82–3.

poetry. It is capable of saving us; it is a perfectly possible means of overcoming chaos.'[63]

Richards's theories were the main formative influence on Cambridge English.[64] His 'practical criticism' soon became independent of the liberal theory of communication on which it rested, and passed into currency as the key instrument of literary analysis in general. In raising literature to a new eminence and responsibility in contemporary culture, he helped to legitimate the aesthetic innovations of Pound and Eliot, Joyce, Woolf and Lawrence, and provided the rationale for more stringent assessments of the literary past. And although few followed him in his rigorously psychologistic interpretation of society and culture, the main arguments of *Science and Poetry* left an ineffaceable impression on the minds of his contemporaries. F. R. Leavis, who as a student had moved from History to English and subsequently become one of Richards's freelances, inaugurated his critical career with a series of pamphlets in which he broached his analysis of the modern social and cultural condition.[65] Its specifically poetic aspect was the subject of his first full-length book, which elucidated the 'new bearings' adumbrated in Hopkins and fixed in the poetry of Eliot and Pound.[66] Q. D. Roth, who had been Leavis's pupil and was soon to marry him, drew on psychology and on contemporaneous experiments in cultural anthropology for her study of the English reading public.[67] In William Empson, mathematical training, the influence of Freud and the poetry and criticism of Eliot fused to produce an intricate, 'metaphysical' poetry and the tirelessly ramified analyses of *Seven Types of Ambiguity*.[68] Another migrant from History to English, L. C. Knights, began with a critique of the naive 'character criticism' of Bradley's Shakespearean studies, and went on to explore the

63. Ibid., pp. 82–3. Richards's epigraph was that of *The Study of Poetry* (see n. 23 above).

64. See, for example, Bennett, Bradbrook and Empson.

65. *D. H. Lawrence*, Cambridge 1930; *Mass Civilization and Minority Culture*, Cambridge 1930.   66. *New Bearings in English Poetry*, London 1932.

67. Q. D. Leavis, *Fiction and the Reading Public*, London 1932. The 'anthropological' work in question was Robert S. Lynd and Helen Merrell Lynd, *Middletown: A Study in American Culture*. Inspired by the work of W. H. Rivers and based on intensive empirical investigation, this book, first published in 1929, explored the effects of industrial development on the 'total situation' of a small American town.

68. See Bradbrook, 'The Ambiguity of William Empson', *Seven Types of Ambiguity* was first published, London 1930.

relations between drama and capitalism in the early seventeenth century, in a book that bespoke the increasing pressure of Marxism and the mediate influence (via Tawney) of Weberian sociology.[69]

It is possible, with due caution, to suggest the overall nature of the 'critical revolution' that these works collectively represent. The effect of the curricular and institutional reforms of 1917 was to license the free interpenetration of certain cultural and social contradictions, which together transformed the character and expanded the field of operation of academic literary study. The ulterior unity and objective cultural import of the new critical practices may be seen most clearly in the work of their pioneer exponent. Richards's emphasis on 'rigour' was, in the first place, a deliberate repudiation of the amateurism of belles lettres, and thus a symbol of the intellectual professionalism to which the rising generation aspired. But it was also a logically necessary consequence of his Arnoldian conception of the social function of poetry. Richards's commitment to an ideally 'scientific' literary criticism was the measure of his belief in the social utility of its judgments: the greater the social power of poetry, the graver the responsibilities laid upon its adjudicators. For all its technicality, his *Principles* was less an academic disquisition on aesthetics than 'a loom on which . . . to reweave some ravelled parts of our civilization'.[70] Thus, the transformation of literary studies was not the only, or even the principal goal of 'the critical revolution'. The changes wrought by Richards and his contemporaries in the internal constitution of literary criticism implied a major revision of its comparative intellectual status. The 'revolution' *in* the discipline was also a revolution *of* literary criticism against the palsied cultural regime of post-war England.

The latter part of the decade has been styled 'the Golden Age' of Cambridge English.[71] 1926-7 saw the ratification of a degree-course devoted wholly to Modern English and the founding of an autonomous Faculty to govern it. The novelties of the early twenties were

---

69. *How Many Children Had Lady Macbeth?*, Cambridge 1933; *Drama and Society in the Age of Jonson*, London 1937.
70. *Principles of Literary Criticism*, p. vii.
71. Bradbrook, 'I. A. Richards at Cambridge,' p. 61.

now enshrined in the syllabus of a stable and independent discipline, whose academic legitimacy was assured by the distinguished performance of its students in university examinations.[72] However, the measures of 1926 were more ambivalent in their effects than this honorific phrase allows. With the creation of the Faculty, the *ad hoc* institutional arrangements that had played so central a role in the intellectual development of the English school were superseded by much more formal and centralized structures of teaching and administration. The freelances were disbanded as a category, and only a few of them could be included in the fixed quota of University Lecturers, appointed through set procedures, who were henceforth to be responsible for all formal lecturing.[73] The effect of the second reform was to weaken the main exponents of the first. For in addition to Richards, Forbes and Tillyard, the new teaching corps included many – among them the former College Lecturers – who were still unreconciled to the initial Tripos reform. Fearing an attempt to reintroduce compulsory Anglo-Saxon, Chadwick decided to place his department beyond their reach, and transferred it to the Faculty of Archaeology and Anthropology.[74] The loss of Chadwick further weakened the triumvirate, whose power and manoeuvrability had already been considerably diminished in the more formal, rule-bound conditions that now obtained. Bored by administrative routine, Forbes was increasingly drawn to outside activities. After the publication of *Practical Criticism*, Richards's absence from Cambridge became longer and more frequent, as the counter-attractions of China and the USA grew stronger. Only Tillyard, intellectually the least adventurous of the three, remained to oversee the process that he later interpreted as a transition from 'creation' to 'consolidation'.[75]

The changes that occurred around the turn of the decade were not, in fact, so serenely evolutionary as this interpretation suggests. The institutional system devised to accommodate the 'critical revolution' was at odds with the structures that had fostered it in the first instance. It appears, rather, that the 'consolidation' of the English school was achieved at least partly at the expense of its 'creative' sources. The

72. Tillyard, p. 120.
73. Ibid., p. 102. The conflict to which this transition gave rise is mentioned but not adequately explained by Tillyard.
74. Ibid., pp. 112–14.
75. Ibid., pp. 120f., 128.

contrasting fortunes of the College Lecturers who had shunned Chadwick's cause and the freelances who had made it their own furnish a symbol of the anomalous course of 'the revolution in English studies'.[76]

It soon became clear that these institutional alterations had induced a significant shift in the intellectual climate of the school. The resentment which the new Tripos had caused, especially in Classical quarters, now found its most uninhibited expression in the Faculty itself, in the person of F. L. Lucas, 'a classic of outstanding brilliance' who had become involved in English and now held a University Lectureship in the subject.[77] Lucas had from the outset been 'openly hostile' to the influence of Eliot;[78] and by the early 1930s, his enmity had deepened to encompass all that the new course represented. In an article on 'English Literature', written for the quasi-official conspectus *University Studies*, he launched a frontal attack on its conduct, its major personalities and its educational objectives.[79] Lucas's main target was the evaluative criticism initiated by Richards. The academic study of literature was, in his view, properly a discipline of 'fact'. But, left in the keeping of the self-appointed critical 'elect', it was in danger of lapsing into 'organized orgies of opinion'. The symptoms of critical debauchery were already discernible, he alleged, in the scripts of Tripos candidates; and in the research work of certain of its postgraduates, they were unmistakably far advanced. In a long and brutally sarcastic account of Q. D. Leavis's doctoral dissertation, *Fiction and the Reading Public*, he railed against the 'angry arrogance' of 'the critical minority' and attempted to diagnose its causes: 'this joyless attitude and its jargon rings, somehow, familiar; until suddenly one recognizes it – the Puritan has risen again. . . . Since the War, it seems as if Religion, growing weaker, had bequeathed to Art (originally her daughter it is said) and to many so-called lovers of Art her least admirable qualities – Pharisaism, asceticism and fanatical intolerance.

76. Tillyard, p. 102f; the quoted phrase comes from the subtitle of his book. It should not be assumed that the freelances were a homogeneously 'progressive' bloc or that their seniors were homogeneously 'reactionary': what can be said is that the former included the most advanced elements and the latter, the least so – in both cases, *among others*.

77. Tillyard, pp. 104–5, 80.

78. Ibid., p. 98.

79. 'English Literature,' Wright (ed.), pp. 259–94. See n. 41 above.

The same anaemic arrogance marks the critical school of Mr T. S. Eliot; though his is a more ritualistic and "higher" tone.' The educational ambitions of the new discipline received equally short shrift. As an intellectual training, Lucas affirmed, English could not compete with Mathematics, the Natural or Moral Sciences, or Classics; and as an education, Classics was peerless: 'the study of its two literatures is saved from the effeminacy of many aesthetic pursuits by its linguistic difficulty, from muddleheadedness by the clarity of the classical mind, from critical crazes by its remoteness.' Literary criticism was, as he had declared on another occasion, 'a charming parasite', a fit pastime for the cultivated but not the stuff of an intellectual discipline. For, as far as he was concerned, 'we are not training reviewers'.

Lucas did not claim official status for his views. But that a senior member of the Faculty could utter such a philippic and go unchallenged was a clear sign that the balance of forces had been decisively altered, to the disadvantage of 'the critical revolution'. However, the process of retrenchment at the centre of the Faculty was matched by the rise of a counter-movement at its periphery. Among the students who had taken it, enthusiasm for the reformed syllabus was strong; and especially so among those who had gone on to join the rapidly growing body of postgraduates in research of an unprecedentedly elastic kind. A small group of these students now began to meet regularly at the home of F. R. and Q. D. Leavis, a couple who were now coming to symbolize the opposition to the Faculty. Since the expiry of his 'probationary' lectureship in 1931, F. R. Leavis had been reduced to a precarious existence as a part-time college supervisor; his partner, her Research Fellowship at Girton College having come to an end, was in a similar situation. Publicly regarded since the publication of their first writings as leading exponents of the new 'Cambridge criticism', both now subsisted in the margins of the English course. The character of these weekly gatherings was recalled thirty years later by Leavis himself: 'The research students and undergraduates who used, in the early thirties, to meet at my house, which was very much a centre, did not suppose that they were meeting at an official centre of "Cambridge English", or one that was favoured by the official powers. They gravitated there because it had become known as a place where the essential nature, the importance and the possibilities of the English Tripos were peculiarly matters of preoccupation.

... We had most of us taken [it]; a couple of us . . . were (without salaries – an important point) teaching for it; the research students aspired to prove that they had subjects in dealing with which they could vindicate conceptions of "research" answering to [its] spirit. . . . Such a milieu favoured discussion of the state of criticism – discussion urgent and unacademic. I mean, we had no tendency to confine ourselves to questions of method or theory, and the "practicality" of the "practical criticism" we were indeed (taking "practical" as the antithesis of "theoretical") concerned to promote was not just a matter of analytic technique and brilliant exercises. What governed our thinking and engaged our sense of urgency was the inclusive, the underlying and overriding, preoccupation: the preoccupation with the critical function as it was performed, or not performed, for our civilization, our time and us.'[80]

The culture of this small circle was consciously a re-creation of the ethos of the early English school. Its major commitment was to defend and further the innovations that the Tripos reform had inspired, to establish the titles of literary criticism as an intellectually serious and culturally significant pursuit. Socially too, the group reinforced the patterns of the formative period. Neither birth nor occupational status fitted its members for the role of the scholar-gentleman. They were, for the greater part, petit or lower bourgeois in origin.[81] 'The discipline of letters' was for them a profession, not a patrimony; and at a time when the contraction of opportunity within the Faculty was compounded with nationwide graduate unemployment, none of them was professionally secure.[82] Committed to the 'vindication' of the English Tripos and yet powerless to influence the institution that housed it, the Leavis circle was impelled into an oppositional role.

80. 'Scrutiny': A Retrospect, pp. 1–2; see also English in Our Time and the University, Appendix III, pp. 190–92.

81. Some years later, reviewing Virginia Woolf's Three Guineas, Q. D. Leavis attacked the class affiliations of Bloomsbury culture and declared, with some pride: 'there is no member of that class on the contributing list of this review' ('Caterpillars of the Commonwealth Unite,' Scrutiny, VII, 2, Sept. '38, p. 203). In an interview given to me in early 1976, L. C. Knights mentioned the role of this social determinant in the formative days of the journal.

82. Bradbrook, 'I. A. Richards at Cambridge,' alludes to 'that critical era of graduate unemployment round 1933–36' (p. 61). See also F. R. Leavis, 'The State of Criticism: Representations to Fr Martin Jarrett-Kerr,' Essays in Criticism III, 2 (April '53), pp. 226–8; idem., to The Listener, November 1, 1956, repr. (John Tasker, ed.) Letters in Criticism, London 1974, p. 54.

They cast themselves as 'outlaws' whose purpose was to save 'the essential nature' of the Tripos from a narrow academicism that now threatened to extinguish it. Their mode of operation was in keeping both with the marginal situation in which they found themselves and with their conception of the ulterior cultural significance of literary criticism. The ideal of intellectual responsibility to which they aspired was represented not by the successful academic but by a failed journal, *The Calendar of Modern Letters*.

For Leavis, *The Calendar* was both an example and a caution. Its critical style, equidistant from academicism and belles lettres, was a model of 'disinterested' journalism. But in contemporary conditions, its life-span was unlikely to be bettered by 'any merely literary review, however lively and intelligent'.[83] The potential audience of any comparable successor would be considerable, 'but if, amid the distractions of the modern scene, they are to be marshalled in sufficient numbers, it must be by finding some way of enlisting a very active conviction that the "contemporary sensibility" matters very much to the contemporary world: the function and the conviction cannot now be taken for granted as they might in other days.'[84] Indeed, such a review would have to prepare to become the focus of a 'movement'. This term was, in some respects, misleading. For, as it transpired, Leavis's goal was the formation of a new social *estate*: a compact, 'disinterested' intelligentsia, united in commitment to 'human values', whose function would be to watch over and guide the progress of society at large.

The outstanding contemporary statement of this position was Julien Benda's *La Trahison des clercs*.[85] But whereas Benda had tacitly assumed that philosophical inquiry would be foremost among the concerns of the clerisy, Leavis accorded priority to literary criticism. The reason for this contrast has already been suggested. In the cultural situation of the twenties – defined by the absence of synoptic social thought at a time of profound political and social crisis – it became possible for literary criticism to reassert its claim to cultural hegemony. This Arnoldian ambition was, as we have seen, perhaps the

83. F. R. Leavis (ed.), *Towards Standards of Criticism: Selections from 'The Calendar of Modern Letters' 1925–7*, London 1976, p. 12.
84. Ibid., pp. 12–13.
85. Paris 1927.

main impulse of 'the critical revolution'; with the emergence of the 'outlaws', it found social anchorage. The marginal anti-*salon* run by the Leavises ('a kind of alternative to Bloomsbury with intellectual but no social links')[86] became the conscious nucleus of this new estate, the vanguard of 'the "highbrow" front' in culture.[87] Its instrument was *Scrutiny*.

III

It remains now to give a brief account of the works in which *Scrutiny*'s leading themes were first set out. Among F. R. Leavis's early productions were two pamphlets, published in 1930 by the Cambridge-based Minority Press. Together with Q. D. Leavis's *Fiction and the Reading Public*, which appeared on the eve of *Scrutiny*'s inception, they constitute a preliminary reconnaissance of its field of operations.

Leavis's first study of D. H. Lawrence was less a literary-critical discussion of his novels than a meditation on their broad cultural meaning. The summary judgments passed on them were, on the whole, subordinate moments in a general evaluation of their author's vitalist ideology. In Leavis's view, Lawrence's affirmation of 'impulse and spontaneity against "reason" and convention' was both a condition of his artistic achievement and a limitation upon it. If it inspired the shorter works, like *St Mawr* and *England, My England*, where 'his genius triumphs again and again', it was also responsible for the 'monotony' of *The Rainbow*, with its 'drama of the inexplicit and almost inaccessible in human intercourse', and for the 'dissipation of genius' that the later novels represented.[88] As a means of social criticism, the Lawrentian ideology was similarly ambivalent. 'It is plain that the

86. Victoria Brittain, 'F. R. Leavis: Half a Century of Arousing Academic Enmity,' *The Times*, February 17, 1975.

87. This phrase comes from 'Scrutiny', a four-page publicity brochure issued by the editors, probably in the summer of 1934. I am grateful to R. G. Cox who brought it to my attention and made a copy for me.

88. 'D. H. Lawrence,' *For Continuity*, Cambridge 1933, pp. 113, 144, 117. This version includes the 1930 text, and two addenda, dated 1932 and 1933. Some of this material also appeared in F. R. Leavis, 'On D. H. Lawrence,' *Cambridge Review*, June 13, 1930.

civilization that he still seems in some way to care for could not exist if no one cared more about "mind" than he does. It is plain that his devotion to the dark God is not so much an evangel of salvation as a symptom; a refuge from the general malady rather than a cure.'[89] Not even *Lady Chatterley's Lover*, which Leavis singled out as Lawrence's most accomplished novel, was exempted from this qualification. 'So far as artistic success can validate his teaching, *Lady Chatterley's Lover* does so'; but 'a complete wisdom ... involves greater concern for intelligence and the finer products of civilization than Lawrence ever manifests.'[90] The real achievement of the novel was to have stated 'the inclusive problem of our time': that of 'industrialism' and its impact on society and culture. The 'fundamental nature' of the problem, Leavis believed, had been grasped in Spengler's phenomenology of urban rootlessness: 'one can, without endorsing the Spenglerian idiom or philosophy, recognize [its] felicity ... as an account of the present situation. The traditional ways of life have been destroyed by the machine, more and more does human life depart from the natural rhythms, the cultures have mingled, and the forms have dissolved into chaos, so that everywhere the serious literature of the West betrays a sense of paralysing consciousness, of a lack of direction, of momentum, of dynamic axioms.'[91] Yet, for all the desolation of these lines, Leavis's vein was not so much the *sic transit* of *The Decline of the West* as what one of his collaborators later termed a 'desperate optimism'; and Lawrence, with his 'splendid human vitality, ... creative faith, and ... passionate sense of responsibility', was its symbol.[92]

The themes of *D. H. Lawrence* were expounded in a more general and analytic form in *Mass Civilization and Minority Culture*. Leavis's purpose in this pamphlet was to argue that the traditional relationship between 'civilization' (the totality of social relations) and 'culture' (the values on which 'fine living' depended) had been strained to the point of rupture by the advance of 'the machine'. Historically, 'culture' had been preserved and transmitted by a minority who, mediating the values of the past in the present, had been able to safeguard the 'currency' on which the general 'standard of living' rested.[93] But the

---

89. *For Continuity*, p. 128. 90. Ibid., pp. 131, 135.
91. Ibid., p. 139. 92. Ibid., pp. 140–41.
93. 'Mass Civilization and Minority Culture,' *Education and the University*, London 1948, pp. 141–71; p. 143f. This essay was actually published some months before

accelerated pace of economic development, and the new patterns of recreation and culture that it entailed, now threatened the integrity of this inherited order. The motor car, symbol of the second industrial revolution, had 'broken up' the family and disrupted social custom.[94] The latter-day evolution of the Press showed that 'mass production' and 'standardization' meant 'a process of levelling-down'.[95] Despite certain appearances, the new media were no less deleterious in their effects: 'the standardizing influence of broadcasting hardly admits of doubt'; the cinema – 'the more insidious' for its 'compellingly vivid illusion of actual life' – relied on the 'cheapest emotional appeals', and tended to induce 'a passive diversion' that was inimical to 'active recreation, especially active use of the mind'.[96] At the same time, the prose of the advertising copywriter, crafted solely for the purpose of psychological manipulation, placed language itself in jeopardy.[97] In effect, 'there has been an overthrow of standards, . . . authority has disappeared, and . . . the currency has been debased and inflated.'[98]

According to Leavis, modern historical change had been so rapid and profound that society was now threatened with 'a breach in continuity'.[99] In the struggle to prevent it, the crucial theatre was language, which, as Richards had argued, was increasingly the sole link between past and present: 'as the other vehicles of tradition, the family and the community, for example, are dissolved, we are forced more and more to rely upon language.'[100] Thus, Leavis argued, 'culture' was actually certain uses of language, 'the living subtlety of the finest idiom' without which 'the heritage dies'.[101] To judge a given use of language was *ipso facto* to assay the values of society; the literary critic was, inescapably, the arbiter of good.[102] But even in this crucial sphere, the progressive dissociation of 'culture' and 'civilization' was well advanced. The survival of 'the finest idiom', and thus of 'culture', was threatened not only by the abuses of advertising, but also by the advocates of linguistic reforms such as Basic English, whose success

D. H. Lawrence (Hayman, p. 11); I have reversed them here for the sake of expository convenience. 'Civilization' and 'culture', defined and opposed in this sense, go back, in English thought, to Coleridge, *On the Constitution of Church and State* (see Raymond Williams, *Keywords*, London 1976, 'Civilization').

94. Ibid., p. 146.   95. Ibid., pp. 147–8.   96. Ibid., pp. 149–50.
97. Ibid., p. 150f.   98. Ibid., p. 152.   99. Ibid., p. 146.
100. Ibid., p. 168n. (from *Practical Criticism*, corrected).
101. Ibid., p. 168.   102. Ibid., pp. 144–5. Here again his authority was Richards.

would herald the final victory of 'mass production and standard-ization'.[103] The growth of a mass market in publishing had disorientated the average cultivated reader, and delivered critical standards into the keeping of literary entrepreneurs like Arnold Bennett or the selection committee of the Book Club.[104] Meanwhile, 'the minority' was more disadvantaged than ever before. The cultivated public was scarcely able to support 'a serious critical organ': *The Calendar* had perished for want of support; only the *New Adelphi* and the *Criterion* (whose stability seemed to depend on 'a specific ecclesiastical interest') remained.[105] The new phenomenon of a specifically 'highbrow' literature dramatized the relationship that now obtained between 'the minority' and society. Isolated and embattled, the custodians of 'culture' were 'being cut off as never before from the powers that rule the world'.[106] It was unclear, moreover, what the terms of any future pact between the two might be. For their divergence was fundamentally the index of an irreducible antagonism: 'some of the most disinterested solicitude for civilization is apt to be, consciously or unconsciously, inimical to culture.'[107] Basic English was one example of this; the Russian Revolution, now caught up in the momentum of the first Five Year Plan, was another. 'It is vain,' Leavis wrote, 'to resist the triumph of the machine. [But] it is equally vain to console us with the promise of a "mass culture" that shall be utterly new. . . . The "utterly new" surrenders everything that can interest us.'[108] Nevertheless, Leavis resisted the fatalism and 'proud philosophic indifference' of Spengler's prognosis. It was not yet impossible to believe 'that what we value most matters too much to the race to be finally abandoned, and that the machine will yet be made a tool.' And although no programmatic solution was in view at that date, there remained the responsibility 'to be as aware as possible of what is happening, and, if we can, to "keep open our communications with the future".'[109]

Fiction and the Reading Public was the logical successor of *Mass Civilization and Minority Culture*, in substance and in method. Its object was to confirm, in a systematic and documented analysis, the diagnosis of the

103. Ibid., pp. 167–8. 104. Ibid., pp. 152f., 159f. 105. Ibid., pp. 158–9.
106. Ibid., pp. 163–5. 107. Ibid., p. 164. 108. Ibid., p. 169.
109. Ibid., pp. 145, 170–71.

earlier work, and to elucidate the aetiology of the malaise. However, the analysis of the literary products of 'civilization' from the vantage-point of 'culture' was *ex hypothesi* problematic. The aim of Q. D. Leavis's study was to provide an account of 'fiction as distinct from literature'. But literary criticism, as she understood it, was necessarily unable to 'take . . . heed of the majority of novels'. Estranged from the moral community of 'culture', they were, in a strict sense, unrecognizable. And yet, 'no theory of criticism is satisfactory which is not able to explain their wide appeal and to give clear reasons why those who disdain them are not necessarily snobs'.[110] This contradiction determined the peculiar logical form of her inquiry. The trichotomy 'highbrow'/'middlebrow'/'lowbrow' was less an analytic discovery than an evaluative representation of the literary field as seen through the optic of 'culture', not the result of the analysis but its unchallengeable presupposition. That the contemporary bestseller was an aberration from the self-understood norms of 'culture' was not in dispute; what needed to be explained was the fact of its existence. Since the relationship between 'culture' and 'civilization' was also a relationship between past and present, the form of this explanation was *historical*. The notion of an original unity of 'culture' and 'civilization', which in F. R. Leavis's argument had been an unobtrusive assumption, was now expounded as the first principle of a theory of cultural history.

According to Q. D. Leavis, this ideal homogeneity had been the hallmark of the 'lusty' traditional culture of early seventeenth-century England, and, to a diminished but still ample extent, of the 'polite' and 'popular' reading publics of the following century. However, the later eighteenth saw the onset of the economic and social changes that were eventually to breach this common order and engulf the cultural 'standards' that it had maintained. Industrialization and urbanization combined with radical alterations in the organization of literary production and distribution to enlarge and diversify the reading public and to debase its inherited values. With the dissolution of the peasantry, the 'halcyon age' of 'the folk' passed away. The masses who had once been privileged to 'take the same amusements as their betters' and, in a later day, been schooled in 'the good life' by Bunyan, were now serviced by the hack writers of the popular Press.

110. London 1932, pp. xiv, xiii, xv.

The degeneration of popular taste mirrored the degradation of the popular condition. Seventeenth-century culture owed its vitality to the traditional life of the peasant; the psychologically exploitative and morally conformist bestsellers of the modern epoch expressed the spiritual indigence of his historic successor, 'the exhausted city worker'.[111]

The culture of the dominant classes underwent a parallel decline. The integrity of the eighteenth-century educated public had been founded on an authoritative moral code which, with certain modifications, was in continuity with the 'court culture' of the Restoration. Mediating between Aphra Behn's 'aristocratic' poise and the new values represented by Defoe, 'the journalist of the bourgeois', Addison and Steele had forged a stable language that nourished writers from Mrs Haywood to Jane Austen. But here too, the latter part of the century saw the beginnings of disintegration. The 'rational code of feeling' that had buttressed the eighteenth-century novel was eroded by the sentimental literature that poured from the circulating libraries, and finally swept away by Romanticism. Critical organs like the *Edinburgh Review* managed to preserve the idiom of the age well into the next century, but among novelists, only Emily Brontë, Mrs Gaskell and George Eliot wrote with the authority of their predecessors. Favoured by the new techniques of publication and distribution, sensation and 'uplift' came to dominate the bestselling novel. The economic reorganization of the Press resulted in an equivalent debasement of journalistic standards. The overriding need to maximize circulation led to a systematic cultivation of conformism, quietism and 'blind optimism', and a corresponding hostility to criticism of any kind. In the organs of opinion, 'critical standards' had been ousted by the solidarities of regiment, club and school, the 'authority' of the *Edinburgh* by the good fellowship of *Punch*.[112]

Thus, Q. D. Leavis believed, there had been an 'overthrow of minority values' at every level of society. The stultification of the masses had been accompanied by the degeneration of 'the governing and professional classes', on whom the transmission of 'culture' had traditionally depended: 'the people with power no longer represent intellectual authority and culture.' But a philistine ruling class implied

111. Ibid., Part II, chs. 1–3; pp. 151f., 85, 97f., 85f., 27, 48.
112. Ibid., pp. 118, 121–6, 128f, 130, 152, 164f, 191f, 198–9.

a powerless 'minority'. How, in these conditions, were the representatives of 'culture' to assert themselves? Given the immensity of the
economic forces ranged against them, she argued, individual initiatives
were futile. 'If there is to be any hope, it must lie in conscious and
directed effort. All that can be done, it must be realized, must take
the form of resistance by an armed and conscious minority.'[113]

The chief tactics in this campaign were to be research into the actual
state of the reading public and dissemination of the results, and an
educational practice specifically directed against the effects of journalism, advertising, the cinema and other manifestations of the modern
historical process. Its weapons were to be 'a non-commercial Press'
and 'an all-round critical organ'. The first already existed, on a modest
scale, in Gordon Fraser's Minority Press. So far, there was no exemplar
of the second. Since the closure of the *Calendar*, England's periodical
culture had regressed towards the traditional pattern that still held
in academic literary studies. Criticism was practised in a spirit of
sociable, conservative amateurism – be it 'civilized', as under the
editorship of Desmond MacCarthy in *Life and Letters*, or affectedly
'common', as in the circle around J. C. Squire and the *London Mercury* –
while the universities were represented only by the devotedly philological *Review of English Studies*. The monthly *Bookman* was indeed open
to the new critical generation (F. R. Leavis reviewed quite regularly
for it in the early thirties) but its editor was also ready to publish
obtuse rearguard attacks on them. A much more serious kind of
intellectual journalism was conducted in the *Criterion* and the *Adelphi*,
but Eliot's organ was guided more and more by its peculiar 'ecclesiastical interest' as the years passed, while the latter was consecrated to
the preoccupations and purposes of its editor, Middleton Murry.[114]
The conscious alienation of 'the minority' from the periodical culture
of the time was conveyed in the scathing generalization with which

113. Ibid., pp. 199, 191, 270.

114. *Life and Letters* was founded in 1928, the *London Mercury* in 1919. The *Review of
English Studies* was initiated by R. B. McKerrow in 1925 and edited by him until
1940. The *Bookman* appeared from 1891 until 1934, when it was incorporated into
the *London Mercury* – which, four years later, was in turn absorbed into *Life and
Letters*. The *Criterion* and the *Adelphi* were founded in 1922 and 1923 respectively.
Leavis's contributions to the *Bookman* included 'Criticism of the Year,' LXXXI, 483
(December '31), p. 180; 'Poetry in an Age of Science,' LXXXII, 487 (April '32), p. 42;
'This Age in Literary Criticism,' LXXXIII, 493 (October '32), pp. 8–9; and 'Shelley's
Imagery,' LXXXVI, 516 (September '34), p. 278.

Q. D. Leavis dismissed it: 'one after another the serious politico-literary periodicals have disappeared or lowered their colours, and there is scarcely one left whose liberty of speech has not been sold to the advertiser or mortgaged to vested interests.'[115]

The possibility of launching a journal comparable in critical quality to *The Calendar* but wider in focus had been discussed in the Leavis circle. As it turned out, the practical initiatives that finally brought the journal into being were taken not by the Leavises themselves, but by L. C. Knights, a young research student from Grantham in Lincolnshire who frequented their circle, and an American acquaintance, Donald Culver. Although he consented to write for the journal and approved the manifesto that Knights had drafted for it, Leavis declined to share editorial responsibility until its intellectual character had begun to take definite shape. The inaugural issue of *Scrutiny*, so named in tribute to *The Calendar*, appeared under the editorship of Knights and Culver, in May 1932.

115. *Fiction and the Reading Public*, p. 272.

Two

Between Past and Future
(1932–1939)

Versions of the Modern Crisis

The first issue of *Scrutiny* was printed in 750 copies at a cost of fifty pounds. Bound in pale blue card, it was ninety-four octavo pages in length, the first sixty-five containing seven articles and two poems, the rest devoted to short notes and reviews. The issue proved a success, critically and commercially, selling out within months. The second issue, brought out in the same number of copies, sold still more quickly and had soon to be reprinted; with the third, the print order was raised to 1,000 copies. Thus, *Scrutiny*'s publishing format and periodicity were soon securely established. For the rest of the decade, it appeared at quarterly intervals, in March, June, September and December. Subscriptions and commercial distribution were taken in hand by a Cambridge bookseller. Within four years the journal had expanded to a constant length of one hundred and twenty pages per issue, of which approximately sixty per cent were devoted to an average of five to six articles, the remainder forming the 'Comments and Reviews' section at the rear.

After the appearance of the second issue, in September 1932, Knights and Harding were joined on the editorial board by F. R. Leavis and Denys Thompson. Then, some twelve months later, Culver went abroad and was immediately replaced by D. W. Harding. The new recruits exemplified the continuities between the early Tripos, the Leavises' 'outlaw' circle and the new journal. Thompson, now aged twenty-five, was the son of an Anglican priest from Darlington in the North-East of England, and had studied under Leavis as a member of St John's College at the end of the twenties. Harding, several months his senior, had been born into an accountant's family in Lowestoft, Suffolk, in 1906; he had been a pupil of Leavis at Emmanuel (the latter's own college) and a contemporary of Knights in the English Faculty.[1] The editorial team brought into being by his entry was to remain unchanged until the summer of 1939.

The relative contributions of the four were from the outset very uneven. For not only was Leavis the senior of his fellow-editors by more than ten years (he was now thirty-eight), and in the cases of two of them, a former teacher; he was also the only one permanently based in Cambridge. The first initiative and early organizational work had been Knights's achievement; but an Assistant Lectureship at the University of Manchester kept him away from Cambridge during 1933–4, and a year later he took up a permanent post there. Harding had joined the research staff of the National Institute of Industrial Psychology after graduating in 1928, and remained in that position until 1933, when he became a lecturer in Social Psychology at the London School of Economics. Thompson was at this time a teacher of English at Gresham's, a minor public school in Norfolk. Hence, while Knights, Harding and Thompson were frequent and important contributors to the journal, inter-editorial communication was perforce intermittent, and collaborative planning extremely difficult to sustain. In practice, Leavis's main collaborator was his wife, Q. D. Leavis, who, although never accorded the formal editorial status that was her due, was among the journal's most prolific authors and bore the main burden of secretarial work for it. Her labour reinforced her partner's position, making the Leavis household the 'centre' from which *Scrutiny* was effectively produced.

At the same time, the dispersal of the editorial board was more than counter-balanced by the much larger group of supporters and collaborators that the Leavises were able to attract in Cambridge itself. Neither held any official position in the Faculty (F. R. Leavis had been editing *Scrutiny* for four years when he was appointed University Lecturer and Fellow of Downing College in 1936; and Q. D. Leavis was never to obtain any official status at any time); but the influence of their teaching and writing was very powerful among undergraduates and research students, and here they found contributors with whom direct and often sustained relations could be formed.

1. Thompson was born in 1907 and graduated from Cambridge in 1930, two years after Knights and Harding. (Sources: *The Cambridge University List of Members, 1976*; the Registrar General's Office.)

About half of the one hundred and fifty-odd individuals who ever wrote for *Scrutiny* were Cambridge graduates, and a majority of these were enlisted through some form of collegiate or academic relationship with the Leavises or the other members of the editorial board. They were, characteristically, recent graduates in their early twenties when their contributions appeared. A substantial number of them were members of three colleges with which the editors had personal links: Emmanuel, F. R. Leavis's old college; Christ's, to which Knights was attached during his years of doctoral research; and above all Downing, where Leavis was to teach for nearly thirty years. Muriel Bradbrook, William Hunter, D. J. Enright and G. D. Klingopulos, all of whom contributed within two years of graduation; R. G. Cox and Geoffrey Walton, who took their degrees in 1935 and remained at Downing to pursue postgraduate research; Wilfrid Mellers, who also read English there and then lodged with the Leavises while studying for a degree in Music; Boris Ford, who had passed from Thompson's tutelage at Gresham's directly into Leavis's at Downing – these were among the membership of perhaps the most compact and youthful writing corps possessed by any journal in England this century.[2]

The aims of the journal were announced in the manifesto that opened its first number. *Scrutiny*, the editors wrote, would not confine itself to purely literary discussion. The troubled social and cultural circumstances of the early 1930s called for a publication 'that combines criticism of literature with criticism of extra-literary activities'. Accordingly, *Scrutiny* was to be 'seriously preoccupied with the movement of modern civilization' as a whole; 'a pervasive interest of the magazine will find expression in disinterested surveys of some departments of modern life in an attempt to increase understanding of the way in which civilization is developing.' Much more was implied here than a modestly 'responsible' catholicity of interest. As we have already seen, the devaluation of the 'purely literary' was the deceptive

2. Bradbrook (born 1909) was the daughter of a Waterguard Superintendent. Cox (born 1914) was the son of a Grantham outfitter's manager, Mellers (also 1914) of a teacher in Leamington in the West Midlands. Ford was born in 1917 in India, where his father was a serving officer in the army. (Sources: *Who's Who*, the Registrar General's Office, and for the other data given above, *The Cambridge University List of Members, 1976*, and direct information.)

outward sign of a profound revaluation of the duties and competence of literary criticism. Apparently a gesture of renunciation, the avoidance of the 'purely literary' was, in essence, an act of realization, an entry into literary criticism truly conceived, in all its cultural potency. The editors hinted as much when they spoke of 'a necessary relationship between the quality of the individual's response to art and his general fitness for a humane existence', and, for this reason, could claim that the critical strategy of the new journal was 'immediately practical and political'.[3] Thus, it might be said that the observable 'surfaces' of the journal gave an inverted image of their intellectual substructure. The predominance of the literary in *Scrutiny*, and its paramount role in the world-view of the *Scrutiny* circle, was the effect of a process of argument that was social and political in character and purpose.[4]

I

Scrutiny's most pressing task was to undertake an investigation of the contemporary world. Produced in the 'play of the free intelligence upon the underlying issues', this investigation was to be guided above all by 'a cultivated historical sense, a familiarity with the "anthropological" approach to contemporary civilization exemplified by *Middletown*, and a catholic apprehension of the humane values'.[5] By May 1932, the meaning of these vague protocols had already been specified in practice, in the early writings of F. R. and Q. D. Leavis. And with the publication in the following year of *Culture and Environment*, the main arguments of those works were powerfully reinforced, in a trenchant analysis of the material foundations of modern culture.

In *Culture and Environment*, F. R. Leavis and Denys Thompson attempted to trace the causal links between industrial 'mass production' and

3. 'A Manifesto,' I, 1 (May '32), pp. 2, 3, 6, 5, 4. All subsequent references to *Scrutiny* are given in this form. On the few occasions when this form is used with reference to other journals not named in the note itself, the context of discussion is sufficient to distinguish the latter from *Scrutiny*.

4. The 'time' of this process is notional, not real. It is not claimed that it can be found in the intellectual biography of any of the individuals concerned, much less in the chronological unfolding of the journal between 1932 and the Second World War.

5. 'A Manifesto,' p. 3.

the patterns of contemporary culture. The main emphases of their analysis fell on two aspects of the industrial economy: the mass market – the new types of commodity displayed there and the means used to sell them – and the labour process of the modern factory. The invariable effects of mass production were, as Leavis had argued some three years before, 'standardization' and 'levelling-down'. This was due, in the first place, to the character of machine-made goods: the 'standardization of commodities' led inexorably to the 'standardization of persons'.[6] This more or less automatic process was fuelled, moreover, by the effects of advertising. In a newspaper industry now dependent on advertising for the bulk of its revenues, editorial practices were inevitably steered by the overriding imperative to maximize circulation towards the unexacting norms of the 'average' reader. In other sectors of publishing, the same drive for mass sales swept traditional standards into disuse, in the name of 'readability'.[7] The cultural effects of advertising were not all the result of the economic constraints that it imposed. Distinct both from the mainly informational notices of the first newspapers and from the merely hyperbolic publicity material of the early popular Press, modern advertising – the systematic investment of commodities with meanings more or less unrelated to their use-values — was itself a genuinely new element in the cultural ensemble.[8] The active cultivation of delusory social values ('optimism', 'Progress', the 'herd instinct') and the discernible stylistic convergence between popular fiction and advertisements were testimonies of the direct action of the copywriter in the sphere of culture.[9]

The deleterious cultural effects of the mass market were aggravated, from the other side, by the conditions of labour in the modern factory. As the division of labour advanced, work became ever more repetitive and devoid of responsibility; craftsmanship withered into 'machine-tending'.[10] Drawing on the writings of George Sturt, Leavis and Thompson contrasted the aesthetic and moral training inherent in the pursuit of traditional skills with the cultural sterility of the

6. *Culture and Environment*, p. 32.

7. Ibid., pp. 38–56.

8. As Leavis and Thompson commented: '[advertising] has ironically been said to be the only Art that has indisputably advanced in the last thirty years' (p. 12).

9. *Culture and Environment*, pp. 46–56.

10. Ibid., p. 29.

assembly-line. The village craftsmen memorialized by Sturt had possessed 'a fine code of personal relations with one another and with the master, a dignified notion of their place in the community and an understanding of the necessary part played by their work in the scheme of things'. But for the factory worker, subjected to a division of labour that robbed labour of interest and its products of significance, and to a process of technological change whose pace neither spared old traditions nor allowed new ones to take root, the only possible value of work was the leisure that it financed.[11] The nature of that leisure was in turn determined by that of the work and its products. The monotony of the work-place was redressed by the distractions and compensatory fantasy-materials of radio and the cinema, which, together with other modern leisure pursuits such as motoring, progressively ate away the surviving remnants of truly 'social', truly 'recreative' play. Fulfilled in labour, Sturt's villagers had little need of leisure; nowadays, men and women sought satisfaction in forms of 'substitute living' as sterile as the frustration and fatigue that they were designed to palliate.[12] The 'gregarious manifestations' of the present (cinema audiences, for instance) were evidence less of 'social life' than of a primordial sense of 'herd solidarity' in individuals bent on 'escape from their loneliness and the emptiness of their lives'.[13] Such, in the view of Leavis and Thompson, was the parched 'environment' of human life in the industrial civilization of the early twentieth century.

Together with *Mass Civilization and Minority Culture* and *Fiction and the Reading Public*, this short 'educational' work effectively established the terms and tendencies of *Scrutiny*'s governing theme: 'industrialism' and its destructive effects on society and culture. Within the journal itself, no single contribution matched the breadth of the first or the

11. Ibid., pp. 104, 105. George Sturt is best known for *Change in the Village*, London 1912, and *The Wheelwright's Shop*, London 1923, issued under the name of 'George Bourne'. For a brief biography see E. D. Mackerness (ed.), *The Journals of George Sturt 1890–1927* (two vols.), Cambridge 1967, vol. 1, pp. 5–31; see also idem, 'George Sturt and the English Humanitarian Tradition,' *Essays and Studies 1969*, XXII, N.S., pp. 105–22.

12. *Culture and Environment*, pp. 99–103.

13. Ibid., p. 65.

historical sweep of the second; and no one discussed the structures of the industrial economy as directly or systematically as the authors of *Culture and Environment* had done. These three works were, then, more than blueprints for future research: jointly, they formed a unitary and comprehensive argument that underlay the relatively discrete analyses that actually appeared in the pages of *Scrutiny*. The majority of these were concerned mainly with cultural questions, and as such will be discussed at length elsewhere. For the moment, it will be sufficient to trace the range and bias of these discussions, especially where they relate directly and explicitly to the general analysis of modern historical development.

For anyone professionally involved in the arts, as practitioner, theorist or critic, the emergence of cinema was an event of immense significance. For literary intellectuals pledged as the *Scrutiny* circle were to the defence of 'culture' in an increasingly hostile social 'environment', it was also a portent. There, where technological innovation and the mass market intersected, giving birth to a new art-form, the actual relations between 'culture' and 'civilization' were made manifest. A short essay by William Hunter, published in the first number of the review, expressed the uneasy interest of 'the fastidious minority' in the advance of 'the art-form of democracy'. Believing that film production was inextricably wedded to commercial interests and, for the greater part, entirely anaesthetic in its effects, Hunter was prepared to accord the new medium only a strictly limited artistic title.[14] The best examples of popular cinema – the work of Soviet directors and, in the West, the films of Chaplin and René Clair – had achieved 'a level sufficiently high to give us excuse for optimism'; but it seemed doubtful, nonetheless, whether film was intrinsically capable of equalling the achievements of the 'high' arts: the 'popular' cinema of Chaplin and Clair was, in his view, 'truer cinema and a finer synthesis of experience than the "advanced" work of Bunuel or Dulac'.[15] However far 'our democratic art-form' progressed, Hunter implied, it would remain an essentially demotic medium, outside the pale of 'minority' interests. 'No film yet produced can justify the serious critical approach demanded (for instance) by a good novel or poem. This needs saying firmly, since the cult of "Cinema" by intellectuals,

14. 'The Art-Form of Democracy?' I, 1 (May '32), p. 61.
15. Ibid., p. 62.

English, French and American, shows how insidious may be the forms of *la trahison des clercs*.'[16] A year later, reviewing Rudolf Arnheim's *Film*, Hunter returned with still greater asperity to 'the "intellectual" cult of cinema', denouncing 'the kind of psychological smokescreen the highbrow will throw out to justify his own surrender to the onanistic flesh-and-underclothing motifs'.[17] For all his aversion from the intellectual devotees of the cinema, Hunter was personally appreciative of its more distinguished products and prepared to grant the medium an inferior station within a corporatist cultural scheme. But in this he was only slightly less isolated than the reviewer of his own volume, *Scrutiny of Cinema*, who was not nearly so suspicious of the mass and commercial character of film and considered it worthy of serious critical attention.[18] The consensual judgment of the *Scrutiny* group on the subject was crushingly negative. Q. D. Leavis saw the cinema as one of the 'disruptive forces' that now threatened to extinguish the traditional culture of the working class.[19] For L. C. Knights, it was part of the coalition of interests that stood ranged against valid cultural ideals.[20] And in the writings of Denys Thompson, as in those of F. R. Leavis, cinema figured in the company of the Press, radio and motoring as a familiar of 'the machine'.[21]

Modern musical forms fared only slightly better at the hands of the *Scrutiny* group. Here too, 'industrialism' was identified as the main instigator of disruption and decay. In the essays of Bruce Pattison, who was responsible for the majority of the journal's music criticism in the pre-war period, the Industrial Revolution was portrayed as having destroyed the social conditions that, until then, had guaranteed the survival of an ages-old musical tradition. Where once the soil of traditional popular song had lain, providing nourishment for a whole musical culture, 'the forces of mass production, shoddy thinking and trivial living' had created a dust-bowl in which nothing could thrive.

16. Ibid., p. 65.

17. II, 2 (September '33), p. 211.

18. J. Isaacs, rev. William Hunter, *Scrutiny of Cinema*, I, 4 (March '33), pp. 414–6.

19. 'Lady Novelists and the Lower Orders,' IV, 2 (September '35), pp. 112–32. In *Fiction and the Reading Public* she had cited Anatole France's desolate judgment: 'le cinéma matérialise le pire idéal populaire.... Il ne s'agit pas de la fin du monde mais de la fin de la civilisation.'

20. 'Will Training Colleges Bear Scrutiny?' I, 3 (December '32), p. 259; see also W. A. Edwards, 'Ideals and Facts in Adult Education,' III, 1 (June '34), p. 91.

21. See for example 'What Shall We Teach?' II, 4 (March '34), p. 380.

The social changes that ensued under the aegis of industry had ruptured the organic bonds between performer and audience. If the broadcasting system now diffused music throughout society, it was in such a way as to redouble the passivity of the audience and the estrangement of the performer.[22] In the rootless, standardized society of modern England, authentically 'national' music had virtually disappeared. 'The musical language of the new uniformity', there and abroad, was jazz, a form with 'the same level of appeal as the popular press and film'. The 'rhythms of the soil' had at length been replaced by 'the inanities of a jazz band or a cinema organ' as the measure of popular life.[23] The general cultural-historical themes of Pattison's criticism were reaffirmed in the much more detailed and extensive writings of his successor, Wilfrid Mellers. Like Pattison, Mellers considered the contemporary 'environment' exceptionally unconducive to sustained musical creativity. The 'mechanized and cosmopolitan' social life of the present was wholly lacking in those 'vital conventions' which in earlier, genuinely 'communal' times had underwritten the work of the individual composer. 'Isolation' was the condition of modern artistic activity, and of its successes, which, though certainly not inconceivable, would be exceptional, precarious and laboriously won.[24] Mellers was more attentive than Pattison to contemporary music and more sanguine about its prospects: if he was unable to endorse 'Stravinsky's callously discarded phases' or the 'desperate shilly-shallying, pastiche and experimentalism' of Schönberg and his followers, he was nevertheless appreciative of the few who, like Vaughan Williams or Bernard van Dieren, had achieved an authentically contemporary relationship with the musical tradition.[25] Their differences on the question of popular music were rather more significant. Pattison would probably have concurred in Frank Chapman's judgment that jazz was a form with 'no root in contemporary life[,] . . . something served out to the people, rather than made by

22. 'Music and the Community,' II, 4 (March '34), pp. 399–404, especially pp. 400, 403; see also 'Eighteenth Century Musical Taste,' IV, 4 (March '36), pp. 425–31. Pattison was a research student in Cambridge in the early thirties.

23. 'Music in Decline,' II, 2 (September '34), pp. 198–205, at p. 204; 'Musical History,' III, 4 (March '35), pp. 369–77.

24. W. H. Mellers, 'Tight-ropes to Parnassus: A Note on Contemporary Music,' V, 2 (September '36), pp. 150–7, at pp. 151–2, 153.

25. 'Bernard Van Dieren (1884–1936): Musical Intelligence and "the New Language",' V, 3 (December '36), p. 266; 'Tight-ropes to Parnassus,' pp. 153–5.

them', and not, therefore, to be dignified with the title of 'modern folk-art'.[26] Mellers, on the other hand, was inclined to accept the accomplished fact of 'the machine' and the cultural fissure between 'popular' and 'serious' forms that it had opened up, and, in that awareness, to weigh the possibility of a popular music valid and creditable in its own terms and within its own restricted sphere. In his essay on 'Jean Wiéner and Music for Entertainment' Mellers set out to define both the potentialities and the limitations of a strictly 'popular music', a variety 'composed to fulfil a social function, written in the first place without regard to its aesthetic value but rather as entertainment'.[27] The work of Wiéner, he held, was a 'remarkably intelligent' example of this genre. Thoroughly modern in its use of 'the mechanical' and written for the functional purposes of dance and the cinema, it showed what 'honestly utilitarian' popular music could and should be.[28] The resemblances between this argument and the corporatism of William Hunter's observations on the cinema were made clearer still in a later essay on the same topic. There, Mellers argued that 'the mechanistic bases of our civilization' precluded any fruitful liaison between 'popular' and 'serious' music.[29] Just as 'utilitarian' music should neither claim nor receive the attention due to 'serious' music, so too no composer with artistic ambitions could think to submit, as Wiéner had done, 'to the conditions of mechanism'. The 'honest composer' could 'create music that is a full artistic expression' or 'construct music that is sincerely adapted to the conventions of industry'; but it was not possible to do both. The only practical course for those who were concerned for the musical taste of the populace was to see that 'everything possible' was 'done to raise the level of commercial music *for what it is and within its own sphere*'.[30]

Mellers's concessions to the musical forms of 'machine civilization' were no more than a paternalistic rearguard action.[31] In the matter of language, the most crucial remaining conduit of 'tradition' in the present, not even that degree of latitude was possible. Here the

---

26. Frank Chapman, rev. Harold Stovin, *Totem: the Exploitation of Youth*, IV, 4 (March '36), p. 448.

27. (December '37), p. 284.   28. Ibid., pp. 285–92.

29. 'Searchlight on Tin Pan Alley,' VIII, 4 (March '40), p. 392.

30. Ibid., pp. 399, 392 (emphasis original).

31. See ibid., pp. 399–400.

watchwords were always those of *Fiction and the Reading Public*. *Scrutiny* distinguished three related forms of degeneration which linguistic practices were judged to have suffered as a result of modern economic development. The first of these was the degradation of journalistic standards in the service of commercial interests. Denys Thompson, whose vigorous polemics accounted for most of *Scrutiny*'s coverage of this area, dated the sickness of contemporary journalism to the 1890s – the decade that saw the introduction of compulsory elementary education and the launching of the *Daily Mail*. In the succeeding decades, the 'pervasively responsible press' of nineteenth-century England, which had 'preserved standards with an authority now inconceivable', had succumbed to the coadjutant pressures of advertising – with its 'Rotarian' glorification of 'the idea of Progress' – and mass readerships.[32] In 'the higher journalism' too, the later nineteenth century saw the beginnings of deterioration, as 'the vocabulary of Progress' and a certain 'rationalist strain bred from Mill' filtered into the idiom of the Victorian periodical. By 1918 or thereabouts the process was complete: 'by increasing the demand for cheap stimuli, and supplying improved machines to meet it', the War finally extinguished the old journalistic tradition.[33] Those who now looked to the Press for 'means to social consciousness' such as the *Edinburgh Review* had once furnished, met only with 'nullity, . . . calculated irresponsibility, . . . complacency and obtuseness'.[34]

In discussions of this type, the relationship between linguistic practice and industrialism was conceived as a culpable abuse of the one in the interests of the other. A second type of discussion turned on the more radical proposition that the peculiar economic and social processes of industrial society had actually sapped the signifying capacities of language. This linguistic debility was, in the first place, a result of the impoverishment of social existence. As Leavis wrote, 'what we diagnose in expression, as inadequacy in the use of words, goes back

32. 'Prospectus for a Weekly,' II, 3 (December '33), p. 247–52; 'Advertising God,' I, 3 (December '32), pp. 241–6. See also idem, rev. A. J. Cummings, *The Press*, IV, (March '36), pp. 458–60; *Culture and Environment*, p. 104; Q. D. Leavis, 'Fleet Street and Pierian Roses,' II, 4 (March '34), pp. 387–92; L. C. K[nights], rev. Jane Soames, *The English Press, Newspapers and News*, V, 4 (March '37), p. 460.
33. 'A Hundred Years of the Higher Journalism,' IV, 1 (June '35), pp. 31, 32.
34. 'Means to Social Consciousness,' III, 1 (June '34), p. 65. These, respectively, were Thompson's judgments on the *Times*, the *Daily Express* and the *Observer*.

C

56

to an inadequacy behind the words, an inadequacy of experience.'[35] Reflecting on a contemporary translation of *Piers Plowman*, Derek Traversi reiterated this theme, arguing that the secular atrophy of Langland's idiom reflected an attenuation of 'personal experience'. Whereas the original *Piers Plowman* attested 'an extraordinary ability to describe personal experience in terms of a common idiom', its twentieth-century translation was marred by the interposition of 'diplomatic generalization between the original emotion and its poetic expression'. This linguistic decline, in his opinion, reflected the historical passage from 'a society closely connected with the land', where 'honest and active emotional responses' came readily, to the desiccated life of a society ruled by 'the deadening forces of modern industrialism'.[36] L. C. Knights's 'Shakespeare and Profit Inflations' advanced the same explanation: the modern English language was the carrier of 'feelings, perceptions and ideas acceptable to the devitalized products of a machine economy'. However, the effect of modern historical development was not a simple reduction of expressivity, mirroring a contraction of experience. Contemporary linguistic usage was 'a hazy medium which smothers [man's] essential human nature, which interposes between him and things as they are'[37] – an *alienated* language that blinded individuals to their own 'essential' purposes and to the truth of the economic 'environment' whose spontaneous emanation it was. This belief was fundamental to the intellectual stance of the *Scrutiny* circle. Behind it lay a distinctive conception of society and social change (whose principles will shortly be examined). It furnished the criteria by which the various current forms of social thought were tried and, for the greater part, rejected: the 'abstract' Humanism of Babbitt or Dewey, the scientistic utopias of H. G. Wells, and, where they aspired to self-sufficiency in social analysis and prescription, the quantitative and nomothetic procedures of the social sciences – all spoke, in one mode or another, the language of a mechanical civilization.[38]

35. 'The Literary Mind,' I, 1 (May '32), p. 22.
36. 'Revaluations (x): The Vision of Piers Plowman,' v, 3 (December '36), pp. 277, 280–1.
37. 'Shakespeare and Profit Inflations: Notes for the Historian of Culture,' v, 1 (June '36), pp. 57–8.
38. See for example F. R. Leavis, ' "Under Which King, Bezonian?",' I, 3 (December '32), pp. 205–14.

Abused and alienated, the language of modern times was also uprooted. *Mass Civilization and Minority Culture* had argued that the substance of 'culture' was, to an ever greater extent, 'actually a matter of the use of words', and that 'without the living subtlety of the finest idiom (which is dependent on use) the heritage dies'.[39] Now, with the decay of the social life that it had articulated, that 'use', on which the entire superstructure of 'culture' ultimately rested, had ceased to be general or to command assent among writers.[40] The major literary achievements of the pre-industrial age had derived their strength from the resources of a vital popular speech rooted in a stable and homogeneous social life. The 'tremendous principle of life' that animated Dunbar's best poetry was, in John Speirs's estimation, the gift of the peasantry of medieval Scotland; Shakespeare's language, Knights maintained, was that of a 'community which forged it as a vital medium'; and there too, in 'the same people that created the English language for Shakespeare's use', was the source of the 'rich, poised and mature humanity' that Leavis cherished in *The Pilgrim's Progress*.[41] The contrasting situation of the modern writer – poet, journalist or critic – was one of rootlessness. Where literature did not actually die of moral inanition, its practitioners and critics, with very few exceptions, slid into an anomic drift. Faulkner's 'Bohemianism', Mallarmé's 'pure poetry' and Joyce's *Work in Progress*, which Leavis dismissed as a kind of dionysiac variation on Basic English, were only the more notorious literary 'cases' of a malady borne by historical change into every cell of society and culture.[42]

II

The meaning that *Scrutiny* discerned in the social history of modern England is by now a legend. The three hundred years from the reign of Elizabeth to the present day saw an old agrarian order governed by

39. *Education and the University*, p. 168.
40. Cf. 'The Literary Mind,' p. 21.
41. Respectively: 'William Dunbar,' VII, 1 (June '38), p. 68; 'Shakespeare and Profit Inflations,' p. 57; 'Bunyan Through Modern Eyes,' VI, 4 (March '38), pp. 464, 463.
42. Respectively: H. A. Mason, 'American and English Earth,' IV, 1 (June '35), pp. 74–9; G. M. Turnell, 'Mallarmé,' V, 4 (March '36), pp. 425–38; F. R. Leavis, 'Joyce and "the Revolution of the Word",' II, 2 (September '33), pp. 193–201.

shared and settled custom driven steadily towards dissolution. The crucial episode in this history was the Industrial Revolution, which fatally disrupted an order already shaken by the social effects of the Civil War and set the country on a course of economic and social advance which, by the early twentieth century, had flushed out the few remaining enclaves of the old way of life. The essence of this process was *decline*, from a homogeneous, naturally ordered and psychologically whole community into an artificial, atomized and psychologically splintered aggregate, from the 'coherent and self-explanatory' life of Sturt's village into the urban-industrial wasteland described and denounced in *Culture and Environment*; in the terms made famous by the German sociologist Fernand Tönnies, a fall from *Gemeinschaft* into *Gesellschaft*, in those of *Scrutiny*, the calamitous loss of 'the organic community'.[43]

Some clear and measured sense of priorities is indispensable, if this matter is to be discussed in a useful way. It would be possible and legitimate to challenge many of the conceptual presuppositions of this historical account,[44] or to follow the example of writers who have shown, in more or less detailed and extensive counter-demonstrations, that its version of English social development is historiographically untenable.[45] But as Raymond Williams has written, 'what we have to inquire into is not, in these cases, historical error, but historical perspective'.[46] If such constructions – and there are many of them – typically lack any sure empirical grasp of the past, it is because they are essentially para-historical figures, whose real significance lies in their ideological function in the present. Our primary concern, then, should be to identify the exact place and function of this patently idealized 'history' within the complex of meanings and

43. The earlier of the two phrases cited is Sturt's (cit. *Culture and Environment*, p. 73). Tönnies's *Gemeinschaft und Gesellschaft* was published in 1887.

44. For example, the dubious psychological thesis of a descent from wholeness, probably derived from Eliot's 'dissociation of sensibility'. As Febvre has argued, the precondition of a psychological history is a genuinely historical psychology, which we do not possess (Peter Burke, ed., *A New Kind of History: From the Writings of Febvre*, London 1973, pp. 1–26). See also Frank Kermode, *Romantic Image*, London 1957, ch. 8.

45. See for example Robert D. Mayo, *The English Novel in the Magazines 1740–1815*, Evanston 1962, especially p. 362f; Raymond Williams, *The Long Revolution*, Part II, especially chs. 2 and 3; idem, *The Country and the City*, St Alban's 1973, passim.

46. *The Country and the City*, p. 20.

values that constituted the ideology of *Scrutiny*. For this purpose, it will be necessary first of all to determine its role in the social thought of *Scrutiny*'s contributors; then, to consider their relations with the opposing theory of historical materialism, and the precise meaning of their differences with it; and finally, to elucidate the logic that bound this retrospective populism to its equally notorious twin, the programmatic elitism of 'the minority'.

In 'A Note on Nostalgia', the essay that opened *Scrutiny*'s founding number, D. W. Harding furnished an oblique proleptic defence of the theme of 'the organic community'. The propensity to nostalgia, as Harding analysed it, expressed the dislocation brought about by individual separation or, more radically, by the failure of group solidarity. It was not, however, to be mistaken for the contiguous psychological propensity to 'regression', in which the 'attitude' of the individual to social loss was quite different. It was both possible and valid, Harding believed, to combine 'nostalgia' with realism, to hold to a belief in the preferability of the past, while resolving to act in and for the present.[47] This, translated into the idiom of social history, was also the position of *Culture and Environment* and, thereafter, of *Scrutiny*. The 'organic community' had vanished, irrecoverably; there could be 'no mere going back'.[48] When Leavis and Thompson asserted that 'the memory of the old order must be the chief incitement towards a new, if ever we are to have one', it was not with any form of 're-gression' in view.[49] For them and for their associates, collective rever-sion to an earlier stage of social development was unthinkable (or, at any rate, impracticable), and the folk-revivalism of individual enthusi-asts, merely derisory.[50] The 'organic community' was essentially the putative historical incarnation of certain social values that the urban-industrial order was deemed to have cast out, with possibly disastrous consequences for itself, a myth that functioned principally as a critical device in a discourse on the actual state and possible futures of modern society.[51]

47. I, 1 (May '32), pp. 8–19.
48. *Culture and Environment*, p. 96.   49. Ibid., p. 97.
50. Denys Thompson, 'What Shall We Teach?' II, 4 (March '34), p. 385; idem, 'England and the Octopus,' III, 2 (September '34), pp. 175–9; Frank Chapman, 'Rural Civilization,' V, 2 (September '36), pp. 219–20; Q. D. Leavis, 'Lives and Works of Richard Jefferies,' VI, 4 (June '38), pp. 435–6.
51. This is not to say that it was consciously deployed as such by its exponents.

Within this common ideological framework, there were certain variations of emphasis that should be recorded.[52] Of the editorial quartet that had come into being by September 1933, Harding was least concerned with 'the organic community'. His main interests at all times were literary criticism and psychology. Leavis was of course strongly identified with this theme (more so perhaps in the 'external' writings of 1930–33 than in the journal itself), holding a position which, despite its variable balance of pessimism and hope, remained constant. 'Is the machine – or Power – to triumph or to be triumphed over, to be the dictator or the servant of human ends?' That, for Leavis, was the decisive social question of the day.[53] In the case of L. C. Knights, more exacting norms of empirical sholarship produced a more nuanced appreciation of social development, accompanied by a greater openness to the possibility of general social progress in the context of industrialism.[54] By contrast, Denys Thompson's alienation from 'machine civilization' was complete. His essays expressed an implacable hatred of the era that had seen 'humanity . . . uprooted and atrophied in an unprecedented way and on an unprecedented scale'.[55] Its factories and houses, its goods and recreations, its cultural institutions and speech patterns – all were denounced without qualification as the work of 'the machine unchained'.[56] Thompson was inclined even to attribute an intrinsic spiritual maleficence to machine-made consumer durables. Chastising a writer who had been 'uncritically romantic over the joy of driving high-powered cars', he commented: 'it would have been more helpful if he had speculated on how such joy affects the man who drives.'[57] So radical a disaffection from modernity, in a writer who yet refused to entertain any attempt at historical regression, was bound to produce some kind of crisis of perspective. The resolution of this crisis took the form of a sideways

52. These are discussed further in the next section.

53. 'Restatements for Critics' (editorial), I, 4 (March '33), p. 320.

54. See for example 'Shakespeare and Profit Inflations,' p. 59; 'Restoration Comedy: the Reality and the Myth,' VI, 2 (September '37), p. 123; and especially 'Elizabethan Reading Matter and Elizabethan Literature,' VI, 3 (December '37), where the resulting analytic tension is manifest.

55. 'A Cure for Amnesia,' II, 1 (June '33), p. 9.

56. Ibid.; 'Advertising God,' pp. 241–6; 'The Machine Unchained,' II, 2 (September '33), p. 187.

57. 'The Machine Unchained,' p. 188; see also 'Progressive Schools,' III, 2 (September '34), p. 214.

displacement of interest, into ruralism. Thompson was not himself its most prominent exponent; his main concern was with the salutary educational potential of ruralist literature.[58] It is noteworthy, however, that ruralism became a constant sub-theme of *Scrutiny* during his editorship, disappearing from its pages after his departure from the board in the summer of 1939.

Thompson's nostalgia for the culture of 'the soil' was always accompanied by a bitter insistence on its irrevocability. But little of this realism was allowed to temper Adrian Bell's celebrations of a rural existence that had not yet wholly succumbed to the bane of plumbing, scientific knowledge and bottled cider.[59] 'Happy ingenuousness' – Q. D. Leavis's phrase – does little to evoke the quality of Bell's religious vision of the countryside.[60] 'Even in splitting logs, in some measure man passes into axe and axe into man. How complex a harmony then is man and scythe; every swing an unconscious reiteration of natural law, which thus became the unfailing intuitive basis of life, growing inevitably more "scientific", yet rooted at the other extreme still in superstition.'[61] But what communion could the town-dweller have with 'the old earth-principle'? Recalling the rural woodworker 'modest before the mystery of timber', he turned piteously to 'that great army of people for whom the waterworks and gasworks are made' and asked: 'where for them is the mystery of water, even of domestic water lying in a well, or the mystery of fire?'[62] For those in whose lives 'Providence' had been 'superseded by the local borough council', no return was possible.[63] What was at issue now was whether the inhabitants of that postlapsarian world, 'with [their] sole power of variousness, transience', could hope to 'realize life at a depth at least equal to that attained in a preoccupation with, say, the qualities of tent-pegs or of besom-brooms'.[64]

58. 'A Cure for Amnesia'; 'What Shall We Teach?' p. 38.

59. See 'English Tradition and Idiom,' II, 1 (June '33), pp. 45–50; 'Change in the Farm,' II, 4 (March '34), p. 409; 'Which England?' III, 2 (September '34), pp. 206–7.

60. 'Lives and Works of Richard Jefferies,' p. 440.

61. 'Change in the Farm,' pp. 409–10.

62. 'Which England?' p. 206.

63. Ibid., pp. 206–7; see also 'Farming Near Skye,' V, 2 (September '36), pp. 224–5.

64. 'Which England?' p. 207. At least one contributor was able to attest the salutary spiritual effects of ruralist literature: 'I enjoyed reading Sturt much as one enjoys making a wheelbarrow or repairing a well-made farm-cart' (F. C. Tinkler, 'There's Only One Sturt,' VI, 3, December '37, p. 325).

His Tolstoyan mysticism notwithstanding, Bell represented a
logically faithful variant of the general *Scrutiny* position. It was, however, an isolated one: no other contributor ever hymned the countryside, past or present, in such tones, and towards the end of the decade,
a more critical estimate of the rural past became current. Reviewing
The Open Air, a ruralist anthology edited by Bell, Frank Chapman
warned against the dangers of sentimental retrospection (which,
seemingly, the editor had contrived to avoid on this occasion). He
stressed the 'incredible hardship and poverty of the rural labourer'
and 'the misery and physical discomfort of much of the work, scarcely
surpassed in the most mechanical processes of mass-production'.
Revivalism was neither practical nor desirable as a solution: 'to senti-
mentalize about the past is a very different thing from realizing the
strength and virtue of the old tradition and endeavouring to incor-
porate them into a state of society which must, whatever the outcome, be vastly different from that in which the tradition was
formed.'[65] Q. D. Leavis's tribute to Richard Jefferies, published some
eighteen months later, in March 1938, was in a similar spirit. The
avowed purpose of her essay was to redeem this nineteenth-century
rural writer from a posterity that remembered him, vaguely, as 'a
word-painter of natural beauties, a sort of early Keats in prose'. The
Jefferies whom she now set out to rehabilitate was, in contrast, a
gifted social historian, thoroughly modern in interests and outlook.
The main emphasis of her presentation fell on the radicalism of his
political and social thought and on his freedom from even 'the
smallest hankering after the Merrie Englande past' – as he himself
had written: 'dearly as I love the open air, I cannot regret the medieval days. I do not wish them back again, I would sooner fight in the
foremost ranks of Time.'[66] The subject and stress of Leavis's essay
suggest quite clearly that – rhetoric aside, perhaps – Jefferies's position
was also hers.[67] The actual meaning of that position, for her and for
Scrutiny, was as Chapman had stated it. How, given the definitive
abolition of 'the organic community', were its constitutive values,

65. 'Rural Civilization,' pp. 219–20, 219.
66. 'Lives and Works of Richard Jefferies,' pp. 435f, 442, 441 and n.
67. Jefferies's early political conservatism and late tendencies to medievalism
are not adequately registered in this essay. For a fuller account see Williams, *The
Country and the City*, pp. 232–8.

now dispersed and weakened, to be reconcentrated and made potent in the contemporary world?

III

The quality for which *Scrutiny* prized this vanished past was its social and cultural homogeneity. In the old rural society, where the byzantine division of labour, stultifying work-routines and ceaseless change of the modern factory were unknown, the labouring population had been able to sustain traditions of social intercourse whose richness and authority had nourished and guided the art of the time. *Scrutiny*'s premiss was that this ideal social state was now irretrievable. No mere regeneration of agriculture, in an England based on industry and towns, could suffice to reanimate it; and conversely, to aim to cultivate its residues was not to suppose that cultural homogeneity could ever again be a 'natural' attribute of social life in general. However, even as the journal elaborated this conception of historical development, an alternative perspective was beginning to gain rapidly in appeal among British intellectuals – a rival social theory that argued, to the contrary, that the economic developments so distressing to *Scrutiny* had in fact laid the material foundations of a new society and culture, richer and more genuinely common than any in recorded history. *Mass Civilization and Minority Culture* had done little more than register the existence of such an analysis. But three years later, some more adequate intellectual reckoning had become unavoidable. Thus, when Leavis came to reprint the essay, along with eleven others from the years 1930–33, he prefaced the collection with a discussion of 'Marxism and Cultural Continuity'.[68]

Leavis's earliest treatment of this question actually pre-dated *For Continuity* (in which it was reproduced) by some months. In the critique of Trotsky's *Literature and Revolution* that marked his entry into *Scrutiny*'s editorial team in December 1932, he had already expressed his profound disagreement with Marxist accounts of culture as it now stood, and could be expected to develop under socialism. Leavis was

68. *For Continuity*, Cambridge 1933, pp. 1–12. In addition to the pamphlet mentioned above, and the other Minority Press publication of 1930, *D. H. Lawrence*, the book contained ten essays by Leavis, all from the first two volumes of *Scrutiny*.

disposed to grant some small merit to Trotsky's distinctively continuist view of the transition from 'bourgeois culture' to the 'human culture' of mature socialism.[69] It was, however, a merit that was visible only in a strictly limited context: if Trotsky had 'some inkling' of matters to which his co-thinkers were blind, the credit was due more to his personal gifts than to his chosen allegiance. For in the end, he was scarcely more aware than they of what the maintenance of 'cultural continuity' entailed. How was 'the delicate organic growth' of 'culture' to be borne safely through a protracted phase of consuming revolutionary struggle, and nurtured thereafter in the conditions of quickened economic development that would succeed it?[70] Where Marxism went fatally astray and disqualified itself as a responsible guarantor of 'continuity', Leavis contended, was in its 'dogma concerning the relation between culture and "the methods of production" '. In the past, this relation had indeed been intimate: 'when England had a popular culture, the structure, the framework, of it was a stylization, so to speak, of economic necessities; based ... on the "methods of production", was an art of living, involving codes, developed in ages of continuous experience, of relations between man and man, and man and the environment in its seasonal rhythm.' But with the onset of the industrial revolution, this relationship had ceased to hold. Now, after the ravages of a century, the remnants of 'cultural tradition' survived only *in spite of* the rapidly changing "means of production" '.[71] It was therefore illusory, Leavis argued, to imagine that the conditions of 'cultural continuity' would automatically be met either by an intensification of industrial development or by the unfolding of the class struggle. On the one hand, the intrinsic nature of factory work would remain incorrigible; 'enthusiasm for Five Year Plans, the sense of a noble cause, [and] romantic worship of mechanical efficiency' could not 'be permanently the sanction of

69. Trotsky criticized the notion, widely entertained by Soviet intellectuals in the 1920s, of a specifically 'proletarian' culture created in 'laboratory' conditions by a revolutionary avant-garde, and argued instead that 'the main task of the proletarian intelligentsia in the immediate future is not the abstract formation of a new culture regardless of a basis for it, but definite culture-bearing, that is, a systematic, planful and, of course, critical imparting to the backward masses of the essential elements of the culture which already exists' (cit. ' "Under Which King, Bezonian?",' p. 209; *Literature and Revolution*, Michigan 1960, p. 193).

70. Leavis, ' "Under Which King, Bezonian?",' pp. 207, 209–10 and n.

71. Ibid., p. 208 (my emphasis).

labour in itself unsatisfying'. And beyond that lay the problems of the 'leisure community' that Marxists projected, but without any clear sense of its cultural implications. What would be the basis of 'culture' in conditions where 'the "productive process' [was] so efficient as no longer to determine the ordering of life'?[72] On the other hand, it was futile to see in the proletariat the well-spring of cultural renewal. Its 'values' were 'inevitably those induced by the modern environment – by "capitalist" civilization'. There were no longer class divisions of the kind that could produce class cultures; the only 'essential' difference between capitalist and worker was economic. To entrust the future of 'culture' to the course of the struggle between them was 'to aim, whether wittingly or not, at completing the work of capitalism and its products, the cheap car, the wireless and the cinema'.[73] Here, in Leavis's judgment, lay the truth of socialism, and of the theory that championed it. The differences between capitalism and socialism were, so far as the prospects of 'culture' were concerned, 'inessential': the latter was no more than the consummation of the historical tendencies established by its predecessor. Apparently critical and revolutionary, Marxism was in fact complicit with 'machine civilization' – so much was disclosed in the note of 'Wellsian exaltation' that sounded in Trotsky's adumbration of 'the dynamic development of culture' under communism.[74] Far from embodying a qualitative break with the prevailing order, 'the Marxian future' was, as he declared on another occasion, simply 'vacuous, Wellsian and bourgeois'.[75]

Leavis's polemic drew a prompt response from a leading Communist intellectual of the time, A. L. Morton, who, writing in the following number of the journal, greeted 'Bezonian' as a 'challenge . . . very welcome to Marxists', and attempted to allay the misgivings of its author.[76] In the first place, Morton argued, Leavis was misled in assuming that Marxism saw the *'methods* of production, as the generative source of 'culture'. It was, rather, the *'mode* of production', 'the totality of productive relationships', that produced the cultural

72. Ibid., pp. 208, 209.
73. Ibid., pp. 211, 212–3.
74. Ibid., p. 213. The last of the phrases quoted here is Trotsky's (*Literature and Revolution*, p. 189).
75. 'Restatements for Critics,' p. 322.
76. 'Culture and Leisure,' I, 4 (March '33), pp. 324–6.

ensemble of any given society. The relationship between the two was thus not 'rigidly determined' and 'mechanical' but 'fluid' and 'dialectical'. Secondly, 'bourgeois culture' was properly to be understood as 'the sum of the ideological superstructure characteristic of the present historical period, in which the bourgeoisie is the ruling class' – including 'much that the Editors of *Scrutiny* would perhaps prefer to call lack of culture'.[77] The purpose to which the journal was apparently dedicated, to nourish what was valuable in this cultural 'sum' and combat what was 'harmful', was 'entirely praiseworthy'. What was in question was how best to pursue this goal. This said, Morton tried to persuade Leavis that the exigencies of socialist revolution were not inimical to 'cultural continuity', and further, that the overthrow of capitalism was in fact necessary to it. The dictatorship of the proletariat, he argued, was not a headlong leap from capitalism to communism, but 'a bridge, a period in which the new is growing out of the old'. Its chief cultural task was the critical appropriation of the 'most valuable elements' of the bourgeois heritage, and these, far from 'delicate', possessed an 'amazing tenacity' that would ensure their survival.[78] Morton turned then to the problem of leisure under socialism.[79] It was incorrect, he wrote, to portray leisure as 'the state of having nothing to do'. Real leisure presupposed the elimination of the 'anxieties and uncertainties' that beset the unemployed and a majority of wage-earners, and the attainment of a condition where work was 'no longer the antithesis of living'. Where drudgery had been minimized and exploitation ended, leisure would no longer be given over to psycho-physical recuperation and ideological mystification. In such a society, there would be no place for 'the mass production novel or the tabloid press'; the arts would cease to be 'the preserve of a parasitic minority or of little groups of honest intellectuals attempting to order chaos with pitifully inadequate resources'. In short, then, the social and cultural values of *Scrutiny* were also the objectives of the socialist revolution. 'Here, and here only, is the "organic community" which Mr Leavis and I are at one in desiring.' It had disappeared 'not with the coming of industrialism, but, long

77. Ibid., p. 324.
78. Ibid., p. 325.
79. Leavis's critical reflections on this topic had in fact been prompted by an essay written by Morton in the *Criterion*, October 1932.

before, with the coming of the State', and, with the overthrow of capitalism and the foundation of the self-dissolving proletarian State, would again become incarnate in history. Morton pleaded with Leavis 'to think things over once again', to ask himself whether 'the struggle to "maintain the tradition of human culture" ' could gain much ground in isolation from the struggle of the working class. *Scrutiny* was 'too valuable a weapon against the Philistines' to be left 'permanently' to lament and contemplative despair.[80]

Morton's response was conciliatory to the point of disingenuousness. He forbore to question Leavis's notion of 'culture', which can hardly have been his own, portrayed the socialist revolution as the only efficacious support of 'culture' so conceived, and was even prepared to style the social objective of the revolution an 'organic community'.[81] But his art was largely wasted. The short, courteous acknowledgement that the editors appended to his essay showed no readiness to participate in this new organicist ecumene. What is more interesting, however, is that such a *démarche* should have been attempted at all. It might be said that the thematic resemblances between the two outlooks were sufficient to create an intermediate zone which, given the ideological disorientation of the intelligentsia in the climacteric of the early thirties, was large and open enough to permit important 'territorial' gains by one side or the other. At all events, some such belief was apparently held by both parties. If Morton's essay can be seen as a bold expansionary initiative in one direction, Leavis's 'Marxism and Cultural Continuity' can be read as a sinuous diplomatic counter-measure. Leavis conceded no more on this occasion than he had done in ' "Under Which King, Bezonian?" ' or was ever to do subsequently. He reiterated his belief that Marxism was in every salient respect the creature of the order that it claimed to contest. The truth of its parentage was especially evident in the inability of its followers to reach a balanced estimate of the possible

80. Ibid., pp. 325, 326.
81. One bizarre aspect of the exchange that cannot have escaped Leavis's attention should be noticed here. Leavis had commended Trotsky's insistence on the moment of continuity in the transition towards the 'human culture' of socialism, but attributed this 'inkling' to a local victory of 'intelligence' over 'orthodoxy'. Morton suggested that Leavis's fears about socialism were at least partly due to Trotsky's erroneous conception of proletarian dictatorship, and proceeded to expound a presumably orthodox corrective, which turned out to be that held by Trotsky in *Literature and Revolution*. . . .

autonomy of 'culture'. Oscillating between scepticism in relation to the present and millenarian visions of the future, they showed themselves congenitally incapable of appreciating the essential problems of 'cultural continuity'; and that 'incapacity' was 'the enemy'.[82] At the same time, the essay displayed an acute sense of an audience ideologically in motion. Here, more than in 'Bezonian', Leavis took pains to dissociate his critique of Marxist theory from any hint of political conservatism or quietism. There could be no doubt, he affirmed, that a political attack on 'economic maladjustments, inequities and oppressions' was urgently needed; but it was also incontrovertible that exclusive concentration on problems of that order was dangerously inadequate, and would actually lead to 'the consummation of the cultural process of capitalism'.[83]

This was the conceptual substance of Leavis's appeal to a readership among whom *marxisant* tendencies were growing rapidly; the pivot of its rhetorical strategy was his discussion of the Soviet Union. He accepted that Soviet state policy 'favours the fostering of cultural values that would be recognized as such by one interested in tradition', and that 'practical Marxism in Russia does appear to have released an impressive volume of energy in cultural directions'. It was, however, incorrect to assume that the Soviet model could simply be transposed into Western conditions. 'In such a country, illiterate, inert and economically primitive, a drive for literacy, economic efficiency and social righteousness might well be expected to bring, along with mechanization, a cultural awakening.' But in developed industrial states like Britain, where a complex economic and social infrastructure was already in place, no comparable line of social advance could be plotted in the expectation that 'cultural values' would 'assert themselves appropriately in their own good time'.[84] If, so to speak, the USSR's achievement was to be emulated, it could not be through a process of imitation. This was precisely the point of Leavis's general argument: Marxism, 'the doctrine, strategy and tactics of the Class War', was inadequate as a solution to the contemporary crisis of civilization.[85] If, as at least one Marxist critic had implied, there was 'a point of view above classes', and 'intellectual, aesthetic and moral activity that [was] not merely an expression of

---

82. *For Continuity*, pp. 5–6, 9–10.   83. Ibid., p. 6; also pp. 8, 12.
84. Ibid., pp. 6–7, 7, 7–8.   85. Ibid., p. 5.

class origin and economic circumstances', then there was indeed 'a "human culture" to be aimed at that must be achieved by cultivating a certain autonomy of the human spirit'.[86] It was not to the point to speak of an 'alternative' to Marxism: 'the form of the insistence is that, whatever else must be done or attempted (and the simple formula should be suspect), *this* is necessary. . . .'[87] The tolerance of politico-ideological syncretism that might be inferred from these words was, as the parenthesis suggests, unreal. If it was at all conceivable to be a revolutionary in politics and yet a guardian of 'cultural continuity', it was because of the complete impotence of the one in the face of the problems that engrossed the other. The crisis of 'continuity' was a feature of industrial society as such. The transition to socialism could not possibly discharge, and might not even alleviate, the cultural responsibilities to which *Scrutiny* was sworn.

As it transpired, the balance of Leavis's 'diplomacy' was quite faithfully reflected in the pages of the journal. On the outermost fringes of the contributing circle there was a definite radicalization of intellectual positions. Discussing 'Advertising and Economic Waste', C. H. P. Gifford argued that critiques of the cultural effects of advertising were inadequate by themselves, and proposed the elaboration of an economics of the phenomenon. Scanning the literature on the subject, he noted that Marshall had ignored it, while in Robinson's *Imperfect Competition* the problem was methodologically excluded, and suggested that 'perhaps the Marxist approach [would] prove profitable'. Gifford's view was that since advertising was a structural feature of developed capitalism, it was impractical to dream of some simple reform of its practices; the 'evils' of advertising were 'yet another argument against the capitalist system'.[88] In similar vein, Uno Åhrén expressed sharp criticisms of naively technicist plans for urban renovation. Planning of this type, he argued, deluded itself that 'reason and the desire to satisfy people's *needs*' were 'decisive in directing the actions of financiers, instead of *profit*'. The logic of capitalist development would frustrate any project conceived in this belief. The plan under review, for example, was 'no more than an attempt at patching up existing

86. Ibid., p. 9. The critic was Edmund Wilson, in an article in the *New Republic*, August 23, 1933. Morton's article left this possibility open; for Trotsky, such a culture was possible only in a classless society.

87. Ibid., p. 12.

88. III, 2 (September '34), pp. 168–74.

society on a gigantic scale instead of attempting to get to the radical necessity – a revision of the present conditions of property and power'.[89] The work of the Bauhaus was praised by Herbert Read who, writing as a socialist, castigated official Soviet art and architecture for its conservatism, and stressed the progressive character of Gropius's distinctively and self-consciously industrial aesthetic.[90] And in an interesting exchange with H. E. Batson in the latter half of 1933, Donald Kitchin attacked the 'bourgeois Cloud-cuckoo land' depicted in the 'value-free' economics of the Austrian school and its English affiliates. Spurning 'the Robbins road', Kitchin hailed the prospect of a revival of classical political economy, whose sole legitimate heir, he believed, was Marx, and whose only valid role now was as 'an apologetic for socialism'.[91]

Initiatives such as these, which in tendency pressed towards the kind of synoptic theory that Leavis found so repugnant in Marxism, were rare even within their own outlying sphere. No one echoed Montagu Slater's view that 'what is toward [in Marxism] is not simply a discussion of business methods, but – a prolegomenon to any future theory of knowledge'.[92] Herbert Butterfield praised the Marxian 'conception of history as the profound structural analysis of a society', but alerted *Scrutiny*'s readers to the threat that it posed in the hands of the philosophically materialist or politically committed.[93] The small number of the latter who wrote for the journal were not demonstrative in its pages – indeed the literary reviews contributed by Rickword and Garman, whose 'surrender to the Marxist conclusion' was an important marker of the cultural tides of the early thirties, were quite free of political connotations.[94] By 1937, when the Marxist

89. ' "Intelligent Ideals of Urban Life" ' (a review of 'J47485', *A Hundred New Towns for Great Britain. A Scheme of National Reconstruction*), IV, 2 (September '35), pp. 133–9. Ahrén was City Architect of Gothenburg.

90. 'Gropius,' IV, 3 (December '35), pp. 313–5.

91. Donald K. Kitchin, 'Will Economics Follow the Robbins Road?' II, 1 (June '33), pp. 165–74; H. E. Batson, 'Mr Kitchin on the Insignificance of Economics,' II, 1, pp. 175–81; Kitchin, 'The Significance of Economics Thus Conceived,' II, 3 (December '33), pp. 258–65; Batson, 'Footnote,' II, 3, pp. 265–6. See also P. Harris, rev. Eric Roll, *A History of Economic Thought*, VII, 2 (September '38), pp. 245–58.

92. Rev. Julius F. Hecker, *Moscow Dialogues*; Henry F. Ward, *In Place of Profit*; H. G. Wood, *The Truth and Error of Communism*: II, 2 (September '33), p. 212. Slater soon rose to a prominent position in the cultural affairs of the British Communist Party.

93. 'History and the Marxian Method,' I, 4 (March '33), pp. 344, 350.

94. F. R. Leavis, *Towards Standards of Criticism*, p. 11. See Edgell Rickword, rev.

cultural offensive reached its climax in Britain, this *marxisant* fringe had disappeared from *Scrutiny*.[95]

The editorial circle and more regular contributors were basically at one with Leavis: ostensibly revolutionary, Marxism was in fact *not radical enough*, in its analyses of the contemporary era or in its programmatic solutions. 'What has disintegrated', Leavis insisted, '. . . is not merely "bourgeois" or "capitalist" civilization; it is the organic community.'[96] No acknowledgement of the capitalist crisis was serious or complete, H. A. Mason argued, without an accompanying 'realization of the breakdown of European *civilization*, and of the particular values maintained by that civilization, values indispensable to any civilization'.[97] Opening another line of attack, E. W. F. Tomlin suggested that the great productive capacity of the advanced industrial economies had rendered Marx's 'production economics' obsolete, and that the economic science of the future should concentrate on problems of consumption, as, say, the theorists of Social Credit were doing. The 'conventional' radicalism of those who still clung to the outworn secular religion of Marxism was not that of the 'effective revolutionary'.[98] Marxist literary criticism was indicted on a similar count by Q. D. Leavis. Philip Henderson's *The Novel Today* was 'not revolutionary', she decided; 'because it is not based on any fundamental,

T. S. Eliot, *Selected Essays*, I, 4 (March '33), pp. 390–3; Douglas Garman, 'Professional Enemy,' I, 3 (December '32), pp. 279–82; idem, 'Art and the Negative Impulses,' II, 2 (September '33), pp. 189–93.

95. This was the year of Christopher Caudwell's *Illusion and Reality*, Alick West's *Crisis and Criticism*, Ralph Fox's *The Novel and the People* and Day Lewis's anthology *The Mind in Chains*.

96. 'A Serious Artist,' I, 2 (September '32), p. 177.

97. 'Oxford Letter,' III, 2 (September '34), p. 113. Mason was one of a small group of Oxford-based supporters of *Scrutiny*; E. W. F. Tomlin was another.

98. 'The Revolutionary Simpleton,' V, 1 (June '36), pp. 75–84; see also idem, 'Marxism and the Modern Mood,' V, 3 (March '37), pp. 306–15. Tomlin was one of two contributors who attempted a technical – philosophical or economic – critique of Marxism; the other was H. B. Parkes ('The Philosophy of Marxism,' VII, 2, September '38, pp. 130–44; *Marxism: A Post-Mortem*, London 1940). These writings were typically erratic, logically and empirically, and altogether lacking in the force of Leavis's polemics. Separate discussion of them would require a lengthy digression and a volume of argument and quotation for which there is no room here. For a short but pertinent review of Parkes's book, see Christopher Hill, IX, 3 (December '40), pp. 277–84. The political aspect of Parkes's position will be discussed below.

deeply-felt reorientation, he has no real insight into the problems he pretends to attack.'[99] The most succinct statement of *Scrutiny*'s dissent from Marxism came from the most radical member of the editorial board, L. C. Knights. He agreed that a rigorous definition of the relations between economy and 'culture' was indispensable, but denied that Marxism had provided it. 'Methods of production and cultural superstructure may be related in the realm of abstract dialectic, but no one (anthropologists dealing with primitive peoples apart) has yet established the relation in terms of fact and experience.' Furthermore, in the beneficent form in which it had existed in the 'homogeneous' rural society of Elizabethan-Jacobean England, this relation no longer existed and could not be reconstituted. On these grounds, Knights was led to reject 'the practical implication [of Marxism] that if the social machine is perfected, if everyone is given his due share of *economic* satisfactions, a satisfactory culture will "inevitably" emerge, as culture may be said to have emerged from the productive methods of the past'. Its merits as an economic remedy notwithstanding, socialism was hardly more propitious an environment than capitalism for 'those qualities that were spontaneously fostered by a non-industrial economy'.[100] The responsibility of those who valued 'culture' was to work consciously to sustain it in conditions where it could not hope to put down roots.

IV

The forms of organization and practice adopted by the *Scrutiny* group in its 'conscious attempt to preserve continuity'[101] were chosen in this perspective. In order to uncover the logical filiation that bound the two, it will be necessary to undertake a short contrastive analysis of the intellectual relationship between *Scrutiny*'s conception of society and social change and that of historical materialism. The dynamics of the enterprise will then emerge more clearly.

'There can be no doubt,' Leavis declared, 'that the dogma of the priority of economic conditions, however stated, means a complete

99. 'Class-War Criticism,' v, 4 (March '37), p. 419. See also section 4 below.
100. 'Shakespeare and Profit Inflations,' pp. 48f., 51, 56–7, 59.
101. Ibid., p. 59.

disregard for – or rather, a hostility towards – the function represented by *Scrutiny*.'[102] The entire issue turns on the way in which this seemingly unambiguous statement actually misrepresented the position of the journal. For if anything has become clear by now, it is that the conflict between the two systems arose rather from opposed versions of 'the priority of economic conditions', from *two distinct conceptions of economic determination.* Our main concern must be to try to disentangle them.[103] Historical materialism defines the economic as the unity of two distinct instances: the *productive forces*, which include the technical forms of labour and their organizational concomitants, and the *relations of production*, whose principal aspect is the mode of allocation of the means of production and of the economic product. The itinerary and fate of any given mode of production – and, in the last instance, of the society that it founds – are determined by the *contradictions* that arise in the union of these distinct structures. The specific character of the contradictions so generated establishes both the limits and the possibilities of social change, whether within the existing system or in a revolutionary break with it (thus, it is the deepening contradiction between the increasingly collective nature of production and the persistence of individual appropriation that destabilizes capitalism and introduces the historical possibility of socialism).[104] In the light of these summary remarks, the constitutive difference of the *Scrutiny* model becomes apparent. Here, in contrast, the productive forces were cast as the defining instance of the economy and, by extension, as the panurgic source of historical development. The crucial distinction to be made between economic systems – the 'essential' difference from which all others followed – was between those rooted in 'the

102. ' "Under Which King, Bezonian?",' p. 206.

103. The limitations of this passage must be stressed. It is not designed to represent *Scrutiny*'s relations with the forms of Marxism contemporaneous with it – Soviet Marxism under Stalin or English Marxism in the thirties – a topic that would require a lengthy study in its own right. Its purpose is simply to capture the specificity of *Scrutiny*'s social-historical conceptions. For suggestive discussions of this cultural-historical passage, by socialist writers who stress the relative superiority of Leavis's critical positions, see Raymond Williams, 'Literature and Sociology: in Memory of Lucien Goldmann,' *New Left Review* 67 (May–June '71), pp. 3–18; Andrew Milner, 'Leavis and English Literary Criticism,' *Praxis* (Berkeley) 2 (Winter, '76), pp. 91–106.

104. Marx's classic résumé of historical materialism is to be found in the Preface to his *Contribution to the Critique of Political Economy* (1859). A valuable account of its main concepts is given in Therborn, *Science, Class and Society*, pp. 353–86.

soil' and those based on 'the machine'. Apparently metonymic labels, these twin phrases were for *Scrutiny*'s purposes conceptually exact. In this vision of English history, it was the passage from field to factory that was above all responsible for the descent from the health and homogeneity of seventeenth-century culture into the sickly, centrifugal civilization of the twentieth. The local variations and instabilities of *Scrutiny*'s historical analyses were themselves the effects of this premiss. For the category of 'industrialism' does not necessarily produce a consistent form of technologism.[105] It is a conflationary term that holds the two structures of the economy in an inchoate unity, in which aspects of the relations of production can make an appearance, but seldom if ever in a logically effectual manner – Bruce Pattison implied, for example, that social classes were the product of industrialism, while Knights maintained, conversely, that the 'common' culture of early seventeenth-century England was by that token not a class-divided culture.[106] Thus, while *Scrutiny* produced both 'Right' and 'Left' variants of the critique of industrialism (Speirs and Knights respectively), the premiss that united them remained intact. One of the more telling effects of this conception may be noted in passing. The work of George Sturt was perhaps the main touchstone of *Scrutiny*'s social criticism in the 1930s. Yet for all its tendencies to ruralist nostalgia, the analysis of *Change in the Village* was fundamentally concerned with the final triumph of capitalist relations of production; the critique of 'suburbanism', the deskilling of labour and so on, was subordinate to this theme in the logical architecture of the book. Thus, in Sturt's view, the forces that had disrupted the old village life were internal to the economic structure of the countryside: it was the enclosure of the local common that had driven the inhabitants into regular wage-labour. Further, he recognized the 'change' as a contradictory process combining 'good' and 'bad', gain and loss, just as the old dispensation had done. Whereas Leavis and Thompson denounced the modern Press as a cultural scandal, Sturt

105. 'Technologism' is the conventional term for social theory that derives the character of societies from their technological infrastructures. The most famous latter-day case of this is Herbert Marcuse's *One-Dimensional Man*, an uncanny leftist mirror-image of certain of *Scrutiny*'s themes. The affinities between the Leavis circle and the Frankfurt School have been noted but never explored.

106. Pattison, 'Musical History,' p. 374; Knights, 'Shakespeare and Profit Inflations,' pp. 56–7.

had in fact welcomed even its yellowest manifestations as positive contributions to a way of life which, having lost its former self-sufficiency, was now mean and narrow. The Sturt invoked in the pages of *Culture and Environment* was one who had been filtered through the grid of a very different social analysis.[107]

What were the consequences of *Scrutiny*'s monist interpretation of history? Historical materialism views the social formation as a complex structure, riven at every level by contradictions whose existence alone creates the possibility of alternatives in history, and thus of purposive and effectual action, economic, political or cultural. In the terms of *Scrutiny*'s schema, no comparable perspective was logically possible. There was no flaw in the constitution of the industrial economy, or in the social, political and cultural forms that it generated, that could serve as a point of leverage for qualitative change, no social force which could emerge from inside the prevailing order as the bearer of a new one. However, these considerations led directly to the problem that eventually confronts all monist analyses. What, in that case, was *Scrutiny*? What was it that underwrote its opposition to this seamless social order, distinguishing it from the illusory opposition that Marxism represented? In order to evade this logical reprise, *Scrutiny*'s unrelieved mechanical materialism was obliged to complete itself with an equal and opposite idealism. The principle of opposition to the course of modern history could only reside in an entity that was somehow not itself implicated in it. That trans-historical instance was 'tradition', a category that acknowledged historicity while denying its effects, the principle of constancy amidst unsparing change. The cumulative meaning of 'the tradition' was 'culture', the sum of those values that industrialism had uprooted but not annihilated, the residuum of 'essential life' that 'slips through the mesh' of Marxist theory, indefinable but recognizable by those who tended its last sanctuary, the tradition of English literature.[108] 'The organic community' was both the 'memory' of the ideal, lost unity of society

107. 'George Bourne' (Geoffrey Grigson, ed.), *Change in the Village*, London 1955, especially pp. 84f, 193f. These few sentences are no more comprehensive than *Scrutiny*'s portrayal was. Ruralism and progressivism, nationalism, socialism and anti-industrialism are interwoven throughout Sturt's work. For his idiosyncratic socialism, hostile equally to Fabian and Bolshevik, see *The Journals of George Sturt 1890–1927*, passim.

108. This phrase is Knights's ('Shakespeare and Profit Inflations,' p. 60).

and 'culture' and a figure that reconciled the antinomies of this intellectual position.

Scrutiny's ambition was to restore these values to some kind of authority in the modern world. The essential aspect of this task was the attempt to cultivate a 'contemporary sensibility' which, free equally from inert traditionalism and anomic modernity, could guide thought and action in the conditions of the twentieth century. Its practical modalities were dictated by the prevailing relationship between 'culture' and society. Whereas the old agrarian order had spontaneously reproduced the values of 'culture' in society at large, the automatic tendency of industrial 'civilization' was to negate them, and to marginalize and disperse their representatives – the fate of 'culture' in the modern epoch was personified in the isolated, mildly ridiculous figure of 'the highbrow'. *Scrutiny*'s strategic objective was accordingly to *organize* the defenders of 'culture' as an effective force. As the 'Manifesto' put it: 'the trouble is not that such persons form a minority, but that they are scattered and unorganized.'[109] Its organizational model was of necessity that of an *elite*. For if the industrial order was constitutionally inimical to 'culture', it followed that none of its given classes or sub-groups could provide a vehicle for 'continuity'. The 'minority' could only function as a compact, 'rootless' oppositional group formed and maintained against the natural bias of society, bearers of 'an autonomous culture, a culture independent of any economic, technical or social system as none has been before'.[110] Its main area of activity was to be *literary criticism*. For in the degree that literature was the main surviving witness of an existential integrity that had disappeared from the social world, then, as Leavis argued, 'literary criticism . . . should be the best possible training for intelligence – for free, unspecialized, general intelligence, which there has never at any time been enough of, and which we are peculiarly in need of today.'[111] The mode of operation of the group, in the

109. I, 1 (May '32), p. 5; see also F. R. Leavis, 'What's Wrong with Criticism?' I, 2 (September '32), pp. 132–46.
110. ' "Under Which King, Bezonian?",' pp. 209–10. This was Leavis's characterization of the only possible mode of existence of 'culture' under socialism; it seems legitimate, all things considered, to read it back as an ideal no less pertinent under capitalism.   111. 'The Literary Mind,' I, 1 (May '32), p. 24.

first instance at least, was in keeping with its mode of cultural existence. Flexible, 'opportunist', positively and even proudly 'occasional' in character, a committed *journalism* was the obvious medium of expression of a group for whom academicism was an abrogation of responsibility and 'rootlessness' both a fact and a principle.[112]

The objective of the journal was to forge an intellectual stratum that did not exist in England: an intelligentsia of the 'classic' type, cohesive, independent and critical of the conventional purposes of its society. For Leavis at least, this project was to some degree one of restoration. In one of his most compelling essays, he returned to the eighteenth century to discuss the rise of the English 'scorn' for 'the "virtuoso" and the specialist', and its social roots, the apotheosis of the Gentleman and Good Form. Among the writers of the Augustan era, he singled out Johnson, who evinced the 'conscious dignity' of the 'specialist spirit' and, motivated by a 'sense of the traditional morality of his craft', left the sphere of 'the polite' to rejoin Pope, the master of the early century.[113] Johnson, and later, Arnold and Stephen, represented an ideal of intellectual comportment that England now lacked, but which France and the USA (two constant poles of contrast) in some measure possessed. 'If England is less Americanized than America,' Denys Thompson wrote, 'it is in the discreditable sense that less resistance to the advance of civilization has been developed: no English university has yet produced a *Middletown*.'[114] The work of the Lynds was one example of the inclusive cultural intelligence that *Scrutiny* aimed to promote; Stuart Chase furnished a second. Reviewing a selection of his books in the first number of the journal, Q. D. Leavis depicted him as the type of the 'middleman of ideas', the talented publicist who transmitted the otherwise inaccessible results of original thought and research to a broad educated public. Writers of this calibre – as distinct from writers like Wells or the bogus 'second-order minds' of the *Criterion* – were in her view indispensable to the well-being of the national culture.[115]

112. See *For Continuity*, pp. 1–2; xx, p. 4.
113. 'English Poetry in the Eighteenth Century,' v, 1 (June '36), pp. 21, 22, 24.
114. 'Advertising God,' p. 24.
115. 'A Middleman of Ideas,' I, 1 (May '32), pp. 69–73. The 'second-order mind' was Eliot's own variation on the idea of the 'middleman'; see *The Sacred Wood*

The reading public that they were to serve, and ideally, lead towards ever greater homogeneity, would be the plenary form of a genuine intelligentsia. *Scrutiny* was to be its advance-party.

(London, 1934, p. xiv) where the idea is expounded with explicit reference to Matthew Arnold.

'The Claims of Politics'

The political disposition of *Scrutiny* in the thirties was tense and unstable, shaped both by the moral and strategic conceptions proper to 'the minority' and the turbulence of a country and a continent deep in crisis.

The programme outlined in the 'Manifesto' was 'immediately practical and political', the editors avowed; but not in any direct sense. For while 'devotion' to politics 'at the party level' was, 'no doubt, somewhere necessary', there remained a task that was 'necessary – and prior' to it. *Scrutiny*'s special commitment, its peculiar 'political ambition', would be to the 'play of the free intelligence upon the underlying issues',[1] for only in this way could the essential ends of political action be clarified. This theme was reiterated constantly in the journal. Denys Thompson emphasized the need to prepare a foundation for valid political thought and action: 'obviously the more people seriously interested in politics the better. What we need to establish is a criterion of seriousness.'[2] According to F. R. Leavis, the crucial task was to 'revive or replace' the tradition that had been dispersed by the march of industrialism, led by science: 'desperate' though such an undertaking might seem, he declared, 'no social or political movement unrelated to such an attempt could engage one's faith and energy.'[3]

The distinctive role of 'the minority' was thus ante-political, logically and, it appeared, in time; for only a dedicated concern for 'culture', the repository of essential human values, could guarantee

1. I, 1 (May '32), pp. 2–7.
2. 'What Shall We Teach?' II, 4 (March '34), p. 386; see also idem, 'Prospectus for a Weekly,' II, 3 (December '33), pp. 247–52.
3. 'The Literary Mind,' I, 1 (May '32), p. 31.

a fruitful approach to the problems of the contemporary world. Leavis stressed that this conception was not a plea for exemption but a grave and indefectible responsibility: 'a consciousness maintained by an insulated minority and without effect upon the powers that rule the world,' he wrote, 'has lost its function.'[4] But how, if not in organized politics, was that 'consciousness' to have practical effect? The immediate answer, *Scrutiny* believed, lay in education, both as a locus of daily practice and as a field of struggle for reform. The *Scrutiny* group did not pretend to know how the political crisis might be resolved, Leavis wrote in late 1932, but it was convinced of the 'essential conditions' of a solution, and for that reason gave priority to its 'special educational interest'.[5] 'Some kind of counter-education is necessary,' Thompson argued: far from acquiescing in the reproduction of the prevailing order, the true purpose of education 'should be to turn out "misfits", not spare parts'.[6] And in the judgment of L. C. Knights, *Scrutiny*'s interest in educational reform was in fact 'practical politics'.[7]

Scrutiny was inclined to justify its aloofness from organized politics by pointing to the confusion in which the national and European political orders then stood. To the charge that 'we are too remote from practice to interest anyone really alive to the plight of the world', the editors answered: 'the impotence of the practical mind to do anything essential in practice is being so thoroughly demonstrated that the retort needs no pressing.'[8] And Leavis, while agreeing that 'the perception of the complexity of problems' could not excuse 'complacent inattention', was insistent that refusal to embrace a 'formula' or 'simple creed' should not be misconstrued as political irresponsibility. 'When people line up so promptly,' he wrote in late 1932, commenting on the spread of political partisanship among the literary intelligentsia, 'one suspects, not only that the appeal of the *chic* has something to do with it, but that the differences are not of a

4. 'What's Wrong With Criticism?' I, 2 (September '32), p. 135.
5. ' "Under Which King, Bezonian?",' I, 3 (December '32), p. 214.
6. 'Advertising God,' I, 3 (December '32), pp. 245–6.
7. 'Scrutiny of Examinations,' II, 2 (September '33), p. 162; see also the Editors, 'The *Scrutiny* Movement in Education,' II, 1 (June '33), see unnumbered pages following p. 110.
8. 'Manifesto,' p. 3.

kind that has much to do with thinking.'[9] However, the circumstances of the early thirties posed problems to which cultural rigorism was plainly inadequate as a response. At home, the political order was in crisis, and unemployment was reaching record levels; and abroad, the advance of fascism was bringing political terror, cultural involution and the threat of a war still more barbarous than the last. The pressures on *Scrutiny* to commit itself in the actual debates and struggles of those days no longer came merely from individuals like Santayana or Morton, from the undergraduate communists of *Cambridge Left* or the 'fashions' of the metropolitan intelligentsia, but from the menace of the political conjuncture itself.[10]

To one contributor at least, the likely course of political events, and the new alignments they would dictate, were apparent from the beginning. Writing on 'The Political Background' in the first number of the journal, Goldsworthy Lowes Dickinson assessed 'the political outlook, as it appears after the four years of war and the fourteen of what can hardly be called peace'. It was not *Scrutiny*'s function, he believed, to discuss party politics, or to examine 'the detailed methods of social or political reforms', but the journal would nonetheless have to attend to 'the broader political issues', for 'in that larger sense, these determine everybody's life'. And, in Lowes Dickinson's estimation, the two commanding issues of the day were 'war and capitalism'. The danger of war was now 'more obvious, and perhaps greater, than it was in 1914'. The current policies of the British, French and us governments amounted to a frankly cynical combination of pacific words and armaments orders. It was therefore imperative, he argued, to support the League of Nations, and the formation of an international 'police' force to maintain order among states. Turning to 'the other great question', that of capitalism, Lowes Dickinson remarked the glaring contradiction between widespread poverty and greatly increased productive capacity, and deplored the waste created by 'our national passions, our class antagonisms, the lack of intelligence in our leaders of industry, and the general ignorance and indifference of our populations'. Contrasting the Soviet Union favourably with capitalist

9. ' "Under Which King, Bezonian?",' pp. 210–11.
10. Morton, 'Culture and Leisure,' I, 4 (March '33), pp. 324–6; John Drummond, 'Culture,' *Cambridge Left*, I, 2 (Winter '33–'34), pp. 46–8 (see also J. D. Bernal, 'The End of a Political Illusion,' *Cambridge Left*, I, 1, Summer '33, pp. 10–15).

Europe, he warned that criticism of the former's violent and authoritarian means should not be permitted to obscure the validity of its ends: 'Russia, in spite of agonies, cruelties and follies is blazing the path for the world. The economic system she is determined to establish is the right one.'[11] Lowes Dickinson clearly felt that on these questions at least, it was essential to take up a concrete and unequivocal stance. On the first – peace or war? – *Scrutiny*'s writers showed little hesitation; their response to the second – the struggle between capitalism and socialism – was to be infinitely more problematic.

I

Anti-war sentiment was prominent in *Scrutiny* from the outset. Dickinson's arguments were echoed in the same issue of the journal by H. L. Elvin, in a review of a number of anti-war publications, among them Norman Angell's *The Unseen Assassins*. Elvin supported Angell's thesis that it was 'foolish to expect world peace while there is world anarchy in the economic and political relations of the different states'; and attacked such 'pre-peace assumptions' as 'the inviolable sovereignty of nations', recommending the removal of any political leader who persisted in clinging to them.[12] On this occasion Elvin was pessimistic about the chances of averting war – they were, he reckoned, 'practically *nil*' – but by the end of 1933 his attitude had become more determined. He rejected individual protest in favour of organized resistance, and, with this in view, advocated the drawing up of practical anti-war proposals and the widest possible dissemination of information on anti-war organizations and publications. War could only be prevented, he argued, by directly political action; and the outstanding political prerequisite of peace was the return of a Labour Government.[13]

Elvin's proposals, although ingenuous in their implicit valuation of British social democracy, were distinguished by a political directness that was rare in the pages of *Scrutiny*. The responses of the editorial circle were much more cautious. They were certainly opposed to

11. I, 1 (May '32), pp. 40, 41, 42; 45, 46.
12. 'Felo De Se?' I, 1 (May '32), pp. 85–87.
13. 'War: Can the Intelligent Stop It?' II, 3 (December '33), pp. 326–9.

war, and suspected that capitalism and war might be intimately linked; but their only concession to activism was to give occasional publicity to pacifist and other anti-war literature, and later, to the activities of organizations for the defence of intellectual freedom and civil liberties. There was never any suggestion that *Scrutiny* might endorse any existing political organization. Individually, the editors seem to have formed sharply divergent estimates of the efficacy of anti-war agitation. D. W. Harding was apparently unimpressed by the success of the Peace Pledge Union and by the overwhelming evidence of the Peace Ballot of 1935, for in an essay published in June of that year, just as the huge anti-war poll was confirmed, he argued that resistance to war propaganda was probably futile. Adducing psychological analyses of bellicose feeling, he stressed the close, complementary relationship between aggressivity and the desire for unity. Although distrustful of the postulate of innate aggression, Harding was insistent on the potency of the desire for unity: intra-national antagonisms tended to lead to inter-national conflicts – a process that could, as it were, be demonstrated *a contrario* from the marked relaxation of domestic tension that customarily followed entry into war. He was thus drawn to the conclusion that campaigns of war propaganda were 'a genuine folk product' from which not even intellectuals were necessarily immune. Those who, in Eliot's words, possessed a 'knowledge of the human heart' would disdain the emollient of wartime solidarity, recognizing that 'the nations [they] know will never be at war over ideals that are worth fighting for'; but public opposition to militarist propaganda, he decided, was ineffectual.[14] Harding's mood of resignation was at the opposite pole to Denys Thompson's vocal pacifism. Thompson made repeated attacks on the jingoist distortions of the bourgeois Press – following one particularly unrestrained denunciation of its anti-Soviet bias, the London *Times* demanded and was given a printed apology.[15] He was enthusiastic about the American tradition of muck-raking journalism and lamented the social and legal conditions that had blocked a parallel English development, but nevertheless commended

14. 'Propaganda and Rationalization in War,' IV, 1 (June '35), pp. 4–16.
15. 'Means to Social Consciousness,' III, 1 (June '34), pp. 65–69; 'The Times in School,' II, 4 (March '35), pp. 378–82; 'Apology to *The Times*,' IV, 1 (June '35), p. 72.

the organs of the Communist Party and the Labour Research Department, and Claud Cockburn's news-sheet *The Week*, for their defiant reporting of 'delicate' information.[16] His reviews of pacifist literature, which included practical recommendations for its circulation and discussion in the classroom, were unsparing in their condemnation of all forms of pro-war sentiment, whatever their source. 'This country has plenty of latent material for a fascism as brutal as the German,' he declared in June 1936.[17] And later that year he wrote, with a cynicism that included a measure of prescience: ' "Preserve the people's front" seems a possible war cry, especially if British imperialists instead of toadying to fascism recognize in it a menace to their own interests. . . . Given a suitable formula, Mr Pollitt and Mr Churchill may yet be seen on the same recruiting platform, inviting us to "break the Fascist front", or even again to make the world safe for democracy.'[18]

We have seen that *Scrutiny*'s response to the upsurge of anti-war agitation was uneven. Thompson's words, from the last text of its kind to appear in the journal, revealed that mere pacificism was in any case a fatally abstract response to the political circumstances of pre-war Europe. The new threat of war was clearly attributable to the inherent expansionary dynamic of the fascist regimes, and its overall impact on imperialism; and fascism, as Thompson himself was aware, was the product of conditions internal to the potentially belligerent states. His statement enacted in its very structure the irreparable disruption of pacifist discourse, its intentional argument – war or peace? – literally submerged in the terms of the very different conflicts that now dominated European history. Nazism was consolidating its internal rule; and Mussolini was advancing through Abyssinia. Two years after Hitler's accession to power, the Seventh Congress of the Comintern had discontinued the disastrous tactics of the 'Third Period' and called for the formation of popular anti-fascist fronts throughout Europe – in France, a Popular Front government was now in office. At home, the British Union of Fascists had grown rapidly in influence, with the public support of a significant portion

16. 'The Robber Barons,' v, 1 (June '36), pp. 2–12; 'Means to Social Consciousness'.

17. 'Recent Pacifist Literature,' v, 1 (June '36), pp. 71–4.

18. Review of Will Lovin, *Propaganda and the News*, v, 3 (December '36), pp. 336–8.

of England's ruling elite, including the large Press magnates; and in October 1936, only two months before Thompson's article appeared, thousands of London workers had defied both the Labour leadership and the State to prevent the BUF from holding a mass rally in the Jewish quarter of the city's East End.[19] Meanwhile, the summer of that year had witnessed the symbolic climax of the struggle between fascism and democracy, with the outbreak of civil war in Spain, where the Soviet Union was aligned with the Republican Government while the Axis dispatched men and *matériel* to the franquist counter-revolution. By the end of 1936, the pertinence of Lowes Dickinson's advice to the young *Scrutiny* had been demonstrated with brutal cogency: the future of peace, and of democracy itself, was indissolubly wedded to the outcome of the other 'great issue' of the time, that of capitalism.

This was the predicament that faced the entire national intelligentsia in the first half of the thirties, and drove thousands of their number to a firm political choice. The chaos and misery of the world-wide capitalist depression, contrasted with the success of Stalin's Five-Year Plan, led to a quickening of interest in Communism and to widespread philo-Sovietism; and as fascism began its international march, exposing the political insolvency of the League of Nations and meeting with palsied conciliation in British and French ruling circles, a whole generation of the English intelligentsia was impelled dramatically to the Left. Among the earliest expressions of this shift was the formation in 1933 of the British Section of the Writers' International, followed soon afterwards by the launching of a monthly organ, the *Left Review*; its most striking expression was the Left Book Club which, three years after its foundation in mid-1936, could claim more than a hundred titles, circulating among an organized readership of more than fifty-five thousand.[20]

The effects of this radicalization were soon evident on the outer

19. Noreen Branson and Margot Heinemann, *Britain in the Nineteen Thirties*, London 1971, pp. 306–8. The overall politico-diplomatic situation at the time is studied in A. J. P. Taylor, *The Origins of the Second World War*, London 1961.

20. John Lewis, *The Left Book Club*, London 1970; for a short general account of the Left intelligentsia in the thirties, see Stuart Samuels, 'English Intellectuals and Politics in the 1930s,' in Philip Rieff (ed.), *On Intellectuals*, New York 1969, pp. 196–247.

fringes of the *Scrutiny* 'connection'. The reviews that Auden occasionally contributed in the early years showed signs of pro-communist
sympathies.[21] The first volume of Trotsky's *History of the Russian Revolution* was welcomed with enthusiasm by W. A. Edwards on its appearance in English in 1932.[22] Montagu Slater, who was eventually to join
forces with *Left Review*, was at that date already drawn towards Marxism and the Soviet Union, and by mid-1933 had obviously been won
over.[23] The contributions of Read, Gifford, Åhrén and Kitchin, on
architecture, advertising, urban planning and economics respectively,
were all written in a socialist perspective.[24] Other contributors were
active in anti-fascist and related popular-front activities: the novelist
Storm Jameson, Joseph Needham, who wrote a volume for the Left
Book Club, and Olaf Stapledon and Richard Church, both of whom
addressed the first public meeting of the LBC's Readers' and Writers'
Group.[25] And in the twin itineraries of Douglas Garman and Edgell
Rickword, from *The Calendar of Modern Letters* to *Left Review* and the
Communist Party, the political migrations of the early thirties found
a symbol that was especially difficult to ignore.[26]

Rather closer to the centre of the *Scrutiny* circle were a small number
of individuals associated to some extent with the Right – notably
Martin Turnell, who before his entry into *Scrutiny* had been a regular
contributor to the Catholic-Right quarterly, *The Colosseum*. The 'programme' of *The Colosseum*, as outlined in its first issue, was Catholic
and anti-communist. Although opposed on Christian grounds to
Nazism and critical of the overseas expeditions of Mussolini's Italy, it
rejected the idea of Catholic anti-fascism: of the contending radical
forces of the day, the editor stated, only Bolshevism was intrinsically
unacceptable to Catholic belief. The strongest positive enthusiasm of
the journal was for the regimes of Dollfuss and Salazar, 'corporative'
states which it portrayed as combining the equity of the Left with the

21. W. H. Auden, rev. Winston S. Churchill MP, *Thoughts and Adventures*, I, 4
(March '33), pp. 410–13; and 'The First Lord Melchett,' II, 3 (December '33),
pp. 307–10.
22. I, 3 (December '32), pp. 301–4.
23. II, 2 (September '33), p. 212.
24. See pp. 69–70 above.
25. See Storm Jameson, *Journey From the North*, vol. 1, London 1969, pp. 293–307;
and John Lewis, *The Left Book Club* – Needham's book, published under the name of
'Henry Holorenshaw,' was *The Levellers and the English Revolution*.
26. See p. 70. above.

'Order' of the Right. Surveying the attitudes of the liberal and Left Press in mid-1934, the editor complained that 'the attempts in Austria or Portugal to defend the liberty of man and organize a positive social form in accord with the nature of man is met with execration'.[27] Upon the outbreak of the Spanish Civil War, *The Colosseum* declared for Franco;[28] and shortly afterwards, Turnell, who had by this time begun to contribute to *Scrutiny*, set up his own journal, *Arena*. The new journal was, as one contemporary observer remarked, less illiberal than *The Colosseum*.[29] It too supported Franco, but the statement on Spain with which Turnell opened its first issue, in April 1937, was qualified in argument and defensive in tone, with considerable effort made to dissociate its stand from general pro-fascist positions.[30] *Arena* also evinced a more inquiring attitude towards Communism, and in late 1937 devoted a special issue to Marxism and the USSR. Among the contributors to this discussion were two other *Scrutiny* writers, E. W. F. Tomlin and Derek Traversi. Tomlin's essay was a critique of Marx's theory of value, similar in approach to his contemporaneous writings in *Scrutiny*.[31] Traversi's dealt with 'Marxism and English Poetry', passing from a negative assessment of Spender and Auden to a general reflection on the politics with which they were then associated: 'Marxism always lacked the moral fibre to sustain its natural revolutionary ardour. Its case against modern society is one which we must respect, but it is still a duty to make a firm stand for all that it neglects, and against its complacent unawareness of its own omissions.' His own ideological preference, again echoing his *Scrutiny* writings, was for the morally-based social criticism of Langland and

27. 'Programme,' *The Colosseum*, I, 1 (March '34); 'Commentary,' I, 2 (June '34), p. 7. Turnell, born in 1908 into the family of a Staffordshire metal manufacturer, had graduated from Cambridge (Corpus Christi College), in 1930. His contributions to *The Colosseum* included an attack on Middleton Murry's para-religious views, and on modern 'spiritual anarchy' in general, of which Lawrence was given as a typical example ('For Mr Middleton Murry,' I, 1, pp. 39–54). Another contributor was Nicholas Berdyaev (see 'The Destiny of Culture,' Parts One and Two, I, 1, pp. 11–17, and I, 2, pp. 61–7). The editor of the journal was Bernard Wall.

28. *The Colosseum*, III, 12 (December '36); two years later there appeared 'The New Spain' by Primo de Rivera, the founder of the Falange (IV, 19, October '38).

29. F. W. Dupee, 'British Periodicals,' *Partisan Review*, V, 1 (June '38), pp. 45–8.

30. 'Spain,' *Arena*, I, 1 (April '37), pp. 8–10.

31. 'Marxist Economics,' I, 3 (October-December '37), pp. 176–86. See also idem, 'The Bankruptcy of Political Thought,' I, 2 (July '37), pp. 116–26.

D

Jonson.[32] Within *Scrutiny* itself, these writers were not politically obtrusive. Their shared opposition to Marxism was hardly distinctive; nor was Traversi's admiration for the anti-acquisitive morality of medieval England. Turnell's pronounced nostalgia for the epoch of hierarchy that had ended in 1789 was the only indication of the possible contemporary political preferences of the votaries of Order.[33]

By the close of 1936, the *marxisant* fringe had disappeared from *Scrutiny*. Their Right-leaning counterparts remained much longer – Turnell's association endured for more than a decade, and Traversi's to the very end – but were no more demonstrative in strictly political matters than the Left had been. And neither current was really central to the life of the journal in the thirties. The editors and their most prominent collaborators were all inflected Leftwards in this period, but their common aversion from the basic forms of modern social organization in general proved as stubborn an obstacle to full socialist commitment as did their anti-dogmatic humanism to any *rapprochement* with the Christian Right. Their Left-wing inclinations, where more than minimal, were fraught with qualification and reserve, becoming settled only at the cost of deep historic pessimism.

D. W. Harding stayed aloof from the larger social debates in which his colleagues involved themselves, preferring to concentrate on literary criticism and on his own profession of psychology, which he regarded as a politically neutral means of social amelioration.[34] Apart from one review in which he praised Herbert Read's anarchism as 'a genuinely different political principle' not concerned with a 'mere variation in state policy, such as dictatorial communism', he remained politically silent.[35] Denys Thompson's polemics were often

32. I, 3, pp. 199–211. Traversi also contributed, among other things, a review of Auden's *Look, Stranger!* and an essay on 'The Novels of E. M. Forster' (I, 1, pp. 64–5 and 28–40 respectively).

33. See however Traversi's wartime review of Butterfield's *Statecraft of Machiavelli*, where he criticized the 'liberalism' of the author, and suspended judgment on the conflict between fascism and the Allied powers ('Machiavelli,' IX, 2, September '40, pp. 186–93).

34. See Denys W. Harding, 'Some Implications of Industrial Psychology,' *The Highway*, XXV, (March '33), pp. 20–22. Harding was at this time a Tutor in the Workers' Educational Association (whose monthly journal this was).

35. Rev. *Poetry and Anarchism*, VII, 3 (December '38), pp. 345–6.

anti-capitalist in effect, but his real antagonist was industrial society as such, and consequently, although the Leftwards shift of contemporary debate induced a certain radicalization of idiom (epithets like 'the Power Age' and 'the Machine Age' giving way to 'capitalism' and 'imperialism'), the struggle between capitalism and socialism was, for him, essentially irrelevant.

F. R. Leavis was notionally open to the prospect of 'communism'. 'If there seems to be no reason why supporters of *Scrutiny* should not favour some kind of communism as the solution of the economic problem,' he wrote in 1932, 'it does not seem likely . . . that they will be orthodox Marxists.'[36] Little weight can be attached to that qualifying 'orthodox', but it is at least apparent that Leavis did not exclude the possibility of an industrially-based economic transformation that would somehow escape the dangers that he sensed in Marxist strategies for revolution. Several months later, he reiterated his belief that 'some form of economic communism' was 'inevitable and desirable', but added: 'the question is . . . what kind?'[37] The Marxist variant – 'so vacuous, Wellsian and bourgeois' – was, as we have already seen, unacceptable on general ideological grounds; and the unfolding history of Europe seemed proof of its political perils. Writing in mid-1933 on 'Marxism and cultural continuity', Leavis alluded to the last days of Weimar Germany and the suicidal role of the German Communist Party in its downfall: were his own cultural proposals any more 'ineffective', he asked, 'than . . . incitements to the Class War that are likely to be effective, if at all, in precipitating some Fascist *coup d'état* with the attendant advance of brutalization'?[38] The mounting terror of Stalin's domestic policy provided the definitive argument. Reviewing Day Lewis's symposium, *The Mind in Chains*, in the summer of 1937 – shortly after the second Moscow Trial and some six months before the biggest and most phantasmagoric of them all – he declared himself convinced by the Soviet experience that Marxism was fatally insensitive to the need for 'a directing and controlling humanity in social and political change'. The collective purpose of Day Lewis's authors was to win the intelligentsia to the cause of socialist cultural revolution – to which Leavis put what was now a

36. ' "Under Which King, Bezonian?",' p. 206.
37. 'Restatements for Critics,' I, 4 (March '33), pp. 320, 322.
38. *For Continuity*, Cambridge 1933, p. 12.

crucial question: 'is it socialism that obtains in Russia?'[39] (Q. D. Leavis too was anti-fascist and anti-capitalist, but equally alienated by what she knew of socialism in power. Commenting on the fate of Thorstein Veblen, 'the economist who diagnosed the diseases of capitalism and died frustrated', she observed: 'the life of a man who suffers from a constitutional inability to say yes would be no less tragic under Communism and probably a lot shorter too.'[40])

The only member of the editorial board to adopt an explicitly Left-wing stance, both outside the journal, where he was involved in Spanish solidarity activities and in the defence of civil liberties, and in its pages, was L. C. Knights. In an early essay devoted to a number of publications in the Catholic 'Essays in Order' series, he firmly rejected the Catholic-distributist prospectus of 'capitalism for all' and challenged the misrepresentation of anti-capitalist thought that it typically entailed, describing one account as 'a travesty of the class war that is only equalled by [Christopher] Dawson's account of Communists as "people who believe in wrecks as a matter of principle" '.[41] And in a later essay, he stated his own position, simply and concisely: 'no one need suppose that I imagine a retreat from a machine economy to be possible or desirable, or that I can envisage a solution of our economic *impasse* on other than socialist lines.'[42] Knights's political views were much less ambivalent than Leavis's, but he was not, on that account, significantly less critical of Marxism, and the negative form of this *prise de position* suggests that his socialist beliefs were not of a conventional kind. As we have seen, he remained adamant that Marxism was incapable of analysing or evaluating cultural phenom-

39. 'The Marxian Analysis,' VI, 2 (September '37), pp. 202, 204. In the review immediately following, Geoffrey Walton deplored the regimentation of literary production in the USSR and explicitly compared the regime there with that in Hitler's Germany ('The Arts in Totalitarian Russia,' VI, 2, September '37, pp. 205–7). For the response of British Communist Party intellectuals to the Trials, see Michael Woodhouse and Brian Pearce, *Essays on the History of Communism in Britain*, London 1975, pp. 219–40.

40. 'Mr Dos Passos Ends His Trilogy,' V, 3 (December '36), pp. 296, 299.

41. ' "Quicunque Vult . . . ",' II, 1 (June '33), pp. 98, 99. Turnell, writing in *The Colosseum*, cited Knights's article as an instance of *Scrutiny*'s incapacity in matters metaphysical (II, 5, March '35, pp. 52–4). Christopher Dawson was a prominent intellectual of the Catholic Right. See below for H. B. Parkes's critique of his perspectives.

42. 'Shakespeare and Profit Inflations, V, 1 (June '36), p. 59.

ena, and that it was wrong in its assumption that socialist revolution would produce, or even optimize the conditions for, a renewal of cultural life. He accepted the economic need for socialism, but insisted that the fate of culture depended on 'a conscious attempt to preserve continuity with those qualities that were spontaneously fostered by a non-industrial economy',[43] and spontaneously uprooted by industrial social organization, be it capitalist or socialist in form. Accordingly, even for Knights, education activity remained paramount. 'Our educational programme,' he wrote in 1938, 'has been conceived from the first in terms of a radical criticism of existing society, including, we may say, its economic and social ordering. ... It is precisely by unfitting his pupils for the environment ... that the educator can hope to change it, and to change it more radically than if he concentrates on "political" issues only.'[44]

The most striking expression of *Scrutiny*'s ambivalent relationship with socialism came not from any of the editors, but from one of their most prominent associates in the later thirties, H. B. Parkes, in his study of the Catholic-Right publicist, Christopher Dawson. Parkes accepted Dawson's central contention that religion was indispensable to 'cultural vitality', as a corrective to nineteenth-century materialism: without some such source of total human significance, he believed, the liberal ideals of progress and individualism would inevitably come to mean 'a mere increase in economic efficiency' and 'the competitive struggle for wealth'. However, he dissented from Dawson's belief that only Roman Catholicism could serve the purpose, and that acknowledgement of a transcendent reality was indispensable – his own expectation was of 'a philosophy derived from Christianity, but shorn of its otherworldly elements'. Parkes went on to attack the political implications of Dawson's position, pointing out that its practical issue could only be a *rapprochement* with fascism, 'the enthronement of brute force and the destruction of rationality'. The only possible course, he suggested, was to distinguish between the ultimate need for 'new philosophical attitudes' and the present need for a political solution; a cultural transformation was certainly essential, but the task of the hour was to resolve the political and economic crisis. Politics was, after all, 'the art of compromise', and whatever the

43. Ibid., p. 59.
44. 'The Modern Universities: A Postscript,' VII, 1 (June '38), pp. 4, 3.

perilous cultural implications of Marxism, the fact was that 'the extension of state control is inevitable, unless we are to relapse into chaos'. Compelled to make a practical choice between capitalism and socialism, Parkes chose the latter: 'immediate exigencies require that the economic system be controlled by the state, and that this control be exercised in the interests of the majority of the people.... The immediate evil is not the tyranny of the state but economic chaos, not the subordination of the worker to the economic machine but the denial to the worker of the wealth which the machine produces.' But if he was convinced that some kind of socialist option was economically inescapable, Parkes placed no confidence in its capacity for political or cultural advance: 'it will also, in course of time, become necessary to defend the liberty of the individual against a totalitarian state, and to prevent human life from becoming subordinated to the processes of the economic machine.' His hope was that 'the diffusion of a wise and humane philosophy [would] make these problems easier of solution'.[45] Parkes' perception of the historical conjuncture was thus, in a strict sense, *tragic*: he saw no alternative to some form of socialized economy, but equally was unable to conceive of the socialist *state* except in the sibling forms of the Fabian blueprints and the Stalinist reality, as a system of hypertrophied bureaucratic control.[46] If his sense of practical exigencies led him to endorse socialism, his deepest cultural instincts told him that he would eventually have to suffer under it.

The partial inclination towards socialism evoked in some of *Scrutiny's* inner circle by the political crisis underwent its decisive test when finally the journal turned to assess the Left Book Club. As an explicitly educational enterprise that combined *Scrutiny's* permanent interests – such as the condition of the reading public – with a political movement of an extremely broad, 'progressive' character, the LBC was the point at which the possibilities of an alliance, however temporary and unexacting, between the purposes of the journal and those of the

45. 'Christopher Dawson,' v, 4 (March '37), pp. 365–75. Parkes's article was attacked in an unsigned article in *Arena* ('Christopher Dawson,' I, 1, April '37, pp. 45–51): 'the discrimination with which Dawson treats fascism is, to say the least of it, preferable to Mr Parkes's blind condemnation.'

46. See also idem, *Marxism: A Post-Mortem*, London 1940.

Left would have to be determined, concretely and with some finality. In 'Education by Book Club?', published in December 1937, H. A. Mason took the measure of the LBC and found it lacking. Despite his evident sympathy with its political aims (and his admiration for its publishing methods), Mason had grave doubts about the intellectual standards maintained by the Club. He charged it with having concentrated on increasing the size of its audience without due regard for their level of critical awareness. It had failed to encourage genuinely critical discussion among its members, and was itself guilty of major critical lapses. The reviews of new titles in Left Book News were often no more than publicity exercises; and a similar abrogation of standards was attested in its unqualified admiration for the USSR. 'What the LBC stands most in need of,' he concluded, 'is a stricter maintenance of the standards they profess [sic].' This aim might be attained by the formation of a more broadly-based directorate with a correspondingly more critical outlook. At any rate, some such reform was necessary if the Club was to surpass its current level of achievement – 'simplification' – and to realize its aim, 'the clarification of the public mind'.[47]

In a letter published in the following number of Scrutiny, Boris Ford (then still an undergraduate) attempted to defend the Left Book Club against Mason's strictures. He reminded Mason that the crisis in which the LBC had been founded and now operated effectively confined it to the pursuit of one limited but urgent objective: the mobilization of 'maximum active opposition to Fascism and war'. In those circumstances, some instability of critical standards was unavoidable. He dismissed Mason's allegation that the Club was sometimes disingenuous in its political dealings, and, adducing the work of Sidney and Beatrice Webb, disputed his evaluation of authoritarianism in the USSR.[48] Mason's rejoinder conceded nothing to Ford's criticism. He reaffirmed his position on the Soviet Union (which, he claimed, was derived precisely from the Webbs' evidence) and, to substantiate the charge of political disingenuousness, cited Gollancz's editorial statements on the relationships obtaining among the Club, the Popular Front and the Communist Party and pointed to the general 'intolerance' with which the 'anti-Communist Left' was treated in the LBC.[49] He rejected Ford's view that the gravity of the political crisis excused

47. VI, 3 (December '37), pp. 240–46.   48. VI, 4 (March '38), pp. 424–6.
49. VI, 4, p. 427.

critical lapses, insisting that genuine education knew no 'short cuts'. Therefore, he concluded, it was necessary to cultivate 'a sort of desperate optimism' and act as though there were sufficient time, while remaining aware of 'the approach of a general collapse'.

Final judgment in the dispute was given by the editors. Ford had been alone among correspondents in his dissent, they reported; all the others had either corroborated Mason's claims or criticized his 'restraint'. They reaffirmed *Scrutiny*'s commitment to struggle 'on behalf of critical standards and critical intelligence' and concluded: 'as for the Left Book Club, if it is doing valuable work, that work, we believe, will be helped and not hindered by such reminders of what serious standards are as Mr Mason provided.'[50]

II

In all these statements, whatever their individual nuances, the same pattern of advance, strain and withdrawal was manifest. The editors and their collaborators shared a tendentially anti-capitalist ideology that had little or nothing in common with the theory and politics of Marxism. Yet, confronted with fascism and economic crisis, they tried in various ways to improvise a relationship with the political Left. None was wholly successful. Thompson was attracted by the defiant investigative journalism of the Left; but his pacifism and anti-industrialism were in essence a rejection of the very bases of contemporary struggles, and as political events moved beyond the purview of pacifism, he fell silent. Leavis was notionally favourable to 'some kind of communism'; but he rejected Marxism and its only major British exponent, the Communist Party, and so remained politically suspended. Knights and Parkes argued that socialism was an economic necessity, but neither believed that it could effect any kind of cultural renewal; Knights was for a time encouraged by Trotsky's struggle against the bureaucratic degeneration of Soviet society, but this political opening was soon lost sight of, obscured by the historical perspective that was his primary commitment,[51] and Parkes was in fact positively convinced that socialism would be politically regress-

50. 'Education by Book Club?' vi, 4, p. 428.
51. Knights recalled this in an interview with the author in May 1976.

ive. Mason was strongly sympathetic to the aims of the Left Book Club; but he refused to consent to a morganatic union in which 'culture' remained subordinate. Outside the Communist Party and its affinal organizations, and the Labour Party, there was no significant forum or organization for intellectuals of socialist leanings who refused to support Soviet and Comintern policy under Stalin. Mason's impossible agenda of 'desperate optimism', and the ostentatiously non-committal editorial statement that terminated the debate on the Left Book Club, marked the effective collapse of any hope of an alliance between *Scrutiny* and socialist politics.

Anti-fascist, anti-war, anti-capitalist, and yet unable to accommodate itself to socialism, even in the latitudinarian popular-frontist version of the late thirties – *Scrutiny*'s eventual recoil from socialist politics was indicative of its general failure to make the practical connection between 'culture' and organized politics. Only one course remained open; and appropriately, it was Mason who set out to explore it, in an essay whose formal occasion was a consideration of '*The New Republic* and the Ideal Weekly'. The main object of his criticism was the conventional separation, in format and in substance, of political and literary discussion in weekly journalism. It was in literature above all, he affirmed, that the 'sense of human values' – the essential moral basis of political judgment – was cultivated; and, given the current state of political thought, it was the duty of 'the literary side of a journal ... to show the way to the political side'. But in this central respect, *Scrutiny* had not fully discharged its responsibilities. It had been 'too content to maintain a negative attitude' towards Marxism, which, as a result, had been allowed to dominate discussion of the relations between politics and literature. 'Exposure of the weakness of the Marxist position does not constitute the whole duty of a quarterly,' Mason argued; and although the journal's criticism had certainly yielded some of the elements of a political position, its 'critical agreements' could not be said to constitute the foundations of 'a unity between [an ideal weekly's] "literary" and ... "political sides" '. The truth was, he argued, in a chiding allusion to the 'Manifesto' of 1932, that 'those "underlying issues" on which the critical mind should freely play make a too infrequent appearance. ... Surely the work undertaken by *Scrutiny* does have political implications.'[52]

52. VII, 3 (December '38), pp. 250–61, 259, 260.

This public self-criticism, unparalleled in the entire history of the journal, was an attempt to draw the lessons of *Scrutiny*'s perplexing first six years. The 'human values' of 'culture' were not acknowledged in the world of 'practical politics'. Those who were committed to the former, and yet aware of their responsibilities to the latter, were therefore condemned to fret through a series of unsatisfactory and unconsummated alliances imposed by changing political circumstance and accepted without zeal, *unless* they made the effort to define a politics that was the consistent practical articulation of their primary intellectual commitment. The question of possible alliances was now replaced by that of a politics peculiar to 'culture' itself.

The impact of Mason's challenge was immediate. In the next number of the journal, the editors proposed the establishment of 'a corresponding bureau' that would permit systematic contacts among their readers, and provide a forum for critical discussion of 'the consensus of opinion apparent in the pages of *Scrutiny*'. The topics singled out by the editors as requiring discussion included 'the sociological (a conspicuous gap in *Scrutiny*) and educational', and the question of 'the political implications of *Scrutiny*'.[53] And finally, six months later, the journal addressed itself directly and at length to its longstanding problem, in a symposium on 'The Claims of Politics'. The editorial preamble to the symposium reported an increasing pressure 'to express political conviction and engage in political action'. Their own concentration on 'culture' was 'not readily accepted as a reason for political non-commitment', but on the contrary was often deemed 'to carry with it special political obligations'. So, in an attempt to determine whether these obligations actually existed, and, if they did, what they entailed, a representative sample of authors had been assembled to give their opinions on the matter.[54]

In certain obvious respects, the eight intellectuals who contributed to the symposium did indeed represent a broad range of political positions. Olaf Stapledon's anti-fascist and cautiously pro-Marxist

53. 'A "Corresponding Bureau"?,' VII, 4 (March '39), p. 430.

54. 'The Claims of Politics,' VIII, 2 (September '39), p. 130. The contributors were Richard Church, 'The Individual in Politics,' pp. 130–34; Geoffrey Davies, pp. 134–6; Christopher Dawson, pp. 136–41; George Every SSM, 'Critical Judgment in Politics,' pp. 141–5; Michael Oakeshott, pp. 146–51; Olaf Stapledon, 'Writers and Politics,' pp. 151–6; L. Susan Stebbing, 'Philosophers and Politics,' pp. 156–63; R. H. Tawney, pp. 163–7.

sentiments were at odds with the deeply conservative, neo-Burkean thrust of Michael Oakeshott's essay. In contrast with George Every's belief that most *Scrutiny* readers favoured the more intellectual style of Left-wing politics, and Geoffrey Davies's contention that aloofness could only 'encourage the worse tendencies' and increase 'the chances of defeat', Richard Church took the view that 'all definitions of the problems of society' were 'false circumscriptions of the facts involved' and that 'action is always an evil because it cuts out nine-tenths of the truth'.[55] R. H. Tawney recommended that *Scrutiny* should arbitrate intellectual standards in politics as it did in literature, while Oakeshott contemptuously denied the very possibility of such standards in public life: 'a mind fixed and callous to all subtle distinctions, emotional and intellectual habits become bogus from repetition and lack of examination, unreal loyalties, delusive aims, false significances are what political action involves.'[56]

However, these divergences were at bottom variations on a single theme. The eight participants disagreed, sometimes sharply, about the general character of political life and about the relative merits of opposing political forces; but, virtually without exception, their definitions of the correct relationship between the intellectual and politics coincided. With a unanimity that was all the more remarkable in the light of these 'secondary' differences, they returned, one after another, to the theme that was most fully elaborated by Christopher Dawson. Dawson began by distinguishing two forms of political activity: administration, which was the business of politicians and statesmen; and the formulation of ideals, which was the function of the great political leader. The second, which transcended politics in the first sense, and which drew its inspiration from 'a community... wider and deeper than the State', was also the proper function of the intellectual. That community was incarnated in 'culture', which transcended political frontiers and national communities alike – thus, he argued, the political conflict between the Western powers and the Axis was not registered, except in contingent ways, in their respective literatures, which partook of 'a common tradition of culture'. He denounced those intellectuals whom he considered to have enlisted in the apostolate of the new barbarism (instancing Nietzsche, Sorel,

55. 'The Claims of Politics,' pp. 133–4
56. Ibid., p. 148.

Marinetti, d'Annunzio and the Bolsheviks) and argued that 'the social responsibilities of the man of letters' could not 'be identified with his duty as a citizen or subordinated to the interests of the State of which he [was] a member'. His role was to act on behalf of 'the interests of culture as a whole'.[57]

This was the general verdict of the symposium. The imperative task, Stapledon decided, was 'to reaffirm and clarify the civilized spirit, which is simply the developed human spirit'. *Scrutiny* should continue to invigilate political affairs, criticizing them in the light of 'the civilized intelligence'.[58] According to Oakeshott, the function of 'those whose genius and interest lie in literature, in art and in philosophy' was to create and re-create society's deepest values, and the primary condition of that activity was 'to be free from the world'.[59] With different emphases but in the same spirit, Tawney, Every and the other contributors echoed this view, effectively endorsing the programmatic imperative (though not necessarily the Inquisitorial imagery) of Geoffrey Davies's conclusion: 'it is the duty of every citizen who, by nature or education, is mentally or spiritually above his neighbours, to continue his own personal development but at the same time to watch every political development around him with the closest attention; to regard himself as a member of a new Holy Office charged with the combating of the appalling and rampant heresies all around him; to employ his interest and authority diurnally to the re-tracing of the road and the recognition of reality.'[60]

The consensus that emerged from the symposium was an unqualified reaffirmation of the position classically defined by Arnold (or equally, Benda: in some of the contributions, the accents of *La Trahison des clercs* were unmistakable). The mission of the intellectual was to serve a transcendent 'culture' or 'humanity', to protect and propagate the values without which civilization was doomed to stagnation or outright regression. The cultural agenda outlined in the 1932 'Manifesto' was thus vindicated and, in one crucial respect, clarified. Cultural exploration was not, as the editors of *Scrutiny* had originally seemed to suggest, the prologue to a future politics in any temporal

57. Ibid., pp. 136–41.
58. Ibid., pp. 153, 156.
59. Ibid., pp. 150–51.
60. Ibid., p. 136.

sense: the former did not simply precede the latter. It was now seen as the permanent precondition of fecund political thought. Ever 'above' and 'beyond' politics itself, 'culture' was a permanent meta-political sanction, the tribunal before which all politics stood judged, in the name of 'the human'.

3

Revolution in Education?

'To say that the life of a country is determined by its educational ideals is a commonplace' – it was in these remarkable terms that *Scrutiny*'s founders announced their own 'political' priorities.[1] The many essays and reviews that the journal devoted to educational topics in the thirties were not nearly so forcefully coordinated as their wartime and post-war equivalents were to be, but they nevertheless constitute, in their sheer volume and variety, a formidable body of argument whose object, in the words of an advertisement placed in the *New Statesman* in mid-1933, was the preparation of a 'revolution in education'.[2]

The parameters of *Scrutiny*'s educational thinking were established in two early statements by F. R. Leavis and Denys Thompson. In 'Restatements for Critics', Leavis named education as the only position from which successful resistance to 'the material environment' could be mounted. 'We assume an "inner human nature", and our recognition that it may be profoundly affected by the "economic process" persuades us that it must rally, gather its resources and start training itself for its ultimate responsibility at once.' On the outstanding issue of the day ('is the machine – or Power – to triumph or to be triumphed over, to be the dictator or the servant of human ends?'), capitalism and socialism were at one in their neglect of that 'ultimate responsibility'; but in education, a 'cogent way in which the human spirit can refute the Marxian theory and the bourgeois negative lies open'. Education, and especially its central discipline of English, could become the forcing-house of effective social thought, 'a centre of real

1. I, 1, p. 6.
2. June 3, 1933, p. 740. The slogan in full was 'Standards in Criticism, Revolution in Education'.

consensus' of the kind 'presupposed in the possibility of literary criticism and ... tested in particular judgments'.[3] Thompson's discussion of advertising expressed similar views, but with greater pungency. Advertising was not only manipulative, he charged: it debased art, thought and religion, and undermined the language. In order to fight it, 'some kind of counter-education' was necessary, 'something like Active Reading', a discipline that would stimulate young people to enquire into the meaning of contemporary truisms and usages. At present, the educational system was 'very busy mass-producing interchangeable little components for the industrial machine'. The concern of a genuine education in these conditions 'should be to turn out "misfits", not spare parts'.[4] These two essays initiated themes that were to remain constant throughout *Scrutiny*'s career: the belief that education, a potentially 'humanizing' activity, was at present complicit with the 'economic process'; that it should be reformed as a centre of opposition to the latter; and that in this effort, the role of literary training was paramount.

I

A large number of the contributions on secondary education were reviews of text-books – anthologies of poetry or prose, critical primers and related publications. About this type of material, which was associated mainly with Denys Thompson, Raymond O'Malley and Frank Chapman (all practising teachers), little need be said, except that it was typically practical in bias, oriented towards the daily problems of the classroom, and that the criteria used in the selection and evaluation of review material were explicitly derived from *Scrutiny*'s general outlook. Thus, for example, Thompson and Chapman advocated the use of the publications of the Council for the Preservation of Rural England and other ruralist literature; and, as we have seen, the former was anxious to see pacifist literature made available to schoolchildren and discussed in the classroom. His review of George Sampson's *English for the English* called for an anti-industrial, anti-commercial, anti-jingoist, anti-war education, and endorsed Sampson's unsurpassable statement of the thesis that *Scrutiny* had made its

3. I, 4 (March '33), pp. 323, 319.
4. I, 3 (December '32), p. 246.

own: 'English is not really a subject at all. It is a condition of existence . . .'.[5]

Scrutiny's analysis of secondary education focused principally on the key component of the 'educational machine', the examination system. In 'Scrutiny of Examinations', published in September 1933, L. C. Knights presented a comprehensive indictment of prevailing methods of assessment, and in particular, of the centrally administered School Certificate in Education. Whatever its possible advantages, standardized assessment was a virtually unattainable goal, he argued; and the actual effects of the system were ruinous. It imposed a regime that dominated and distorted the educational process, degrading learning to the accumulation of suitably profitable material, and restricting the range of work to the officially 'relevant' (one correspondent cited in this essay testified to the 'moral strain' of teaching English for the School Certificate). It was imperative, he concluded, to abolish the external examination system, in favour of a more flexible and responsive system of internally designed syllabuses and examinations.[6]

Some time later, Chapman supplemented Knights's general criticisms with the detailed observations of a practising teacher. He deplored the arbitrary and confined range of texts prescribed by the examining bodies, and commented cynically on the criteria that shaped the School Certificate course: 'précis is said to be useful in "business": hence, I suppose, its very prominent place in the examination.' Chapman was pessimistic about the chances of even minor reforms, and saw little possibility of 'the abolition of the School Certificate and the examination system, as a whole, . . . in the present framework of society'.[7] The social rationality of the examination system was explored further by D. W. Harding in an essay on intelligence testing. In important respects, he argued, this mode of assessment corresponded to the functional requirements of 'industrial civilization': it excluded self-criticism, measured only the capacity to solve problems posed from without, disregarding the examinee's capacity to formulate new problems, and simply discounted incorrect answers. Designed to produce efficient functionaries rather than

5. 'What Shall We Teach?' II, 4 (March '34), p. 380.
6. II, 2 (September '33), pp. 137–63.
7. 'English for the School Certificate,' IV, 4 (March '36), pp. 358, 359.

self-determining individuals, intelligence tests merely reflected 'the peculiarities of the civilization that produced them'.[8]

The conviction underlying these attacks on the examination system was that current educational thought and practice were marked by strong tendencies towards standardization and abstraction whose origins lay in the economic and political system, and whose effects were culturally destructive. Further studies traced these tendencies in every sector of education, from the Public Schools to the 'progressive' theories of Dewey, Neill and Montessori.

The Public Schools were seldom praised in *Scrutiny*'s early volumes. The 'nasty mess of Kipling, commerce and uplift' that composed the Public School thought-world was attacked by Thompson, who alluded also to the 'maladjustments caused by monasticism'.[9] But these skirmishes never developed into a full-scale assault, and were scarcely comparable with the campaigns that were contemporaneously launched against these institutions from other quarters. In fact the only extensive essays on the Public Schools to appear in *Scrutiny* were written from a basically sympathetic standpoint. Martin Crusoe's overview of 'The Development of the Public Schools', printed in the first number of the journal, described the social function of the schools in the past, and recommended certain changes which, he argued, were necessary if they were to retain that function in the altered conditions of the twentieth century. England was fortunate in that its 'Renaissance foundations' had survived down the centuries, as 'the one really powerful bulwark against bureaucratic instruction'. They had survived because they had successfully adapted to changing social needs. In the nineteenth century, they had incorporated certain mechanisms – the prefectorial system, compulsory games and religious observance – designed to produce 'a type satisfactory to the Victorian middle classes', and had gone on to modify these as circumstances demanded, undergoing 'a steady process of civilization comparable to that which has occurred in the Middle

8. 'The Cultural Background of Intelligence Testing,' vi, 2 (September '37), pp. 144–54.
9. 'Progressive Schools,' iii, 2 (September '34), p. 209; 'What Shall We Teach?' p. 385; compare W. H. Auden, 'Private Pleasure,' i, 2 (September '32), pp. 191–4.

Class itself'.[10] But now they were threatened with sclerosis. Acquiescing in 'the pathetic belief of the business world' in tangible tokens of attainment, they had 'most regrettably' accepted the School Certificate, 'just such an instrument as an increasingly bureaucratic and banausic system of education finds apt to its purpose, the standardization of thought'. The old mechanisms of socialization had 'lost force and application' and the expansion of the curriculum had fragmented their former unity of purpose – 'dogmatism has moved from the Chapel to the Laboratory'. It was urgently necessary, therefore, for the Public Schools to find a new 'unifying principle that [would] relate life and learning,' and that principle, Crusoe believed, could only be the pursuit of truth: 'no living educational force can come to birth without passion for the truth, and it is precisely the absence of this passion that has sterilized our educational system as a whole.' Moreover, 'there is only one object of education, to live abundantly'. But this 'splendid and exalted conception, this religion', had now petrified into 'one or another form of Pharisaism'. Nevertheless, Crusoe believed that 'the circumstances of Public School life [were] such as to make an education based on truth and the love of truth the most obvious in the world', and, on this assumption, offered several concrete proposals. He recommended that the system of pastoral care be reorganized so as to facilitate a more sensitive and informed response to the problems of adolescence; that the science curriculum be reorganized to commence with biology (if not physiology) so as to accommodate the adolescent's 'intense preoccupation . . . with the physical'; and that written English should become the advance-post of the 'search for truth'.[11]

The main obstacle to this plan, Crusoe argued, was the psychology of the average schoolmaster. As he wrote in a later essay on the same topic, it was 'inherently probable' that the schoolmaster was psychologically regressive, 'a frozen adolescent seeking his natural milieu, the bosom of his Alma Mater or her substitute'.[12] Such men were not only incapable of guiding their charges through the squalls of puberty; they also threatened to retard the development of English as the central component of the curriculum. They themselves exploited poetry as a narcotic, and communicated this habit to their

10. I, 1 (May '32), pp. 47–8.   11. Ibid., pp. 50, 51, 53.
12. 'English Work in the Public School,' I, 4 (March '33), p. 370.

pupils; they were incapable of using English as an intellectual and emotional training, for the nurture of critical capacity and 'aggressive' rather than 'regressive imagination'. As long as 'adults manqués' continued to throng the common rooms of Public School England, education would remain blocked in its attempts to thwart the designs of bureaucracy and mass-production. Now that 'the middle class' had become in effect the dominant class, 'the specifically bourgeois virtues of complaisance, safety, the golden mean' could not adequately prepare its children for their special role: 'a stronger, freer-minded aristocracy is needed, and unless the Public School creates it it will deservedly die of atrophy, for it must justify the social privileges gained in the past by present function.'[13]

For all his idiosyncrasies, Crusoe's preoccupation with the psychological and sociological dimensions of education was characteristic of much of the educational thinking of the inter-war period. The Hadow Reports of 1931 and 1933, on primary and nursery education respectively, laid strong emphasis on the psychological needs and propensities of children, and on the merits of child-centred curricula. The work of child psychologists like Susan Isaacs and Jean Piaget was widely discussed.[14] And initiatives in progressive education – the theory and practice of Montessori, A. S. Neill's Summerhill experiment, John Dewey's conception of education for citizenship – attracted considerable attention. In a number of essays and reviews published in the early years of its existence, *Scrutiny* offered its own characteristically ambivalent estimate of these developments. Although personally in favour of a libertarian, child-centred pedagogy which, as far as possible, would cater for each pupil individually, Raymond O'Malley remained reserved about the value of Neill's work. He criticized the 'widespread habit of hygienic, rootless ratiocination' and recourse to 'meaningless abstractions' in progressive educational theory, and upheld the Lawrentian 'religious sense' which, opposed equally to all dogmas and observances, was 'almost

13. 'The Development of the Public School,' p. 59.
14. See S. J. Curtis and M. E. A. Boultwood, *An Introductory History of English Education since 1800,* fourth ed., London 1966, pp. 187f, 220f. For reviews of Piaget and Isaacs in *Scrutiny,* see I, 3 (December '32), pp. 308–10; I, 4 (March '33), p. 420; II, 3 (December '33), pp. 321–3 – all by D. W. Harding.

the only means of organized resistance to the forces of the new illiteracy'.[15] In a short piece on ' "Englightened" Education', Alan Keith-Lucas attacked the theories of Montessori and other progressive educationists, suggesting that the former's methods were the educational analogue of Fordism.[16]

Reviewing *The Educational Frontier*, a collaborative volume from the United States, Knights seconded the authors' belief in education as a vital factor in social advance but complained of the abstractness of their arguments: there was 'much talk of "culture", yet, politics apart', the book contained 'nothing that need disturb an educational Babbitt'. He insisted that ' "an integrated and unified attitude" of any value can *only* be achieved by the careful and intelligent discrimination of the quality of thought and emotion expressed in particular instances. The study of literature, of the use of words, . . . must be the basis of any educational programme worth the name.' This, the first principle of *Scrutiny*'s humanism, was profoundly at odds with the views of the contributors to *The Educational Frontier* (among them John Dewey), whose upper-case Humanism of Progress and Improvement linked them with the 'rotarians' of Middletown.[17] The progressive critique of the authoritarianism and hierarchical rituals of orthodox education, especially in the Public Schools, was welcomed by Eric Capon in his review of L. B. Pekin's *Progressive Schools, Their Principles and Practice*; but Denys Thompson's comment on this piece reiterated the customary complaint about the facile generalizations of progressive pedagogics, and maintained that although they certainly constituted the foundations of an improved education, the distinctive innovations of the progressive school were not in themselves sufficient. (Elsewhere, Thompson enumerated what he considered to be the foremost negative 'manifestations of the Progressive': 'aggressive rationalism, a clinical and morbid interest in sex, an impercipience beyond present psychology, an immature, arrogant faith in "science".') The most important precondition of

15. 'Culture and Early Environment,' III, 3 (December '34), pp. 223–33. O'Malley, who had graduated from Trinity College in 1931, was now Head of English at Darlington Hall School. See also idem, rev. E. Sharwood Smith, *The Faith of a Schoolmaster*, IV, 2 (June '35), p. 108; and 'The Rigour of the Game,' II, 3 (December '33), pp. 319–20.

16. I, 2 (September '32), p. 98.

17. 'Good Intentions in Education,' II, 2 (September '33), pp. 215–19.

educational advance, he concluded, was the provision of adequate personnel: it was necessary to educate the educator.[18]

II

Two fairly definite shared conclusions emerged from these discussions, despite the many differences of opinion that they revealed. The first was that the well-being of culture and society required an education specifically designed to resist the ethos of the modern industrial economy, but that no existing programme of educational reform held out this possibility; the second, that the immediate prospects for educational reform were largely determined by the quality of the teaching personnel. Accordingly, *Scrutiny* concentrated its energies in an attempt to organize the teaching community, and in a strategic emphasis on the sector of higher education, where teachers were produced.

In December 1932, Knights published 'Will Training Colleges Bear Scrutiny?', a report on the findings of a questionnaire circulated among staff and students in training colleges around the country. 'Behind the educational system', he charged, stood 'the cinema, newspapers, book societies and Big Business – the whole machinery of "Democracy" and standardization', and his evidence suggested that, in training colleges at least, the ill-effects of this association were already pervasive. He attacked the conservative, philistine routines that dominated these institutions. The condition that he depicted was one of authoritarianism and mediocrity among academic and administrative staff, producing dull, servile and personally arrested students. In the next issue of the journal he returned briefly to the subject, to report that his observations had been favourably received by the numerous correspondents, both staff and student, who had written to corroborate his main points from their own experience. 'Already,' he announced, 'more than a nucleus of an informal educational association has developed.'[19]

18. Capon, 'How Shall We Teach?' III, 1 (June '34), pp. 102–4; D.T., 'Another Point of View,' p. 104; idem, 'Progressive Schools,' III, 2 (September '34), pp. 210.
19. I, 3 (December '32), pp. 247–63; 'Training Colleges: Repercussions,' I, 4 (March '33), p. 389.

The following summer, the editors convened a meeting of sympathetic teachers at the Leavises' house in Cambridge, and it was decided there to work towards a 'movement' based on loosely federated 'cells'. Reporting on 'the *Scrutiny* movement in education', the editors described their initiative as an 'unusually practical form of politics' that approached contemporary social problems with an entirely new pertinence. This educational emphasis, they declared, was 'the political strength of the movement'. Very little is recorded of the progress of the 'movement' in the next few years. No further mention was made of it in *Scrutiny*. However, by the end of the decade it was evident that a *Scrutiny* current existed among secondary-level teachers, geographically quite widespread and possessing its own specialist organ, *English in Schools*.[20]

Scrutiny's educational interests remained fairly catholic throughout this period, but of the various sectors of the system, the one that dominated discussion in the journal was the university. Stimulated and encouraged by current transatlantic debates on the role of the university, F. R. Leavis set out 'to present the Idea of a University in terms appropriate to the modern world'.[21] 'Why Universities?', published in September 1934, was Leavis's first major statement on the organization and function of university education and a comprehensive outline of the blueprint for a new 'English School' that was to follow some eight years later.

The key social problem, in Leavis's view, was that of *control* – control of 'the enormous technical complexity of modern civilization' through the 'coordination' of 'knowledge and understanding'. It was the task of the university to achieve this coordination, by submitting the 'specialist knowledge and training' of the expert to the guidance of 'humane culture'. Against Marxist analyses of university problems ('the most insistent criticism that academic institutions are

20. II, 1 (June '33), following p. 110. *English in Schools* was founded by Thompson in 1939. For further details, see Chapter Three.

21. III, 2, pp. 117–32. For discussions of US thought and experimentation in this field, see Willard Thorp, 'How High is the Higher Education?' (rev. Abraham Flexner, *Universities: American, English and German*), I, 1 (May '32), pp. 73–6; F. R. Leavis, 'An American Lead,' (rev. Alexander Meiklejohn, *The Experimental College*), I, 3 (December '32), pp. 297–300.

likely to be receiving'), he asserted 'a certain autonomy of the human spirit' and the consequent need to protect and extend the 'autonomy' of the universities, whose seclusion from 'the common grind' permitted not only 'cloistral vegetation' but also 'a free play of spirit' that was impossible elsewhere (it is at the universities that Public School boys, from well-to-do bourgeois homes, become Communists. That is as it should be.').[22]

Leavis's contention was that 'the Educated Mind' was at present gravely hampered in its attempt to resist the centrifugal forces of specialization, in intellectual life and in society: 'the idea of liberal culture' had 'been defeated and dissipated by advancing specialization' at a time when it was more than ever necessary 'to produce specialists who are in touch with a humane centre'. The constitutive discipline of this 'centre' could only be literary criticism, for literature was the prime depository of 'humane values', of 'the inherited wisdom of the race'. No one who was unable to distinguish between 'the living in contemporary literature' and the 'Book Society classic' could be relied upon to think effectively about contemporary civilization.[23] However, if university English was to perform this function, to produce genuinely mature and critical individuals, it would have to be reformed. The examination system, which merely tested 'examinability', encouraged glibness and subverted 'the system of instruction and guidance', could not continue; and in the organization of teaching, lectures would have to be replaced, largely or even wholly, by more collaborative structures – like, say, the Cambridge 'supervision'. These were among the reforms that were necessary if 'humane culture' was ever again to be a force in social life.

Leavis's essay inaugurated a series of more detailed analyses of the content and organization of university education. E. W. F. Tomlin undertook a 'scrutiny' of the Oxford School of 'Modern Greats' (politics, philosophy and economics) in order to establish whether the latter – the forcing-house of the English political elite – was adequate as a study of modern civilization. He attacked the conservative forces whose Classical prejudices blocked the development of

22. 'Why Universities?' pp. 119–20, 130–**31.**
23. Ibid., pp. 121, 124, 125.

the School as a coherent course of study. At present, it was a 'confused medley'. But its case was not hopeless. It had been founded to meet the 'genuine need' for instruction in economics, and, for all its failings, 'at least saves [students] from the London School of Economics'.[24] Tomlin doubted, nevertheless, whether Modern Greats could ever be 'an *education*'. English apart, only the Classics-based School of 'Greats' could claim to be this 'in the highest sense'. As it stood, the School was only 'capable ... of turning out minds seething with information, ... sophisticated, but quite illiterate'.[25]

H. A. Mason brought the study of English still nearer to its educational apotheosis in his discussion of the role of Classics in a 'revised education'. The residual claims of Latin and Greek, he argued, rested on their literatures: the languages, and the educational routines associated with them, could not be justified. 'Our approach to the values of the past must be from the present', and accordingly, the civilizations of Greece and Rome were to be considered principally as sources of critical norms for the analysis of the present. Mason called for translations that rendered 'in the modern idiom the poetry of the past': the value of ancient literature was directly proportionate with its modernity, and the paramount educational requirement was a critical revaluation of the classics. Revisions of this nature would improve classical education, Mason believed, but nothing could ever restore Classics to the exalted position from which Leavis's 'Why Universities?' had dismissed it: English was now 'the humane study *par excellence*'.[26]

If this was so, it was all the more necessary to combat the powerful conservative forces whose influence threatened to retard the development of English studies. Knights's 'Mr C. S. Lewis and the Status Quo', published simultaneously, was an attack on one of the leading representatives of the academic rearguard. Knights attacked Lewis's systematic exclusion of 'all awkward fundamental questions' in favour of such secondary issues as the relative merits of Classics and Old and Middle English as tributaries of English literature, and also his belief in specialization and 'learning for its own sake', and reaffirmed his own preference for 'the study of a particular culture as a

24. IV, 4 (March '36), pp. 344–57, at p. 351.
25. Ibid., p. 355.
26. 'Classics and Education: A Note,' VIII, 1 (June '39), pp. 32–5.

whole', for 'the development of genuinely individual taste and critical intelligence' and 'the sharpening of tools that [could] be used outside any limits that the teacher may impose'.[27]

These discussions were primarily concerned with what *Scrutiny* called 'the older universities' or 'the ancient foundations': the conception of English studies defended by Lewis was that in force at Oxford; Tomlin's and Mason's studies also referred – the first directly, the second indirectly – to the Oxford curriculum; and Leavis's suggestions for university reform were obviously written with Cambridge in mind.[28] This emphasis was immeasurably strengthened by Knights in his most important contribution to these pre-war discussions, an examination of the educational potential of 'the Modern Universities' published in March 1938. He began by rebuking theorists who underestimated or denied the potentially critical social role of the university sector: 'we know that Capitalism – as represented by Ford, Beaverbrook or the National Government – is strongly anti-educational. But it is, I think, academic theorizing to assert – as the Marxists assert – that because England is a capitalist country the universities, in so far as they are not mere servants of the economic system, are impotent.' To ignore 'their potential value as schools of social thought and independent criticism' was 'enormously to decrease the chances of intelligent social change', and possibly to court positive dangers: it might easily 'prove an effective way of fostering a totalitarian state of mind'. Knights himself had no illusions about the collusive role of the universities – he cited one correspondent's charge that they were 'the tied houses of the commercial and industrial minds' – but held that this was the effect of passivity and deficiency: 'the modern universities are not at present – whatever the politically minded may say – merely flunkeys of the capitalist system. They serve the modern world not by toadying to this or that "interest" but simply by *not* producing a sufficient number of men who are educated enough to make any fundamental criticism of society as they find it.'[29]

27. VIII, 1, pp. 88–92 (a review of Lewis's *Rehabilitation and Other Essays*).
28. Compare his *How to Teach Reading: A Primer for Ezra Pound* (1933) which, as he explicitly affirmed, presupposed a bias towards Cambridge (letter to *The New Statesman*, June 10, 1933; reprinted in John Tasker, ed., F. R. Leavis, *Letters in Criticism*, London 1974, p. 28).   29. VI, 4, pp. 361, 372–3.

If the universities were not to betray their 'essential function', they would have to be organized around 'one ideal aim'; for 'the only way of discovering what most needs *doing* is to establish certain positions in the light of an ideal which does not vary.' Knights went on to amplify (if hardly to clarify) the meaning of this educational ideal: it entailed the nurture of a 'sensitive and flexible intelligence' capable of addressing the problems of contemporary life, 'a potentially mature sense of values' (that is, the capacity to understand the possible relevance of the past to the present), and 'a sense of the relativity of one's immediate standards'. Without these qualities, the most obvious purpose of education – the inculcation of the 'ability to use with precision the instruments of knowledge in some field of human effort' – degenerated into mere vocational training.

The value of any given university education, according to Knights, was practically determined by three factors: the quality of the teaching system (the abilities of the staff, the nature of the curriculum and of the structures of teaching and assessment), the opportunities provided for 'self-education', and 'the extent and quality of those informal contacts outside "classes" which largely determine the prevailing intellectual climate'. On the first and second counts, Oxford and Cambridge were only slightly favoured. No university was free of 'narrowly specialized' curricula, 'excessive' lecturing and an intellectual life tyrannized by 'the constant pressure of examinations'. In 'the newer universities, where economic pressure is both more potent and more obvious', these problems were much more pressing. But it was on the third count that the modern foundations suffered most. Because of their non-residential character, their members were dispersed, hourly and daily; and this, combined with understaffing and over-lecturing, frustrated the development of extra-curricular contacts between teachers and students. The material conditions that would enable them to function as real intellectual *centres* were unalterably absent. In place of the 'self-education' and informal contact that Knights saw as essential to a vigorous intellectual climate, there was only 'the mass-production of BAs'. Furthermore, the world into which these intellectual atoms were daily scattered was deeply inhospitable. In the provincial centres, the 'cultural tradition inherited from the eighteenth century' had atrophied; these cities were now 'simply business centres' exhibiting 'all the symptoms, economic and cultural, of the dominance of middle-class acquisitive ideals'. Knights carefully avoided any blunt counterposition of 'the ancient foundations' to 'the modern universities', but the implication of his analysis was unmistakeable. There could be no healthy issue from the marriage of the university and *Manchestertum*.[30]

It would not in any case have been easy to establish a neat antithesis between the two types of institution, as Q. D. Leavis in particular was aware. 'It is time,' she wrote, 'that a realistic account of the older universities was put into circulation'; and in her justly famous 'diagnosis' of 'the case of Miss Dorothy Sayers' she provided that account with a memorable exordium. With great pungency and wit, she assailed the 'combination of literary glibness and spiritual illiteracy' that Sayers's career seemed to her to epitomize. 'People in the academic world who earn their livings by scholarly specialities are not as a general thing wiser, better, finer, decenter or in any way more estimable than those of the same social class outside. The academic world offers scope for personal aggrandisement much as the business world does, with the results you might expect. No one who has had occasion to observe how people get a footing in the academic world, how they rise in it, how appointments are obtained, how the social life is conducted, what are its standards, interests and assumptions, could accept [the] romanticizing and extravagant claims' of Sayers's Oxford idyll, *Gaudy Night*. Between frivolity and philology, between the novels of Dorothy Sayers and the 'kind of scholarship [that] never gears in with life', the fit was perfect.[31]

Sayers's antitype was Leslie Stephen, 'Cambridge critic'. In a tribute to Stephen published in March 1939, Q. D. Leavis contrasted 'the oppressive spirit of the old Oxford atmosphere' with the intellectual astringency of 'the Cambridge tradition' that he exemplified. For her

30. Ibid., pp. 362f, 371.
31. vi, 3 (December '37), pp. 334–40, at pp. 337, 338, 340. See also her partner's scornful comment on Oxford's decision to confer an honorary doctorate on P. G. Wodehouse: 'Miss Dorothy L. Sayers is also widely thought in universities to write well. Admirers of hers in the world at large are now wondering whether the well-known constitutional anti-feminism of Cambridge means that Cambridge has no chance of catching up with Oxford.' ('The Function of the University,' viii, 2, September '39, p. 209.)

generation, Stephen had been a model of critical probity. Yet he had left Cambridge, and then precisely on a point of moral principle – his loss of religious belief – and the values that he had upheld were now at a discount in the university. Cambridge, it appeared, was unequal to its own highest standards; in present conditions, remembrance itself was an act of defiance.[32] Nevertheless, beset and dishonoured though it was by the contingent university of the thirties, the 'essential' Cambridge remained, as an inspiration and – perhaps – as an opportunity. In the years that followed, it was to be chosen as the strategic pivot of the 'revolution in education'.

32. VII, 4 (March '39), pp. 404–15. The phrase concerning Oxford is Stephen's. For his life, see Noël Annan, *Leslie Stephen*, London 1951. Leavis's essay is resumed more fully in the next section.

Standards, Currencies and Values

'We take it as axiomatic that concern for standards of living implies concern for standards in the arts.'[1] I have argued that this, *Scrutiny*'s first word, was in actual logic its last; that this founding 'axiom' and the distribution of attention dictated by it could only be understood as the manifest form of an argument whose real scope and purpose were much wider. Having examined *Scrutiny*'s conception of modern historical development, the effects of this on the political disposition of the review and the educational strategies that it indicated, we can now turn to this dominant concern, to see what it meant in practice and to specify the nature of the 'necessary relationship between the quality of the individual's response to art and his general fitness for a humane existence'.[2]

The generic term 'the arts' suggests a comprehensiveness that *Scrutiny* did not often attain. Film was the subject of several short essays in the very early numbers of the journal, but appeared thereafter only as an exhibit in the case against modern 'civilization'. Ballet was discussed briefly on several occasions, as were the new movements in art and design associated with Moholy-Nagy and Gropius. Modern painting and art criticism received a certain amount of attention, mainly in the later thirties, and books on these and related topics continued to claim a small though fairly constant part of *Scrutiny*'s reviewing space.[3] However, D. W. Harding was alone among the inner circle of contributors in writing on any of these

1. 'A Manifesto,' I, 1 (May '32), p. 2.   2. Ibid., p. 5.
3. See, for example, William Hunter, 'The Art-Form of Democracy?' I, 1, pp. 61–5; J. Isaacs, rev. Hunter, *Scrutiny of Cinema*, I, 4 (March '33), pp. 414–16; Erik Mesterton, 'The Criticism of Ballet,' III, 4 (March '35), pp. 424–7; Vladimir Kameneff, 'Post Obitum (Diaghileff, Pavlova),' IV, 4 (March '36), pp. 401–6; J. M.

topics;[4] and with the important exception of Wilfrid Mellers's music criticism, initiated in late 1936, the critical energies of the journal were at all times concentrated in the field of literature.

The pre-eminence of literature was the consequence of its special relation to 'tradition'. In the usage of Eliot's *Sacred Wood*, 'tradition' signified a purely literary order, only contingently implicated in historical time and, despite its conventional Europocentrism, without any strict geographical reference. In Leavis's usage, and that of *Scrutiny* generally, the notion underwent three related modifications. 'Tradition' was henceforth predicated of actually existing national societies, individually or in combination; at the same time, its trans-historical quality came to be understood as the result of identifiable developments that were themselves historical; and therewith, literature came to be seen as a part of 'tradition' which, through a process of historical attrition, had become virtually the whole – not all of 'tradition', but all that survived of it.[5] The relations between the lost world of seventeenth-century England, its 'tradition' and the literature that it had handed down, were succinctly defined in Knights's essay on 'Tradition and Ben Jonson', published in the autumn of 1935. Jonson's work, he wrote, was now 'one of the main channels of communication with an almost vanished tradition. That tradition cannot be apprehended in purely literary terms, but we can learn something of it through literature, just as to feel our way into the technique of Jonson's verse is to share, in some measure, that steady, penetrating scrutiny of men and affairs.'[6]

Harding, 'A Public for Art in Industry,' III, 4 (March '35), pp. 428–32; Storm Jameson, 'The Methods and Theory of the Bauhaus,' VIII, 1 (June '39), pp. 81–8; Richard March, 'The Swallow's Egg,' V, 3 (December '36), pp. 243–56; idem, 'The Apotheosis of Post-Impressionism,' VII, 1 (June '38), pp. 21–33. For fuller lists see the Indices in vol. XX.

4. See (with J. M. Harding), 'Art for the Common Reader,' II, 4 (March '34), pp. 393–9; and (with Erik Mesterton), 'A New Critic of Ballet,' IV, 4 (March '36), pp. 435–8.

5. Eliot's use of the term became broader as his non-literary interests became more pronounced. Leavis may have been influenced by this broader usage, even though he dissented from the positions that it subserved in Eliot's own writings – see Leavis, 'T. S. Eliot: A Reply to the Condescending,' *Cambridge Review*, February 8, 1929. See also Donald Davie, 'Second Thoughts: III. F. R. Leavis's "How to Teach Reading",' *Essays in Criticism* VII, 3 (July '57), pp. 231–41, where a different interpretation of this relationship is given.

6. IV, 2 (September '35), p. 157.

To re-cast the notion of 'tradition' in this way was to invest the problem of 'tradition and the individual talent' with a new historical meaning. The poet, as Leavis argued in *New Bearings*, was 'at the most conscious point of the race in his time'; poetry had the power to 'communicate the actual quality of experience with a subtlety and precision unapproachable by any other means'. But 'if the poetry and the intelligence of the age lose touch with each other', as a result, say, of the prevailing conception of the poetic, then 'poetry will cease to matter much, and the age will be lacking in finer awareness'.[7] Although he did not press them on this occasion, the larger implications of Leavis's argument were clear. The progressive weakening of English poetic language had been set in train by the same historical process that had uprooted 'tradition'; the final exhaustion of the one would signal the death of the other, and, therewith, the extinction of the very memory of human community. A year or so later, introducing his selection from *The Calendar*, Leavis described this historical crux in more general and forthright terms: 'the fact that the other traditional continuities have . . . so completely disintegrated, makes the literary tradition correspondingly more important, since the continuity of consciousness, the conservation of the collective experience, is the more dependent on it: if the literary tradition is allowed to lapse, the gap is complete.'[8]

The main task of a culturally responsible criticism was to recover and enforce the 'standards' on which the development of an authentically 'contemporary sensibility' depended; to combat those who obstructed the promulgation of authoritative 'standards'; to provide, through a rigorous assessment of literary history, an eligible past that could guide poetic practice in a detraditionalized society, and thus to avert that catastrophic 'lapse'. However, the importance of literary criticism was not limited to its role in literary production. It could also claim a definite cultural efficacy on its own account: by virtue of its relationship with literary language and the values incarnated in it, literary criticism possessed a special heuristic capacity that was essential to contemporary intellectual life in general. Where the prevailing modes of discourse on society were content to manipulate abstract 'counters', literary criticism held fast to the concrete and

7. *New Bearings in English Poetry* [1932], London 1963, pp. 19–20.
8. *Towards Standards of Criticism*, p. 8.

particular; where political and economic thought dwelt exclusively on 'means', literary criticism returned constantly to the problem of 'ends'. It was, in Knights's words, 'the keenest instrument we have for the understanding of human values',[9] and hence an indispensable control in the culture as a whole. At that point of control stood 'the critical minority', witness to the moral community of the past and incarnation of the possibility, foreshadowed in the act of literary judgment itself, of a new 'centre of real consensus'.[10]

I

This 'minority' was not socially given. 'The standards that, maintained in a living tradition, constituted a surer taste than any individual as such can pretend to, have gone with the tradition,' Leavis wrote; 'there is now no centre and no authority.'[11] The 'centre' envisaged by *Scrutiny* would have to be fought for, in a campaign against the powerful economic and cultural forces that dispersed and misled its potential membership.

Polemical, occasional and sometimes bitterly *ad hominem* in character, *Scrutiny*'s assessments of the dominant literary culture of the day were yet something more than piecemeal documentation of personal malfeasance. They constituted, rather, a relatively coherent attempt to provide 'sociological' corroboration of a sense of cultural crisis. The first line of analysis, a continuation of Leavis's first Minority pamphlet, was concerned with the intermarriage of 'culture' and 'civilization', and its offspring, the 'middlebrow'. The operations of 'the literary racket', Leavis argued, were yet another symptom of 'the advance of civilization'. Commercial considerations had displaced traditional standards in the conduct of literary life. 'The supply of literature' was now 'an industry subject to the same conditions as

9. ' "The Economic and Social Background",' iv, 2 (September '35), p. 203. Cf. F. R. Leavis, 'The Literary Mind,' i, 1 (May '32), p. 24; and *Towards Standards*, p. 9.

10. F. R. Leavis, 'Restatements for Critics,' i, 4 (March '33), p. 319. The spiritual unity of the old 'traditional' community and twentieth-century 'minority culture' was confidently asserted by Q. D. Leavis: 'Bunyan's religious vocabulary has only to be translated into the more general language of conduct and sensibility for it to become evident that he is on the side of the highbrow' (*Fiction and the Reading Public*, p. 100).

11. 'The Literary Mind,' p. 21. Cf. 'A Manifesto,' p. 5.

the supply of any other commodity'; and at the same time, the pressures of advertising had deflected the critical reviews from their true purpose, forcing even the most promising talents to subordinate the exercise of judgment to the exigencies of making a living.[12] So much had already been argued, in identical terms, in *Mass Civilization and Minority Culture*. What distinguished the polemics that appeared in *Scrutiny* was a shift of emphasis away from the commercial agencies of 'levelling' and 'standardization' towards their academic accomplices. Leavis's essay, 'What's Wrong With Criticism?', based on a pamphlet that T. S. Eliot had commissioned and then rejected, traced the power of 'the Walpole–Priestley *régime*' through a network that included 'the Book Society, Ltd.', the fashionable London intelligentsia, the Royal Society of Literature, the English Association and thus the universities themselves.[13] Time and again *Scrutiny*'s reviewers belaboured the academic supporters of this '*entente*' for their obscurantist stand against 'the moderns' in poetry and criticism. Frank Chapman derided Lord David Cecil's *Early Victorian Novelists* as 'creation *manqué*'. Oliver Elton's *English Muse* was dismissed by Douglas Garman as 'sixteen bob's-worth of culture'. Harding and Knights joined in mockery of the stoutly philistine *London Mercury* and its academic counterpart, Housman's *Name and Nature of Poetry*. And John Sparrow was repeatedly attacked for his *Sense and Poetry*, an exercise in 'comfortable prejudice' designed to meet 'the onslaught of the hated highbrow'.[14] The social motivation of the academic rearguard was laid bare by Q. D. Leavis: beneath the abstracted scholarship and 'spiritual illiteracy' of academic traditionalism lay a solid foundation of class privilege.[15]

The same modes of explanation were utilized in a second, more sustained line of analysis, devoted to 'minority culture' as it actually fared in the keeping of England's 'highbrows'. Although the *Scrutiny* group took the side of these figures against the common enemy, and

12. 'The Literary Racket,' I, 2 (September '32), pp. 167–8.
13. I, 2 (September '32), p. 139f.
14. Garman, 'Sixteen Bob's-Worth of Culture,' II, 1 (June '33), pp. 86–7; Chapman, rev. Cecil, III, 4 (March '35), p. 423; Harding and Knights, 'Flank-Rubbing and Criticism,' II, 2 (September '33), pp. 183–6; Hugh Gordon Porteus, rev. Sparrow, II, 4 (March '34), pp. 419–22. See also H. A. Mason, 'Oxford Letter,' III, 2 (September '34), pp. 113–14.
15. 'The Case of Miss Dorothy Sayers,' VI, 3 (December '37), p. 337.

E

on at least one occasion claimed the adjective for their own project, it appears that in their more considered statements 'highbrow' was used to denote a certain disorientation of intellectual life, conditioned historically by the loss of cultural homogeneity and direction.[16] Without the support of shared and binding values, 'disinterestedness' and commitment were now more often than not reduced to eclecticism and caprice, and authentic 'discrimination' to 'pharisaism' or complacency; the ideal of 'the common pursuit' was scarcely recognizable in the conduct of the self-sustaining coteries who now dominated the intellectual organs of the capital. If the formation of these coteries had been induced by the' advance of civilization', entry to them and success within them were regulated by the prevailing order of social privilege. So many elements in a circuit that linked the Public Schools, Oxford and Cambridge and the salons of fashionable, rentier London, they were sustained by a system of solidarity and censorship based on personal relationships – prone to extremes of partisanship in the service of contemporary vogue but governed always by the reflexive loyalties of class.

Scrutiny's earliest polemics were aimed mainly at the 'middlebrows'; analyses of the coterie phenomenon tended to stress the objective historical tendencies that fostered it; the new 'consensus' envisaged by the Leavis circle was seen not as a monolith but as a space mapped out in exchanges among a plurality of 'centres'; and some prominent members of the rising literary generation were invited to contribute to the journal. But, as it became clear that the metropolitan 'highbrows' were not prepared to rally to the journal, or even engage in debate on terms that it found acceptable, diplomacy gave way to outspoken criticism.[17] The lapses and aberrations of the 'highbrows' soon

16. See F. R. Leavis, ' "This Poetical Renascence",' II, 1 (June '33), pp. 68, 73; idem, 'What's Wrong With Criticism?' I, 2 (September '32), pp. 137–8.

17. Geoffrey Grigson (the editor of *New Verse*) contributed one review, in the first volume; by the end of 1935, Auden had ceased to contribute; L. C. Knights recalls that Stephen Spender was invited to write for *Scrutiny*, but declined. The reception of its 'forlorn stand for standards' evoked this comment from one sympathetic London editor: 'if there is one name in the literary world today the mention of which is likely to cause acrimonious discussion, that name is Leavis. It has become a red rag to all sorts and conditions of bulls. Young, middle-aged, old; "best-sellers" and "serious artists"; budding poets and fading critics – all alike

became the main object of attack. Among the earliest targets was the *Criterion*. Eliot's poetry and early literary criticism were touchstones of contemporary excellence for *Scrutiny*, and remained so throughout its career; and even his later critical and social writings, inspired by a dogmatic Anglo-Catholicism to which the review's inner circle was deeply unsympathetic, were treated with respect.[18] But his editorial practice, mingling narrow and abstract dogma with apparently uncritical patronage of *marxisant* literary intellectuals, displayed a familiar kind of eclecticism that was all the more serious in a writer who had once led the struggle for 'standards'. According to the *Scrutiny* manifesto, the *Criterion* was, with all its defects, 'still the most serious as it is the most intelligent of our journals'. Shortly afterwards, in a note on Lawrence, Leavis spoke distantly of those 'who a good while ago formed the habit of taking the *Criterion* seriously'. Three months later, he finally dismissed the journal, observing that its name was now a 'dismal . . . irony'.[19]

The hospitality extended to the new literary Left by a London journal whose 'official bent' was towards Anglo-Catholicism and Action Française provided *Scrutiny* with a further argument against Marxism. According to Leavis, 'the appeal of the *chic*' was one of the most notable causes of the political divisions now emerging in the literary intelligentsia[20]. Their disagreements were 'inessential', and not only at the level of social and cultural understanding: the conflict of ideologies was carried on within a tacit consensus whose ultimate sanction was the common social provenance of the opposing parties. The intimate connections between literary Marxism and the reigning

---

seem infected with what can only be described as *leavisphobia*' ('Notes at Random,' *Bookman*, LXXXVI, April '34, pp. 1–2).

18. See, for example, Harding, 'Mr Eliot at Harvard,' II, 3 (December '33), pp. 289–92; F. R. Leavis, 'Mr Eliot, Mr Wyndham Lewis and Lawrence,' III, 2 (September '34), pp. 184–91; idem, 'Mr Eliot and Education,' V, 1 (June '36), pp. 84–9.

19. Respectively: I, 1 (May '32), p. 3n; F.R.L., 'Reminiscences of D. H. Lawrence,' I, 2 (September '32), p. 190; idem, ' "Under Which King, Bezonian?",' I, 3 (December '32), p. 214. Eliot's failure in the 'test' of Lawrence was an important cause of Leavis's disenchantment, but not so obviously so then as it appears now. See his comments in the 'Retrospect 1950' included in the second edition of *New Bearings* (London 1963, p. 187); and also 'T. S. Eliot as Critic' (1958), in *'Anna Karenina' and Other Essays*, London 1967, pp. 177–96 – a sweeping assault on Eliot's critical and editorial 'conventionality'.

20. ' "Under Which King, Bezonian?",' pp. 210–11.

social-intellectual elite were constantly emphasized by *Scrutiny*. H. A. Mason characterized Communism at Oxford as a blend of doctrinaire rigidity and Public-School sentimentalism.[21] The *marxisant* literary-critical productions of the period were repeatedly castigated for their aesthetic conventionality – on the evidence of Philip Henderson's *The Novel Today*, Q. D. Leavis concluded, 'the new gang' seemed unlikely to 'differ materially from the old gang'.[22] R. G. Cox was still more explicit: 'if a revolution leaves the Public School Communists in privileged positions (as they seem sure it will) and follows the lines of their writings, it is impossible that the triumphant new culture of the classless society should be anything more than our present intellectual and moral chaos writ large.' The activities of the literary Left were both typical of the 'highbrow' circles in which they moved and indicative of the actual complicity between those circles and the agents of 'civilization': 'if you wear the right colours and know the right people you need observe no higher standards than those of the best-selling thriller and the middle-class novel with a purpose. Mr Day Lewis, it will be remembered, is on the selection committee of the Book Society.'[23] Far from revolutionary, 'Public School Communism' was, in *Scrutiny*'s eyes, doubly implicated in the existing cultural dispensation.

London's most prestigious literary court was Bloomsbury, and for *Scrutiny* it came to epitomize all that was modish, arrogant and sciolistic in the 'minority culture' of inter-war England. Wherever brittle cerebration was paraded as 'intelligence' or glib modernity as genuine adjustment to the contemporary, wherever purely social loyalties were substituted for principled intellectual collaboration or 'currencies' wantonly 'inflated' without regard for the 'standards' that underwrote them, *Scrutiny* discerned and denounced the influence of 'Bloomsbury'.[24] This general condemnation was not applied absolutely to its individual members. Lowes Dickinson, one of Bloomsbury's Cambridge associates, was commissioned to write for the first

21. 'Oxford Letter,' p. 114.
22. 'Class-War Criticism,' v, 4 (March '37), p. 419. See also Frank Chapman, rev. R. D. Charques, *Contemporary Literature and Social Revolution*, II, 4 (March '34), pp. 422–4.
23. 'Left-Wing Allegories,' VII, 1 (June '38), p. 92.
24. See, for example, Q. D. Leavis, 'Lady Novelists and the Lower Orders,' IV, 2 (September '35), pp, 112–32; 'English Novelists and Higher Reviewers,' v, 1 (June '36), pp. 93–9; 'Mr Aldous Huxley,' v, 2 (September '36), pp. 179–83.

issue of the journal, and did so. And if the Leavises wrote critically on
E. M. Forster, it was with an open respect that few of his contemporaries were accorded. However, the 'weaknesses' that qualified Forster's
'real and very fine distinction' were unmistakeably those of 'the very
inferior social-intellectual milieu' that he frequented, of 'the Bloomsbury which (to confine ourselves to one name) produced Lytton
Strachey and took him for a great writer'.[25] This cult was offered as
the most telling evidence of Bloomsbury's delinquency. Reviewing
Characters and Commentaries in December 1933, T. R. Barnes attacked
Strachey's belle-lettrism, and went on to show how he had combined
its traditional devices with the tactics of 'Metro-Goldwyn-Mayer' to
produce a highly saleable line in iconoclasm. Furthermore, Barnes
charged, the deleterious influence of his biographies was not confined
to their 'middlebrow' audience: 'he set a tone which still dominates
certain areas of the highbrow world – *e.g.* that part of Bloomsbury
which has a well-known annex in Cambridge. The deterioration and
collapse represented by Mrs Woolf's latest phase . . . is one of the
most pernicious effects of this environment.'[26] Barnes's verdict on
Virginia Woolf was representative. Reviewers of her later novels
recorded a precipitate decline from the achievement of *To the Lighthouse*.[27] In the same way, Denys Thompson contrasted the subjectivist
recommendations of her *Common Reader: Second Series* with its predecessor's appeal for binding norms of literary judgment.[28] Woolf was
the main focus of *Scrutiny*'s pre-war campaign against Bloomsbury. The
appearance of *Three Guineas* provided the occasion for one of the most
ferocious invectives ever printed in the journal, Q. D. Leavis's 'Caterpillars of the Commonwealth Unite'. Woolf's claim to speak for her
sex was invalidated, Leavis maintained, because of the social assumptions that attended it. What she thought of as 'the educated class'
was no more than the propertied cultural elite to which she herself
belonged; and her book was merely 'a sort of chatty re-statement of

25. 'E. M. Forster,' vii, 2 (September '38), pp. 200–1, 185; compare Q. D. Leavis's
review of *Abinger Harvest*, 'Mr E. M. Forster,' v, 2 (September '36), pp. 100–5; and
see also F. R. Leavis, *D. H. Lawrence*, where *A Passage to India* is placed as a counter-
weight to *Lady Chatterley's Lover*.

26. 'Lytton Strachey,' ii, 3, pp. 301–3.

27. W. H. Mellers, 'Mrs Woolf and Life,' vi, 1 (June '37), pp. 71–5; F. R. Leavis,
'After "To the Lighthouse",' x, 3 (January '42), pp. 295–8. See also M. C. Bradbrook, 'Notes on the Style of Mrs Woolf,' i, 1 (May '32), pp. 33–8.

28. i, 3 (December '32), pp. 288–9.

the rights and wrongs' of its female component. Apparently intended
to meet the educational needs of women in general, her proposals
were actually a recommendation of 'boudoir scholarship', designed
'to penalize specialists in the interests of amateurs' like herself. Her
conception of 'the art of living' was that of 'a social parasite'.
She was in general 'quite insulated by class' – and, Leavis added,
'there is no member of that class on the contributing list of this
review'.[29]

In this way, the *Scrutiny* group quickly came to believe that if the
endoxa of 'mass civilization' was inimical to 'standards', England's
reigning 'minority' was scarcely less so. To ignore or misapprehend,
as they did, the impending breach in 'continuity' was in effect to
hasten it. Anglo-Catholic, Marxist or simply 'civilized', the 'highbrows' were themselves part of the crisis.

Dmitri Mirsky once observed that England's 'highbrows' were quite
distinct as a phenomenon from what other cultures termed 'the
intelligentsia';[30] and in this, if in little else, *Scrutiny* was inclined to
agree with him. Q. D. Leavis's criticisms of the Bloomsbury ethos were
fundamentally concerned with its internal organization and external
relations with the social order, and were explicitly premissed on an
alternative conception of intellectual activity, which *Scrutiny* was
assumed to exemplify. Against the socially privileged amateurism
represented by Virginia Woolf, she argued for the *carrière ouverte aux
talents*, regulated always and only by the criterion of professionalism.
Against Aldous Huxley's 'flair for embodying the *Zeitgeist*', she emphasized the importance of the responsible 'middleman of ideas' in a
healthy culture.[31] And against the aimless literary gatherings typified
by Derek Verschoyle's critical anthology, *The English Novelists*, she
insisted that collective work could only succeed where it was braced

29. VII, 2 (September '38), pp. 203–14. Leavis's own proposals included co-
education from primary level onwards and democratization of access to
higher education; she also suggested research into the social construction of
gender.

30. *The Intelligentsia of Great Britain*, London 1935, pp. 89–90.

31. 'Mr Aldous Huxley.' For other assessments, see Joseph Needham, 'Biology
and Mr Huxley,' I, 1 (May '32), pp. 76–9; and Denys Thompson, rev. *The Olive
Tree*, V, 4 (March '37), pp. 458–9.

by the sort of intellectual unity exemplified in Rickword's *Scrutinies* or F. R. Leavis's collection, *Determinations*.[32]

Where, other than in isolated local ventures, were these codes respected? France was commonly invoked in approving contrast to England during *Scrutiny*'s early years; and Henri Fluchère's reports on French cultural life were a regular feature of its first five volumes.[33] However, these contrasts were seldom elaborated beyond the level of conventional half-truths concerning French intellectuality and 'love of culture'; and at the end of the decade, in the first extended discussion of its kind to appear in the journal, Martin Turnell delivered a mixed verdict on the record of French literary criticism, combining admiration for the prestige that it enjoyed at home and commanded abroad with distrust of its intellectualistic proclivity for 'system'.[34] In this context – though not in others – 'France' functioned less as an independent object of investigation than as a contrastive device intended to expose certain failings in English intellectual life. Comparative analyses of the United States were more searching and sustained. For *Scrutiny*, the USA was both the homeland of modern 'machine civilization' and the advance post of opposition to it. The symbol of its dual distinction was *Middletown*, the Lynds' 'anthropological' critique of industrialization in a Mid-Western town. The exemplar of Q. D. Leavis's 'middleman' was the American publicist, Stuart Chase.[35] Her partner's proposals for university reform took strength from the contemporaneous 'liberal revival' in American educational thought.[36] The novels of John Dos Passos were praised repeatedly for their analyses of the modern social condition in the USA, and adduced in criticism of the inferior productions of his

32. 'English Novelists and Higher Reviewers,' p. 99.

33. See, for example, F. R. Leavis, 'What's Wrong with Criticism?' p. 146; Q. D. Leavis, 'Fleet Street and Pierian Roses,' II, 4 (March '34), pp. 387–92; W. H. Mellers, 'The Composer and Civilization: Notes on the Later Work of Gabriel Fauré,' VI, 4 (March '38), pp. 386–401. Henri Fluchère, 'Surréalisme,' I, 3 (December '32), pp. 219–33; 'The French Novel of Today,' II, 1 (June '33), pp. 51–58; 'French Literary Periodicals,' II, 3 (December '33), pp. 239–46; 'The Novels of Jean Giono,' III, 3 (December '34), pp. 258–67; 'French Intellectuals and the Political Crisis,' V, 3 (December '36), pp. 232–42.

34. 'Literary Criticism in France,' Parts 1 and 2, VIII, 2 (September '39), pp. 167–83, and VIII, 3 (December '39), pp. 281–98.

35. 'A Middleman of Ideas,' I, 1 (May '32), pp. 69–73.

36. 'An American Lead,' I, 3 (December '32), pp. 297–300; 'Why Universities?' III, 2 (September '34), pp. 117–32.

English co-aspirants.[37] Q. D. Leavis sponsored Santayana's writings as a corrective to 'the insular Nordic Protestant limitations' of English culture.[38] And in his reflections on the nature of 'the ideal weekly', H. A. Mason dwelt at length on *The New Republic*, among whose chief virtues he numbered an 'immunity from respect for established English values'.[39] The relative superiority of American over English culture was explored further by Q. D. Leavis in 'The Background of Twentieth Century Letters', and traced to the differential formation of intellectuals in the two countries. While the United States had experienced 'an evolution out of chaos and futility to a general recognition of standards and an agreement as to abiding values', she wrote, English literary criticism remained complacently erratic, guided by nothing more constant than the etiquette of a certain social round. Contrasted with the education and society depicted in Cyril Connolly's *Enemies of Promise*, 'the advantages Americans enjoy in having no Public School system, no ancient universities and no tradition of a closed literary society run on Civil Service lines, can hardly be exaggerated'.[40]

The opposition England/America was seldom so flatly asserted. For F. R. Leavis, America was also the land of Irving Babbitt and 'abstract' Humanism. H. A. Mason warned that *The New Republic*'s 'immunity' did not preclude 'a distressing tendency to take over Bloomsbury values without question'.[41] Q. D. Leavis's second discussion of Santayana was in notable contrast to its predecessor, stressing his disabling anglophilia and associating him with Pater, another 'victim of the feminine charm of Oxford'.[42] And in his first-hand reports on 'The American Cultural Scene', which appeared in *Scrutiny* between March 1939 and June 1940, H. B. Parkes expressed more general misgivings about the United States. The emphasis of Parkes's analyses fell on the cultural consequences of the USA's distinctive history, past and present. Its educational system, admirably 'democratic' but qualitatively

37. F. R. Leavis, 'A Serious Artist,' I, 2 (September '32), pp. 173–9; Q. D. Leavis, 'Mr Dos Passos Ends His Trilogy,' V, 3 (December '36), pp. 294–99; R. G. Cox, 'Left-Wing Allegories.'
38. 'The Critical Writings of George Santayana,' IV, 3 (December '35), p. 288.
39. ' "The New Republic" and the Ideal Weekly,' VII, 3 (December '38), p. 253.
40. VIII, 1 (June '39), pp. 72–7.
41. ' "The New Republic" and the Ideal Weekly,' p. 253.
42. 'The Last Epicurean,' IV, 3 (December '35), pp. 325, 328.

inferior to those of Europe, posed in its most acute form the problem 'inherent' in any democracy: that of the fate of 'cultural standards in a society . . . dominated by egalitarian ideals'.[43] Its novelists, lacking an 'established social structure' and common moral code, were largely disqualified from the 'moral exploration' that preoccupied the best twentieth-century writers, and were impelled towards a 'sociological' fiction that 'necessarily exclude[d] large areas of human experience'.[44] Moreover, the 'critical environment' of American literature had been impoverished by the ideological effects of the country's founding historical experiences. Puritanism, the colonial enterprise and industrialization together had induced a 'hypertrophy of the will' and a 'Northern' mentality that was typically pragmatic, utilitarian and prone to 'disembodied intellectuality and idealism'.[45] Parkes's sympathies were drawn not to the dominant, Eastern intelligentsia, but to the writings of the Fugitives, elegists of the aristocratic, agrarian ante-bellum South.[46] The American contrast, although real, was so far from a genuine alternative that, viewed in close-up, it inspired little other than a transatlantic reprise of *Scrutiny*'s English dispositions.

The cultures of contemporary France and America were not sufficiently different from that of twentieth-century England to furnish *Scrutiny* with a working model of intellectual practice. Thus, although both countries continued to interest the journal, their role as critical contrasts was ultimately secondary to that of the English past. Denys Thompson's 'Prospectus for a Weekly' (December 1933) looked back across decades of journalistic decline to a time when, in De Quincey's words, 'almost all the world had surrendered their opinions and their literary consciences into the keeping of the *Edinburgh Review*'. If 'our present plight' was to be mitigated, he argued, some of that power of normative, centralized judgment would have to be recovered, in an

43. 'The American Cultural Scene: (III) Education,' VIII, 3 (December '39), pp. 257–64.
44. 'The American Cultural Scene: (IV) The Novel,' IX, 1 (June '40), p. 4.
45. 'The American Cultural Scene: (II) Criticism,' VIII, 1 (June '39), pp, 4, 6.
46. See VIII, 1, pp. 9–10; IX, 1, p. 7; 'The American Cultural Scene: (I) Political Thought,' p. 370f.

organ capable of assembling an 'intelligent, educated, morally responsible and politically enlightened public'.[47] In the later thirties, R. G.
Cox set out to define and document the substantive achievement of
'the Great Reviews'. Their essential cultural strength, he suggested,
was derived from the eighteenth century: secure in the common
codes of that time, and confident still of a relatively homogeneous
reading public that honoured them, they wrote with an authority
that marked them out as the 'legitimate successors' of Addison and
Johnson. Cox went on to survey the critical record of the *Edinburgh*,
the *Quarterly* and *Blackwood's Magazine*, citing their consistent though
discriminating anti-Romanticism and early recognition of the novel
in evidence of their quality. These organs 'never doubted', he concluded, 'that literature deserved the serious concern of the adult
intelligence, and that it was their business to maintain standards of
taste which had behind them the consensus of educated opinion.
They consistently refused to pretend that excellence was "common
and abundant", and with their extraordinary influence and authority,
they played the major part in creating for the writers of their age
that informed, intelligent and critical public without which no
literature can survive for very long, and which is so conspicuously
lacking today.'[48]

As the nineteenth century progressed, the robust periodical culture
of its first quarter began to falter; by its close, death was only years
away.[49] But amid the debilitating vapours of Victorian romanticism
and positivism, two figures stood out as representatives of what was
best in 'the higher journalism' and exemplars of the critical probity
that *Scrutiny* sought to emulate in its own practice. The earlier and
more eminent of the two, Matthew Arnold, was discussed by F. R.
Leavis in two essays published in 1938–39. The purpose of 'Arnold as
Critic' was to correct the judgment of Eliot's *Sacred Wood*. Arnold was,
Leavis agreed, a distinguished 'propagandist for criticism': his 'plea for
critical intelligence and critical standards and the statement of the
idea of centrality . . . are made in memorable formulations of classical

47. ıı, 3 (December '33), pp. 247, 250; compare idem, 'A Hundred Years of the
Higher Journalism,' ıv, 1 (June '35), pp. 25–34.
48. 'The Great Reviews,' Parts 1 and 2, vı, 1 (June '37), pp. 2–20, and vı, 2 (September '37), pp. 155–75; see p. 175.
49. 'A Hundred Years of the Higher Journalism,' p. 31; 'The Great Reviews (ı),'
p. 78.

rightness'. But he was also a *critic*, as the 'sensitiveness and sure tact' of his comparative evaluation of the English Romantic poets made plain. Furthermore, his literary-critical gifts were the real source of his moral and cultural insight. His 'best work is that of a literary critic, even when it is not literary criticism: it comes from an intelligence that, even if not trained to some kinds of rigour, had its own discipline; an intelligence that is informed by a mature and delicate sense of the humane values and can manifest itself directly as a fine sensibility.'[50] The signal importance of Arnold's work was that in it the cultural potential and responsibility of literary criticism were acknowledged and made actual. What it represented, for Leavis and for *Scrutiny*, was 'the unspecialized intelligence asserting its rights and duties in a modern industrial civilization and devoting itself with courage to the problem of restoring the unity of culture'.[51]

Arnold's successor in this 'great tradition' was the near-contemporary Leslie Stephen. In a tribute published around the same time as these essays on Arnold, Q. D. Leavis recalled his formative influence on the generation of 'the critical revolution'. 'We were grateful to Leslie Stephen not so much for what he wrote – though that was considerable – as for what he stood for, implied and pointed to. He seemed to us to be in the direct line of the best tradition of our literary criticism, to exemplify the principal virtues of a literary critic, and to exhibit a tone, a discipline and an attitude that were desirable models to form oneself on.' His life too was exemplary. 'Stephen was not academic – it is only one of his virtues, but it is the fundamental one for a critic – he was not conventional, timid or respectable in his findings.'[52] And his decision publicly to announce his loss of religious faith, resign his Fellowship and join the London *Saturday Review*, was a touchstone of moral authenticity. Stephen's role in the *Scrutiny* ideology was crucial: in him, the critical lineage of Johnson and Arnold, the 'higher journalism' and the 'spirit' of Cambridge coalesced to form a luminous image of the 'tradition' that inspired and vindicated the work of the journal.

50. 'Arnold as Critic,' VII, 3 (December '38), pp. 319–20, 321, 326, 323.
51. 'Arnold's Thought,' VIII, 1 (June '39), p. 98.
52. 'Leslie Stephen: Cambridge Critic,' VII, 4 (March '39), pp. 404–8. Annan's *Leslie Stephen* includes a facetious account of the intellectual affiliations between Arnold, Stephen and the *Scrutiny* circle.

II

The specifically aesthetic premises of *Scrutiny*'s critical work appear paradoxical. Leavis agreed with Eliot that 'tradition' was the necessary ground and goal of individual literary effort, but rejected his attendant anti-expressive interpretation of 'impersonality' in favour of one that was closer to I. A. Richards's sense of the term.[53] At the same time, while accrediting literary language with special and irreplaceable heuristic powers, Leavis repudiated Richards's neo-Arnoldian belief that poetry would inherit the plenipotentiary moral functions of religion, and ridiculed his 'romantic' account of poetic practice for its ignorance of the place of 'tradition' in history.[54] In order to account for these logical tensions, it will be necessary to look again at the tacit redefinition to which the terms of Eliot's 'Tradition and the Individual Talent' were subjected by *Scrutiny*.

'Impersonality,' as Eliot understood it, referred firstly to the poet's voluntary submission to the objective demands of 'tradition', and secondly, to certain imputed characteristics of poetic production, in which 'the man who suffers' and 'the mind which creates' were ideally distinct.[55] *Scrutiny*'s conception, in keeping with the altered meaning of 'tradition', was at once social, moral and aesthetic. 'Impersonality' now came to signify a certain moral and psychological poise which had characterized the lost 'community' of the past, and now survived *in potentia* in England's inherited literary language. It was the gift of 'tradition' and, conversely, the hallmark of its presence in contemporary literature. The highest form of 'impersonality' was evinced in that Wordsworthian preoccupation with 'a distinctively human naturalness, with sanity and spiritual health' which Leavis and his

53. How soon and how consciously Leavis rejected Eliot's notion of 'impersonality' is not clear. His 1929 article, 'T. S. Eliot: A Reply to the Condescending', praised it; and nearly thirty years passed before he publicly attacked the essay that had expounded it ('T. S. Eliot as Critic'). It seems, however, that the sense of 'impersonality' current in *Scrutiny* was never Eliot's. According to Richards, 'to say that we are *impersonal* is merely a curious way of saying that our personality is more *completely involved*' (*Principles of Literary Criticism*, London 1967, p. 198). Compare D. W. Harding, 'Aspects of the Poetry of Isaac Rosenberg,' III, 4 (March '35), pp. 358.

54. F. R. Leavis, 'Dr Richards, Bentham and Coleridge,' III, 4 (March '35), pp. 391–3; compare 'Arnold as Critic,' p. 323.

55. *The Sacred Wood*, pp. 52, 54.

circle called 'the religious sense'.[56] In this phrase, oddly enough, the substantive divergence between the two conceptions of 'impersonality' was most evident. For 'the religious sense' was explicitly counterposed by *Scrutiny* to dogma of all kinds and did not necessarily imply belief in the supernatural. What it signified, above all, was allegiance to supra-individual codes of perception and valuation that were common and binding in the way that religion had once been.[57]

The language that bore these qualities into the present was not simply an accumulation of literary usages. It was essentially 'the language of Shakespeare'. Formed in 'a genuinely national culture . . . rooted in the soil,' Shakespeare's mature art was not a model to be imitated but a measure of the capacities of his native language, and thus a standard by which to assay the literary achievements of his posterity.[58] Accordingly, it was to Shakespeare that Leavis normally referred when discussing the formal modes of 'impersonality'. The most important of these modes was identified in his comparative analysis of *All For Love* and *Antony and Cleopatra*. Whereas Dryden's language displayed 'eloquence', he argued, Shakespeare's breathed 'life'. *All For Love* was 'merely descriptive', confined to 'saying and relating' even in its intentionally affective moments; *Antony and Cleopatra*, on the other hand, was typically concrete, 'immediate' and 'sensuous', giving 'an effect of re-creation'. Dryden's was an art of *statement*; Shakespeare's, one of *enactment*.[59] The distinction suggested

56. See especially F. R. Leavis, 'Wordsworth,' III, 3 (December '34), p. 242. Vincent Buckley has correctly emphasized the importance of Wordsworth in Leavis's thought: see 'Leavis and His "Line",' *Melbourne Critical Review* 8 (1965), pp. 110–20, and for a more general discussion of 'impersonality' and 'the religious sense,' idem, *Poetry and Morality*, London 1959, pp. 189, 193–213. See further, Leavis, 'Restatements for Critics,' pp. 316–8; Harding, 'Aspects of the Poetry of Isaac Rosenberg,'; Mellers, 'Bernard Van Dieren (1884–1936): Musical Intelligence and "the New Language",' V, 3 (December '36), p. 265.

57. 'Wordsworth'; idem, 'D. H. Lawrence and Professor Irving Babbitt,' I, 3 (December '33), pp. 273–9; Raymond O'Malley, rev. E. Sharwood Smith, *The Faith of a Schoolmaster*, IV, 1 (June '35), pp. 102–6. The notion of 'the religious sense' can fruitfully be compared with Durkheim's view that religion was the original, and still paradigmatic, form of social solidarity (see Göran Therborn, *Science, Class and Society*, London 1976, pp. 256–70).

58. F. R. Leavis, 'Joyce and "the Revolution of the Word",' II, 2 (September '33), p. 199; *New Bearings*, pp. 73, 137f. Compare Knights, 'Shakespeare and Profit Inflations,' V, 1 (June '36), p. 56f.

59. ' "Antony and Cleopatra" and "All for Love": a Critical Exercise,' V, 2 (September '36), pp. 158–69.

here, between a literary language that merely reported pre-existing or absent meanings and one that produced its meanings, as if plastically, was analysed further in three studies which, in their mutual qualifications, fixed the essential relationship between the individual artist and the moral-aesthetic state of 'impersonality'.

The first of these, a review of Joyce's *Work in Progress*, was concerned to distinguish the 'liberties' taken there with the English language from those of Shakespeare. Unlike the later Joyce, Leavis maintained, Shakespeare was not motivated by interest in his 'medium'; his mature work was ruled 'tyrannically' by 'the command from within'. The 'organization' of *Work in Progress* was 'external and mechanical', whereas in Shakespeare's plays, 'the words are the servants of an inner impulse or principle of order; they are imperiously commanded and controlled from an inner centre.'[60] Despite appearances, Leavis's distinction was not between an art that was expressive and therefore valuable, and one that, failing in expressivity, was of inferior worth. For him and for his fellow-critics, art was *per se* a mode of 'expression': in their own terms, 'sensibility' was the author of 'technique'. As Leavis's contrasting 'revaluations' of Keats and Shelley made clear, literary worth was dependent on the quality of the expressive subject.

Although Leavis gave due consideration to the proto-Aestheticist limitations of Keats's poetry, his main concern was the 'vitality' that had strained against them, pressing 'major' from the themes and occasions of 'minor' art. True, the flight from the 'uncongenial' in the name of Beauty did sometimes result in 'devitalization', but 'so strong a grasping at fullness of life implie[d] a constitution, a being, that could not permanently refuse completeness of living.' Thus, the 'rich local concreteness' of his *Ode to a Nightingale* was to be seen as 'the local manifestation of an inclusive sureness of grasp in the whole'. The 'tactual' effects of the *Ode to Melancholy* – 'one of the most obviously decadent developments of Beauty-addiction' – exemplified 'not merely the voluptuary's itch to be fingering, but [a] strong grasp upon actualities – upon things outside himself . . .'. And the most distinguished passages of the revised *Hyperion* achieved 'the profoundest kind of impersonality'. Here, in a way remarkable for the Romantic period, there was 'no afflatus . . ., no generous emotionality. The

60. 'Joyce and "the Revolution of the Word",' pp. 194, 195.

facts, the objects of contemplation, absorb the poet's attention completely; he has none left for his feelings as such. As a result, his response, his attitude, seems to us to inhere in the facts, and to have itself the authenticity of fact.'[61] If Keats's best poetry exemplified the aesthetic modes of 'impersonality', the great bulk of Shelley's bore the marks of their absence. The 'essential trait' of the latter's poetry was its 'weak grasp upon the actual'. The incoherent imagery of the *Ode to the West Wind*, and the confusion of 'the metaphorical and the actual, the real and the imagined, the inner and the outer' in *Mont Blanc*, were signs of a radical perceptual instability whose source was the devaluation of reason in favour of emotion. Unlike Keats's, Shelley's poetry was the issue of 'inspiration', its emotions generated not by real 'objects of contemplation' but by the estranged, hypertrophied Romantic self. Unsurprisingly, then, the 'Shakespeareanizing' experiment of *The Cenci* failed utterly to emulate the 'sharp concrete particularity' of its model, producing a pastiche of 'wordy emotional generality' in its stead.[62] In Leavis's judgment, Shelley's poetic traits were rooted in a moral condition: in a 'radical lack of self-knowledge' and, at times, in 'radical disabilities and perversions'; the 'easy objectivity' of Keats's *Ode to Autumn*, in contrast, had been won by 'moral and spiritual discipline'.[63] The failure of Shelley's poetry and the successes of Keats's were alike to be read back into the 'sensibilities' whose expressions they were.

None of these studies was expressly designed to elucidate the idea of 'impersonality'. Read in conjunction, however, they reveal its full meaning and, thereby, the logic that bound *Scrutiny*'s literary, social and moral concerns into a cohesive discourse. 'Impersonality' was, in a crucial sense, the cultural trace of 'community'. Its aesthetic modalities were so many tokens of a state of *unity* – within the psyche, among individuals and between society and the non-human world – that had once formed the ethos of a whole social order, founded on settled relations among its individual members and between them and nature. No longer socially given, this state was still morally attainable, through the resources of the language: it was through 'moral and spiritual discipline' that Keats acceded to his 'native English strength'

---

61. 'Keats,' IV, 4 (March '36), pp. 388, 379, 390, 392, 398, 399.
62. 'Shelley,' IV, 2 (September '35), pp. 160, 165, 176.
63. Ibid., p. 167; 'Keats,' p. 399.

– a strength, as Leavis wrote elsewhere, that belonged to 'the very spirit of the language – a spirit that was formed when the English people who formed it was predominantly rural'.[64] In this way, the main logical figure of *Scrutiny*'s social and cultural analysis was repeated within the smaller compass of its aesthetics. In both cases, qualities that had once been instinct in a whole social order, and then, through a process of radical change, been displaced, were to be recovered and sustained in an action whose essence was *moral*.

III

A full account and assessment of *Scrutiny*'s literary-critical production is not feasible in this study. The narrow purpose of this section is to record the distribution of literary-critical attention in the pre-war phase and to identify and illustrate its main themes.

The main general characteristics of this phase were a strong concentration on *poetry* and a relatively high level of attention to *contemporary* literary production. Poetry claimed over three times as many essays as the novel, and, together with drama (the great majority of it from the seventeenth century), more than four fifths of the literary criticism published in the front of the journal. In the reviews section, poetry received almost twice as much discussion as the novel, accounting for nearly two thirds of all reviews of literary works. The distribution of interest between *twentieth-century* poetry and prose fiction was much less unequal, reflecting the relatively close attention paid to contemporary literature in the pre-war years; but here too, the coverage of poetry was more comprehensive.[65] Within this general pattern, there were four major areas of interest: English literature in the sixteenth and seventeenth centuries, with an associated, secondary interest in medieval Scottish and English literature; modern French

64. 'Joyce and "the Revolution of the Word",' p. 200.
65. All these calculations are per *item*, irrespective of length. In the first eight volumes (May '32–March '40) the distribution of articles was: poetry – 58%; the novel – 18%; drama – 2%. Reviews were distributed as follows: poetry – 62%; the novel – 33%; drama – 2%. Poetry and the novel accounted respectively for 28% and 23% of discussion on contemporary literary topics (criticism and literary culture in general claimed 46% and drama 3%) which themselves formed nearly one third of the whole.

poetry and drama; the history of modern English poetry; and contemporary literary production in England and the United States.

The literature of late-sixteenth- and seventeenth-century England was *Scrutiny*'s most constant interest, in this and in the two succeeding phases of its life-time. This was in part a particular instance of a general bias in English literary culture which, emerging in the late nineteenth century, became powerful in the twenties and persisted for some thirty years after the First World War. But its chief stimulus was the special role of the period in *Scrutiny*'s rendering of English history: the leading motif of these studies in the literature of the seventeenth – and preceding – centuries was the social and cultural theme of 'community'. John Speirs's writings on Henryson and Dunbar were wholly shaped by his distinction between the rooted language of medieval Scots poetry and the dissociated idiom of its posterity.[66] Derek Traversi used the occasion of a new translation of *Piers Plowman* to record his sense of a secular impoverishment of language, naming Spenser, Milton and the poetics of the Victorian era as the three main coordinates in the downward curve from Langland's day to the present.[67] Ben Jonson (singled out by Traversi as one of Langland's successors) was reinterpreted by L. C. Knights as a quintessentially English author whose 'classicism' consisted really in 'an equanimity and assurance' drawn from 'the strength of a native tradition'.[68] And in a literary-sociological analysis of *The Revenger's Tragedy*, L. G. Salingar ascribed Tourneur's achievement to the organizing principle of his art, the application to 'the contemporary world' of 'the standards of the medieval social tradition, as it had survived through the sixteenth century'.[69]

Much more than documentary evidence was at stake in these analyses. The social and cultural conditions of Old England had, in

66. See 'Dunbar and "the Scottish Renaissance",' II, 1 (June '33), pp. 79–81; 'Henryson, Chaucer and the Scottish Language,' II, 3 (December '33), pp. 296–8; 'William Dunbar,' VII, 1 (June '38), pp. 56–68.

67. 'Revaluations (x): The Vision of Piers Plowman,' V, 3 (December '36), pp. 276–91.

68. 'Tradition and Ben Jonson,' p. 147.

69. ' "The Revenger's Tragedy" and the Morality Tradition,' VI, 4 (March '38), pp. 420–1.

Scrutiny's view, fostered values of perdurable 'human' significance. However, these values were not directly available. It was necessary to 're-create' them, by means of a literary criticism capable of recognizing and assaying their significance, historical and contemporary. This purpose was manifest in essays such as Speirs's or Traversi's. It appeared more sharply focused in essays whose concern was less with 'sociological' analysis than with forwarding the practice of 'genuine' literary criticism. Knights's rebuke to 'abstract' theoreticians of comedy – notably Bergson and Meredith – drew its authority from 'practical criticisms' of *Volpone*, *Henry IV* and *Henry V*.[70] F. R. Leavis's drastic assessment of Milton was presented in express defiance of opponent critical tendencies, those with 'the kind of intellectual bent that produced Humanism', and the more powerful 'academic mind'.[71] W. A. Edwards's 'revaluation' of Webster (the first in the long series of that name) and James Smith's essay on Chapman were notable early examples of the new critical technique in operation.[72]

Scrutiny's central preoccupation in this chronological area was Shakespeare. Of all the essays and reviews devoted to the late sixteenth and seventeenth centuries in the pre-war phase, more than a third of the former and nearly two thirds of the latter were on this topic. Shakespeare's importance was twofold. As the 'pre-eminently ... English' author, he embodied the full moral potential of the national literary tradition; and as the conventionally recognized apex of English literature, he represented the 'high ground' on which any new literary-critical campaign depended for victory. In *How Many Children Had Lady Macbeth?*, published in 1933 by the Minority Press, L. C. Knights set out to dislodge the reigning orthodoxy in Shakespeare studies, in the name of the new literary criticism. The main object of this polemic was the 'character' criticism associated chiefly with A. C. Bradley's *Shakespearean Tragedy*. 'Character,' he argued, was, like 'all our other critical counters', no more than 'an abstraction from the total response in the mind of the reader or spectator, brought into being by written or spoken words.' A Shakespeare play, properly

70. 'Notes on Comedy,' I, 4 (March '33), pp. 356–67.

71. 'Milton's Verse,' II, 2 (September '33), pp. 123–36; 'In Defence of Milton,' VII, 1 (June '38), pp. 104–14.

72. 'John Webster,' II, 1 (June '33), pp. 12–23; 'George Chapman,' Parts 1 and 2, III, 4 (March '35), pp. 339–50, and IV, 1 (June '35), pp. 45–61.

understood, was 'a *dramatic poem*'.[73] Knights did not claim complete novelty for his views: the early works of G. Wilson Knight, with their conception of the Shakespeare play as an 'expanded metaphor', were among the pioneers of the critical 're-orientation' to which he alluded in the opening sentences of his essay. Nevertheless, he shared his colleagues' misgivings about the ulterior philosophical purposes of *The Wheel of Fire* and *The Imperial Theme* ('a preoccupation with imagery and symbols, unless minutely controlled by a sensitive intelligence directed upon the text, can lead to abstractions almost as dangerous as does a [Bradleian] preoccupation with "character" ') and insisted that, 'read with attention, the plays themselves will tell us how they should be read'.[74] His own critical ideal was an astringent exercise of sensibility: 'we start with so many lines of verse on a printed page which we read as we should read any other poem. We have to elucidate the meaning (using Dr Richards's fourfold definition) and to unravel ambiguities; we have to estimate the kind and quality of the imagery and determine the precise degree of evocation of particular figures; we have to allow full weight to each word, exploring its "tentacular roots", and to determine how it controls and is controlled by the rhythmic movement of the passage in which it occurs. In short, we have to decide exactly why the lines "are so and not otherwise".'[75]

Knights's essay struck the main hallmarks of *Scrutiny*'s Shakespeare criticism. His caveats were sounded again and again in reviews of

73. *How Many Children?* was based on a paper read to the Shakespeare Association. It was reprinted, slightly amended, in Knights's *Explorations*, London 1946, pp. 1–39.

74. *Explorations*, pp. 4, 5. The passage quoted in parenthesis was omitted from the revised version, but was recorded in the Preface to *Explorations*, where Knights acknowledged his 'extensive indebtedness' to the author of *The Wheel of Fire*. Leavis, reviewing the latter's early work, stood aloof from its metaphysical concerns but expressed the hope that its methodological advances might prompt some 'young man' to write 'the first good literary criticism of Shakespeare' ('Criticism of the Year,' *Bookman*, LXXXI, 483, December '31, p. 180). Compare R. O. C. Winkler, 'Mr Wilson Knight,' VIII, 2 (September '39), pp. 232–6. Knight himself insisted on his leading role. '*Scrutiny* can hardly be said to have broken new ground in Shakespeare,' he wrote in the early sixties. It had adopted his 'spatial analysis,' only modifying it to take account of the temporal axis of drama; and compared with his own exploration of the 'superstitious' and the 'cosmic,' its 'moral' and 'psychological' approach was narrow and mundane ('*Scrutiny* and Criticism,' *Essays in Criticism*, XIV, 1, January 1964, pp. 32–6).

75. *Explorations*, p. 16. Richards's 'fourfold definition' of meaning included 'sense, feeling, tone and intention' (*Practical Criticism*, III, 1).

narrowly philological or critically obsolete studies of the plays; and his precepts laid down the basic working discipline of his collaborators' substantive contributions in this area. The variety of occasion and approach displayed in this body of work indicates Shakespeare's central importance in the outlook of the journal. Knights himself attempted to make good the lack of 'genuine criticism' of the *Sonnets*, in a 'revaluation' that traced the 'technical' development of the poems, seeing this as the manifestation of a 'development and unification of sensibility'. The age of Shakespeare formed the concrete ground of a later essay by him, devoted to a critique of Marxist approaches to cultural history.[76] F. R. Leavis's 'Diabolic Intellect and the Noble Hero' sought to recover *Othello* from a century of misguided interpretation, rejecting psycho-biographical speculation about 'characters', insisting on the difference between 'art' and 'life', and re-directing attention to the play as a specific and irreducible organization of words. His comparison of *Antony and Cleopatra* and *All For Love* was a 'critical exercise' addressed polemically to both 'literary fashion' and 'academic' criticism, and designed to elicit the enactive quality that distinguished the Shakespearean from lesser modes of literary 'organization'.[77] Traversi, who from 1937 onwards was *Scrutiny*'s most prolific writer on Shakespeare, stressed the abiding political relevance of *Coriolanus*. The play's analysis of Roman society was 'fundamental', he maintained, 'precisely because it was not merely political, like so many of the fashionable accounts of the contemporary situation by Left-minded writers, but based upon a sensation of fine living . . .'. *Coriolanus* suggested 'how valuable might be a sensitive artist's study of a social situation, what weight a fine experience could add to otherwise ephemeral political discussion'.[78]

Among non-Anglophone cultures, France was *Scrutiny*'s most consistent interest. Its coverage of French culture began early on, and was quite systematically organized in the form of regular reports transmitted by Henri Fluchère, whom Leavis had known in Cam-

76. 'Shakespeare's Sonnets,' III, 2 (September '34), pp. 133–60; 'Shakespeare and Profit Inflations.'

77. VI, 3 (December '37), pp. 259–83; ' "Antony and Cleopatra" and "All for Love".'

78. 'Coriolanus,' VI, 1 (June '37), pp. 43–58.

bridge in the twenties and who was now editor of the *Cahiers du Sud*.[79] Between 1932 and 1936, Fluchère contributed five reports in all, dealing with contemporary currents in the arts, critical culture and politics. The first of these evoked the cataclysmic impact of the War on French intellectual life, and went on to trace the emergence and current range of surrealism, whose exponents he lauded as 'the artisans of a new spiritual progress, . . . fierce and imperious defenders of the dignity of man'.[80] The next was a brief survey of 'the French novel of today'.[81] In his third report, Fluchère described the salutary influence – on writers and public alike – of French literary periodicals, instancing in particular the anti-bourgeois *Europe* and the *Nouvelle Revue Française*.[82] This was followed, a year later, by his 'introduction to Jean Giono for the English reader', in which he sketched a profile of the novelist and the remote Basses-Alpes that formed the ambience of his books, referring – in an uncharacteristic echo of Adrian Bell – to 'the persistence of ancient memories . . . which no amount of science or republicanism will ever destroy'.[83] His last report, published at the close of 1936, dealt with 'French Intellectuals and the Political Crisis', expressing sympathy with the Popular Front and upholding the Left as 'the last refuge of the dignity of man'.[84]

Fluchère's contributions were essentially informational in character: although highly selective, and therefore not uncritical, they were surveys rather than analyses. It was only with the entry of Martin Turnell in September 1936 that *Scrutiny* acquired a critic of French literature akin in his procedures and objectives to its own writers on English literature.[85] Turnell's earliest contributions were devoted to modern poetry. The first of these concerned a poet who, through the sponsorship of Eliot, had become a standard reference in discussions

79. Leavis had already done Fluchère the complementary service: his 'La Poésie anglaise et le monde moderne: étude de la situation actuelle,' appeared in *Cahiers du Sud*, vi (1930), pp. 595–615.
80. 'Surréalisme,' p. 233.
81. ii, 1 (June '33), pp. 51–8.
82. 'French Literary Periodicals.'
83. 'The Novels of Jean Giono,' p. 265.
84. v, 3, pp. 234–42.
85. Douglas Garman's 'Art and the Negative Impulses' (ii, 2, September '33, pp. 189–93), an enthusiastic review of Céline's *Voyage au bout de la nuit*, and William Hunter's 'Céline' (iii, 2, September '34, p. 193), a short notice of the English translation, were the only other contributions on French literature in this period.

of English poetic modernism: Jules Laforgue. Turnell began by analysing the main features of Laforgue's technique, comparing them with those of the Russian cinema, and then proceeded to a detailed comparative discussion of his style and that of Eliot. At the same time, he questioned the coherence of Eliot's personal 'tradition', with its collocation of Laforgue, Corbière and Donne, and disputed the implicit association that underlay it, between seventeenth-century England and late-nineteenth-century France.[86] The significance of this objection emerged more clearly in his subsequent reflection on Mallarmé. The defining characteristic of Mallarmé's poetry, he argued, was estrangement. Its stylistic elegance, far from validating his work socially, was 'used to hide a fundamental rootlessness'. Its deepest obscurities were to be attributed 'either to a genuine failure to communicate experience, or more often to an abuse of the function of language' consisting in 'a progressive dissociation of language and experience'. Mallarmé's 'pure poetry' was in Turnell's view 'a deliberate attempt to create an unnatural cleavage between literature and life' and, as such, 'a symptom of the state of the civilization in which we are living'.[87]

Against Mallarmé's 'elegance', which depended on 'the deliberate exclusion of whole tracts of human experience', Turnell cited that of Racine, which was 'the expression of something real and living in the society of his time'.[88] As he argued on a later occasion, the recurrent items in Racine's vocabulary were not to be mistaken for 'poetic jargon'. Rather, his 'society was such that these words [signified] completely realized and often incomparably presented emotional states'; they exemplified a 'correspondence' between words and things that was 'always the sign of a very high degree of civilization; and it is a remarkable fact,' he continued, 'that as soon as civilization begins to decline language tends to lose its power of translating sensation into precise terms.'[89] The fate of 'civilization' was the core preoccupation of Turnell's studies on 'the classical moment' of

86. 'The Poetry of Jules Laforgue,' v, 2 (September '36), pp. 128–49.

87. 'Mallarmé,' v, 4 (March '37), pp. 425–38. Of Rimbaud, Turnell wrote: '[his] poetry is proof of the supreme difficulty of preserving one's human integrity in a world like our own' ('Rimbaud,' vii, 4, March '39, p. 465; see also 'The Poet of Revolution,' vii, 2, September '38, pp. 223–34). Mallarmé was also discussed by James Smith (vii, 4, March '39, pp. 466–78).   88. 'Mallarmé,' pp. 430–2.

89. 'Racine,' vi, 4 (March '38), pp. 450–7.

French drama, published in *Scrutiny* between 1938 and 1944.[90] His essay on 'the great and good Corneille' dwelt on the politico-moral disorder of late-feudal France. Corneille, he wrote, was 'the champion of youth in revolt against the corruption and pretence of an older generation'. The main figure of his drama was 'initiation' – initiation compelled by the irruption of crisis in the formalized life of the court. His constant 'propaganda for absolute monarchy' was a call for the rule of 'reason', which alone could subdue the worsening 'violence' of the realm. 'The social order which emerges from *Cinna* is therefore concerned with the problems of the ruling class, for it is assumed – not unnaturally – that reconstruction starts from above.' A major trait of this *œuvre* was its 'religious' quality; and 'what is religious in all Corneille's best work,' Turnell judged, 'is not the subject or the setting, but his sense of society as an ordered whole and man as a member of this hierarchy'.[91] In his study of *Athalie*, written in the first months of the war, Turnell returned to these general issues with a sharpened sense of actuality. Racine's work was presented here as a response to the 'disintegration' of the old and essentially 'sane' social order, amidst the rise of 'unbridled individualism'. *Athalie* itself dramatized the conflict between a 'religious order' based on the law of God (and embodied in Port Royal) and a regime of despotism, apostasy and corruption, 'a pagan order based on force and bolstered up by ignoble superstition'. Analysing the language of the play, Turnell showed how Racine's social order, unlike that of Corneille, was arrested at the level of potentiality, and related this failure of realization to his personal discouragement. By this time, 'Racine had come to feel that his great hope – the creation of a truly Christian society on the ruins of the society analysed in the secular plays by a synthesis of all the disparate elements – was not destined to be realized'. Turnell's retrospective judgment affirmed the validity of Racine's premonition: 'the history of the past hundred and fifty years has abundantly justified his pessimism,' he concluded; and 'at a time when we are fighting to preserve the faith and the civilization that produced Racine's poetry, it is a question that Christians might meditate in a spirit of humility and repentance'.[92]

90. *The Classical Moment* was published in 1947 (London).
91. ' "The Great and Good Corneille",' vii, 3 (December '38), pp. 277–301.
92. ' "Athalie" and the Dictators,' viii, 4 (March '40), pp. 363–89.

Turnell's criticism represented a secondary tendency within *Scrutiny*; neither identical nor antagonistic to Leavisian criticism, it was *collateral* with the dominant line of the journal. His emphatic commitment to Christianity, and the marked doctrinal accents of his reflections on French literature and history, were foreign to the majority of the *Scrutiny* circle at this time.[93] Yet there was an unmistakeable kinship between his procedure and perspectives and those of his fellow-contributors. His criticism, like theirs, was conceived as a 'first-hand response' to verbal organizations, and was avowedly contemporary in its valuations; and his reading of French history, its angular metaphysical vocabulary notwithstanding, was evidently analogous to the main *Scrutiny* interpretation of England's historical trajectory. This pattern was to remain stable throughout the period of his association with the journal.

The most important single component of *Scrutiny*'s literary-critical activity in this period was its treatment of pre-twentieth-century modern English poetry. Its first eight volumes included fourteen essays in this field, and a further two on modern Scottish poetry. These essays fell into two categories, distinct in character and separate in time.

Those in the first category appeared in the first and last three years of the pre-war phase, and were diverse in authorship and emphasis; akin in that their range of interest and approach was recognizably that of the new critical generation to which *Scrutiny* belonged, they were distinguished nevertheless by their restricted and sometimes specialist analytic focus. Empson's note on 'Marvell's "Garden"' was an application of the method initiated in *Seven Types of Ambiguity*.[94] W. H. Gardner's contributions on Hopkins studied the Scotist inspiration of the poet's aesthetic, and the relationship between priesthood

93. Some eighteen months before his first contribution, Turnell had expressed his qualified enthusiasm for *Scrutiny*, supporting its cultural stance but underlining its deficient awareness of metaphysical issues (*Colosseum* II, 5, March '35, pp. 52–4). His own view was that, all other things being equal, the committed Catholic was the better critic, by virtue of the incomparable wholeness of vision that faith made possible ('The Function of a Catholic Critic,' *Colosseum* II, 8, December '35, pp. 267–75).

94. I, 3 (December '32), pp. 236–40.

and poetic activity as it figured in his life and work.[95] The main theme
of John Speirs's essays on Burns and on the Scottish ballads of the
eighteenth century was the social preconditions of artistic achievement.[96] A similar emphasis was struck in Geoffrey Walton's discussion
of Cowley, where 'the decline of Metaphysical poetry' was explained
by reference to the social changes of the middle and later seventeenth
century.[97] James Smith's 1933 essay 'On Metaphysical Poetry' set out
fastidiously to elucidate the exact meaning of this literary-historical
tag, arguing that 'verse properly called metaphysical is that to which
the impulse is given by an overwhelming concern with metaphysical
problems; with problems either deriving from or closely resembling,
in the nature of their difficulty, the problem of the Many and the
One'.[98] Philosophical themes were also prominent in his 'preliminary
survey' of Wordsworth, published some five years later.[99]

These essays helped, in various ways, to consolidate *Scrutiny*'s literary-
critical advance, but they did not in themselves form a cumulative
and coherent body of work. This was the distinction of the second
category: the series of essays published between September 1933 and
June 1936 in which F. R. Leavis re-mapped the 'tradition' of modern
English poetry. Few of the main features of this map were his own
discoveries. What was genuinely original was its new 'projection' of
the terrain in which they stood. And this was the result of the deliberate and avowed intentions of the survey that produced it. Leavis's
first full-length work had analysed the 'new bearings' of contemporary English poetry, assessing the legacy of the late Victorian era,
elucidating the nature and circumstances of the work of Eliot and
Pound, and arguing that the innovations of the two men had laid the
groundwork of an authentically contemporary poetic. In *Revaluation*,
the book that these essays of the mid-thirties eventually became, he
set out to provide 'the full perspective' that *New Bearings* had implied,
'to define, and to order in terms of its own implicit organization, a

95. 'A Note on Hopkins and Duns Scotus,' VI, 1 (June '36), pp. 61–70; 'The
Religious Problem in G. M. Hopkins,' VI, 1 (June '37), pp. 32–42.

96. 'Revaluations (III): Burns,' II, 4 (March '34), pp. 334–47; 'The Scottish
Ballads,' IV, 1 (June '35), pp. 35–44.

97. 'Abraham Cowley and the Decline of Metaphysical Poetry,' VI, 2 (September
'37), pp. 176–94.

98. II, 3 (December '33), pp. 222–39.

99. 'Wordsworth: A Preliminary Survey,' VII, 1 (June '38), pp. 33–55.

kind of ideal and impersonal living memory' – in effect, the 'point of view . . . of someone living in the present'.[100]

The 'memory' composed by *Revaluation* – including Jonson, Donne, Carew and Marvell; Pope and Johnson; Wordsworth and Keats – was not of a singular or unbroken lineage. Leavis's analysis moved across the actual lines of poetic descent, making detailed discriminations among and within their individual components, to elicit a canon that did not simply correspond either to a selection of whole *œuvres* or to movements in the history of poetry. The main distinction of this canon was its access to a common, objective world, whether direct – through biographical-historical circumstance – or indirect – through the resources of the tradition itself, and most notably the developed potential of the English language. Donne's 'talking voice' utilized 'the sinew and living nerve of English'; Jonson figured here as a 'native' poet whose relationship with the classics was one of active appropriation.[101] Pope was 'as much the last poet of the seventeenth century as the first of the eighteenth'; his moral intensity was sustained by the stable Augustan ethos, and his 'wit' – 'Metaphysical as well as Augustan' – was directly descended from Marvell's.[102] The revaluation of Wordsworth cut through the 'illusion' of philosophic exposition to concentrate on the 'wisdom' of his best poetry, and on its source, a 'social-moral centrality' whose origins lay 'deep in the eighteenth century'.[103] Leavis's most damaging judgments were occasioned by departures or lapses from this traditional norm. His famous strictures on the 'monotony' of *Paradise Lost*, on 'the routine gesture, the heavy fall, of the verse, . . . the foreseen thud that comes so inevitably, and, at last, irresistibly', evoked a whole battery of argument on the relations between individual, language and tradition: 'the mind that invented Milton's Grand Style had renounced the English language, and with that, inevitably, Milton being an Englishman, a great deal else.'[104] The poetic depression of the mid-eighteenth

100. Necessarily so, for the critic 'endeavours, where the poetry of the past is concerned, to realize to the full the implications of the truism that its life is in the present or nowhere; it is alive in so far as it is alive for us' (*Revaluation* [1936], London 1972, pp. 9–10).

101. 'English Poetry in the Seventeenth Century,' IV, 3 (December '35), pp. 237, 238, 242–3.

102. 'Revaluations (II): The Poetry of Pope,' II, 3 (December '33), pp. 269–84.

103. 'Wordsworth,' pp. 234–57.

104. 'Milton's Verse,' pp. 124, 130.

century, amidst which Gray's *Elegy* and Collins's *Ode to Evening* were exceptional achievements, was attributed to the conditions of a culture which, although still stable and homogeneous, had been attenuated by the social changes attendant on the Civil War and its aftermath.[105] The themes of Wordsworth's late, 'public' poetry were seen as a falsification of experience, appropriately registered in a formal, and formalistic, turn towards the Miltonic.[106] The language of a characteristic poem by Shelley was deplored as that of a mind estranged from the world of common perception.

Leavis conceived *Revaluation* as a 'history': not an empiricist chronicle of things past, but a record of what was 'significant' in the line of English poetry.[107] More precisely, its domain lay in the *trans*-historical realm of 'tradition', in *Scrutiny*'s strongest sense of that term – a locus of values which, although discoverable more or less widely in history, were neither bound to it nor fundamentally alterable by it. The 'morality' of *Revaluation* was, then, reciprocal: the book had been written out of a compelling sense of the present, and it was in the present, if anywhere, that its canon should hold good.

Scrutiny's coverage of contemporary literature was inevitably less systematic than its discussions of the past. It was undertaken, for the greater part, in short reviews; and the contingencies of publishing, the influence of contemporary vogue and the insuperable circumstantiality and allusiveness of reviewing as a form combined to produce a record which, forty years later, can sometimes seem enigmatic and wayward in its emphases. Within these limits, its pattern of interest is fairly clear. Poetry remained predominant (though less so here than in pre-war literary discussion as a whole), both in quantity and in the type of attention that it commanded. While the quantitative representation of the novel increased, nearly equalling that of poetry, discussions of it were with very few exceptions occasional and partial. The greatly reduced representation of drama marked the only

105. 'English Poetry in the Eighteenth Century,' v, 1 (June '36), pp. 13–31.
106. III, 3 (December '34), pp. 255–7.
107. See W. W. Robson, 'Literary Studies,' *Universities Quarterly* x, 2 (February '56) pp. 154–61; Leavis, 'Literary Studies: A Reply,' in the same journal, XI, 1 (November '56), pp. 14–25; and Robson, 'Mr Leavis on Literary Studies,' XI, 2 (February '57), pp. 164–71.

qualitative difference from the general pattern of literary discussion in this phase.[108]

The journal's criticism of the contemporary novel resists summary definition. It was wide-ranging, including writers as diverse in character and origin as Joyce, Hemingway and Sayers, Céline, Lagerkvist and Mulk Raj Anand, Kafka and Amabel Williams-Ellis.[109] At the same time, it was often inconsistent, in its selections and in its distribution of emphasis: Dorothy Richardson was noticed, but not the more sympathetic Storm Jameson;[110] the later productions of Woolf and Joyce were severely criticized, but the preceding works with which they were disobligingly contrasted were never given comparable attention, either individually or in balanced assessments of the two *œuvres* taken as wholes.[111] No straightforward preferences – say, of style or subject – can be discerned: the close and enthusiastic attention with which the progress of John Dos Passos's trilogy was followed by *Scrutiny* stood in contrast equally with its dismissal of other 'experimental' work and with the critical reception accorded to most of the committed Left-wing novels of the time. What was evident, however, was a shared belief in the potential of the novel as a means of social-moral exploration and judgment, and a correspondingly explicit concern with the ideological issues raised by the novels under discussion.

It was this orientation, as much as the prevailing cultural trends of the day, that dictated the amount of space given to 'proletarian' or otherwise 'progressive' fiction in the reviews pages of the journal.

108. Poetry was the subject of just over half of all items on contemporary literary production (51% approximately). The novel accounted for some 43%.

109. Respectively: F. R. Leavis, 'Joyce and "the Revolution of the Word" '; W. H. Mellers, 'Hollywooden Hero,' VIII, 2 (December '39), pp. 335–44; Q. D. Leavis, 'The Case of Miss Dorothy Sayers'; Douglas Garman, 'Art and the Negative Impulses'; Norman Shrapnel, 'Lagerkvist,' V, 2 (September '36), pp. 186–7; Boman Mehta, rev. Anand, *Untouchable*, IV, 1 (June '35), pp. 81–2; R. O. C. Winkler, 'The Significance of Kafka,' VII, 3 (March '39), pp. 354–60.

110. Q. D. Leavis, rev. Richardson, *Clear Horizon*, IV, 3 (December '35), pp. 328–30 (see 'Lady Novelists and the Lower Orders,' pp. 116–17n.).

111. M. C. Bradbrook's 'Notes on the Style of Mrs Woolf' (I, 1, May '32, pp. 33–8) were, as their title and brevity suggest, very limited in scope. *The Years* was reviewed by Mellers ('Mrs Woolf and Life'). F. R. Leavis's review of *Between the Acts* ('After "To the Lighthouse"',' X, 3, January '42, pp. 295–8) was offered as a 'stop-gap'; but the full evaluation for which it did temporary service never appeared.

The considerations that guided these discussions of Left-wing writing were variable. H. A. Mason faulted John Lehmann's *New Writing* on the grounds that its contributors were 'all deficient as *artists*'. The 'integrity which has gone into these campaign documents ... is capable of doing a service,' he conceded, 'but it is a service which is primarily social and political'.[112] R. G. Cox's 'Left-Wing Allegories' took issue with the substance of its subjects' social and political commitments, criticizing Rex Warner's *Wild Goose Chase* for its dependence on 'the values of Public School communism and Bloomsbury enlightenment' and Edward Upward's *Journey to the Border* for the inadequacy of its Marxist eschatology.[113] Class condescension and modish philo-Sovietism were the main counts in Q. D. Leavis's case against Naomi Mitchison and Amabel Williams-Ellis: she contrasted the productions of these 'lady novelists' with Grace Lumpkin's prize-winning proletarian novel, *To Make My Bread*, which, she averred, 'leaves the reader convinced' that the Southern mill-hands depicted there, 'given economic freedom, could live to exemplify the best possibilities of humanity'.[114]

A more sustained critical contrast was furnished by Dos Passos, whose work was eagerly received and sponsored by *Scrutiny* in the mid-thirties – as Q. D. Leavis wrote, reviewing *The Big Money* in 1936: 'America is fortunate in having a novelist whose work makes that of our contemporary Bloomsbury school and its Paris-American affiliation look both frivolous and pinchbeck.'[115] Cox echoed this judgment in his critique of Warner and Upward. And of *Forty-Second Parallel*, F. R. Leavis wrote: '[it] established Mr Dos Passos as an unusually serious artist – serious with the seriousness that expresses itself in the propagandist spirit. Unlike Mrs Woolf, his antithesis, he cannot be interested in individuals without consciously relating them to the society and the civilization that make the individual life possible.'[116] Yet there were deep misgivings. Q. D. Leavis's political verdict on *The Big Money* was ambivalent in formulation and still more so in tone: 'Mr Dos Passos's negative propaganda has this advantage, that all men

112. Rev. *New Writing* 1 and 2, v, 3 (December '36), pp. 315–16.
113. vii, 1 (June '38), pp. 89–92.
114. 'Lady Novelists and the Lower Orders,' p. 116. Lumpkin's novel won the Gorky Prize for Proletarian Literature for 1933.
115. 'Mr Dos Passos Ends His Trilogy,' p. 299.
116. 'A Serious Artist,' p. 174.

of goodwill must agree with him, and they can respect his earnestness accordingly, as they frequently cannot respect the earnestness of the righteously positive souls. Nor does it incite to the asking of awkward questions, for instance whether such a character and talent as Veblen's would be any better off under Communism than Capitalism – the reader does not have to reflect that the life of a man who suffers from a constitutional inability to say yes would be no less tragic under Communism and probably a lot shorter too.'[117] Her partner's most fundamental objection to the trilogy was not to its 'propagandist spirit' but to the main theme of the propaganda itself: the hope of revolution. 'What has disintegrated – this is the point – is not merely "bourgeois" or "capitalist" civilization; it is the organic community.'[118] Thus, in so far as these commentaries on the Left-wing novel of the thirties, with their judicious distinctions and contrasts, seemed open to the possibility of an 'ideal' instance of the genre, they were misleading. Hostility to the established economic and political order and concern for the social condition of the working class reduced but could not abolish the distance between the basic assumptions and perspectives of the proletarian novel and those of the Leavis circle.[119]

Scrutiny's distance from the proletarian novel as a form was, then, fundamentally ideological. In the few affirmative judgments passed on contemporary novels in this period, the primacy of ideological concerns was equally explicit. The only practising English novelist to be discussed favourably and at length in the thirties was L. H. Myers. In a full-length essay published in June 1934, D. W. Harding paid tribute to Myers's 'intuition of the undying conflict that exists between sensitive and cultured individuals and the world of commercial values and social competitiveness', and compared him with Henry James. His novels, Harding argued, were communications with a value distinct from the aesthetic, such was their 'clear and sensitive

117. 'Mr Dos Passos . . .,' p. 299.
118. 'A Serious Artist,' p. 177.
119. Q. D. Leavis's comment on Ruth Adam's *I'm Not Complaining* illustrates the nature of *Scrutiny*'s Left-wing sympathies very exactly: 'her enlightenment is apparently unattached to politics of any shade, her social criticism is not from a *parti pris*,' and was 'likely to awaken a social conscience in people who would remain unmoved by all the recommendations of the Left Book Club' ('"Femina Vie-Heureuse" Please Note,' VII, 1, June '38, pp. 84–5).

insight into the conditions of adult and self-responsible lives in a civilized society'.[120] Over the next six years, Myers's work was discussed as it came out. Reviewing *The Root and the Flower*, Harding praised him for his contribution to the formation of 'an adequate psychology'. Geoffrey Walton's regard for *Strange Glory* was captured in the Arnoldian tag that headed his review – 'criticism of life'. *The Pool of Vishnu*, Myers's 'statement of positives', was reviewed – again by Harding – in 1940: although critical of its bias towards the manner of the *roman à thèse*, Harding praised the novel for the 'development of thought and feeling' attained in its central theme, friendship's critique of a money-dominated society.[121]

Myers figured as a major point of comparison in the only comprehensive assessment of a contemporary English novelist to appear in the journal before the war – F. R. Leavis's essay on Forster. Designed to clarify 'the oddly limited and uncertain quality of [Forster's] distinction – his real and very fine distinction' – Leavis's essay was itself precariously balanced.[122] Much of it was devoted to a pertinacious examination of the flaws in 'the work of a significantly original talent' which, as he stressed, he held in high regard and took to be securely established in general recognition. Although suggestive in one aspect of 'no one less than Jane Austen', and, in his 'radical dissatisfaction with civilization – with the finest civilization of personal intercourse that he knows' – of Lawrence, Forster appeared to lack the 'maturity' that his ambitions required. Hence, Leavis argued, the radical 'inequality' of the four pre-war novels. *Where Angels Fear To Tread* was, in his view, 'decidedly a success', and *Room With a View*, although 'essentially trivial', was 'far from being a failure'. But in *The Longest Journey* and *Howard's End*, where the 'sure easy poise' of the less ambitious works was disarrayed by the pressure of deeper moral and social interests, Forster revealed a proneness to 'disabling immaturities' in valuation, to 'crudity' and sentimentality. *A Passage to India*, published after fourteen years' silence, was free of 'these staggering discrepancies'; it was, Leavis agreed, 'a classic: not only a most significant document of our age, but a truly memorable work of

120. The 'Work of L. H. Myers,' III, 1 (June '34), pp. 44–63.

121. 'L. H. Myers,' IV, 1 (June '35), pp. 79–81; 'Criticism of Life,' V, 1 (June '36), pp. 108–9; 'A Statement of Positives,' IX, 2 (September '40), pp. 161–5.

122. 'E. M. Forster,' p. 185.

literature'. Yet even in this work there was evidence of 'uncertainty' and 'a curious lack of grasp' that stylistic accomplishment could transfigure but not conceal, and which pointed to an abiding deficiency in its author. It was at this point that Myers entered the argument. Leavis was insistent that Forster's limitations as a writer were largely personal in origin, and to a significant extent attributable to the 'inferior' Bloomsbury milieu with which he had associated himself. The more penetrating social and moral exploration undertaken in *The Root and the Flower* was proof that they were not endemic in the liberal cultural tradition. By the same token, they did not disqualify Forster as a participant in it. Speaking now of both novelists without distinction, Leavis declared: 'they represent, the spokesmen of the finer consciousness of our time, the humane tradition as it emerges from a period of "bourgeois" security, divorced from dogma and left by social change, the breakdown of traditional forms and the loss of sanctions embarrassingly "in the air"; no longer serenely confident or self-sufficient, but conscious of being not less than before the custodian of something essential. It is, in these representatives, far from the complacency of "freedom of thought", but they stand, nevertheless, for the free play of critical intelligence as a *sine qua non* of any hope for a human future. And it seems to me plain that this tradition really is, for all its weakness, the indispensable transmitter of something that humanity cannot afford to lose.'[123]

Scrutiny's coverage of the contemporary novel formed a loose and incomplete mosaic, clear and polished in places, its separate tesserae always sharp, but uncertain in overall design. Its coverage of contemporary poetry was much more coherent. For in *New Bearings*, with its analysis of the 'new start' that was now open to English poetry, Leavis had already provided *Scrutiny* with the essential means to a sustained and coordinated critical effort: an analysis of the present conjuncture and an interventionist critical strategy designed to unlock its cultural potential.[124]

Leavis's perspective on the decade then opening had been relatively sanguine, albeit qualified by a grave sense that the prospects

123. Ibid., pp. 186, 200–202.
124. *New Bearings*, ch. 6.

of the 'new start' were not assured. The critical record of the journal over the next eight years showed a growing inclination towards discouragement and exasperation. The general analysis of *New Bearings* was upheld, as were its particular judgments on the existing corpus of modern English poetry; but as the decade wore on, the measure of hope that Leavis had drawn from them was gradually drained away.

Eliot's poetry, largely unprejudiced by the doctrinal turn which so disquieted *Scrutiny* in his critical prose, remained pre-eminent; but its future seemed uncertain. Writing in praise of *Ash Wednesday*, Harding declared: 'this may be called religious submission, but essentially it is the submission of maturity.' Harding was critical of *The Rock* for its 'false' counterposition of social disorder and the Church, but the main stress of his review fell on the originality of the poem: it had achieved 'a tone that is new to contemporary verse', he argued, and in its novelties of technique, interest and stance, formed 'a transition to a stage of Mr Eliot's work which has not yet fully defined itself'. It was Eliot's most recent poem that drew his highest praise: *Burnt Norton* was in his view remarkable for its 'linguistic achievement, in this case an achievement in the creation of concepts'.[125] The dramas which formed the bulk of Eliot's verse production in the later thirties were more controversial. *Murder in the Cathedral* was welcomed by T. R. Barnes as the successor of *Ash Wednesday*, even if, as he judged, its art was 'not concealed' and 'often a little cold and academic'.[126] But *The Family Reunion* provoked Martin Turnell into a frontal attack, not only on the play itself but on the course that its author now seemed to him to be taking. It was 'with the solitary exception of *The Rock*, . . . the worst poem of any pretensions' that he had yet written. Effectively overturning Harding's earlier estimate of Eliot's future development, Turnell concluded that 'there seems no reason to hope that we shall ever get anything but abstractions after this'.[127]

Scrutiny's reception of Pound confirmed the judgments and prognosis of 1932. He remained, for Leavis and his circle, 'the author of *Hugh Selwyn Mauberley*'. The only unequivocally laudatory discussion of

125. 'The Rock,' III, 2 (September '34), pp. 180–3; 'T. S. Eliot 1925–35,' V, 2 (September '36), pp. 171–6.
126. 'Poets and the Drama,' IV, 2 (September '35), p. 191.
127. 'Mr Eliot's New Play,' VIII, 1 (June '39), pp. 108, 114.

F

his work was John Speirs's review of the reissue of *Homage to Sextus Propertius*, a hitherto inaccessible composition from the same period as *Mauberley*.[128] Ronald Bottrall's critical account of Pound's aesthetic was exceptional in its sympathetic attention to the later work.[129] The normal reaction of reviewers was to disparage the *Cantos* as a grandiose diversion, ingenious, pedantic and pointless.[130] Reviews of Yeats's poetry traced a decline from the outstanding late achievement of *The Tower*. Leavis's discussion of *The Winding Stair* dwelt on the loss of the 'proud sardonic tension' of the earlier volume – a loss disclosed in the 'sterile bitterness' of 'Byzantium' and the 'relaxed grasp' of the Crazy Jane poems.[131] On the appearance of the *Last Poems and Plays*, shortly after Yeats's death, Leavis returned to this theme, developing it finally towards a summative judgment: 'the major quality and the element of greatness cannot be denied. But the sense of a heavy price paid and of power wasted and of results incommensurate with effort becomes stronger as we are able to look back and take stock. His pride and beauty, limited and qualified positives as they must in any case appear to us, are not there in any substantial creation. What he has to give us is an attitude, defined in a manner and an idiom.'[132]

The poetry of Isaac Rosenberg was the occasion of the only major amplification of *New Bearings* to be undertaken in *Scrutiny* during this period. In his chapter on 'the situation at the end of the War', Leavis had paid passing tribute to Rosenberg, describing him (along with Owen) as 'remarkable'. By 1937, a fuller appreciation was possible. In March 1935, the journal had carried a selection of previously unpublished poems by Rosenberg, with an accompanying essay by Harding, who was at this time engaged in editing the *Complete Works*.[133] Reviewing the volume on its appearance, some two years later, Leavis hailed it as 'a rare document of invincible human strength, courage and fineness'. Rosenberg's 'interest in life', he affirmed, was 'radical and

128. 'Mr Pound's Propertius,' III, 4 (March '35), pp. 409–18.
129. 'xxx Cantos of Ezra Pound (An Incursion into Poetics),' II, 2 (September '33), pp. 112–22.
130. See Speirs, 'Recent Verse,' IV, 2 (September '35), p. 199; and H. L. Bradbrook, 'Tuesday's Hash,' VI, 2 (September '37), pp. 226–7.
131. 'The Latest Yeats,' II, 3 (December '33), pp. 293–5.
132. 'The Great Yeats and the Latest,' VIII, 4 (March '40), pp. 437–40.
133. III, 4, pp. 351–7, and 'Aspects of the Poetry of Isaac Rosenberg,' pp. 358–69.

religious in the same sense as D. H. Lawrence's' and, moreover, was braced by 'an extraordinarily mature kind of detachment' that made him the better artist of the two.[134]

Eliot's poetic progress seemed, for all the transcendent distinction of its best moments, uncertain. Pound was apparently fixed in the perverse trajectory of the *Cantos*. Yeats's poetry voiced an increasing bleakness and exacerbation of spirit, as death approached. Rosenberg's canonization was by no means an insignificant event, but the honour was posthumous. It was evident that responsibility for the 'new start' had passed to the new, 'post-Eliot' generation.

The appearance of Michael Roberts's anthologies, *New Signatures* (1932) and *New Country* (1933), and the launching of Geoffrey Grigson's *New Verse* (1933), marked the self-conscious, collective entry of the new generation into English poetry. Reviewing these ventures together with individual volumes by Stephen Spender, Cecil Day Lewis and others in June 1933, Leavis gave his estimate of the situation and prospects of what Roberts had heralded as 'this poetical renascence'.[135] At the centre of his reflections lay the problem of *audience*: its indispensability in the development of poetry, its actual absence, and the difficulty of reviving it. 'To assemble the nucleus of an actively and intelligently responsive public,' he wrote, 'and to form in commerce with it the common critical sensibility that every individual critic assumes, and has to assume if he is to be a critic at all, is a desperately difficult business.' He acknowledged the 'notable determination' exhibited in *New Signatures*, but felt compelled to question its results. The poets assembled under Roberts's editorship did not form a genuine community; the project was wanting in the essential impulse of any 'renascence' – 'moral seriousness'; and in the more gifted contributors, there was a 'lack of that sureness of self-realization, that awareness of essential purpose, which registers itself in technique ...'. The predicament disclosed in the anthology was, in Leavis's view, 'just what one would expect in the absence of an intelligent public'. Without such an audience, the poet was exposed to two complementary perils. The first was the 'uncritical acclamation' of reviewers and publicists, which had been the 'misfortune' of Auden

134. 'The Recognition of Isaac Rosenberg,' vi, 2 (September '37), pp. 229–34.
135. ' "This Poetical Renascence".'

in particular and already seemed likely to impair the promise of his early *Poems*, and which, heaped upon the less resilient Spender, was simply disabling. The second peril was that of 'the Group'. While accepting that the absence of 'an intelligent public' made some such form of solidarity indispensable, Leavis warned that 'the very circumstances that make the Group essential enhance its disadvantages and dangers . . .'. Esotery and major misjudgments were its likely effects. Day Lewis's *Magnetic Mountain* exemplified these effects, he suggested, reflecting 'in [its] uncertainty of purpose and level a confusion, very natural where the Group counts for so much and is the only certain audience, of the public occasion and context with the familiar'. There was a careful avoidance of finality in even the most adverse of these literary judgments; and although he paused to mention the 'psychological interest' of Public School Communism, Leavis refrained from pressing his criticisms of the cultural tendency that it represented. His express purpose was to intervene constructively in the course of the new poetry. 'That a group of young writers, uniting a passionate and responsible concern about the state of contemporary civilization with a devotion to poetry, should have won some kind of public recognition is something. It would be a pity if a serious propagandist spirit should let itself get confused with a kind of higher boy-scouting, or the new poetic movement degenerate into a new Georgianism . . .'.[136]

One earnest of *Scrutiny*'s intentions in this field was its decision to publish new poetry in its own pages. Volume One included two contributions from Ronald Bottrall – one of them a section from *Festivals of Fire* – and two poems each by C. H. Peacock and Selden Rodman.[137] Bottrall and Peacock appeared again in the second volume, as did E. M. Wilson's verse translation of Góngora's *De la Brevedad Engañosa Dela Vida*, together with the original text.[138] The third year of publication brought the selection from Rosenberg and 'The Return of Odysseus' by Richard Eberhart – who, like Empson, had come to

136. Ibid., p. 76.

137. Respectively, 'On a Grave of the Drowned,' 1 (May '32), p. 39; 'Festivals of Fire, I,' 3 (December '32), pp. 215–8; 'Release,' 1, p. 60, and 'Excursion,' 2 (September '32), pp. 164–5; 'Car: a Poem' and 'This is a Woman: a Poem,' 3 (December '32), pp. 234–5.

138. Respectively, 'Festivals of Fire, II,' 1 (June '33), pp. 24–7; 'To Maecenas,' 2 (September '33), pp. 163–4; Góngora, 3 (December '33), p. 267.

Leavis's notice through his contribution to *Cambridge Poetry 1929*.[139]
Volume Four contained only one poem (Bottrall's 'Preamble to a
Great Adventure'), the fifth volume, none; and the last poem to be
published before the war, again by Bottrall, appeared in the issue for
December 1937.[140] The list was scarcely notable for bulk or range; and
it could not be said, either by contemporary canons or in retrospect,
to be at all 'representative'. Yet, in its exclusiveness and brevity (only
two more poems, both by Bottrall, were ever to appear after 1937), it
was appropriate. For by the later thirties, *Scrutiny*'s hopes for the new
generation were near collapse.

Pessimism and exasperation became pervasive in its reviews, as disappointment followed disappointment. H. L. Bradbrook's conclusion,
arrived at in 1937 on the occasion of new works by Pound, MacNeice,
Madge and Warner, was essentially at one with the emerging judgment of *Scrutiny* as a whole: 'today we confront a depressing situation
in which the elder poets seem to have spent themselves and the
younger ones can achieve nothing.'[141] Leavis's observations on 'Public
School Communism' and 'the Group' were quickly sharpened into
weapons of attack. 'The Old Boy may have gone Left,' wrote John
Speirs of Day Lewis's *Time to Die*, 'but he remains true at heart to the
Old School.'[142] The course of Spender's work over the decade was
taken to corroborate Leavis's early warning of the perils of 'uncritical
acclamation': a sequence of harsh reviews culminated, in late 1938,
in H. A. Mason's judgment that 'his career . . . has in short been one
of literary frustration and dissipation'.[143]

The outstanding, and most lamentable, case of the 'Group' syn-
drome, as *Scrutiny* perceived it, was Auden. The crux of *Look, Stranger!*,
Leavis argued, was that of a poet whose indubitable technical prowess
was exercised without anything of 'that with which a poet controls
words, commands expression, writes poems'. His 'embarrassing uncertainty of tone and poise', his celebrated 'irony' – 'self-defensive,
self-indulgent or merely irresponsible' – his excessive dependence on

139. 1 (June '34), p. 64.
140. 1 (June '35), pp. 2–3; 'Revengers Against Time,' VI, 3, p. 303.
141. 'Tuesday's Hash,' p. 226.
142. 'Recent Verse,' p. 198.
143. See Mason, 'Poetry 1934,' III, 4 (March '35), pp. 402–9; E. S. Huelin, V, 1
(June '36), pp. 118–19; and for this judgment, 'Mr Spender's Play,' VII, 2 (September
'38), pp. 219–22.

personal memories and neuroses, his facile elisions of the public and the private: these were all symptomatic of a fundamental and persistent 'immaturity'. Turning to *The Ascent of F.6.*, Leavis traced this 'immaturity' to 'the habits of the group world' in which the poet moved, and, beyond that, to its matrix in the ethos of the Public School. The values instinct in the play, extended into adult literary life, ensured its acceptability, to its authors and to a certain tangible audience. The 'kind of badness' that *F.6.* exemplified, 'when a writer of Mr Auden's gifts is led into it, implies not only a complete absence of exposure to criticism, but also a confident awareness of an encouraging audience. In other words, the present is the time when the young talent needs as never before the support of the group, and when the group can, as never before, escape all contact with serious critical standards.' Leavis's belief in the efficacy of critical intervention appeared to be weakening at this point: 'in such a time,' he concluded, 'it often seems a hopeless undertaking to promote by criticism the needed critical stir.'[144] Auden's development over the next four years confirmed his pessimism. 'He has made a technique out of irresponsibility,' Leavis wrote in 1940, 'and his most serious work exhibits a shameless opportunism in the passage from phrase to phrase and from item to item – the use of a kind of bluff. That poised knowledge-ableness, that impressive command of the modern scene, points to the conditions in which his talent has lost itself. We must still feel that he ought to have been a poet, but the possibility of development looks very frail.' All that could be allowed in favour of *Another Time* were its 'one or two' exceptional poems, and an invidious concession: 'perhaps, however, he is more unequivocally conscious of his immaturity than before.'[145]

Further reason for discouragement was given by the poets in whom Leavis had placed his main hopes. He had observed, in his review of *New Signatures* and *New Country*, that Eberhart was not noticeably progressing, and that Empson's poetry seemed 'less and less likely to develop' beyond gratuitous intellectualism.[146] The appearance of their first collections added substance to his fears. He saw in Eberhart's *Reading the Spirit* a decline from the early work, while H. A.

144. 'Mr Auden's Talent,' v, 3 (December '36), pp. 323–7.
145. ix, 2 (September '40), p. 200.
146. ' "This Poetical Renascence" '.

Mason greeted Empson's *Poems* with mixed feelings, echoing his colleague's praise for the earliest (pre-1929) pieces but complaining of the indulgence in 'subtlety for its own sake' that had become general in the succeeding work.[147] Ronald Bottrall stood higher, for longer and more securely in *Scrutiny*'s regard than any of his coevals, but not even his reputation was proof against erosion. Harding queried Leavis's opinion of his work as early as May 1932.[148] And Leavis himself, although he continued to sponsor the author of *The Loosening* – on one occasion alleging the currency of a 'general taboo on Bottrall' – was before long obliged to conclude that, like his contemporaries, he was proving 'very disappointing in development'. Intellectualistic contrivance ('a too imperious determination from above') coupled with an abstract interest in technique was the main negative tendency of Bottrall's verse, in Leavis's view;[149] it also formed the main grounds of R. O. C. Winkler's criticism of *The Turning Path*, on the eve of the war. Winkler did not demote Bottrall to a lower rank among contemporary poets, but even his commendations were reserved in manner, suggesting not only his own distance from *The Turning Path* but also Bottrall's decline from his own highest achievements.[150]

IV

Scrutiny's discourse on literature was defined by negation.[151] When Leavis and his colleagues discussed the question of 'criticism' as such, it was usually to deprecate its miscarriages in the practice or theory of others. The most common symptom of these miscarriages was 'abstraction'; their cause was the illegitimate intrusion of positivist or speculative concerns into literary studies, to the detriment of authentically 'critical' judgment.

Scrutiny's earliest and most protracted campaign was against the

147. v, 3 (December '36), pp. 333–4; 'William Empson's Verse,' iv, 3 (December '35), pp. 302–4.
148. i, 1, p. 90.
149. 'Auden, Bottrall and Others,' iii, 1 (June '34), pp. 80–83; and rev. *The Faber Books of Modern Verse*, v, 1 (June '36), p. 117.
150. 'Ronald Bottrall,' viii, 2 (September '39), pp. 215–18.
151. Martin Greenberg, 'The Influence of Mr Leavis,' *Partisan Review* xvi, 8 (August '49), p. 856.

positivism of traditional literary scholarship. The 'value-free' assumptions of conventional academic research were repeatedly challenged by the journal's reviewers, and its conclusions dismissed as inadequate, conformist or simply worthless. Caroline Spurgeon's quantitative analyses of Shakespeare's imagery were met with suspicion by R. G. Cox, who insisted that there could be 'no substitute for literary criticism'.[152] One 'fatally academic' study of Pope prompted Geoffrey Walton to reiterate 'the *Scrutiny* commonplace that academic ideas of technique go along with a preference for the Romantic in poetry'.[153] L. C. Knights faulted the scholarly contributions to Herbert Grierson's memorial volume for their lack of 'that sharp sense of relative values which should guide even the most laborious work with the pick and shovel', and, in another review of seventeenth-century scholarship, dismissed as mere 'lumber' any literary inquiry that ignored the exigencies of 'the present time'.[154] The criterion implied here was obviously not to be met simply by seasoning scholarship with 'judgment'. Thus, although sympathetic to the efforts of his fellow-contributor Muriel Bradbrook to combine scholarly with critical methods, Knights feared that her *Themes and Conventions of Elizabethan Tragedy* would serve to comfort opponents of the new discipline.[155] Derek Traversi, meanwhile, poured scorn on E. M. W. Tillyard's attempts to refurbish his scholarship with 'a type of criticism he [did] not understand': 'one might deduce from this book alone that Dr Tillyard is connected with Cambridge, where he has evidently been assiduously keeping to touch with the latest developments.'[156] Of the many academic specialists criticized on these grounds by *Scrutiny*, only F. W. Bateson defended his work in its pages. Replying to F. R. Leavis's critique of his *English Poetry and the English Language*, Bateson insisted that literary history and literary criticism were constitutionally distinct activities. Literary history set out to construct a causal order; its paradigm was 'A derives from B' and its statements were amenable to verification. The purpose of literary criticism, in con-

152. 'Statistical Criticism,' IV, 3 (December '35), pp. 309–11.
153. 'The End and the Means,' VI, 4 (March '38), pp. 433–4.
154. 'The Academic Mind on the Seventeenth Century,' VII, 1 (June '38), p. 99.
155. 'Elizabethan Drama and the Critic,' IV, 1 (June '35), pp. 90–95.
156. 'Shakespeare's Last Plays,' VI, 4 (March '38), p. 449; see also Harding, rev. Tillyard, *Poetry Direct and Oblique*, III, 1 (June '34), pp. 89–90; and F. R. Leavis, 'In Defence of Milton.'

trast, was evaluation; its paradigm was 'A is better than B' or 'A is good', and its statements, expressions of 'opinion' rather than determinations of 'fact', were not similarly verifiable.[157] It was evidently incorrect, within the terms of this schema, to judge either discipline in the name of the other. What was desirable, Bateson concluded, was to strive towards a more critical scholarship and a more scholarly criticism. Leavis's rejoinder yielded nothing of his original position. Literary history could not legitimately ignore the priorities implied by contemporary needs, he argued; no work qualified for attention simply because it was extant, or had once been widely read. All significant literary history was laden with value-judgments. The student of literature was obliged 'to justify his treating as a fact of the public world something that [could not] be tripped over, passed from hand to hand, brought into a laboratory, or, in any literal sense, pointed to . . .'.[158] For Leavis, the only relevant past was the *significant* past, the 'tradition' composed by a literary criticism whose values were grounded in the needs of the present.

Scrutiny was equally averse to any form of literary criticism whose norms of analysis and evaluation were derived from 'external', general systems. Psychoanalytic criticism was seldom mentioned, and then dismissively.[159] G. Wilson Knight's theological preoccupations were deplored as trammels that confined and disabled a potentially 'fine critic'.[160] And Marxist criticism, which drew its explanatory and evaluative concepts from a general theory of society, became a by-word in *Scrutiny* for its 'shamelessly uncritical use of vague abstractions and verbal counters'.[161] It was in these terms that Leavis rejected Jack Lindsay's *John Bunyan: Maker of Myths*: 'like most Marxist writers who undertake to explain art and culture, he produces the effect of having emptied life of content and everything of meaning.'[162] H. A. Mason

157. 'Correspondence,' iv, 2 (September '35), pp. 181–5; see Leavis, 'Criticism and Literary History,' iv, 1 (June '35), pp. 96–100.

158. iv, 2 (September '35), pp. 185–7.

159. See Richard March, 'Psychology and Criticism,' v, 1 (June '36), pp. 32–43; F. R. Leavis, 'This Age in Literary Criticism,' *Bookman* lxxxiii, 493 (October '32), pp. 8–9; and, for a solitary contrast, Harding's remarks on March (v, 1, pp. 44–7).

160. F. R. Leavis, rev. G. Wilson Knight, *The Christian Renaissance*, ii, 2 (September '33), pp. 208–11; T. R. Barnes, rev. *The Principles of Shakespearean Production*, v, 3 (December '36), pp. 328–9; Winkler, 'Mr Wilson Knight.'

161. ' "Under Which King, Bezonian?",' p. 212.

162. 'Bunyan Through Modern Eyes,' vi, 4 (March '38), pp. 461–8.

argued that the logical architecture of Caudwell's *Illusion and Reality* actually inverted the proper order of a valid study of literature in society: 'the metaphysical sweep of the dialectic merely beats the air if it neglects the strict discipline of the sciences it attempts to embrace. . . . As has been insisted often enough it is only through the strict practice of literary criticism that the data are available for those who would establish the relation of literature to society.'[163] L. C. Knights made still larger claims for genuine 'literary criticism', and still more damaging an assessment of Marxism's heuristic competence: upholding 'literary sense' against the 'meaningless generalities' of Philip Henderson's *Literature and a Changing Civilization*, he championed 'literary analysis' as 'the keenest instrument we have for the understanding of human values'; and elsewhere he expressed the corollary judgment on 'the Marxian method', which 'applied to a people's culture leaves us with only a few formulae; essential life slips through the mesh.'[164] In another book by Henderson, Q. D. Leavis detected 'the same inability to make value-judgments and the same substitution for them of "ideas" and generalizations divorced from any actuality in experience, the same helplessness where particular analysis is needed . . .'. Henderson, she concluded, understood nothing 'less external than the class struggle and the Fascist-Communist battlefield'.[165]

It was in Martin Turnell's study of 'Literary Criticism in France' that the separate themes of these discussions were most coherently assembled and expounded. His general admiration for French literary-critical culture notwithstanding, Turnell devoted the greater part of his argument to what he saw as its congenital weakness: 'the French love of systems'. Thus, while commending Taine's sociological precepts, he objected to the documentary use of literature that they engendered in practice. He also believed that Taine's criticism was essentially conformist: in refusing seriously to question the values at work in literary texts, it had abdicated from its 'true function'. Turnell traced the same intellectualist currents in the writings of Sainte-Beuve, whose characteristic flaw, in his view, was a lack of interest in

163. 'The Illusion of Cogency,' vi, 4 (March '38), p. 430.

164. ' "The Economic and Social Background",' pp. 203–4; 'Shakespeare and Profit Inflations,' p. 60.

165. 'Class-War Criticism,' v, 4 (March '37), p. 419.

the detail of his chosen texts. Both *œuvres*, with their ambitious typological schemes and persistent bias away from literature towards 'culture and ideas', displayed a 'love of speculation' that dulled the 'sensibility' on which 'genuine literary criticism' relied. In opposition to these exercises in the 'natural history of minds', Turnell invoked Lawrence: 'we judge a work of art by its effect on our sincere and vital emotion and nothing else. . . . A critic must be able to *feel* the impact of a work of art in all its complexity and all its force.'[166]

This first basic distinction was associated with a second, between 'historical' and 'actual' criticism – the one represented by Sainte-Beuve, Boileau and Voltaire (and in England, by Dryden and Johnson), the other by Baudelaire and Gourmont (and by Coleridge and Arnold).[167] 'Actuality' was, in the first place, a certain virtue of 'sensibility' that made possible a quasi-scientic rigour distinct from Taine's scientism, and a 'taste' relatively immune from passing cultural fashion. At the same time, it retained the sense of its French original, connoting a standard of contemporary relevance. The distinction between 'historical' and 'actual' did not correspond to any simple opposition between past and present. As Turnell's contrast between Sainte-Beuve and Baudelaire implied, 'actual' criticism was defined rather by its *non-relativist* approach to the past: 'like most Frenchmen,' Sainte-Beuve was 'aware of tradition in a general way, but his attitude [was] historical and [had] nothing of the extraordinary actuality of Baudelaire's criticism'.[168] This second sense of 'actuality' was crucially related to the first. For 'tradition', the distinguishing preoccupation of 'actual' criticism, was a trans-historical order whose coherence and value were actively determined in relation to present needs; and these could only be discerned by criticism that was 'actual' in its capacity for concrete, personal judgment. Those who defected from this kind of judgment, in the name of some 'abstract' scheme of analysis and evaluation, inevitably lost purchase on the *significant* past and succumbed to relativism and conformity, thereby negating the 'true function' of criticism.

166. 'Literary Criticism in France (I),' VIII, 2 (September '39), pp. 167–82.
167. 'Literary Criticism in France (II),' VIII, 3 (December '39), pp. 281–98, at 283–4.
168. Ibid., pp. 283–4.

Turnell's arguments were consistent with *Scrutiny*'s general stance, above all in their effective lack of positivity. 'Actuality' was largely a polemical term that served to expose the shared failings of professedly divergent critical strategies; it did little to resolve the apparently discrepant grounds of *Scrutiny*'s objections to them. The study of literature was not in any circumstances to be conceived as an empiricist registration of 'fact'; as Leavis had argued in his reply to Bateson, and Mason in his critique of Caudwell, literary criticism was the irreplaceable arbiter of factual relevance – and not merely a selective principle that supervened on a notionally separate process of empirical investigation, but, according to Mason, the very condition of appearance of the relevant data: 'the essential facts do not exist for observation until a certain degree of cultural awareness is reached.'[169] The effect of these anti-empiricist avowals was paradoxical: to all appearances, they seemed to undermine the critique of 'abstraction' that accompanied them. If it was really the case that the object of analysis was in some sense constituted in accordance with the presuppositions – or, in Mason's nebulous phrase, 'awareness' – of the analyst, then it became logically impossible to refute the 'abstract' and 'external' theorizings of a Taine, a Richards or a Caudwell in the name of the empirically given. But what, then, was the logical status of *Scrutiny*'s appeals to 'concreteness' and 'particularity'? If not the *names* of self-evident data of perception, these key words could only be *terms* in a discourse – that of 'genuine literary criticism' – whose logical substructures were in principle no less 'systematic' and 'abstract' than those of Marxism or Ricardian hermeneutics. Few episodes in *Scrutiny*'s career are more widely known or more often recalled than the Leavis–Wellek exchange of 1937, in which this crux formed the explicit point of debate. The exchange was largely unproductive, neither party conceding anything of substance to his adversary; and subsequent reflections on it have been, for the greater part, correspondingly limited.[170] It is

169. 'The Press,' VII, 3 (December '38), p. 343.

170. The most important of these are: Martin Jarrett-Kerr, 'The Literary Criticism of F. R. Leavis,' *Essays in Criticism* II, 4 (October '52), pp. 351–68; Ian Gregor, 'The Criticism of F. R. Leavis,' *Dublin Review* CCVI, 457 (1952), pp. 55–63; Renford Bamborough, 'Literature and Philosophy,' in idem (ed.), *Wisdom: Twelve Essays*, London 1974, pp. 274–92; Michael Tanner, 'Literature and Philosophy,' *New Universities Quarterly* XXX, 1 (Winter '75), pp. 54–64. See also Andor Gomme, 'Why Literary Criticism Matters in a Technologico-Benthamite Age,' in the same issue of *New Universities Quarterly*, pp. 36–53.

arguable, however, that the most revealing aspect of the occasion was precisely its unsatisfactory outcome: that failure was pre-ordained by the issues involved and is therefore to be seen as an important symptom of their basic significance.

The occasion of the exchange was the appearance of *Revaluation*, in the latter part of 1936. Wellek wrote privately to Leavis, expressing his admiration for the book, which he regarded as 'the first consistent attempt to rewrite the history of English poetry from the twentieth century point of view'. However, having lauded the many 'acute critical observations and brilliant interpretations of texts' that it contained, he went on to take issue with certain aspects of its critical procedure and to detail what he saw as their negative local effects. Leavis's initial response to these comments was to request permission to publish them in *Scrutiny*. Wellek agreed, and in March 1937 his letter appeared under the title, 'Literary Criticism and Philosophy'. Wellek's first and most important point concerned Leavis's reticence in matters of theory. 'I could wish,' he wrote, 'that you had stated your assumptions more explicitly and defended them systematically.' The underlying evaluative 'norm' of *Revaluation* was one that he found sympathetic, but it was necessary 'to defend [it] more abstractly and to become conscious that large ethical, philosophical and, of course, ultimately, also aesthetic *choices* are involved'.[171] He went on then to observe that Leavis's tacit inclination towards philosophical 'realism' entailed an aversion from the idealist tradition and a corresponding tendency to under-estimate the Romantic world-view;[172] and finally, to suggest how philosophical information, relevantly deployed, could assist analysis of the poetry of Blake, Wordsworth and Shelley, and thus help to adjust imbalances of critical assessment.[173]

Leavis replied promptly in the next issue. 'I knew I was making assumptions (even if I didn't – and shouldn't now – state them to myself quite as [Wellek] states them) and I was not less aware than I am now of what they involve.' But if Wellek felt the need of an abstract exposition, it was because he was a philosopher; Leavis was not, and doubted 'whether in any case I could elaborate a theory that he would find satisfactory'.[174] Literary criticism and philosophy were, in Leavis's view, 'quite different and distinct kinds of discipline.'

171. v, 4, p. 376.   172. Ibid., p. 377.   173. Ibid., pp. 377, 378–9, 379–83.
174. 'Literary Criticism and Philosophy: A Reply,' vi, 1 (June '37), p. 59.

Although it was no doubt possible to enhance criticism by philosophic training, and to combine the two disciplines in various ways, it was necessary 'to have a strict literary criticism somewhere and to vindicate literary criticism as a distinct and separate discipline'.[175] Their radical difference, which rendered any working alliance problematic, was one between contrary modes of reading. Philosophy was 'abstract', and poetry 'concrete'. To read poetry was 'not to "think about" and judge but to "feel into" or "become" – to realize a complex experience' that was 'given in the words'. The 'fuller-bodied response' and 'completer responsiveness' demanded by the poetic word were thus 'incompatible with the judicial, one-eye-on-the-standard approach suggested by Dr Wellek's phrase: "your 'norm' with which you measure every poet." The critic – the reader of poetry – is indeed concerned with evaluation, but to figure him as measuring with a norm which he brings up to the object and applies from the outside is to misrepresent the process. The critic's aim is, first, to realize as sensitively and completely as possible this or that which claims his attention; and a certain valuing is implicit in the realizing. As he matures in experience of the new thing he asks, explicitly and implicitly: "Where does this come? How does it stand in relation to ... ? How relatively important does it seem?" And the organization into which it settles as a constituent in becoming "placed" is an organization of similarly "placed" things, things that have found their bearings with regard to one another, and not a theoretical system or a system determined by abstract considerations.'[176] Leavis was prepared to concede that certain principles and 'formulable norms' might perhaps be elicited *a posteriori* from an achieved corpus of particular judgments; but generalizations of this order were inevitably secondary to the main business of criticism, and were, in his view, to be kept separate from it. His 'whole effort' was precisely 'to work in terms of concrete judgments and particular analyses', so avoiding 'clumsy' generalities. His arguments were addressed to 'readers of poetry as such. I hoped, by putting in front of them in a criticism that should keep as close to the concrete as possible my own developed "coherence of response", to get them to agree (with, no doubt, critical qualifications) that the map, the essential order, of English poetry seen as a whole did, when they interrogated their experience, look

175. Ibid., p. 60.   176. Ibid., pp. 60–61.

like that to them also.' It was debatable whether generalization could add force to these judgments: 'I think I have gone as far in explicitness as I could profitably attempt to go, and . . . I do not see what would be gained by the kind of explicitness [Wellek] demands (though I see what is lost by it).'[177] That said, Leavis proceeded to a defence of the disputed passages of *Revaluation* and to criticize the general argument on which Wellek's objections were based, concluding that it demonstrated nothing other than the extreme difficulty of wedding philosophy and literary criticism.[178]

Much of Leavis's reply was, in one sense, irrelevant: Wellek's first and most important point – concerning the 'ethical, philosophical and . . . aesthetic' presuppositions of *Revaluation* – was logically distinct from the second – concerning the auxiliary function of philosophical information in critical analysis – and was not affected by objections to it. Leavis's elision of the two may have been partly the fault of Wellek's exposition, which did not register the distinction with due formality and emphasis; it was at any rate central to the logic of his counter-argument. By discussing the first problem in the terms of the second, he was able to consign all reflection on 'abstract' questions of 'system' to the domain of philosophy, whose affairs were not those of literary criticism proper. A curious dual argument then followed. Leavis gradually withdrew from the ground on which Wellek had challenged him. Having at first agreed that he had made 'assumptions' – but cast doubt on his ability to expound them to his critic's satisfaction – he passed quickly to a consideration of the difficulties facing any 'working alliance' between philosophy and literary criticism. He later conceded that certain general principles might eventually be discoverable, through retrospective codification of particular judgments, but then went on to question whether the imputed benefits of 'explicitness' could outweigh its obvious perils. At the same time, and in express counterposition to Wellek's request for an abstract and systematic statement of principles, he described a 'process' – a mode of reading and judgment that deployed specific faculties in specific operations – which he presented as the distinctive activity of the literary critic. But here, in what purported to be a description of a technical process, structured simply by the demands of its material, certain fundamental ideological 'assumptions' became

177. Ibid., pp. 62–3.　　　　　178. Ibid., p. 63f.

unmistakeable. Leavisian literary criticism presupposed, first, that the critic could and should achieve unmediated community with his text, and with his presumed audience, the 'readers of poetry as such'; and, second, that this triune relationship was realizable only in 'the concrete'. That these, or any other, tacit assumptions should have underlain *Revaluation* was in itself unremarkable. What was striking was that Leavis, challenged directly, should have refused to declare them, and then proceeded to an apparently technical account in which, paradoxically, they became manifest. A reticence so obdurate, and so enigmatic in its effects, cannot have been merely idiosyncratic. It was, rather, the consequence of a specific ideological commitment that was shared by the majority of the *Scrutiny* circle. The meaning of that commitment, already discernible in the assumptions of Leavisian literary criticism, can most conveniently be viewed in the sidelight cast by a less renowned but equally important essay published in *Scrutiny* some four years earlier: Harding's critique of I. A. Richards.

Harding's main concern in this essay was the aporia of Richards's theory of value. 'It is clear,' he argued, 'that it cannot, even hypothetically, give us grounds for judgment when a difference of opinion rests on a fundamental constitutional difference between two people.' This insight was unquestionably apt, but its supporting argument was curious: 'Richards . . . condemns swindling and bullying because they lead to a thwarting of important social impulses: the implicit assumption is that the swindler and the bully in question possess the "normal" social impulses. If they do not, they cannot be condemned along these lines. You might as well try to convince a tiger of its misfortune in not being a buffalo.'[179] As Harding perceived, the mainstay of Richards's value theory was the assumption of an essential equivalence among individual human subjects; where this was lacking, objectively valid (that is, consensual) judgment was, strictly speaking, beyond reach. But Harding approached this crux only to evade it. The simile of the tiger and the buffalo, ostensibly designed to highlight the problem of 'constitutional difference', served in fact to displace it from the field of inter-individual relations into that of the

179. 'Evaluations (I): I. A. Richards,' I, 4 (March '33), p. 329.

relations among distinct biological species. Therewith, the challenge to Richards's theory was tacitly withdrawn.

Harding's second approach to the problem was more curious still. His purpose now was to reconcile theoretical accommodation of individual 'difference' with the ideal of critical agreement that Richards had striven to reach. 'The conclusion that [Richards's] account of value gives a basis for agreement only when "normality" (or identical abnormality) is assumed, might seem to leave us no defence against an endless variety of critical opinions, each justified by an appeal to a fundamental constitutional peculiarity in the critic. Since innate differences do of course exist, we must perhaps admit that in the end we shall have to recognize distinguishable "types" of critical opinion founded on psycho-physiological differences in the critics, and irreconcilable.' However, this consideration was 'too remote' to be of immediate practical significance: 'it is still possible to show that differences of opinion in literary matters frequently arise from errors of approach which even those who make them can be brought to recognize. With people who assert that they know what they like the one hope is to demonstrate to them that in point of fact they *don't*, that according to standards they themselves recognize elsewhere their judgment here is mistaken. As these inconsistencies are faced and abandoned, the possibility of agreement with other people grows greater. We cannot tell how far this principle may be pushed, but undoubtedly we have a very long way to go before innate psycho-physiological differences are the sole cause of disagreement between us.'[180] Two observations should be made here. The first is that Harding's argument concerning 'constitutional difference' was effectively self-cancelling. The notion was at best insubstantial, referring only to residual peculiarities of psycho-physiological constitution. But to argue, as he did, that these peculiarities were too remote to be important as factors of critical disagreement was to disqualify them as significant grounds of objection to Richards's theory of value. It is also apparent that, here as in the preceding argument, a displacement occurred: analytic attention was switched from the abiding problem of inter-individual differences to the less intractable question of the discrepancies within a given individual corpus of judgments. Harding averred that the two were intimately related: that the development of

180. Ibid., p. 334.

self-consistency was *pari passu* an extension of agreement, and that Richards's work on communication could assist the unfolding of this dual process. It was not surprising, however, that the point was left unargued, for its premiss was precisely that of the theory of value: the postulate of an essential equivalence among individuals. To the exact degree that this theory was faulty, so too was the companion theory of communication. It was not logically possible to separate them, or to set their common premiss against itself for the purpose of theoretical modification or correction.

The conclusions of Harding's essay help to explain the paralogisms of its main argument. Richards, he suggested, 'sees [poetry] both as the practised reader who has acquired his standards of culture imperceptibly, and as the plain man of common sense and faith in science who needs *convincing*, without a gradual process of education, that poetry might be of some importance to him. A large part of Richards's work can be regarded as an attempt to find common ground for these two points of view; to find a set of standards recognized by the second man which will lead logically to the position of the first.' While accepting that Richards's procedures were educationally valuable, Harding was not persuaded that 'the intelligent and friendly Philistine' could be won over. Nevertheless, he concluded, 'it may be that his work fulfils its purpose by giving those who already value poetry a new assurance that their concern for it is a development, and not a distortion, of "ordinary practical living". If this is one of its functions it bears witness to the growing need of those with minority views to justify themselves at the bar of the main community. The main community may not be convinced; perhaps the fundamental need is that the minority should be.'[181] Harding's reservations about Richards's cultural strategy were, at first sight, no more than the logical outcome of his objections to the theoretical conceptions that underpinned it: if 'the intelligent and friendly Philistine' was unlikely to be won to 'minority' positions, it was because of 'the remoteness and elusiveness of the common denominator chosen – the impulse' which Richards identified as the universal basic element of the human psyche. But to assert this was to disallow the claim of 'the minority' to general cultural authority: without a common denominator there could be no common standard. And for one whose stance was *Scrutiny*'s, this was

181. Ibid., p. 338.

an impossible admission. It was this antimony that condemned Harding's analysis to irresolution. Aware of the vulnerability of Richards's theory, he was nevertheless unable to strike decisively against it, because its first principle – the assumption of a human essence – was one that he shared in practice. The logical 'behaviour' of his essay was that of a critique brought face to face with its own repressed assumptions.

The 'process' described by Leavis in his reply to Wellek was, in the same strict theoretical sense, *humanist*. His conception of literary criticism as an act of unmediated communication between critic, text and interlocutory co-reader, was logically dependent on the idea of a human essence – which, at the same time, relegated major problems of communication to the status of interference, sometimes blameless (the difficult but remediable effects of historical distance) but more often malign (the derangement of critic, text or co-reader by the modern 'environment'). Leavis did in fact formulate this idea, on at least two occasions;[182] but his overriding inclination was to avoid and deprecate discussion of basic theoretical issues, and here, where theoretical clarification was essential, he refused it altogether. This silence was itself logically necessary – determined by certain theoretical assumptions whose peculiar characteristic was that they were debarred, on pain of self-refutation, from announcing themselves.

Leavis's critical epistemology has been termed 'nominalist', and traced back to the powerful empiricist traditions of English – and especially Cambridge – philosophy.[183] These ascriptions are certainly not inapt; but they cannot account for those elements in his work that were, and are, quite alien, indeed hostile, to that tradition. If the critic of Wellek was simply an empiricist, what was the critic of Bateson? The central problem in any analysis of Leavis's criticism is the seeming contradiction that dominates it – what one writer has described as 'the logical paradox of an insistent metaphysical vocabulary combined with a positivist methodology'.[184] It is there that analysis should properly begin.

182. See *For Continuity*, p. 9; and 'Restatements for Critics,' p. 323.

183. Greenberg, p. 857; also Tanner, p. 54.

184. Perry Anderson, 'Components of the National Culture,' *New Left Review* 50 (May-June '68), p. 51.

Apparently contradictory, the two poles of Leavis's criticism were in fact logically interdependent: his 'positivist methodology' was the determinate effect of his 'metaphysics'. The most notable feature of Leavis's humanism was its obdurate anti-scientism. The improper aggrandisement of the established sciences of nature and society, and misconceived attempts to transpose their models into the domain of culture, were in his view among the greatest threats posed by contemporary 'civilization' to human integrity. Their inevitable consequence was 'abstraction', and 'abstraction' meant the death of 'unambiguous and effective meaning'. Leavis's anti-theoretical insistence on 'concreteness' and 'particularity' was thus not a defence of mere fact-gathering – an activity no less 'abstract' in his estimation than the most rarefied exercises in concept formation. It was, rather, an affirmation of certain *qualities* to which 'abstraction' was at best insensitive and at worst inimical. These qualities, conversely, represented that which the merely scientific could never encompass: the specific and integral reality of the human. The apparent contradiction in this position (the notion of an essential humanity was itself abstract and therefore unacceptable) was muted by the term chosen by Leavis to describe his supreme moral value. 'Life' was not so much *essence* as *plenitude*; not an abstraction, but a totality whose compass was such as to dwarf even the most audacious theoretical system. More, it did not simply 'place' categories of more limited reference; it dissolved them in a protean flux of particulars that no 'system' could hope to channel. The peculiar timbre of the word, evoking both a human totality and the minutiae of lived experience, was the sign of its pivotal logical function: by the grace of 'life', particularity became the proper form of appearance of the most general of abstractions.[185] 'Metaphysics' and 'positivist methodology' were linked in Leavis's thought, not as the poles of a 'paradox' but as the latent and manifest levels of a logical whole. The nature of the whole dictated the manner of its defence. Premissed upon a refusal of 'abstraction', Leavis's 'system' could not consistently be defended – except in the name of a 'process'

185. More than one admirer of Leavis has defended this position on the ground that the general has no real existence outside of particular instances (see Bamborough, pp. 276, 280; Gomme, p. 45). This defence seems to substitute the metaphysical question of *universals* for the quite different question that concerned Wellek: the 'abstract' conceptual grid, the *problematic*, that governed Leavis's reading of 'particulars'.

offered as the alternative to 'abstraction' and 'system' as such. For the system as a whole, reticence was the price of cohesion.

This literary-critical 'process' has so far been considered only as the point at which Leavis's 'assumptions' were involuntarily laid bare; it can now be examined in its own right. Martin Greenberg has drawn attention to the characteristic form of Leavis's critical essays: 'they are not, for the most part, shaped from within, but mechanically borrow such order as they have from the texts they consider.'[186] Its rationale has been concisely stated by L. D. Lerner: 'most of the assumptions of [Leavis's] practical criticism are simply those of literature itself . . .'.[187] In these two judgments – one critical, the other appreciative – the dominant trait of Leavisian literary criticism is clearly delineated. The act of criticism was in essence maieutic, performed to facilitate an operation in which criticism itself had no productive role. To criticize was to bear witness to meanings that were already adequately constituted in the words on the page, needing only to be 'realized' in the consciousness of the reader. The most vital of these meanings were indefinable – as Leavis was to put it, years after *Scrutiny*'s closure: 'in our time it is very necessary to insist that the most important words – important for those troubled about the prospect that confronts humanity – are incapable of definition. You can't by defining them fix and circumscribe their life – for in any vital use they will *live*, even disconcertingly: and there lies their importance for thought.'[188] Definition was an intellectual mode proper to thought that strove for 'system'. The typical gesture of Leavisian criticism, in contrast, was *recognition* – recognition and, where appropriate, affirmation of what was immanent in the concrete literary word. This criticism was, therefore, a form of intuitionism: specifically, it consisted in *the intuition of moral values in literary experience.* The judgments derived from it were saved from tautology by the imputed identity of its participants: the essential humanity intimated by the text, elicited by the critic and corroborated ('. . . with, no doubt, critical qualifications' – but no more) by his audience, the 'readers of poetry as such'.

186. Greenberg, p. 857.
187. 'The Life and Death of *Scrutiny*,' *London Magazine* ii, 1 (January '55), p. 73.
188. *Nor Shall My Sword*, London 1972, p. 163.

V

Two final observations are in place here, the first a further specification of *Scrutiny*'s literary-critical practice, the second concerning the logical and programmatic relations between this practice and the *Scrutiny* project as a whole.

The conclusion that the literary criticism of the journal was dominated by a problematic of 'recognition' seems to beg two important questions. How can the depreciatory and dismissive judgments for which *Scrutiny* became notorious be depicted as instances of 'recognition'? And how, if this conclusion is granted, can the 'sociological' strain in its criticism be accounted for? To some extent, these questions must be left as reminders that *Scrutiny*'s literary criticism was not utterly monolithic: although its dominance was never seriously challenged, Leavis's criticism was not the paradigm of his collaborators' every judgment. But to a much more important extent, they begin to answer each other. For it was more or less in the measure that the values discerned in a given text diverged from those tacitly held by the critic – so becoming 'unrecognizable' – that some form of 'explanation', sociological or psychological, became necessary. The inverse proportionality of the two modes was apparent both between and within individual analyses: while Leavis simply affirmed the qualities of Keats's poetry, without reference to their conditions of existence, his contrasting assessment of Shelley was strongly marked by cultural-historical and psychological speculation; and in the one instance where he paid unqualified tribute to the latter's work – the paragraphs on *The Mask of Anarchy* – the 'explanatory' mode was temporarily suspended.[189] The *locus classicus* of this peculiar dual methodology was perhaps Q. D. Leavis's *Fiction and the Reading Public*. Her introductory remarks were quite explicit: literary criticism proper could 'necessarily take no heed of the majority of novels'; for the purpose of analysing these novels, examples of 'fiction as distinct from literature', criticism and scholarship required the assistance of a third method which could 'explain their wide appeal and . . . give clear reasons why those who disdain them are not necessarily snobs.'[190]

189. See 'Shelley,' pp. 161–2, 176, 177.
190. *Fiction and the Reading Public*, pp. xiii–xv.

The status and function of her 'anthropological' inquiry were thus made clear: its task was to *explain* a literature that 'criticism' could not, in either sense of the word, *recognize.* Conversely, her analysis of 'genuine' literature was concerned mainly with its plight in a hostile environment, and with the 'highbrow' indirection that had arisen in tactical response to it; the values that these tactics were deemed to subserve were simply taken for granted.[191]

This dualism was itself subject to one major variation. The working arrangement between 'recognition' and 'explanation' was settled according to the ascribed relations between 'culture' and 'civilization' in the given field of inquiry. Where these were harmonious, as in the 'community' of the late-medieval era, the two critical modes tended towards unison, one explaining what the other intuited and endorsed. Thus, John Speirs attributed the vitality of Dunbar's best poetry to the 'living speech' of his ' "locality", which was not without its place in the still homogeneous medieval European community'; L. G. Salingar saw 'the medieval social tradition, as it had survived through the sixteenth century,' as the source of Tourneur's dramatic strength, and its absence as the condition of Webster's relative inferiority; and for F. R. Leavis, Shakespeare's artistic achievement was inexplicable apart from the community that had shaped and sustained his means of expression.[192] Even here, the fusion of the 'critical' and the 'socio-logical' was not complete. Already, the social bases of artistic excellence seemed residual or insecure, in a world increasingly agitated by the forces that would eventually bring it down. As *Scrutiny's* analytic focus moved forwards, the temporal distance between individual literary achievement and its presumed social sources became marked: Johnson's distinction was traced back to the culture of an older generation; the stable and exacting standards of the *Edinburgh Review* were entered to the credit of the previous century; the novels of Emily Brontë, Mrs Gaskell and George Eliot were seen by Q. D. Leavis as isolated survivals of an idiom long since dissipated by romantic extravagance.[193] As the estrangement of 'culture' from 'civilization'

191. Ibid., p. 257.
192. Speirs, 'William Dunbar,' p. 57; Salingar, ' "The Revenger's Tragedy" and the Morality Tradition,' pp. 421–2; Leavis, 'Joyce and "the Revolution of the Word".'
193. See respectively, 'English Poetry in the Eighteenth Century,' p. 24; Cox, 'The Great Reviews (I),' pp. 2–4; *Fiction and the Reading Public*, pp. 128–30.

deepened into virtually absolute alienation, the sources of individual achievement were displaced into 'tradition', an impalpable meta-community whose relations with actual history were increasingly nominal; and at the same time, a definite division of labour became established in *Scrutiny*'s criticism. In its discussions of twentieth-century topics, 'sociological' analysis was reserved for deficiency, aberration and failure – in conventional *Scrutiny* parlance, for the 'diagnosis' of 'cases'. At its most accomplished – in the hands of Q. D. Leavis – it was a mode of denunciation. The rare and usually qualified successes of contemporary literature were not, in this sense, subjected to analysis. Tributes to authorial 'character', 'intelligence', 'sensibility', 'disinterestedness' and 'impersonality' formed the staple of a critical process of recognition and affirmation whose culminating occasion, towards the end of *Scrutiny*'s career, was F. R. Leavis's evaluation of Lawrence.

The relationship between this critical methodology and *Scrutiny*'s cultural programme was of direct practical importance. As Leavis wrote, the 'centre of real consensus' projected by the journal was 'such a centre as is presupposed in the possibility of literary criticism and is tested in particular judgments'.[194] The most striking aspect of this central strategic conception was its logical reversibility. Literary criticism appeared simultaneously to depend on the prior existence of 'consensus' and to provide a practical warrant of its attainability in some notional future: conclusion was possible only if assumed in advance. In Leavis's thought, this logical circle was a constant cause of unease. 'For Matthew Arnold,' he wrote, in the opening lines of *Mass Civilization and Minority Culture*, 'it was in some ways less difficult. . . . Today one must face problems of definition and formulation where Arnold could pass lightly on.'[195] Nevertheless, he continued to defend Arnold's mode of discourse against its critics, arguing that 'there may be an important function for an intelligence that, in its sensitive concern for the concrete, its perception of complexities, and its delicate responsiveness to actualities, is indifferent to theoretic rigour or completeness and does not mind incurring the charge of incapacity for strict thinking'. Arnold's 'persuasiveness', he maintained, was not

194. 'Restatements for Critics,' p. 319.
195. *Education and the University*, London 1948, p. 143.

derived from 'convincing analysis, rigour of definition and the logical cogency of his argument'; it was rather 'a matter of reminding his public of what they know already' – a perfectly viable writing strategy in a period when 'the sense of what a civilization should be was as yet far from extinguished'.[196] Leavis's defence was dearly bought. For in vindicating Arnold's procedures, he exposed the inborn disability of his own. The values implicit in 'literary criticism' were drawn from his 'sense' of a community that he and his collaborators could neither identify in the real nor define in thought – except as part of a circle of meanings whose interdependence was exclusive and absolute. The perimeter of the circle marked the limits of persuasion: what *Scrutiny*'s audience did not 'know already', it could not be told.[197]

The logical circle was thus a form of practical confinement, and as such boded ill for the journal's overall cultural programme. From the beginning of his writing career, Leavis had been adamant in his repudiation of cultural 'pharisaism' or any other form of self-righteous withdrawal on the part of 'an insulated minority'.[198] But given that *Scrutiny* was, in one very precise sense, 'insulated', how were its perceptions to have their due effect? How was the meta-community of 'culture' to become a real force in the actual society? The journal's record in the thirties gave few indications. Collective political commitment had turned out to be impracticable – and not principally because the editors and collaborators were irreconcilably divided: although significant political differences did exist, there was a clear general bias towards the Left. A more critical factor was their shared cultural perspective which, demoting the political as such to secondary status, rendered these differences, and hence their possible resolutions, 'inessential'. Other forms of institutional anchorage had proved equally hard to find. The 'movement in education' launched in 1933 did indeed exist, but only as a small oppositional tendency in certain grammar schools and universities. Leavis himself was now more securely established, in Downing College; but the university as

196. 'Arnold's Thought,' pp. 95, 96–97, 98.

197. Leavis was always uneasily aware of this. 'What this means it is perhaps impossible to bring home to anyone who is not already convinced of the importance of poetry' – this sentence, from *New Bearings* (p. 20), typifies a figure of argument that recurs constantly in his work.

198. Cf. 'What's Wrong with Criticism?' p. 135.

176

a whole had shown little readiness to rally to his cause. In metropolitan literary circles, *Scrutiny*'s initiative had been met largely with
complacency, suspicion or outright hostility. By the end of the
decade, its main strategic problem was still unresolved.

Three

New Bearings (1939–1945)

The drastically altered conditions of wartime created organizational difficulties for *Scrutiny*, and brought hazards that threatened its very existence. In December 1939, the editors announced: 'the reply to the many flattering inquiries that have been made is that the Editors intend to carry on while it remains possible to do so.' Within eighteen months, the problems anticipated on that occasion had materialized. Apologizing for the late appearance of the number for June 1941, the editors stressed the difficulty of maintaining 'the essential collaboration with a sufficient team'. If they could attract one hundred new subscribers, they wrote, the journal could continue for another year. This target was apparently reached, and the editorial team was strengthened by the addition of Wilfrid Mellers, who was now established as one of *Scrutiny*'s most productive contributors. Meanwhile, however, the more intractable problem of paper shortages had arisen. The number for January 1942 – Mellers's first as editor – was twenty pages short of the normal one hundred and twenty, and the next issue was reduced by the same amount again (though by now the type was more closely set and the margins had shrunk considerably). Around the same time, their printer's premises narrowly escaped destruction in a bombing-raid on Cambridge. Acknowledging the impossibility of maintaining schedules in these conditions, the editors discarded their usual monthly dating system and adopted a more flexible seasonal rubric. In the years that followed, they complained of the futility of any attempt at long-term planning, of the impossibility of extending the print-run to accommodate the growing demand for subscriptions, and, repeatedly, of the dispersal of 'the connection' in the various theatres of war.[1] *Scrutiny* survived the war

1. See VIII, 3 (December '39), p. 309; x, 1 (June '41), p. 87; XI, 1 (Summer '42), p. 59.

years, suffering only minor breaches of publishing continuity, but, as Leavis afterwards recalled, only by the strenuous efforts of a greatly diminished nucleus of active collaborators.[2]

The first intellectual task of the journal was to take stock of the decade now ended. There were a few belated echoes of the controversies of the thirties – notably the exchange between Christopher Hill, who reviewed *Scrutiny*'s culminating counter-thrust, *Marxism: A Post-Mortem*, and its author, H. B. Parkes[3] – but when, in June 1940, F. R. Leavis looked back on the decade, it was as if from the far side of an abyss. He recalled the 'tremendous' pressure 'to wear red or some colour recognized as its opposite', and his journal's successful resistance to it. *Scrutiny*'s 'negative' preoccupation – anti-Marxism – had been unremitting, he declared, as had its 'positive' corollary, the struggle to preserve 'the humane tradition ... representing the profit of a continuity of experience through centuries of economic and material change'. If Leavis's recollections of *Scrutiny*'s relations with Marxism had evidently been somewhat edulcorated, they were nevertheless consonant with his revised estimate of the political problems that had taxed his circle during that 'barren decade': they were so many 'distractions', memorable chiefly for their adverse effects on literary production.[4] L. C. Knights, whose political interests had been both more pronounced and more radical than his colleague's, went still further in his retrospective devaluation of the Left culture of the thirties. He seconded the view now espoused by Stephen Spender, that poetry, the repository of 'ultimate' human values, should remain 'above' political strife; and, not wholly persuaded by the latter's 'generous' account of the radicalization of English poetry, expanded it to include 'the individual's need for rebellious self-assertion combined with the need for a dogmatic religion, and the influence of fashion in the comparative security of middle-class life in England in the '30s'.[5]

2. *Scrutiny: A Retrospect*, pp. 21–2.
3. Editorial Note, 'Mr Parkes on Marxism,' and Christopher Hill, rev. Henry Bamford Parkes, *Marxism: a Post-Mortem*, IX, 3 (December '40), pp. 277 and 277–84 respectively; H. B. Parkes, 'Correspondence (*re* Marxism),' X, 1 (June '41), pp. 2–3.
4. IX, 1 (May '40), pp. 70–72.
5. 'Poetry and Politics,' X, 3 (January '42), p. 383.

These sentiments were clearly in the spirit of the 1939 symposium, which had concluded, in virtual unanimity, that the primary political duty of 'the minority' was to abstain from factional allegiances, instead promoting the essential values of 'culture' and submitting all political initiatives to their judgment. Coming now from Knights, the most Left-wing of *Scrutiny*'s editors, they bore witness to a deeply altered political climate. The Left in Britain had already been gravely demoralized by the shocks of the later thirties – the Moscow Trials, the defeat of the Spanish Republic and the Molotov–Ribbentrop Pact. Now, in the unique conditions of the war, it was also beginning to weaken in political definition. For the new national consensus that began to emerge after the fall of Chamberlain – not the transcendent 'unity' figured in the legend of Dunkirk, but a complex web of disparate and often basically antagonistic political interests – was formed in a *general radicalization* of British society, producing an unprecedented political and ideological fusion of 'the social question' and 'the national interest'.[6] By the end of 1941, when Knights was writing, Keynes was in the ascendant at the Treasury, the Beveridge Report was in progress, Churchill and Bevin sat in the same Cabinet, and England was allied with the Soviet Union in the war against the Axis: it was as if the evils that had driven the Left into bitter combat in the thirties were now to be attacked and extirpated under the leadership of the British State. In such circumstances, where social compassion appeared to be becoming an attribute of the political as such, the 'claims of politics' lost much of their power to divide; and the ideal community of 'culture' could with relative ease project itself as the 'best self' (Arnold) of the nation.

Although the war was the most important single condition of *Scrutiny*'s reassertion of the autonomy of 'culture', it brought with it its own cultural hazards. The ideal that the editors had upheld throughout 'the Marxist decade' was now imperilled by the upsurge of contending national chauvinisms. Just as once they had defended their notion of the autonomy and historical continuity of 'culture' in their duels with Marxism, so now the editors reaffirmed its supranational aspect, against both official government propaganda and the

6. This complex development is studied in Paul Addison, *The Road to 1945*, London 1975.

new forms of *la trahison des clercs* – the jingoist misappropriation of 'culture' and the consequent risk of a new and destructive parochialism.

Little space was given to official propaganda. The reviews that dealt with the subject simply warned of its ubiquity, and recommended books that exposed or provided a method for analysing its mechanisms.[7] More attention was given to the intrusions of patriotism into the traditional domains of intellectual life. Thus, A. J. Woolford's essay on 'The Interpretation of History' collocated two books by Herbert Butterfield, of which the first, *The Whig Theory of History* (1931), had criticized the moralism and retrospective teleology of Whig history as ideological stratagems designed to validate the *status quo*, while the second, *The Englishman and His History* (1944), argued exactly the reverse, extolling and itself exemplifying the genre that its author had criticized only thirteen years before. Woolford deplored the intellectual atavism that transmuted English history into a pageant whose grand finale was 'the story of 1940', and reaffirmed the independent, 'scientific' spirit that had animated Butterfield's earlier work.[8] In the same issue of the journal, and in similar spirit, F. R. Leavis described Trevelyan's *English Social History* as an example of 'that higher advertising of England which has employed so many distinguished pens of late'.[9]

In its main form, however, *Scrutiny*'s resistance to the patriotic deformation of 'culture' was rather more oblique. Beginning in early 1942, the journal published a series of essays and reviews by D. J. Enright on German literature. These pieces, dealing with Rilke, Hölderlin, George, Mann and Goethe, were distinguished not only by their subject-matter, but by an evident solicitude for the fortunes of German literature in Britain. This 'ambassadorial' concern was displayed in a long and meticulous account of *Faust* that sought to free the play from misleading association with its English namesake; in an analysis of Stefan George which, rather ingenuously perhaps, discounted allegations concerning the poet's 'shaky political views'; and most clearly, in Enright's constant attention to problems of

7. See Frank Chapman, 'How to Read a Newspaper,' VIII, 4 (March '40), pp. 430–31; D. W. Harding, 'A Scientist on Propaganda,' IX, 3 (December '40), pp. 284–5.
8. XIII, 1 (Spring '45), pp. 2–11.
9. XIII, 1, p. 79.

translation, which culminated in an essay on the work of J. B. Leishman, whose translation from the German he held in high regard.[10] Enright's essays, together with Traversi's contemporaneous studies of Manzoni, Machiavelli, Leopardi and Carducci, literary representatives of another enemy nation, constituted a practical affirmation of Christopher Dawson's belief that national cultures subsisted on an ideal plane that transcended the temporal antagonisms of their parent countries, and that the duty of the intellectual, therefore, was to defend 'the interests of culture as a whole'.[11] Or as Leavis was to put it, some two decades later: the decision 'to give to [Goethe], at that time, so much space was in a sense our "politics" '.[12]

I

Scrutiny's main interest in this period was neither the immediate past nor the present. None of its contributors showed any inclination to prolong the inquest on the thirties; and cultural Europeanism, though sustained, was a secondary theme. The correspondent who found the issue for September 1940 'unreal' and expressed puzzlement at its failure even to mention the war 'except as an aside' was, in one sense, justified.[13] For the air of suspension that enveloped the journal in the war years was only partly the result of organizational depletion. By some of the group at least, the war was consciously treated as an historical adjournment, a time for reflection, consolidation and, most important, preparation. For Leavis, it was 'by common consent an occasion for radical searchings and stock-takings', the more so since it would certainly be followed by accelerated social change, for which it was necessary to prepare.[14] Thus, the *Scrutiny* group began almost immediately to address itself to the anticipated problems of the post-war world.

10. See below, pp. 25–6.
11. See pp. 97–8 above.
12. *Scrutiny: A Retrospect*, p. 8. The four instalments of the essay on Goethe totalled seventy pages – almost one whole issue of the journal.
13. IX, 3 (December '40), p. 259.
14. 'Education and the University: Sketch for an English School,' IX, 2 (September '40), p. 100; 'Education and the University: Considerations at a Critical Time,' XI, 3 (Spring '43), p. 162.

G

'Talk, with which we half frighten and half flatter ourselves, about the hectic speed of the changes which humanity is undergoing in our century is excited bla.'[15] While Harding's scornful riposte to the broodings of Eliot's *Idea of a Christian Society* can hardly be taken to have expressed the 'official' standpoint of the journal at this or any other time, it did nevertheless have symptomatic significance. For the war years brought a new measure of optimism to *Scrutiny*. The political perspectives of the journal appeared to have been vindicated by events. The 'impotence of the practical mind' had indeed been 'thoroughly demonstrated' by the behaviour of the parliamentary parties over the past decade, and their Communist opponents were now in political and ideological disarray. Social change was now inevitable, but its exact bearings were as yet indeterminate. The vigour and unwonted concreteness that distinguished *Scrutiny*'s discussions of social policy in this period were signs of a certain confidence in the future, and of a belief that 'the minority' would be able to participate in its formation.

This heightened sense of opportunity was most immediately registered in a twofold revision of emphasis in the journal. On the one hand, there was a more positive appreciation of industry, science and, especially, of social planning, which now became a major preoccupation. That social planning was objectively necessary was apparent to C. E. Lucas, who made frequent contributions on the topic during the war; its results would of course be conditional on the values that controlled the planning process, but its social potential was not in doubt.[16] At the same time, there occurred a complementary shift towards a more nuanced appraisal of 'the organic community'. In its most extreme forms – Bell's ardent lyricism or Thompson's philippics against the motor-car – this theme had in fact faded from the journal several years before, and by the end of the thirties it was seldom aired at all. Now, in an essay on Bacon published in 1943, Knights took his distance from obscurantist versions of the notion, bluntly rejecting ' "anti-scientific" hocus-pocus' in all its forms, and counterbalancing his analysis of the losses entailed in the seventeenth-century 'dissociation of sensibility' with a strong insistence on its positive aspects, in particular the 'necessary' step forward

15. VIII, 3 (December '39), pp. 309–13.
16. See n. 34 below.

to a language capable of methodical, rational and scientific formulation.[17] The traces of this double revision were clearest in two short articles by J. C. Maxwell, published in 1941–42. In the first, a review of 'essays on culture and civilization', Maxwell went so far as to suggest that 'some form of democratic socialism' might prove capable of alleviating certain problems, such as that of 'responsibility in work', which writers like Bell and Thompson had seen as inherent in industrial production.[18] The second, an account of how Swift and Rousseau had made use of an idealized version of Augustan Rome to define and validate their 'moralistic revulsion' from their own societies, was not ostensibly related to the first; but whatever Maxwell's conscious intentions may have been, it is difficult not to read in his essay, with its clear perception of the character and function of this 'memory', a displaced critique of the structurally identical mechanisms of 'the organic community'.[19]

This new access of hope, limited and partial though it was, raised the old question of the thirties afresh. If indeed there were real opportunities for change, how were they to be seized? How was the intellectual 'licence' (Leavis) of wartime to be exploited in practice? Initially, fidelity to 'culture' had been seen as implying some form of political commitment, but mainly as the crucial precondition of a valid commitment. Then, having momentarily entertained the suggestion that there might be a politics peculiar to 'culture', *Scrutiny* concluded that the civic responsibility of 'the minority' was meta-political: its role was to invigilate the political domain in the name of 'the human', without entering it in its own right. This process of involution was now pressed to its logical end. Henceforward it was to be assumed that the practices of 'culture' were in themselves a quasi-political force. Such a view had been expressed before (notably in Knights's suggestion that educational reform was an 'unusually practical

17. 'Bacon and the Seventeenth-Century Dissociation of Sensibility,' xi, 3 (Summer '43), pp. 268–85.
18. ix, 4 (March '41), pp. 388–91.
19. 'DemiGods and Pickpockets: The Augustan Myth in Swift and Rousseau,' xi, 1 (Summer '42), pp. 34–9. See also Maxwell's review of John Speirs's *The Scots Literary Tradition* ('Scottish Literature,' ix, 2, September '40, pp. 193–6), where he dissents from Speirs's deep pessimism.

politics'), but it was only now that it became actually operative in the work of the journal; and again, as in 1932, it was D. W. Harding who furnished the perspective with its oblique theoretical warrant.

'The Custom of War and the Notion of Peace', published in December 1940, was primarily concerned to identify the conditions of a 'radical peace' that would be qualitatively distinct from the 'aim-inhibited warfare' of the 'interlude' of 1918–39;[20] but its main interest lay not so much in this conjunctural preoccupation as in the general assumptions that underpinned it. Harding's major premiss was that the purpose of all social violence, of which war was the extreme case, was to alter the social relations obtaining among the participants. In present conditions, peace was distinguished only by the predominance of non-violent – chiefly economic – forms of coercion. Thus, war and peace were the alternative manifestations of a social organization founded on 'domination'. Most current political and social thought was cast in the logic of domination, concentrating on 'social elites, the direction of the masses by propaganda, shifts of power within social groups, and the alignment of individuals and classes with the forces operating in social process'. The outstanding social priority, therefore, was to find a means of eradicating dominative-submissive behaviour, so as to achieve a genuine 'social integration' that would not depend on mere compromise, or share the 'mild amiability' that reacted to conflict by denying its rationality. An authentically 'integrative social intercourse' would be one in which 'difference' meant not 'deference' but mutual 'respect'.[21]

The role accorded to political and economic measures in this effort was decidedly secondary. In so far as the dominative urge was engendered by insecurity, and that in turn by 'the expectation of violence', any reform that produced 'greater resistance to war' was to be supported. However, Harding warned, 'political maturity' could not be expected to 'outrun social maturity'. Similarly, while endorsing any reform that relieved material hardship and promoted opportunity, he criticized 'the common misunderstanding' that such reforms should be 'primarily intended to make things better for the underdog'. On the contrary, 'the most important reforms – for the present purposes – are not those which aim at lifting the lowest classes to the

20. ix, 3 (December '40), pp. 202–30.
21. Ibid., p. 213f.

economic, moral and hygienic level of the stratum above them, but those which could apply to the life of people of all classes'. For 'insecurity' and 'jealousy' were not peculiarly working-class traits; 'the prevailing organization by deference' affected all social classes. The children of the wealthy, for example, were restricted in their choice of vocation by their parents' 'insecure' fixation on the 'deference-value' of occupations. And in the sphere of consumption the working class were perhaps in advance of their betters: 'gusto in spending, for instance, and the vivid interpretation of money in terms of the direct satisfactions it can bring are fairly usual among the very poor but almost beyond the capacity of the middle classes.'

Harding's diagnosis of social contradictions as problems of attitude led him to allot a privileged role to psychological techniques. In his comments on work, for example, he denied that 'aridness' and 'disharmony' were inherent in modern factory life: 'industrial psychology has already done something and could do vastly more, to remove them.' And speaking of the family, he suggested that preventive psychotherapy, administered to parents and children, would counteract the dominative urges and 'taboo on tenderness' induced in children by the contradiction between the mother-centred home and the male-dominated society outside it. However, his major emphasis fell neither on political and economic reforms nor on techniques of psychological adjustment, but on the desirability of self-transformation and the power of individual example. It was incumbent upon each individual, he declared, to relinquish, as far as possible, his or her own dominative attitudes: 'to break the vicious circle of domination and submission at one point is probably as important as anything in the power of the individual person. The greater his social power, the more influence his achievement of integrative behaviour is likely to have.'[22]

The core of Harding's argument was a species of psychological reductionism. In it, the component structures of society were dissolved and presented as a sum of inter-individual relationships; objective inequalities of wealth and power became the contingent attributes of individuals whose behaviour was governed by subjective propensities – to domination or submission, deference or jealousy, and so on. Its effect was to undermine the intelligibility of politics as

22. Ibid., pp. 220, 223, 224, 225–9, 222.

a social practice. The social, repressed in the scheme of his analysis, returned in the form of an abstract ideal, to be pursued (or not, as the case might be) by the abstract individual. Social progress was now to be achieved not by the working out of contradictions in the social structure but by the striving of individuals towards an ideal of 'social integration' which, represented by none, excluded none. Thus, despite his claim to the contrary, Harding denied the rationality of political conflict: its very existence testified to the 'custom of domination' and precluded 'social integration'. His solution was to abolish it; for in society so conceived, political struggle could only be individual moral effort.[23]

In the notion of 'social integration', Harding at once discovered the political aspect of 'culture' and effected a cultural dissolution of politics. In so doing, he perfected the conception towards which his collaborators had long been tending. His theses had two consequences. which together were to transform the complexion of the journal. First, politics was now fractured into administration – the technical business of government – and ethics: political analysis now turned on the moral evaluation of individual political agents. At the same time, the moral development of the individual became the supreme 'political' question, and accordingly, education and its central discipline, literary criticism, were confirmed as the privileged vantage-points from which to identify and promote the 'essential interests' of society. Harding's essay was the last significant venture in contemporary political analysis by any member of the *Scrutiny* circle (and even here a displacement had occurred, into the idiom of psychology). Henceforward, political ideas were produced as asides in, or as effects of, other discourses – chiefly those of education and literary criticism – which, charged now with this political burden, were themselves to undergo significant modifications. In both cases, these were most dramatically registered in the work of F. R. Leavis.

II

Scrutiny's concern for educational reform was now redoubled. The

23. Cf. ibid., p. 213.

first and clearest sign of this change was the departure of Denys Thompson to found *English in Schools*. Launched with *Scrutiny*'s blessing, the new journal was a specialized continuation of the educational interests with which Thompson had become identified during the previous seven years; its contributors included the most prominent among *Scrutiny*'s writers on secondary education, notably Frank Chapman, Raymond O'Malley and, of course, Thompson himself.[24] Within *Scrutiny* itself, there occurred a simultaneous intensification of educational interest: the issue containing the symposium on 'the claims of politics' (the first to appear without Thompson's name on the masthead) was followed in December 1939 by the editors' first extended collective statement – on the Spens Report on secondary education.[25]

The editors opened their symposium with the declaration that 'it is still possible to believe that the obvious drift – or drive – of civilization doesn't exhaustively represent the "hopes, the knowledge, the values, the beliefs" of the society to which we belong. And in fact it is in that society conventionally assumed that education should be in some way concerned with countering certain characteristic tendencies of civilization. Those of us who are not completely pessimistic are committed to believing that this assumption is in some measure justified by a correspondent reality, one which we ought to do our utmost to make more effective.' The contributors to the symposium, most of whom were 'educationists engaged in practice within the system', had been brought together to assess the significance of the Spens Report in that regard.[26]

Although its emphasis on English was generally welcomed, the

24. 'English in Schools,' VIII, 4 (March '40), p. 430. Other *Scrutiny* contributors to *English in Schools* included T. R. Barnes, Sylvia Legge, Boris Ford, J. C. Maxwell, L. G. Salingar, Bruce Pattison, G. D. Klingopulos and George Every. In all, in the first four years and eight issues of its career, *English in Schools* published eleven *Scrutiny* contributors, past, current or future.

25. 'The Spens Report: A Symposium-Review,' VIII, 3 (December '39), pp. 242–56. Published in late 1938, the Spens Report recommended parity within the secondary sector, which it proposed to enlarge by the incorporation of the junior technical schools, thus creating a tripartite system. Its authors were, however, reluctant to support 'multilateralism', the amalgamation of the three branches into composite secondary schools with flexible internal transfer systems. The Report also favoured English studies as the central element of the school curriculum (Curtis and Boultwood, p. 190).

26. 'The Spens Report,' pp. 242, 243.

Report was subjected to severe criticism by the unnamed correspondents whose quoted statements made up the bulk of the printed text. One writer attacked its timorous compromise over the School Certificate, arguing that so long as the external examination system was retained, in however liberal a form, education would be forced into 'standardization, mass-production, rigidity, uniformity and the rest'. Furthermore, the Spens Committee had omitted to consider 'the real reason' for the retention of the examination: 'the profits made by the examining bodies'. Another attacked the 'thoroughly reactionary' class rationale of the Report; the numbers entering secondary education were to be restricted, in favour of an expanded technical sector, because the Government, as part of its preparations for war, was determined to restore academic secondary education as a ruling-class preserve, and 'to make higher education for the masses suitable to their station in life'. While a strictly educational case could be made for the Spens proposals, their 'social and political context' endowed them with a dangerously reactionary meaning: 'it is a two-edged sword. But I'm sure which edge is being sharpened in Whitehall.'[27]

However, these sentiments did not predominate. Most space was given to a critique which, though also 'radically adverse', was quite distinct, and more in keeping with *Scrutiny*'s established positions. According to this correspondent, the fact that the Report could 'confess the optimistic faith of 1895 [was] its sufficient condemnation'.[28] Then, an 'obsequious Providence, or the natural evolutionary forces (biologic, economic or – for the higher-minded – merely metaphysic) may have seemed a sufficient guarantee for future, as they had proved of present prosperity'. But now, 'in 1939, ... most people have shared in or witnessed one great war, and four major revolutions which are far from merely political; a yet greater revolution is at any rate conceivable, and a second war upon us'. In its covert attempt to reduce secondary education to vocational training, the Spens Report reaffirmed the panglossian delusions of the late nineteenth century, where it should have stressed the detached, contemplative function of a truly 'liberal education'. For 'society's demands'

27. Ibid., pp. 245, 246f.
28. Ibid., p. 250. The author's reference was to the Royal Commission on Education of 1895, which the Spens Report cited as its own basis.

were 'no longer clear; and what would seem to be so is that in the past blind acquiescence in such demands was at least conducive to evil'.[29] The author went on to denounce the absolute separation of work and leisure that prevailed in contemporary society, and those who, by depicting this separation as 'right, proper and founded on nature', helped to perpetuate it. 'They give up hope of rescuing out of a barren isolation the two halves of life which, if they could be brought together, might be immeasurably fruitful.' Modern life was an alternation between work and the seaside, and modern cultural pursuits – as the Spens Committee apparently saw them – no more than 'an intellectual Brighton, . . . well cleaned and well policed, but still a Brighton'. By reiterating the nostrums of 1895, Spens could only aggravate the modern condition. Comparing the philosophical training of the French *lycée* with the intellectual regimen of the English secondary school, the author attacked Spens's adherence to the cherished belief that 'as Englishmen are by nature unintellectual, they may be excused the labour of being so'. The greater maturity of the average *lycéen* was due in large measure to the philosophical ingredient in the French curriculum, where 'the professor implies and the pupil acknowledges what is rarely acknowledged or under-stood in England – that it is not only possible but desirable for the intellect to play a part in the conduct of life'. The Spens Report, it was concluded, sought to complete the destructive work of the Indus-trial Revolution and, to this end, was 'willing to sacrifice what is still conceivably of value – the remains of a liberal tradition in our schools'.[30]

The symposium on the Spens Report was the only extensive dis-cussion of secondary education to appear in *Scrutiny* during the war years. For with the subsumption of politics into education, there occurred a strategic reorientation whose most obvious effect was a transfer of attention from the secondary to the university sector of the system. In December 1940, one reader wrote to express his dismay at the abstracted nature of this interest: surely 'an article on "Evacu-ation and Education" or some such topic would have been a great

29. Ibid., p. 250.
30. Ibid., pp. 255–6.

deal more timely than a programme, however admirable, for a hypothetical English School'?[31] But Leavis understood his wartime responsibilities rather differently. The series of essays on 'Education and the University' which began in September 1940 were in his eyes eminently practical, and of much greater long-term importance.

In 'Why Universities?' Leavis had argued that the outstanding social and political issue of the time was that of control of the modern industrial economy in the interests of 'essential' human ends.[32] By 1940, the possibility of actual breakdown was much more remote; but with the widespread use of planning to meet the exigencies of war production, and the prospect of its generalized application in the post-war period, the problem of control – in particular, of the type of control – had become highly topical.[33] The problems of scientific social planning became a constant preoccupation in *Scrutiny* during these years, and particularly in the contributions of C. E. Lucas. The fundamental issue, for Lucas, was not whether planning was necessary – it evidently was – but rather what aims it should serve. He denied that science could in any sense be socially 'neutral', concurring in R. S. Lynd's view that 'the variables in the social scientist's equations must include not only the given set of structured institutions, but also *what the present human carriers of those institutions are groping to become*'. But science could not itself provide that insight; and again Lucas followed the co-author of *Middletown*: '. . . novelists, artists and poets provide valid insights into our culture that go beyond the cautious generalizations of social science and open up significant hypotheses for study.' In these practices, 'social science has the most sensitive index to the qualitative human adequacy of . . . our . . . institutions'. Culture was the discoverer of 'a core of richly evocative common purposes'. C. H. Waddington, also quoted approvingly by Lucas, summarized this view concisely: 'it is from present-day culture that we can learn what sort of being modern man should be, and it is only when we know this that we can decide what political and economic system we must try to create.'[34] Thus, only a value-laden science could con-

31. Cit. F. R. Leavis, 'Education and the University: Criticism and Comment,' IX, 3 (December '40), p. 259.

32. III, 2 (September '34), p. 120.

33. See Addison, passim.

34. C. E. Lucas, 'Science and Values,' X, 3 (January '42), pp. 317–24, a review of Lynd, *Knowledge For What?*, and Waddington, *The Scientific Attitude*, from which these

tribute to social advance; and the supreme locus of human values, the most profound and inclusive mode of apprehension of 'the human world', was literature. Leavis's 'political' purpose in his blue-print for a new English School was to devise an institution that would incarnate this viewpoint and give it practical effect.

He began by restating the theses of 1934. The major problem, in the university as in society, was the division of labour. But it was mani-festly inadequate simply to evade the objective contemporary need for specialists and to resurrect the ideal of 'the educated man'. What was crucial was that the specialist should be 'in touch with a humane centre'. The duty of the university now was to produce ' "educated men" with . . . various tendencies towards specialization'. That centre was, of course, literary criticism, which trained, 'in a way no other discipline can, intelligence and sensibility together, cultivating a sensitiveness and precision of response and a delicate integrity of intelligence – intelligence that integrates as well as analyses and must have pertinacity and staying power as well as delicacy'. The narrow-ness of an education revolving around practical criticism was decep-tive: 'the more advanced the work the more unmistakeably is the judgment that is concerned inseparable from that profoundest sense of relative value which determines, or should determine, the import-ant choices of actual life.' Rigorously practised, literary criticism constantly led outside itself to neighbouring disciplines; it demanded an interdisciplinarity in which it would be dominant.

There was no master-key to the problems raised by this agenda, Leavis warned; solutions would inevitably be local, partial and 'oppor-tunist'. But for all that, he believed, the Cambridge English Tripos 'might be held to be as promising an opportunity as the academic world has to offer'. Because of its 'emancipation from Anglo-Saxon and the associated encumbrances', its adherence to the notion of literary criticism 'as a training of sensibility and intelligence', and its relative openness to other literatures and to non-literary disciplines, it was unusually amenable to reform. The English School was to be established within Part Two of the existing Tripos, and – 'this would be a condition of its influence and importance – would be essentially

quotations come. See also idem, 'Science and Society,' x, 1 (June '41), pp. 100–104; and Olaf Stapledon, 'Tradition and Innovation,' IX, 1 (June '40), pp. 33–45.

designed for an *élite*'. The main reforms concerned the systems of teaching and assessment, and the syllabus. Final examinations would remain, but would no longer determine the final assessment, which was to be based on course-work. Lectures would be superseded by 'a full and flexible use of discussion and seminar procedures'. The outstanding substantive innovation of the English School was to be the centre-piece of its syllabus, a special study of the seventeenth century as a whole, 'as a key phase, or passage, in the history of civilization'. For the study of that century, the epoch of the dissolution of feudalism and of the rise of capitalism and modern science, was nothing less than 'a study of the modern world'. 'Such a study would have the necessary comprehensiveness, complexity and unity: it would be a study in concrete terms of the relations between the economic, the political, the moral, the spiritual, religion, art and literature, and would involve a critical pondering of standards and key-concepts – order, community, culture, civilization and so on.' The critical ends that Leavis sought to serve were analogous to those of Meiklejohn's comparative studies of Athenian and contemporary American civilization, but there was one decisive difference. The seventeenth century was neither the modern world nor simply, like Athens, culturally other: it was the period that 'enacted' the reciprocal criticisms of the medieval and the modern.[35]

The 'Sketch' was filled out over the next two years by three articles in which Leavis amplified two key conceptions that had been criticized in unpublished correspondence: the roles of 'the elite' and of literary criticism. His notion of 'the elite' had been faulted on the grounds that it bore little relation to the 'real' elite of politicians, civil servants and trade-union officials who would occupy the commanding positions of the 'new planned society', and that the 'mechanical' qualities that he despised were precisely those that any government required in its functionaries. Leavis denied that he desired the formation of '*the* elite', or that he despised the 'mechanical', but warned that 'if the qualities required in a great Government office are what we should be thinking about, then we had better drop the English Tripos altogether'. At the same time, the elite that he envisaged was not to be merely a cultural Resistance: it was to be an 'active and

35. 'Education and the University: Sketch for an English School,' pp. 101, 102; 98–9, 99–100; 102–3, 105, 106, 107.

potent' force, able to 'check and control the blind drive onwards of material and mechanical development, with its human consequences'. It was to be a new and duly incorporated *intelligentsia*, whose relationship with power would be mediate but nonetheless actual: a new levy of 'authors, publicists, editors and journalists, such as might fitly provide for the reading' of the governing elite, and 'help to supply those intelligent and well-informed journals and reviews, the flourishing of which would be evidence of the existence of an intelligent and well-informed public'.[36] It was incorrect, therefore, to construe his emphasis on literary criticism as a purely professional interest in its institutional well-being: 'I have no doubt that it will make the student a better literary critic, but the test of his having profited duly by his course of studies will be his handling of a historical or a sociological work as much as his handling of a novel or a book of poems.'[37] Literary criticism as practised in the Leavisian English School would be nothing less than the discipline of 'non-specialized intelligence' which, by virtue of its privileged access to the values of 'tradition', would unite the new intelligentsia that was to form the conscience of the social order.

The strategic significance of *Scrutiny*'s redoubled emphasis on higher education, and increased concern with the practicalities of institutional reform, should now be clear. What they betokened was the supersession of a policy of relentless struggle mounted 'from without' by one of institutionalized critical cooperation – tensely and profoundly critical, certainly, but cooperative nonetheless, in so far as its projected institutional base could not be built and maintained without official consent. Whereas Thompson, the predominating educational voice of the thirties, had been above all aware of the complicity of 'the educational machine' with the prevailing order, and therefore convinced that the purpose of a 'humane education' should be to produce 'misfits', Leavis now called for the formation of an educational 'centre'

36. 'Education and the University: Criticism and Comment,' pp. 259–64; 'Education and the University: Considerations at a Critical Time,' p. 163f; '... Criticism and Comment,' p. 265.

37. '... Criticism and Comment,' pp. 266–7. See also 'Education and the University (III): Literary Studies,' IX, 4 (March '41), pp. 306–22, which also outlines the structure of the revised Tripos.

that would become 'active and potent' in public life, not merely resisting but positively 'check[ing] and control[ling]' contemporary society.

The historical context of this strategic shift was one of change for the national intelligentsia as a whole: change not only in its politico-ideological dispositions, but also and crucially, in the structural relationship between one of its elite components and the State. Between 1939 and 1941, the political dissensions that had torn the national culture in the thirties were largely resolved, and the factions of that time regrouped in a new consensus that was at once 'progressive' and 'patriotic'. In the same period, and as an important part of this process of reunification, a hitherto relatively inconspicuous segment of the intelligentsia began to enjoy an entirely new prestige and influence in Britain's public affairs. Based occupationally in the social sciences and united politically by a belief in the efficacy of liberal-technocratic social reform, these intellectuals were not so much a faction as a congeries of experts; their blueprints, incubated in the same crises that had induced the intellectual schisms of the thirties, came to maturity just as the revolutionary programmes were cut short by disorientation and defeat, and found ready patronage in the political coalition that now governed 'the Home Front'.[38] *Scrutiny*'s course was broadly congruent with the development of the intelligentsia as a whole. In the thirties, its interventions had been directed mainly against competing intellectual factions, within a shared disaffection from the prevailing political and social order. Now, amidst the exceptional conditions of war and clear signs of a major long-term reorientation of social policy, it sought to establish a new, institutionalized relationship with the leading agencies of State and society. However, the circumstances of Leavis's projected 'elite' were evidently not quite as he defined them. For even by the end of 1940, 'checks' and 'controls' were beginning to be devised and applied on an unprecedented scale; henceforward, the onward drive of 'material and mechanical development' was, in one sense at least, to be less 'blind' than it had ever been. His 'Sketch for an English School' was a remote, antiphonal response to the blueprints of another, very different intellectual elite whose influence amongst the population

38. Addison, pp. 35–44 and ch. VI; see also Arthur Marwick, 'Middle Opinion in the Thirties,' *English Historical Review*, April 1964, pp. 285–98.

and in the State was already considerable and was soon to become irresistible.[39]

The 'Education and the University' series was followed in June 1941 by Wilfrid Mellers's 'Towards a Musical Academy', a set of proposals conceived as an extension of Leavis's programme. If the 'barriers' that separated 'the "academic" musician' from 'the rest of the civilized world' were to be lowered, Mellers believed, musical education would have to be reorganized. The prevailing conception of musical education as the 'manufacture of performers' was wasteful: all but a small minority of students 'would be better employed in educating themselves to form a responsible and discriminating audience for the talented'.[40] Some of the main difficulties in such an undertaking were inherent in the art: its abstract, non-conceptual character conduced to a 'brazen' subjectivism, undisciplined by knowledge, that resulted in ignorance of the 'social necessity' of musical forms, which led in turn to an 'insensitivity to emotional climates' and thus to technical errors of interpretation. Only a musical education based on 'the inculcation of the Historical Perspective' could restore music to the social context that alone gave it meaning. History was the only possible foundation for interpretation, and equally, the condition of music's future vitality: '. . . if there is to be a future for music as a social manifestation, musical academies will have to acquire a sense of social responsibility. Music must be an aspect of human life, not the property of the academic or the aesthete.' For this reason, Mellers advocated the study of the 'functional' music of the theatre and the cinema: 'serious' musicians who sincerely believed that 'functional' music was 'debased' were obliged for that very reason to interest themselves in it, for the sake of 'the spiritual health of the populace'. Mellers's proposals, a composite of 'technical' reform and cultural paternalism, lacked the coherence and verve of Leavis's 'Sketch', but his valuation of the cultural significance of his discipline was no less vaulting: 'precisely because it is, as Roussel said, of all arts the most "inaccessible", it is the strongest fortress of "spiritual values" in times when these values are most violently besieged. One should not need

39. Addison, chs. viii–x.
40. x, 1 (June '41), pp. 4–5.

to justify further the urgency of musical education, however remote it may seem from "the present conflict".'[41]

Some time later, Knights returned to the subject of 'the modern universities', in his review of Bruce Truscot's *Redbrick University*. He repeated the substance of his earlier criticisms: in non-collegiate institutions, the student body was inevitably dispersed; the university thus became 'predominantly a teaching and examining institution'; and inadequate financing resulted in a 'rudimentary tutorial system' and hence, over-lecturing. But on this occasion, 'with "reconstruct-tion" looming, it is to the positive proposals that one turns with most interest'. He seconded Truscot's appeal for more money, supervisions and hostels, fewer lectures and an end to assessment based on exam-inations, but regretted 'the lack of a conception of function, nourished from the actual, strong enough to permeate all the major proposals for reform and direct them towards the desired end'. It was necessary, Knights believed, in some fashion to reconcile humane education and specialization. To this end, he endorsed Leavis's plan for a 'centre' that could re-shape humane education, as the only way of super-seding the contradiction between 'disinterested research' and 'the needs of industry'.[42]

The strategic shift that these essays attest presupposed at least a modicum of belief in the possibility of a successful intervention in the policy and practice of British education. How substantial that belief actually was, is a question that must remain. The Preface written by Leavis for the book-publication of *Education and the University*, although characteristically guarded, conveyed a strong impression of prac-ticality: its form, he explained, was 'that of a sketch, addressed to specific existing conditions, for a practical experiment at a particular place.... I am anxious to make the practical intention, the direct-ness of the drive at practice, unmistakeable, and to avoid any sugges-tion of the Utopian. Hence, then, the hypothetical start from an actually existing school in a specified university, and hence the hypothetical compromise, with its limiting consequences.'[43] At the

41. Ibid., pp. 20, 20–21.
42. 'The Modern Universities,' xii, 1 (Winter '43), pp. 59–64.
43. *Education and the University* [1943], London 1948, pp. 9–11.

same time, however, Q. D. Leavis's concurrent studies of English academic *mores* provided a sardonic commentary on the likely fate of optimists.

Her essay on 'The Discipline of Letters' was a comprehensive and unrestrained assault on the intellectual and social character of traditional English studies, instigated by the publication of the *Letters* of G. S. Gordon.[44] These documents, among the few that he left, were now of some importance, she believed, 'for if any educational reform as a whole is to be achieved in this country after the war – and everything suggests that attempts in that direction will be made – it must centre on the universities, and there on the humanities.' Gordon was an outstanding example of academic reaction, as his Inaugural Lecture of 1923, *The Discipline of Letters*, made plain: 'as late as 1923 Gordon, who evidently lived in a literary backwater, was unaware of any challenge to what he stood for.' The 'discipline of letters' was incarnated in Oxford English, a combination of linguistics and the unwearying pursuit of the perfect text; the suggestion that English should replace Classics as a serious cultural study was 'an affront to life'. But between this early pronouncement and his *Poetry and the Moderns*, delivered from the Oxford Chair of Poetry in 1934, 'the deluge had occurred, as far as literary criticism [was] concerned'. That lecture, with its cheap appeals to 'the stock responses of the herd' was one missile in 'the academic war against contemporary poetry and literary criticism which [raged] from about 1925 for a dozen years or more'. Gordon had been formed by Raleigh, Oxford's first Professor of English, who, in a manner exactly the reverse of Leslie Stephen's, had prized collegiate comfort and traduced his intellectual responsibilities; and it was from him that Gordon had inherited his distinctive tastes, disinterested scholarship and good mixing. In the social-academic caste that he represented, these normally went together: 'its social standards and its conventional literary and cultural values

44. XII, 1 (Winter '43), pp. 12–26. Gordon came to Oxford from Glasgow as 'a brilliant classic,' but eventually, under Raleigh's influence, gravitated towards English – 'notoriously the prerogative of your classic (generally of your not-good-enough classic)'. He was successively English Fellow at Magdalen, Professor of English at Leeds, Raleigh's successor in the Merton Chair at Oxford (1922), President of Magdalen (1928) and finally, from 1934, Oxford Professor of Poetry. His extra-curricular interests included membership of the Selection Committee of the Book Society.

are only different aspects of the same mentality.... This "mode of life" has a vested interest in the profession of letters identical with its economic interests.... The Discipline of Letters is seen to be simply the rules of the academic English club.' And there, she declared, lay Gordon's value to his class.[45] (In the same way, David Cecil's *English Poets* presented 'not judgments of literary criticism but gestures of social solidarity – the only kind of criticism that isn't Bad Form'.)[46] It was essential for the survival of English studies, she argued, that the Gordons be evicted from their strongholds. Otherwise, 'an impatient revolutionary movement in education, the new order that is more than likely to follow the peace, will be tempted to send the whole system down the drain, not only the academic club but the humanistic studies that they have discredited.... There is no future for an order that is incarnated in a Gordon; and it deserves the fate it has invited.' She demanded a 'new deal for English', including a complete break with 'the classical-scholarly tradition' and a radically interdisciplinary approach of the kind adumbrated by her husband.[47] However, she did not share the ostensible optimism of *Education and the University*: 'can anyone be so optimistic as to believe that any university reform less violent than a bloody revolution would make such a programme possible?'

In another 'academic case history' written around the same time, Q. D. Leavis described the long struggle to establish Anthropology as an academic subject at Cambridge, and the treatment suffered by the chief protagonist, A. C. Haddon, and his associates. Again she attacked the ethos of the scholar-gentleman, the methods of professorial *Realpolitik* and 'the forces of native stupidity reinforced by that blind hostility to criticism, reform, new ideas and superior ability which is human as well as academic nature', and lamented the passing of the freelance lecturing system which in the past had provided opportunities for innovators like Haddon, but which had now been replaced by a system of closed, self-perpetuating Faculties, jealous of their prejudices and vested interests.[48] She concluded with a reflection

45. Ibid., pp. 18, 19–20. She instanced his 'deplorable' reaction to the General Strike of 1926 (*Letters*, pp. 181–3).

46. Ibid., p. 21.

47. Ibid., pp. 23, 24–6.

48. 'Academic Case History,' XI, 4 (Summer '43), pp. 305–10, at pp. 307–8, 309.

on the case of S. H. Ray, a dedicated and original Oceanic linguist whose only official recognition had been an MA. 'When one thinks how much money there was to dispose of in the universities, where comfortable livings seem to have been available for so many insignificant scholars and posts for so many without vocation, where young men have so freely been elected into fellowships on promissory notes that have not by any means invariably been honoured, and where, in short, the most casual glance round would reveal a number of people who seem to have no reason for being supported with income and status except their strong sense of their right to be – the tragedy of a Ray seems unnecessary.'[49]

The associations of this passage are not spurious. This series of articles on academic life, beginning in the late thirties with essays on Sayers and Stephen and continuing with these studies of Haddon and Gordon, were in fact so many parables, telling of the ways of the academic world and the fate of the 'moral hero' abroad in it. The first and last, both set in Oxford, depicted the reign of intellectual corruption; the second and third, the efforts of principled Cambridge innovators and the obstinacy and ingratitude with which they had been met – Stephen had preserved his intellectual integrity only at the cost of forsaking collegiate life for a career in critical journalism; Haddon had retired in 1925, after twenty years of struggle and nearly a decade before the foundation of a Chair in his subject; Ray, deprived of support during his working life, had remained an assistant elementary schoolmaster in London's East End, and been fobbed off in the end with a piece of parchment. Together, these essays formed a sombre record of defeat, and an early and eloquent warning of the fate of the 'Sketch for an English School'.[50]

49. Ibid., p. 309.
50. F. R. Leavis actually accepted the appellation of 'moral hero', though in a typically oblique way. Recalling the hostility aroused by his early polemics in *Scrutiny*, he wrote: 'an advanced Cambridge intellectual, who had the art of being advanced without offending anyone, and of being anti-academic while remaining academically respectable, said to me, I remember, at about the same time, with quiet admonitory irony: "*I* am not a moral hero." ' (*Scrutiny: A Retrospect*, p. 3). Q. D. Leavis has stated that the 'advanced Cambridge intellectual' was I. A. Richards (interview, March 1976).

III

The topical composition of *Scrutiny*'s literary criticism remained much the same during this period. Its basic elements were the literature of late-medieval and early modern England, modern English-language literature, and their counterparts in the literature of continental Europe; and both within and beside the essays devoted to these topics, the defence and illustration of 'genuine literary criticism' remained a prominent concern. At the same time, however, there was a notable alteration of proportion. Enright's and Traversi's contributions, on German and Italian literature respectively, augmented Turnell's ongoing studies in French literature, giving the journal's criticism a more international coloration. Medieval topics began to gain in importance, and there was a slight recession of interest in contemporary literature. But more striking than any of these was the major shift of critical attention from poetry to the novel. In the pre-war phase, poetry accounted for more than half of all essays on literature, the novel for less than a fifth; between 1940 and 1945, the representation of the novel nearly doubled, to claim more than a third of all essays on literary topics, while that of poetry fell by over forty per cent, accounting now for rather less than a third of the whole.[51]

The seventeenth century was represented almost exclusively by its drama, and that, by the plays of Shakespeare. Knights's essays on Bacon and on Herbert, and Enright's on Jonson, formed a small minority in a five-year period that saw nine studies directly or indirectly concerned with Shakespeare – one each on *As You Like It*, *Hamlet* and *Henry V*, two on *Cymbeline*, three on *Measure for Measure*, and one more general discussion of tragedy that took Shakespeare as its touchstone. The foremost common preoccupation of these essays, as of their predecessors in the early phase, was what might be termed

51. Representation of the novel increased from 18% to 35% approximately, while that of poetry fell from 58% to 32% approximately – respectively, a growth of around 94% and a decline of around 45%. Meanwhile, representation of drama increased from 24% to 33% approximately. In the reviews section, there was a small proportional decline in coverage of the novel (33–30% approximately) and a modest increase in that of poetry (62–70% approximately).

the 'moral sociology' of the seventeenth century, and its general significance.[52] Thus, according to Enright, the *leitmotiv* of Jonson's drama was ' "spiritual modesty", or the acknowledgement by the individual of his proper and ordained position in the universe'; and the chief object of its satiric 'indignation' was 'the extravagant assertion of the individual self', of which 'the economic capitalism of the era was the nearest and most outstanding example'. The plays treated this antagonism between individualism and order in a series of deepening gravity and within a constant narrative pattern of 'crime and punishment'.[53] The terms in which Knights analysed *Measure for Measure* were essentially the same; but in this case the antinomy between impulse and restraint, liberty and law, was seen as invading the moral core of the play, engendering an ambiguous idea of authority in which justice and expediency mingled uneasily. In this, Knights argued, it was the product of a transitional society: descended from the old Moralities, it was deprived by social change of their steadiness and clarity of moral perception, and thus of the possibility of resolution.[54] A. A. Stephenson's criticism of *Cymbeline*, in contrast, located the problem of the play in its 'relentlessly' uniform and abstract imagery of commerce, exchange and assay. In representing 'an ideal perfection, an absolute value', which coincided with 'the attainment of a harmonized experience', *Cymbeline* emptied itself of antagonism, of development and thus of time, to arrive at an essentially undramatic stasis.[55]

The second major theme of *Scrutiny*'s work in this area was Shakespeare criticism itself; and it was here that the stress of F. R. Leavis's contributions fell. 'The Greatness of "Measure for Measure" ', his reply to Knights's essay, was largely a defence of the play's moral

52. James Smith's ' "As You Like It" ' (IX, 1, June '40, pp. 9–32) was, characteristically, literary criticism of a relatively 'technical' variety; so too, rather less characteristically, was L. C. Knights's 'Prince Hamlet' (IX, 2, September '40, pp. 148–60).

53. 'Crime and Punishment in Ben Jonson', IX, 3 (December '40), pp. 231–48.

54. 'The Ambiguity of "Measure for Measure",' X, 3 (January '42), pp. 222–33. Derek Traversi's analysis of the play, written without knowledge of Knights's, discussed the theme of ' "liberty" in its relation to the moral order' (' "Measure for Measure",' XI, 1, Summer '42, pp. 40–58).

55. A. A. Stephenson s.j., 'The Significance of "Cymbeline",' X, 4 (April '42), pp. 329–38. This essay was among other things a criticism of an earlier essay on the play by F. C. Tinkler (' "Cymbeline",' VII, 1, June '38, pp. 5–20).

design; but it was also concerned to establish the reasons for Knights's divergent conclusions. In effect, Leavis argued, his colleague had failed to analyse the text itself in an adequate manner, but instead 'imported' extraneous considerations; implied a hypostatized separation of technique ('mere arbitrary theatre-craft') and moral-thematic pattern ('the essential design'); and been led astray by a naive conception of character, so aligning himself with the 'bad prepotent tradition' of Shakespeare criticism. The resulting arguments were especially surprising, Leavis commented, coming from 'the author of *How Many Children Had Lady Macbeth?*'; for they stemmed from 'that incapacity for dealing with poetic drama, that innocence about the nature of convention and the conventional possibilities of Shakespearean dramatic method and form which we associate classically with the name of Bradley'.[56]

Shakespeare, the criticism of his plays and the general issue of Tragedy were commingled in the meditations of 'Tragedy and the Medium', one of Leavis's most important essays on the relations between the poetic and the moral.[57] The purpose of the essay was to counter the arguments of Santayana's 'Tragic Philosophy' (published by *Scrutiny* in March 1936), which had contrasted the art of Dante and Shakespeare, relating the intentionally 'transparent' language of the one to his prior philosophical commitments and the predominantly suggestive ('rich and thick') language of the other to his lack of a 'previously defined' position. To argue in this way, Leavis objected, was to misapprehend 'the poetic – and the essentially dramatic – use of language that Shakespeare's verse supremely exemplifies'. For, rather than 'a "medium" for "previously definite" ideas', this use of language was one that 'created' what it 'conveyed': its essential process was not 'statement' but 'enactment'. Santayana was aware of the relation between Shakespearean language and the tragic, but, perceiving the former as 'exuberance', was drawn to define the latter as a mode of catharsis; thus, to challenge his conception of language was, implicitly, to question the conception of Tragedy that accompanied it. The main source of Leavis's counter-argument was a text from Lawrence. Citing the novelist's diatribe against the modern

56. x, 3 (January '42), pp. 234–47. See also Leavis's reply to Stephenson: 'The Criticism of Shakespeare's Late Plays: A Caveat,' x, 4 (April '42), pp. 339–45.

57. xii, 4 (Autumn '44), pp. 249–60.

'state of disintegration wherein each separate little ego is an independent little principality by itself', he wrote: 'it is an essential part of the definition of the tragic that it breaks down, or undermines and supersedes, such [individualist] attitudes. It establishes below them a kind of profound impersonality in which experience matters, not because it is mine – because it is to me it belongs or happens, or because it subserves or issues in purpose or will, but because it is what it is, the "mine" mattering only in so far as the individual sentience is the indispensable focus of experience.' The tragic awareness was one that reached coherence at the highest pitch of 'impersonality', and, as such, was attainable only through that complexity of 'organization' whose mode was the poetic use of language. Leavis went on to elaborate his theme, calling on Shakespeare and on Rosenberg, on Yeats's view of Tragedy and, uneasily, on the Nietzschean notion of the Dionysiac; and finally, in a passage that was both a further specification and a final verdict, to discuss the apparently similar conceptions of I. A Richards's *Principles of Literary Criticism*. Here too, 'impersonality' and Tragedy were intimately associated, and Richards's definition of Tragedy as 'perhaps the most general, all-accepting, all-ordering experience known' was evidently close to Leavis's own. However, in asserting that the experience could be 'given by a carpet or a pot or a gesture as unmistakeably as by the Parthenon, . . . through an epigram as clearly as through a Sonata', Richards's theory reached an impasse that was ultimately the impasse of his neo-utilitarian psychology, with the evasions that that entailed. 'This may seem, so late in the day, too obvious a kind of criticism to be worth reiterating,' Leavis wrote; 'but I want to give it a special point in relation to my main argument. No theory of Tragedy can amount to more than a blackboard diagram, a mere schematic substitute for understanding, unless it is associated with an adequate appreciation of the subtleties of poetic (or creative) language – the subtleties that are supremely illustrated in the poetry of Shakespeare.'[58]

At the end of the thirties, *Scrutiny*'s foreign-language critical repertoire was extended to include German and, secondarily, Italian literature.

58. The quotation from Lawrence came from the *Letters*; those from Richards, from *Principles* (second ed., 1967), pp. 194, 195.

The chief *differentia* of Enright's German studies, already mentioned, was their express awareness of a cultural context vitiated by the chauvinism of wartime, and an associated, more technical concern with problems of translation and presentation.[59] In other respects, in range and thematic stress, they showed definite elective affinities with the journal's English-language interests. Hölderlin, 'a genuinely philosophical poet', was compared with Wordsworth; and Rilke, whose preoccupations with continuity and the responsibility of the individual for and to the cultural heritage were described in terms strongly reminiscent of *Scrutiny*'s, found ready sympathy for his alienation from 'a world where the tools of living come from Woolworth's and hardly last long enough to acquire the aura of tradition'.[60] In 'Stefan George and the New Empire', the two aspects of Enright's criticism were explicitly united. George was 'a truly fine poet', he wrote, who communicated 'in very telling fashion certainly reasonably traditional ideas of mental and emotional vivacity, of good taste united with a proper regard for the instinctive springs of life'; in this, he was the superior of England's pallid and 'abstract' Aestheticists. Suspicions concerning his 'shaky political views' were unfounded, Enright insisted. He emphasized the poet's remoteness 'from any organized political or ethical programme' and 'refusal to cooperate' with Hitler's government. The Nazi exploitation of George's poetry was not something for which the poet himself could be blamed, and in any case involved a 'deliberate misapplication of his ideas'. What these ideas actually represented was 'a milder, more dignified Nietzscheanism. Nietzsche attacked the decadence of society with the pungent wit of an Elizabethan pamphleteer, whereas George condemned its aimlessness with strong scornful words, always a little aloof, for he lacked that streak of energetic hopefulness which runs through *Also Sprach Zarathustra . . .*'. And besides, Enright observed, 'it is an ill-boding omen that any philosophizing, however vague, which desiderates cultivation of the spirit and accepts the inevitable exclusion of the majority should these days immediately come under suspicion of fascism'.[61]

59. See 'Rilke and Hölderlin in Translation,' XII, 2 (Spring '44), pp. 93–104; 'Tristan and Isolt,' XII, 4 (Autumn '44), pp. 302–8; and 'J. B. Leishman and the Art of Translation,' XII, 4, pp. 282–91.

60. 'Hölderlin: Poet of the Gods,' XI, 2 (December '42), pp. 158–60; 'Rilke and Hölderlin in Translation,' pp. 97, 98.   61. XII, 3 (Summer '44), pp. 162–71.

Traversi's studies in Italian literature were fewer and less sustained than Enright's on that of Germany, and seemed less conscious of the adverse pressures of cultural chauvinism. They were, however, more obviously congruent with *Scrutiny*'s main lines of analysis and argument. His essay on Giovanni Papini, published early in 1939, concentrated on a literary-sociological analysis of fourteenth-century Italian culture – 'Boccaccio's prose is the expression, vigorous and assertive, of the prosperous middle-class life of the Italian cities. . . . One has only to compare his prose with Dante's, on the one hand, and with that of the medieval chroniclers and *novelle* on the other, to see that his work represents something new in Italian literature.'[62] His unfinished essay on 'the development of modern Italian poetry' traced the historically determined specificities of the Italian language and the native literary consciousness of them, discussing the poetry of Leopardi and Carducci, and going on to analyse the dispersal of the classicist and humanist tradition under the impact of nationalism.[63] One major representative of that tradition was Manzoni, who was 'classical' in being 'firmly established in an artistic tradition and fully conscious of unquestioned moral standards'. And the achievement of his *Promessi Sposi*, Traversi argued in his study of the novel, was to have braved 'the threat of anarchy' – 'personal anarchy due to the absence of objective sanctions for his moral instincts, and social anarchy proceeding from the lack of any rational check to destructive self-interest'. His significance lay in his attainment of 'personal coherence', of a balance between the moral and the social, 'in the light of Christian teaching'.[64]

Traversi's closest intellectual affinities in this context were with Martin Turnell – his fellow-contributor in the Catholic-Right quarterly, *Arena* – whose essays on French literature remained the centrepiece of *Scrutiny*'s foreign-language critical work during the war. Turnell's 1940 'Postscript on Verlaine' set out to redeem the poet from those aspects of his work which had commended him to the

62. 'Giovanni Papini and Italian Literature,' vii, 4 (March '39), pp. 415–25, at p. 418.
63. 'The Development of Modern Italian Poetry (i),' x, 2 (October '41), pp. 143–56. The indicated sequel or sequels to this essay never appeared in *Scrutiny*.
64. 'The Significance of Manzoni's "Promessi Sposi",' ix, 2 (September '40), pp. 131–48.

artists and critics of the nineties. Verlaine's 'nineteenth-century trappings', he argued, 'concealed, and nearly succeeded in stifling, a genuine folk-poet, a direct descendant of an almost extinct race.' The poet's deepest affinities were with 'the anonymous writers of the middle ages (who used an almost identical verse-form)'; and 'it was because he belonged, properly speaking, to a line that was anterior to literary nationalism that his verse appeals so directly to English as well as to French readers.'[65] Meanwhile, Turnell continued his work on classical drama with the study of *Athalie* and further articles on Racine in the Catholic *Tablet* and the newly-founded *Horizon*.[66] The themes of these essays came under attack in *Scrutiny* in early 1941, when R. C. Knight wrote accusing Turnell of 'misrepresenting' the dramatist. Knight disputed their portrayal of Racine as critic of 'a moral chaos resulting from the dissolution of a Catholic world-order which Mr Turnell idealizes'. What the latter represented as a façade concealing progressive social and moral disequilibrium was in fact a positive decorum, shared by Racine and the milieu in which he worked.[67] Turnell appeared undisturbed by this criticism. His essay on *Phèdre*, which appeared some three years afterwards, showed no alteration in his terms of argument, and, indicating the direction of Racine's subsequent work, drew conclusions which implicitly reaffirmed the positions of the essay on *Athalie* that had drawn Knight's fire.[68] His only other contribution on the French classical drama of the seventeenth century was an essay on 'the greatest of Molière's plays', *Le Misanthrope*, of which he concluded: 'the "message", if we must have one, is that we must have the courage to create our own "order", whatever the cost, instead of yielding to the temptation of an easy escape.'[69]

The controlling historical theme of Turnell's criticism – the inexorable inner atrophy of a late-feudal Catholic order through the agency of corruption and excess – persisted into his writings on the novel, which began to appear in *Scrutiny* as the series on classical drama

65. IX, 3 (December '40), pp. 249–58.

66. ' "Athalie" and the Dictators,' VIII, 4 (March '40). This essay has already been discussed, p. 141 above.

67. 'The Politeness of Racine,' IX, 4 (March '41), pp. 323–33.

68. ' "Phèdre",' XII, 4 (Autumn '44), pp. 271–81.

69. ' "Le Misanthrope",' Parts 1 and 2, XI, 4 (Summer '43), pp. 242–58, and XII, 1 (Winter '43), pp. 27–34.

neared its end. It was appropriate, then, that the first novelist to be treated in this new series should have been the Comtesse de La Fayette, an almost exact coeval of Racine, and the novel in question, 'the finest of the seventeenth century', a work almost exactly contemporary with *Phèdre* – *La Princesse de Clèves*. The main burden of the novel, as of all her writing, he wrote, was 'the disruptive influence of sexual passion on society'; the story it told was of 'feverish underground activity going on beneath the tranquil polished surface of society'; and the ethos in which its action unfolded was one ruled by a precarious lay morality in which 'the common virtues' retained their position but no longer with the support of 'traditional sanctions'. *La Princesse de Clèves* was 'a searching criticism' of this world, of 'a highly civilized and to a great extent a homogeneous society which nevertheless contains within itself the germs of its own dissolution'. It was also, in Turnell's opinion, 'a warning we should do well to heed'.[70] The second novel studied by Turnell – this time a work of the early nineteenth century – was also concerned with 'an order which is disintegrating from within.' Benjamin Constant was for him a 'champion of civilization and the natural order, . . . the intellectual aristocrat, the remorseless critic of a sham nobility'; and 'the fate of the natural human being in an unnatural society [was] one of the central themes of *Adolphe*'. Turnell saw Constant's novel as the first great response to a new historical condition, 'the disintegration of the unity of the individual in a hostile environment' – superior to Balzac's 'artificial' unities of character or to Flaubert's 'emptiness', a touchstone of modern novelistic attainment.[71]

Scrutiny's interest in contemporary literary culture and its immediate social circumstances did not lapse in this period. Q. D. Leavis used the occasion of Edwin Muir's *The Story and the Fable* and George Orwell's *Inside the Whale* to reiterate *Scrutiny's* analysis of 'Bloomsbury' culture, presenting the former as the anti-type of its social-intellectual presumption, and the latter, with his 'special kind of honesty', as one who, having originated in that privileged circle, had nevertheless transcended it and 'grown up'. Looking at the 'little world' of Bloomsbury,

70. 'The Significance of the "Princesse de Clèves",' x, 3 (January '42), pp. 256–71.
71. 'Benjamin Constant and "Adolphe",' xi, 2 (December '42), pp. 125–45.

she wrote, 'one can see the kind of pressure to which the *Criterion* succumbed early on in its career and why the literary side of the *New Statesman* was foredoomed'.[72] At the same time, the United States was still seen as providing at least some elements of a cultural alternative: recommending Edmund Wilson's *The Wound and the Bow*, F. R. Leavis noted that the constituents of the volume had first appeared in the *New Republic*, and asked: 'what could one find in an English journal that would bear reprinting as well – or at all?'[73] However, none of these themes was as prominent in *Scrutiny* during the war as in the thirties. They were muted now, in the slight but general recession of interest in contemporary literary activity brought about in part by the material restrictions and privations of wartime and in part by what was now almost a habit of disappointment.[74]

Amidst the crowded literary history of the thirties, Leavis wrote in his 'Retrospect of a Decade', only the appearance of *The Root and the Flower* and the discovery of Rosenberg were of real significance.[75] In his review of *Between the Acts*, he dwelt on Virginia Woolf's 'failure to develop', singling out *To the Lighthouse* as the only artistically successful product of a career that had gone astray for want of critical guidance.[76] In his journal, two poems by Ronald Bottrall ('Farewell and Welcome' and 'Evidence Evalued') were the only reminders of an aspect of editorial policy that had all but lapsed.[77] The after-life of literary Marxism was monitored by R. G. Cox, in reviews of the periodical *Folios of New Writing* that were seldom more than lenient and most often dismissive. His interest was briefly quickened by a debate in its pages over the role of the writer in society (involving, among others, Woolf, Orwell, Upward and MacNeice), but his judgment on the literary art of the *Folios* was unhesitatingly negative: 'the "poetical renaissance", which began with the publication of Auden's best work in 1930, has petered out in vapid mannerisms and stale clichés.'[78]

72. 'The Literary Life Respectable,' ix, 2 (September '40), pp. 170–76.

73. 'An American Critic,' xi, 1 (Summer '42), pp. 72–3.

74. See F. R. Leavis, 'Retrospect of a Decade,' ix, 1 (June '40), pp. 70–72; and idem, 'After Ten Years,' x, 4 (April '42), pp. 326–8.

75. 'Retrospect of a Decade,' p. 71.

76. 'After "To the Lighthouse",' x, 3 (January '42), pp. 295–8.

77. xi, 1 (Summer '42), pp. 17–22; xi, 2 (December '42), pp. 82–4.

78. ' "New Writing" in the Thirties,' ix, 1 (June '40), pp. 73–5; rev. *Folios*, ix, 3 (December '40), pp. 286–8; 'The Thirties' Reply,' x, 2 (October '41), pp. 189–93. The statement quoted above appears in the first of these; the debate is discussed

Cox's verdict might have been transposed into any of a large majority of his collaborator's poetry reviews. Eberhart was exempted from the general condemnation, as were Frederick Prokosch and Hugh Mac-Diarmid;[79] but Spender, Day Lewis, MacNeice and Dylan Thomas met unsparing criticism.[80] Auden's reception differed mainly in its greater emphasis on the conditions that had thwarted his talent. Commenting on Francis Scarfe's *Auden and After: the Liberation of Poetry 1930–41*, Leavis insisted that the 'liberation' had in reality been 'from all critical inhibition: standards are out of sight and out of surmise'. He reiterated his judgment on the 'intellectual and spiritual hobble-de-hoydom' of the milieu that had been able to 'arrest even a real talent [like Auden's] at an embarrassing stage of immaturity', but this time with an express sense of futility. Direct attacks on that 'corporate ethos' were now pointless, he decided. To those who had taken heed of them, the arguments were by now commonplace; and those who in the thirties had orchestrated 'the gang-war response' to *Scrutiny*'s 'tactful' criticisms had ceased to listen.[81]

There remained the commanding figure of Eliot. As editor and critic, Eliot was viewed with regretful but blunt disfavour by *Scrutiny*. Q. D. Leavis ascribed the failings of the *Criterion* to the debilitating influence of 'Bloomsbury'; R. O. C. Winkler mourned the eclipse of the early 'empiricist' criticism by doctrinally induced generalization and abstraction; and Boris Ford deplored his having 'lowered himself' to sponsor the verse of Kipling, the 'embodiment of a world that it has become so imperative to alter'.[82] But all these lapses and transgressions were cast into deep shadow by the appearance, between 1940 and 1942, of the second, third and last of the *Four Quartets*. Harding had

---

in the second and last. *New Writing* (1–5, 1936–38, and N.S., 1–3, 1938–39) was succeeded by *Folios of New Writing* in 1940.

79. See, respectively, W. H. Mellers, 'Cats in Air-Pumps (or Poets in 1940),' IX, 3 (December '40), pp. 289–300; T. R. Barnes, 'Poets in Wartime,' IX, 4 (March '41), pp. 374–80; and John Durkan, 'Hugh Mac Diarmid,' XII, 1 (Winter '43), pp. 72–3.

80. See, for Spender and Thomas, W. H. Mellers, 'The Bard and the Prep-School,' IX, 1 (June '40), pp. 76–80; for Day Lewis and MacNeice respectively, Barnes, 'Poets in Wartime,' and R. G. Lienhardt, 'Louis MacNeice,' X, 1 (June '41), pp. 91–3; and for Spender again, D. J. Enright, 'Ruins and Warnings,' XI, 1 (Summer '42), pp. 78–80.

81. 'The Liberation of Poetry,' XI, 3 (Spring '43), pp. 212–15.

82. See Leavis, 'The Literary Life Respectable,' p. 173; Winkler, 'Crumbs from the Banquet,' X, 2 (October '41), pp. 194–8; and Ford, 'A Case for Kipling?' XI, 1 (Summer '42), pp. 33, 26.

hailed *Burnt Norton* shortly after its first appearance in 1935.[83] The publication of *East Coker*, some five years later, was greeted by Wilfrid Mellers as a rare warrant for cultural hope – 'it is difficult to see where else those who are concerned about poetry today are likely to find direction and sustenance.'[84] F. R. Leavis used the occasion of *The Dry Salvages* for a general discussion of Eliot's 'later poetry', examining its distinctive procedures and purposes and assessing its contemporary cultural significance.[85] And the fourth 'quartet' was greeted with rapture: 'for me,' Harding declared, in his review of *Little Gidding*, 'it ranks among the major good fortunes of our time that so superb a poet is writing.'[86] One of the main themes of *Scrutiny*'s discussions of the *Four Quartets* was the relative autonomy of the work as poetry from the religious beliefs of its author. As Leavis argued, following Harding, to conflate the two was to mistake the essential process of the poetry, which was not one of statement or illustration, but rather an exploration, carried on 'below the conceptual currency', with the aim of creating a concrete analogue of the attitudes of 'acceptance' and 'belief'. As such, it was a remarkable exhibition of concrete thought *tout court*, and a test of all ready-made intellectual positions. 'To have gone seriously into the poetry is to have had a quickening insight into the nature of thought and language; a discipline of intelligence and sensibility calculated to promote, if any could, real vitality and precision of thought; an education intellectual, emotional and moral. From such a study it would be impossible to come away with a crudely simplifying attitude towards the problems facing the modern world, or without an enhanced consciousness of the need both for continuity and for "new starts".'[87] One particular corroboration of Leavis's estimate was furnished almost immediately by Winkler, in a review on 'scientific attitudes' which graduated from conventionalism into a tacit agnosticism, sanctioned and represented by *East Coker*'s meditations on 'the knowledge derived from experience'.[88] His own

83. 'T. S. Eliot 1925–35,' v, 2 (September '36), pp. 171–6.

84. 'Cats in Air-Pumps.'

85. 'Eliot's Later Poetry,' xi, 1 (Summer '42), pp. 60–71.

86. ' "We Have Not Reached Conclusion",' xi, 3 (Spring '43), pp. 216–9. See also R. N. Higginbotham's 'Objections to a Review of "Little Gidding",' and Leavis's reply on Harding's behalf, 'Reflections on the Above': xi, 4 (Summer '43), pp. 259–61 and 261–67.

87. 'Eliot's Later Poetry,' pp. 70–71.

88. 'Scientific Attitudes,' xi, 2 (December '42), pp. 151–7.

appreciation of the poem's cultural value was given practical form with his decision to include the review-essay on the 'later poetry' as an appendix to his main strategic work, *Education and the University*.[89]

In the general field of modern English literature, between the seventeenth century and the immediate contemporary period, *Scrutiny's* critical focus now switched to the novel. This genre claimed the overwhelming majority of literary-critical essays in the journal after 1940.[90] And, as in the field of education, it was Leavis himself who most clearly signalled the new turn: his major productions in the thirties were *New Bearings* and *Revaluation*; the forties was to see *The Great Tradition* and the inception of *D. H. Lawrence: Novelist*.

The first novelist to be discussed at length in the new phase was Jane Austen. The theme of the essay that D. W. Harding devoted to her in March 1940 was her strategy of 'unobtrusive spiritual revival'. These novelistic critiques could not have been other than 'unobtrusive', he argued: for the society in which 'the people she hated were tolerated, accepted, comfortably ensconced' was, for all its shortcomings, 'the only human society she knew'. None the less, her successive appraisals of the relation between social circumstance and intrinsic spiritual worth – the 'Cinderella theme' that so fascinated her – were unwavering in their moral cogency and of undiminished relevance: the title of his essay was 'Regulated Hatred' and its object, to bring Austen to the attention of 'those who would turn to her not for relief and escape but as a formidable ally against things and people which were to her, and still are, hateful'.[91]

Some twelve months after the appearance of Harding's essay, *Scrutiny* commenced publication of a second, much longer study of Austen. This study, by Q. D. Leavis, was unusual not only by virtue of its length – some ninety pages, printed in four instalments – but

89. Second, 1948 ed., pp. 87–104.
90. Only three essays on eighteenth- or nineteenth-century English poetry were published during the war: Marius Bewley, 'Revaluations (XII): The Poetry of Coleridge,' VIII, 4 (March '40), pp. 406–20; D. W. Harding, 'The Theme of "The Ancient Mariner",' IX, 4 (March '41), pp. 334–42; and F. R. Leavis, 'Evaluations (IV): Gerard Manley Hopkins,' XII, 2 (Spring '44), pp. 82–93.
91. 'Regulated Hatred: An Aspect of the Work of Jane Austen,' VIII, 4 (March '40), pp. 346–62.

also because of its pronounced dependence on a work of traditional literary scholarship, R. W. Chapman's edition of Austen's writings. However, its main concern was 'critical' in *Scrutiny*'s sense: 'in Jane Austen,' Leavis affirmed, 'literary criticism has ... a uniquely documented case of the origin and development of artistic expression, and an inquiry into the nature of her genius and the process by which it developed can go very far indeed on sure ground. Thanks to Dr Chapman's labours we have for some time had at our disposal a properly edited text of nearly all her surviving writings, and scholarship, in his person chiefly, has brilliantly made out a number of interesting facts which have not yet however been translated into the language of literary criticism.' Leavis's purpose was to accomplish this work of 'translation', both as a practical demonstration of that 'critical' utilization of scholarship on which *Scrutiny* had long insisted, and in order to subvert the customary academic-bellelettrist account of Austen's art. Thus, in arguing, from the documentary evidence, that *Mansfield Park* had originated in the epistolary 'Lady Susan', she was mainly concerned to illuminate the immediate social circumstances in which the novels had been written, and to emphasize the conscious and exacting labour that their composition had entailed – in short, to establish them as the socially intelligible work of a 'serious' artist.[92]

A similar concern was evident in F. R. Leavis's 'revaluation' of Conrad, the first-published of the studies that later made up *The Great Tradition*. The object in this case was to redirect attention from the popularly acclaimed 'Kipling of the South Seas', the seagoing master of the 'Malayan exotic', to the conscious artist who claimed 'fellowship in craft with Flaubert'. Leavis laid ample stress on those elements, good and bad, of Conrad's work that had won him his popular renown – the vividness of description and narration, the 'glamour' and the gesturing towards unnameable 'profundities' – but the overriding concern of his 'revaluation' was with the works in which the novelist's plastic faculties were controlled by essentially moral pur-

92. 'A Critical Theory of Jane Austen's Writings,' x, 1 (June '41), pp. 61–87, at p. 61; 'A Critical Theory...(II): "Lady Susan" into "Mansfield Park",' x, 2 (October '41), pp. 114–42; '... "Lady Susan" ...(ii),' x, 3 (January '42), pp. 272–94; 'A Critical Theory...(III): The Letters,' xII, 2 (Spring '44), pp. 104–19.

poses. The canonical novels, to which Conrad owed his place in 'the great tradition', were *Nostromo* and *Under Western Eyes* – 'the two unquestionable classics of the first order that he added to the English novel . . .' – *The Secret Agent*, *Victory* and *Chance*.[93]

Leavis's evaluative criticism of Conrad was grounded in a definite conception of the novel as a literary form, whose source was C. H. Rickword's 'Note on Fiction', first published in the *Calendar of Modern Letters*. The core of Rickword's argument was that the novel was an art of *language*. To speak of it as a concatenation of 'character', 'situation' and 'incident' was therefore to misconceive its nature: what these 'speciously technical terms' signified were not separable aspects of composition, but 'secondary manifestations', 'emergent qualities', 'precipitates' of a certain type of verbal organization. The artistic value of a novel was determined not, say, by the 'knowledge of human nature' that it displayed but by its 'rhythmic coherence', which grew out of 'the writer's conception of life and the adequacy thereto of his vehicle'.[94] The effect of Rickword's theses on the novel, so clearly parallel to Knights's critique of Bradleian Shakespeare criticism, was to illuminate the substantial unity of the literary arts (as Leavis commented, introducing the 'Note on Fiction' in *Towards Standards of Criticism*, 'the differences between a lyric, a Shakespeare play, and a novel, for some purposes essential, are not in danger of being forgotten; what needs insisting on is the community'); and so, to authorize an extension of Leavis's established critical methods into the domain of the novel. Here, as with poetry, 'criticism . . . must be in the first place (and never cease being) a matter of sensibility, of responding sensitively and with precise discrimination to the words on the page.'[95] Leavis's study of Conrad, with its copious quotation and close attention to verbal texture, was a clear demonstration of this approach to the criticism of the novel. It also revealed the distinctive stress that he had introduced into Rickword's original conception. In this and in the studies that followed it, the fundamental 'rhythm', the organizing principle and basic condition of value, of the novel was the moral sensibility. His praise for *Nostromo*, for example, was of

93. 'Revaluations (XIV): Joseph Conrad,' x, 1 (June '41), pp. 22–50; '. . . Joseph Conrad (II),' x, 2 (October '41), pp. 157–81.
94. See F. R. Leavis (ed.), *Towards Standards of Criticism*, pp. 29–43.
95. Ibid., pp. 19–20, 17.

H

'a rich and subtle but highly organized pattern' that subsumed 'every detail, character and incident', a 'pattern . . . of moral significances'; and in *The Secret Agent*, a novel 'truly classical in its maturity of attitude and the consummateness of the art in which this finds expression', a 'sophisticated moral interest' was 'the controlling principle'.[96] The essential unity of the moral and the aesthetic in Leavis's thought was made manifest in a later comment on another exemplar of 'the great tradition': 'when we examine the formal perfection of *Emma*,' he wrote, 'we find that it can be appreciated only in terms of the moral preoccupations that characterize the novelist's peculiar interest in life.'[97] 'Form' was intrinsically a moral achievement. The term 'design', to which he often turned on critical occasions of this kind, conveyed his point with all possible succinctness: denoting both (aesthetic) pattern and (moral) purpose, it was a key-word not of a simply 'moralist' inflection of literary-critical 'technique', but of a rigorously sustained moral monism, in theory and in practice.

However, 'moralism' is the natural associate of moral-monist critical conceptions, and the novel criticism of Leavis and his collaborators was also, obviously and crucially, 'moralist'. The 'lesson' that it sought to communicate was made explicit in this passage from the discussion of *Victory*: 'the characteristic Conradian sensibility is that of the creator of Heyst; that of the writer so intimately experienced in the strains and starvations of the isolated consciousness, and so deeply aware of the sense in which reality is social, something established and sustained in a kind of collaboration . . .'.[98] The idea of the sociality of the individual, pervasive in all Leavis's writings and those of his co-thinkers, was the ruling theme of his novel criticism from this time onward. It was, in his view, the central insight to which the practice of criticism led, and, as he argued in a lecture delivered in 1943 at the London School of Economics, the ground of its political relevance. The study of literature, he affirmed on that occasion, was, 'or should be, an intimate study of the complexities, potentialities and essential conditions of human nature'. And what it taught, above all, was the illusoriness of the Romantic – and utilitarian – opposition between 'individual' and 'society'. The 'new recognition' to which

96. Respectively, 'Joseph Conrad,' p. 40, and 'Joseph Conrad (II),' p. 165.
97. *The Great Tradition* [1948], London 1972, pp. 17–18.
98. 'Joseph Conrad (II),' p. 164.

the critic was thus compelled exemplified 'the inevitable way in which serious literary interest develops towards the sociological'. However, he warned, this heuristic process was not reversible: 'the sociologist can't learn what Jane Austen has to teach about the part played by the family in the life, individual and social, of her times, . . . without being, in reading her, a much more intelligent critic than any professional authority he is likely to have gone to for guidance. Nor, without being an original critic, adverted and sensitized by experience and the habit of critical analysis, can the social psychologist learn what Conrad has to teach about the social nature of the individual's "reality".' The unique 'evidence' of the novel would yield only to literary criticism, and without it, 'the thinking that attends social and political studies will not have the edge and force it should'.[99] Leavis's lecture was a full and emphatic declaration of a conviction that had already been stated or implied, by himself or his collaborators, on many previous occasions. It was implicit, for example, in Harding's valuation of *The Root and the Flower*, in Q. D. Leavis's commendation of Dos Passos or, later, Koestler's *Darkness at Noon*, and patent in a passage by Henry Parkes which, although divergent in certain respects, was all the more arresting for its 'reverse' formulation of the same essential point: 'good history resembles good fiction in that it gives us the same sense of the independent and living reality of other human beings, that it presents their behaviour not as explicable in terms of scientific law but as pre-destined in terms of character and situation – an intuition which is at the root of all drama – and that the generalizations which it suggests belong – to use a trite distinction – to wisdom rather than to knowledge.'[100] The outcome of this shared conviction, particularly in the work of Leavis himself, was a distinctive compound discourse whose relation to politics was peculiarly intangible: the 'claims of politics' seemed almost obsolete in the case of a discourse on literature that was by its nature exclusively competent to determine certain fundamental social needs and realities, which performed a unique and indispensable political function simply by being itself.

It is in this light that *Scrutiny*'s critical shift to the novel can best be

99. 'Literature and Society,' xii, 1 (Winter '43), pp. 2–11.
100. Respectively, 'The Work of L. H. Myers,' iii, 1 (June '34), pp. 44–63; 'A Novel to Recommend,' xi, 2 (December '42), following p. 160; and 'The Historian's Task,' vii, 4 (March '39), p. 436.

understood. There were, no doubt, relatively autonomous critical motives for this change of course. It was now nearly a decade since the Leavises had made their separate complaints about the under-development of novel criticism relative to that of poetry, and nearly three years since Q. D. Leavis's call for a history of the English novel 'rewritten from the point of view of the twentieth century'.[101] The apparent exhaustion of the 'renascence' in poetry must also have prompted some revision of critical priorities. But technical reasons alone are hardly sufficient to explain so major and punctual a shift; and it cannot be forgotten that for *Scrutiny* the 'purely critical' was an invalid, if not unreal, consideration. What seems more likely, given all the evidence, is that the turn towards the novel that occurred in 1940 was induced by the contemporaneous change in the political disposition of the journal. For as long as *Scrutiny* remained open, willingly or not, to the possibility of an 'external' relationship between 'the minority' and politics, poetry and its criticism were in effect taken as the paradigmatic instance of 'culture'. It was only after this possibility had finally been discounted that *Scrutiny* turned to a literary form that embodied an 'internal' union of the two realms – the novel. At once literary and sociological, 'dramatic poem' and privileged mode of moral insight, the novel was a compensatory middle term, the symbolic attainment within literary criticism of a union of politics and 'culture' that had proved unattainable in history.

IV

The latter half of 1942 saw the decisive turn of the War; by the summer of 1943, the victory of the Red Army at Stalingrad, the defeat of Rommel and the involution of Italian Fascism had made eventual Allied success almost certain. In Britain, meanwhile, official blue-prints for 'reconstruction' were nearing completion: with the appearance of the Beveridge Report in December 1942, followed six months later by Butler's report on education, vague and distant images of a

101. See Q. D. Leavis, *Fiction and the Reading Public*, p. 213; F. R. Leavis, *Towards Standards of Criticism*, p. 15f; Q. D. Leavis, 'Gissing and the English Novel,' VII, 1 (June '38), p. 80. Around this time the Leavises had in mind a book that would 'deal with the grounds and methods of the critical study of novels' (see *Education and the University*, p. 126n.). No such book ever appeared.

possible future were resolved into a clear diagram of the post-war world.

As official thinking on educational reform settled into recognizable shape, *Scrutiny*'s determined optimism began to falter. Early in 1943, Knights spoke out on behalf of 'those who are profoundly dissatisfied with much of the current talk about "education for democracy" – not because they do not believe in democracy but because they believe in education . . .'. Educational reform must begin in the universities, he insisted, not only because it was there that teachers were formed, but also because, far from being more democratic, the planned society of the future would depend on meritocratic elites with enormous social responsibilities, and it was imperative that these elites be schooled in a 'humane tradition'.[102] This was an argument in the spirit of the 'Sketch for an English School'; but by the time Leavis's proposals appeared in book-form, in November 1943, the sense of opportunity that had inspired them was already fading, and little that was new or important was to be added thereafter.[103] The primary focus of *Scrutiny*'s mounting alarm was the secondary sector, where – it was by now evident – the main thrust of reform was going to come.

The Norwood Committee's recommendation that the old School Certificate should be reorganized so as to permit internal compilation and assessment of the examination instigated a debate that continued until 1947, when the General Certificate of Education was finally established. Among the earliest contributions to this debate was J. L. Brereton's *The Case for Examinations*, which argued that the competition – among pupils, teachers, classes and schools – engendered by the examination system would ensure optimum educational performance and that the system was thus 'one of the most potent instruments of progress in human society'. Denys Thompson denounced this argument, and the 'tidy planner's world' that it evoked: it was 'a portent and a warning', exhibiting 'in the educational field the vitiating effects

102. 'Education for Democracy,' xi, 3 (Spring '43), pp. 225–9; cf. Geoffrey Walton, 'How Shall We Teach?' xii, 2 (Spring '44), pp. 141–6.
103. See H. A. Mason, 'Reform It Altogether?' xiii, 3 (Autumn-Winter '45), pp. 218–24 (on Oxford Greats); F.R.L., 'For Whom Do Universities Exist?' xiv, 2 (December '46), pp. 136–7; 'A Pupil' [Q. D. Leavis], 'Professor Chadwick and English Studies,' xiv, 3 (Spring '47), pp. 204–8; J. C. Maxwell and 'Redbrick', dissenting comments on the last-mentioned xiv 4 (September '47), p. 252f.

of the doctrine of progress in its 1944 dress – the belief that all we have to do is to get the machinery right'.[104] Within the year, the time of portents and warnings had passed: by August, a new Education Act based on Butler's White Paper and providing for extensive social and administrative reforms of the educational system was in force. In 'Hail Butler!', published the following spring, Thompson spoke sourly of 'the beautiful uniformity, the inspiring equality, of Mr Butler's plan', and attacked the destruction of the 'grammar school tradition' and the 'levelling-down on which the Ministry seems bent'.[105] Later in the year, he returned to the subject. The 'monasticism' that he had once deplored in the English Public School now appeared in a more favourable light, as a prophylactic against the infections of advertising, the cinema and professional sport. The grammar schools represented an educational ideal that went beyond mere vocational training, but now, ' "pearlharboured" by the Act', were unlikely 'to maintain even their present modest level'. He went on to attack the new Act which, he claimed, had been forced into law by 'political and trade union pressure' against the better judgment of 'informed MPs of all parties'. Its positive aspects – the proposals to reduce class sizes and to raise the school-leaving age – would be overriden by its dangers. 'It is very easy to . . . lose a sense of proportion. But on the most dispassionate possible view one cannot escape the conclusion that the attack on the grammar schools – unless it is called off – will set back education everywhere.'[106]

The disaffection voiced in these short, topical pieces was to become general in *Scrutiny* after the War. For although its ideological disposition did not preclude a certain sympathy with Butler's proposals to facilitate more democratic access to education – which, after all, implied no more than the passage from a *noblesse de sang* to a meritocracy, a prospect in itself very congenial to the *Scrutiny* group – the centralization and 'levelling' of which the new Act was a symbol affronted far deeper convictions, with a grievousness that these pre-

104. 'Co-Prosperity?' XII, 3 (Summer '44), pp. 222–7.
105. XIII, 1 (Spring '45), pp. 72–3.
106. 'The Grammar Schools,' XIII, 3 (Autumn-Winter '45), pp. 230–35, at pp. 234, 235.

liminary complaints scarcely conveyed. Henceforward, educational issues were to furnish the occasion of a discourse rich in political and philosophical connotation, more elaborate and formal than any that had preceded it and unequivocally conservative in cast.

Similar developments – more oblique, inevitably, but often strikingly direct – were to occur in the literary criticism of the journal. The motives and tendencies already discerned in its discussions of the novel would become more pronounced, reaching their full amplitude in Leavis's late essays on Lawrence. The seventeenth century would be made the object of a new kind of retrospect, manifestly political in character, and would itself be drawn into a process of retrogression that ran back into the medieval era and beyond.

Four

'The Modern Bezonian'
(1945–1953)

Into the Post-War World

Scrutiny's post-war fortunes were deceptive. The normalization of civilian contacts between England, Western Europe and the United States was immediately reflected in its foreign coverage, which now seemed likely to return to pre-war levels, and also in its personnel, among whom the young Americans now coming to study English at Cambridge were increasingly prominent. With the demobilization of the Allied armies, the most obvious material obstacle to planned collaborative work was removed, and the prospect of a revitalized and enlarged 'connection' became tangible. The reputation of the journal was by now considerable, at home and throughout the English-speaking world. Demand for copies, frustrated for a time by restrictions on the supply of paper, was eventually to double the original print-order of 1932.[1]

Yet, in spite of appearances, *Scrutiny* was now passing into a crisis of organization. For as its regular audience expanded and the 'outer circle' of contributors was replenished, the crucial 'inner circle' of editors and writers began to disperse. In September 1947, Harding resigned from the board to take over the editorship of the ailing *British Journal of Psychology*; he was replaced by Mason, who was by then a colleague of Leavis at Downing College. A year later, Wilfrid Mellers left Downing, where he had been College Lecturer in Music and a Supervisor in English since the end of the War, to take up a post at Birmingham University; he resigned from the editorial board, and

1. By late 1947, the print-run was being held down to 1,000 by 'the dearth of paper' (xiv, 4, p. 259n.). At the time of closure it had reached 1,500 (speaking to C. L. R. James shortly afterwards, F. R. Leavis gave a figure of 2,500 and rising; however, *Scrutiny: A Retrospect* mentions 1,500, a figure which Leavis also gave in conversation with me in March, 1976).

was not replaced. Knights, now Professor of English at Sheffield, agreed at Leavis's request to retain titular membership of the board, but wrote little for the journal and took no part in its affairs.[2] Cox went on contributing after the War, but lectureships at Aberystwyth and then Manchester took him away from Cambridge for good. Parkes, who was now settled in the United States, wrote nothing for the journal after 1940. Chapman's last contribution appeared in 1944, Thompson's in late 1945, O'Malley's two years later, in December 1947. By the end of the decade, Martin Turnell had ceased to contribute. The most damaging blow of all came when serious illness deprived *Scrutiny* of one of its most forceful and prolific writers and most energetic organizers, Q. D. Leavis, thereby imposing a punishing threefold burden of domestic, collegiate and editorial responsibility on the only remaining active member of the old *équipe*, her husband, who was now in his fifties.[3]

These circumstances were, in F. R. Leavis's words, 'the immediate cause' of *Scrutiny*'s decline.[4] The young disciples gathered around him at Cambridge helped to fill the pages of the journal, and indeed one of the more senior among them, Marius Bewley, became an important and prolific contributor; but many of them were, like Bewley, Americans whose stay in England would be relatively short, and this circumstance alone disqualified them as the 'adequate collaborating team' on which the future depended. Moreover, it can be seen now – though it could not have been at the time – that the rising literary-critical generation in England were not, in the main, looking to *Scrutiny* for intellectual leadership, or even for a publishing outlet, but instead were writing for new periodicals like *The Cambridge Journal* or *Politics and Letters*, and especially, from 1951 onwards, *Essays in Criticism*.[5]

2. Harding had offered his resignation on at least two prior occasions, one as far back as 1941, believing that his limited role in the direction of the journal did not warrant the public title of editor, but was dissuaded by F. R. Leavis (correspondence with the author, January 20, 1978). Knights told me of his post-war relationship with *Scrutiny* in an interview given to me in May 1976.

3. See Storm Jameson, *Journey from the North*, vol. 2, p. 234f., and especially Q. D. Leavis's letter to her, quoted at length on p. 235. Cancer was conclusively diagnosed in September 1948.

4. Ibid., p. 298.

5. It would be an exaggeration to represent this *general tendency* as a categorical choice. *The Cambridge Journal* and *Scrutiny* had a number of contributors in common. *Politics and Letters* and its companion-journal, *The Critic*, published a strikingly large number of *Scrutiny* authors; however, reciprocation was very uncommon.

In any case, neither category could have replaced a practised team of writers formed in the singular cultural conditions of 'the critical revolution'.

To view *Scrutiny*'s organizational crisis in this light is to realize that it was not merely 'technical' in character and that the role of personal accident, however real and disabling, was not decisive in its unfolding. It was rather the reflection of a complex of changes, in the general politico-cultural history of the country and in the particular institutional history of literary criticism, which was now disrupting *Scrutiny*'s project, narrowing and reducing it, driving it into involution and abstraction and, in its 'militant' collaborative form, towards dissolution.

I

The third and last phase of *Scrutiny*'s career was also the period in which the basic contours – and fault-lines – of the new world political order were brought to definition. It opened with the American nuclear attack on Japan and the beginnings of the Greek civil war, and ended with the Korean armistice, the suppression of the Berlin workers' revolt by Soviet arms, and French withdrawal from Northern Vietnam – fitting parameters of an eight-year span that saw a massive extension of American political and economic power in Western and Southern Europe, the overthrow of capitalism in the East of the continent, and in Asia and Africa, a new surge of colonial revolt. In Britain, it was the period of the first majority Labour government, which, in a demure sub-plot of this global action, introduced a series of major social reforms, conceded self-determination to India and formalized the Anglo-American alliance of wartime into a 'special relationship' that was to subsist for more than a quarter-century to come.

Scrutiny's reflections on this changing political landscape were infrequent, abstract and ambivalent. Aversion from Labour's reforms was deep and lasting, at least in one section of the contributing circle, but as we shall see, it was not expressed in direct comment on contemporary politics. The Leavis circle remained by and large aloof from the cultural mobilizations of the Cold War then beginning, but this was as often as not a matter of simple omission: the promulgation of

Zhdanov's cultural policy in the USSR, which was widely discussed in the intellectual journals of the time, and the still more notorious 'Lysenko affair' of 1948, passed unnoticed.[6] On the few occasions when the broader international issues of the late forties were discussed, it was at the instigation not of movements or events but of novels.

Scrutiny's major reference in this area was the work of Arthur Koestler. As early as 1942, Q. D. Leavis had likened him to Conrad, as a novelist of 'similar creative gifts' and 'an intellectual with moral, ethical and sociological preoccupations'. *Darkness at Noon* was 'that rarest of things, a really intellectual piece of fiction which provides absorbing matter for speculation'. It was in her view 'the only plausible explanation yet offered of the Moscow Trials' and one whose 'creation in fiction' was 'invaluable particularly as there is now considerable danger that the history of the Russian Revolution, with its painful lessons for humanity, is going to be forgotten in enthusiasm for the defenders of Stalingrad'.[7] Four years later she returned to Koestler, this time to review his fictional treatment of contemporary Palestine, *Thieves in the Night*. While judging the novel inferior both to *Darkness at Noon* and to the 'classic' colonial fiction, *A Passage to India*, she argued that Koestler's account of Palestine was fundamentally more serious than Forster's of India. The former wrote 'from the underdog's point of view while Forster [was] still one of the ruling caste, even though blushing for his compatriots' bad manners'. For this reason, *Thieves in the Night* was unlikely to have comparable impact. Forster's satire was 'not unacceptable: he accused the Anglo-Indians (old style) of nothing worse than bad manners and lack of imagination. Of the darker side of British rule in India he made no mention.' Koestler, on the other hand, was 'less tactful and he is not charming'.[8]

H. A. Mason's judgment of Koestler was more qualified. He welcomed the effort of *The Yogi and the Commissar* to isolate 'the conditions of spiritual rebirth in Europe' but argued that a residually Marxist belief in historical 'necessity' and in the cultural value of scientific development had condemned it to failure. The bricolage of 'Western revolutionary humanism' and orientalism that formed its substance

6. See, for example, *Modern Quarterly*, Winter '46 and Spring '47; *Horizon*, October '46; and *Politics and Letters*, Summer '47.

7. 'A Novel to Recommend,' XI, 2 (December '46), n.p. (inside back cover).

8. 'A Passage to Palestine,' XIV, 2 (December '46), pp. 138–41.

was vague and undirected, betraying an uncertain grasp of 'the essential human values' and leading the author to a rash absolutism, both in his praise for the early days of Soviet power and in his condemnation of the latter-day USSR. Koestler was as yet only 'a partial convert', Mason decided, at 'a transitional stage' that limited 'his value as a thinker and a novelist' – but however great its failings, *The Yogi and the Commissar* was not to be compared with *Animal Farm*.[9]

G. D. Klingopulos echoed this sentiment, arguing that by comparison with the 'insular' Orwell, Koestler was 'much the more serious writer'. Yet the general thrust of his essay was sweepingly negative, effecting a virtually point-by-point reversal of Q. D. Leavis's conclusions. He began by attacking Koestler's interpretation of the Moscow Trials as an oversimplification that had more in common with 'highly-charged propaganda' than with the 'understanding and impersonality of art'. The celebrated 'intensity' of *Darkness at Noon* was in reality a kind of 'emotional bullying'. Koestler's fictional dehumanization of his enemies lent credence to the charge that he was at heart 'a disappointed commissar'. The next object of Klingopulos's attack was the 'disgruntled internationalist' blind to nationalism as 'a social positive'. Koestler was largely unaware, he maintained, 'that national feeling makes the pattern of significant differences which is Europe, that it is the focus of the most complete and intimate agreements and shared meanings, one of the disinterested ideals or "values" that Europeans will live for in the struggle of the rival materialisms of America and Russia'. Only in his portrayal of Jewish settlers in *Thieves in the Night* did he show any understanding of 'national feeling', of the rootedness of values and the fatuity of social engineering. In other respects, however, Klingopulos was deeply critical of this novel. He referred rather distantly to its passages of 'comedy – much indebted to Mr Forster but rather shrill – at the expense of British colonial life', accused the novel of attempting 'to provoke intense feelings against the Arabs' and declared: 'the Palestine affair

9. 'A Partial Convert?' XIII, 4 (Spring '46), pp. 305–11. T. R. Barnes summed up Orwell in these words: 'as far as horse-sense, honesty, and wide, unsectarian interests in economic and social relationships will lead him he will go and is well worth following.' His 'main limitation' was 'a certain bluntness of sensibility' (rev. *Critical Essays*, XIII, 4, pp. 320–21). Orwell seems to have subsisted on the very margins of *Scrutiny's* collective consciousness, unobtrusively present but very little discussed – at least in print.

is an ugly example of international expediency, and cannot even be discussed in ethical terms.' Thus, when he cited Conrad's political fiction, it was to Koestler's disadvantage, contrasting the 'fastidiousness' of the one with the 'journalistic opportunism' of the other. Koestler, he concluded, was a 'gifted propagandist', intelligent but 'thoroughly unscrupulous', and wholly lacking in the essential artistic quality of 'impersonality'.[10]

The Koestler discussion, and especially Klingopulos's contribution to it, epitomized the internal shifts that had occurred in *Scrutiny*'s discourse. The responsibilities laid upon the novel, through the commanding moral-aesthetic criterion of 'impersonality', were emphatically moral and even quasi-political in character; and conversely, it was the novel that furnished the main occasion for the journal's few, glancing allusions to contemporary politics. At the same time, the categorial status of the political was profoundly altered: political phenomena were volatilized into culture (the Europe of 1949 sublimated into a 'pattern of significant differences', the USA and USSR portrayed and equated as 'rival materialisms') and political choice was supplanted by ethical discrimination (the crisis in the Middle East shunned as a pragmatic abomination). Both in form and in substance, these essays confirmed the displacements that had begun in the early forties.

Around this time too, the general logic that they observed was finally summarized, in clear and expressly political terms – but not, as it happened, in *Scrutiny* itself. The occasion for the essay in question was provided rather by the newly-founded *Politics and Letters*. The editorial ambition of *Politics and Letters* was to unite Leavisian 'criticism'and Left politics, and it was on this general theme that R. O. C. Winkler was asked to contribute. The result, published in the journal's first issue, was 'The Critic and Leviathan'.[11] Winkler began by affirming

10. 'Arthur Koestler,' XVI, 2 (June '49), pp. 82–92.

11. The editors of *Politics and Letters* (1947–48) were Raymond Williams, Clifford Collins and Wolf Mankowitz, of whom the latter two had acquaintances in the *Scrutiny* circle at Cambridge. Other *Scrutiny* writers who contributed to it included Grattan Freyer, Lionel Elvin, R. C. Churchill, Geoffrey Walton, G. H. Bantock and F. R. Leavis. *The Critic* (1947) published D. J. Enright, Raymond O'Malley, H. A. Mason, John Peter, A. I. Doyle and, again, Churchill. Of the editorial trio, only Mankowitz (a former Downing student) contributed to *Scrutiny*.

that it was possible and necessary to reconcile progressive political positions with 'humane' and 'cultured' resistance to the 'mechanical' society of the present. He went on then to rehearse *Scrutiny's* case against modern civilization, pointing to the disruption of 'community' by industry, the marginalization and atrophy of the family in urban-industrial conditions and the emotional 'standardization' induced by such contemporary cultural institutions as the cinema. At the same time, he was insistent that these problems be confronted directly and in the terms of the present. Social retrogression was impossible. Localized attempts to preserve 'tradition' were inadequate: intellectual 'currencies', good and bad alike, would continue to circulate in the world outside, and could only benefit from the reclusion of the 'cultured' few. Furthermore, modern social forms were not wholly damaging to human relations; as well as portent-value they had potential which it was desirable to release. The real problem, therefore, was to create 'the conditions in which the efficient could be the expression of the moral'. What these conditions were and how they might be established, Winkler did not say; but the strategically central role allotted to literature and criticism was, as ever, clear. Literature was the locus of 'the moral', of the values that alone could direct 'the efficient'; the critic, *qua* critic, internalized these values, so becoming the arbiter of social good. It was not – as Winkler took pains to emphasize in conclusion – that the existing political parties were of no importance: merely that the peculiar 'politics' of criticism was ultimately decisive.[12]

The arguments of 'Critic and Leviathan' were challenged by Christopher Hill in a 'Comment' immediately following. Hill rejected the 'false antithesis' on which Winkler's analysis was based and the political conflation of Right and Left that it logically entailed. The social problems identified in the essay resulted from the historically specific relations of *capitalist* production, he insisted; and the values in whose name Winkler denounced them were equally 'not permanent and static' but historical in character. That said, he recalled 'the minority' to what he considered its true political duty: 'literary values are human values: those who cherish literary values must associate themselves with a political movement which sets human values first: or they must reconcile themselves to being the ineffective

12. *Politics and Letters*, I, 1 (Summer '47), pp. 32–9.

bewailers of a dying civilization which Mr Winkler repudiates.'[13] Hill was answered in turn by F. R. Leavis. The case put by Winkler was 'so obviously reasonable', Leavis began, that it had scarcely seemed to need reiteration; but Hill's comments had shown that this was not so. To consider values historically, he contended, was *ipso facto* to be heedless of them. 'Those of us who are concerned to preserve the continuity of a higher cultural tradition are concerned to preserve for the race the ability to draw on its most significant experience, so that political action can be in the fullest sense intelligent, and there may be some point in men and women being "potentially free to dispose of their lives", since they won't be free of traditional skill, insight and wisdom.' Literary criticism consisted in 'a trained and cultivated ability to be relevant – to see where a given kind of relevance is required and, in attending to interests and making judgments, to sustain it'; its practical, plenary organizational form was the English School, 'a higher centre of coordination, a focus of knowledge, conscience, human awareness and political will, capable of real influence in the community at large'.[14]

Very little in this exchange was substantively new. Winkler's position was based on a well-established body of argument, and his inclination towards the political Left was familiar from the thirties; Hill's criticisms were a near-replica of Morton's, made fifteen years earlier; and Leavis's rejoinder was a summary statement of all that he had been saying from his first Minority pamphlet onwards. The chief interest of 'Critic and Leviathan' was that, its own declared objectives notwithstanding, it effectively uncovered and underwrote the ulterior political logic of Harding's psychological theses on domination. Winkler's given topic was the relationship between progressive politics and 'culture'; his purpose was to establish the political relevance of the latter by showing what it could contribute to a critical understanding of society. But in arguing his case, he advanced a definition of the central social 'problem' whose effect was to undermine the logical possibility and strategic point of the relationship that he had set out to sponsor. The distinction between 'efficiency' and

13. 'A Comment,' pp. 40–42.
14. 'Literary Criticism and Politics,' *Politics and Letters* 1, 2–3 (Winter-Spring '47-'48), pp. 58–61. The Winkler–Hill exchange was also discussed by an early contributor to *Scrutiny*, Lionel Elvin, from a pro-Labour standpoint more sympathetic to Winkler than to Hill ('David and Goliath,' 1, 2–3).

'morality' – which was a specialized instance of the basic dualism of 'civilization' and 'culture' – led logically to a purely technical conception of society and an idealist conception of the means of reforming it. The economy appeared as a more or less adequate mechanism of material provision, the State as its administrative control-point and the wider domain of politics as the ground on which competing administrative options were debated and judged, while all that pertained to social relations, to 'ends' and 'values', was displaced into a transcendent 'culture' whose constituency was 'the human' and whose *modus operandi* was 'morality'. It followed, then, that the objective of truly radical initiatives for reform was not to transform social relations through political struggle but to alter the ethical posture of administration, to irradiate power with 'morality'. Politics, its social premises consigned to the realm of 'means' and its programmatic objectives sublimated into a transcendent realm of 'ends', was emptied of rationality. In this way, Winkler revealed what the circumstances of the thirties had obscured, what Harding had only, albeit clearly, implied and what he himself was even now loath to recognize: that the basic logical drive of a 'political' discourse grounded in the 'culture'-and-'civilization' antithesis was towards the categorial dissolution of politics as such, in its modern sense. It was for this reason that Hill's appeal (itself in contradiction with the criticisms that preceded it) was pre-destined to ineffectuality; and for this reason too that Leavis, showing greater consistency than either of his interlocutors, moved directly to the theme of 'the English School'.

To speak of 'political' strategy was to speak of education: that was the ulterior logic of *Scrutiny*'s discourse and the position to which Leavis had committed himself in his 'Sketch for an English School'. How had his proposals fared in the years after their first appearance in the early forties? In one sense, their reception had been very favourable. *Education and the University* was reprinted within a month of publication in late 1943. The occasion was marked by an editorial in the *Times Literary Supplement*, which expressed virtually unqualified admiration for the book and respect for its author, who 'needs no introduction to those who take literature and literary criticism seriously'. Leavis 'states his grievance, after twenty years of teaching, modestly, but surely with authority,' the editor declared; 'and his [book] deserves a wide public. Its subject, indeed, is nothing less than the mental health of the nation.'[15] In Cambridge, Leavis's authority and appeal as a teacher were growing; and by the end of 1947, just before the appearance of a second, expanded edition of *Education and the University*, it appeared to his editorial and academic colleague H. A. Mason that the strategy for 're-equipping society with the means of self-direction' was beginning to take practical shape, in the English school at Downing College.[16] Yet neither the general success of the book nor the local prestige of its author was translated into formal institutional advance. Nothing at all resembling Leavis's design was included in governmental blueprints for educational 'reconstruction' after the War; and its impact on the official bodies of his own university had been, in his own estimation, actually counter-productive: 'my *Education and the University* has never been recognized to exist, even to disagree with, at Cambridge,' he wrote in the early fifties. 'What it did was to confirm my life-long exclusion from any say in the English [Faculty].'[17]

Thus, the cast of post-war discussions of the university was increasingly abstract and discouraged. Q. D. Leavis concluded her series on 'the Cambridge tradition' with an evocation of 'Henry Sidgwick's Cambridge', a world 'where it was possible to be a moral hero and find plenty of backers', but 'already so remote as to be almost mythical and apparently almost forgotten'.[18] And when her partner returned to the subject, it was no longer to expound a programme of reform, but to denounce a fallen Cambridge where the spirits of Keynes, Russell and Moore held sway.[19] Educational policy continued to be discussed in the journal, as we shall see; but where it regained the cultural reach of the thirties and early forties, it was at the expense of

15. 'Readers and Critics,' January 15, '44, p. 31.

16. 'F. R. Leavis and *Scrutiny*,' *The Critic* I, 2 (Autumn '47), pp. 21–35. For one student's testimony to Leavis's power as a teacher, see Martin Green, 'British Decency,' *Kenyon Review* XXI, 4 (Autumn '59), pp. 505–32; and idem, *Children of the Sun*, London 1977, pp. 475–8 and passim.

17. From a letter to Storm Jameson, reproduced in *Journey from the North*, vol. 2, p. 298. Leavis's own phrase, 'the English *School*' (my emphasis), is misleading in this context.

18. XV, 1 (December '47), pp. 2–11.

19. 'Keynes, Lawrence and Cambridge,' XVI, 3 (September '49), pp. 242–6; and 'Keynes, Spender and Currency-Values,' XVIII, 1 (June '51), pp. 45–56.

all that had ever underwritten *Scrutiny*'s claim to be a cultural van-guard.[20]

II

In the area of foreign cultural coverage, however, *Scrutiny* seemed set to equal, if not to improve upon, the record of the thirties. The war had scarcely ended when the first of Mason's reports on contemporary cultural developments in France was published; and the United States now became an important focus of literary-critical and more broadly cultural discussion, much of it contributed by American research students associated with the Leavis circle.

The main objects of Mason's attention in the first two post-war years were Jean-Paul Sartre and Albert Camus, and the diffuse and hetero-clite cultural phenomenon of existentialism whose twin leaders they became, in the eyes of their swelling international audience. His main concern, in introducing these writers to *Scrutiny*'s readership, was to emphasize the artistic difficulties created by the marked association of literary and philosophical purposes in their work, and, especially in the case of Sartre, to draw notice to the strain of fashionability that he discerned in the existentialist 'movement' – his first report, written from Basle, was largely 'a comment on the way this new fashion has developed in Switzerland' and was 'offered for comparison with the mode as it develops in London'. Among the defining features of Sartre's reception, Mason reported, was a tendency to discuss his literary productions in terms of their philosophical counterparts. His own procedure, inversely, was to examine the effects of Sartre's pre-existing philosophical theses in his novels and plays, which, as literary works, could be judged only on the terms of literary criticism. It was in this sense that he contrasted *La Nausée* and *Les Mouches*. In *La Nausée*, 'philosophical speculation' functioned so as to 'integrate and vivify the whole', but in *Les Mouches*, 'the philosophical theses remain outside the play which thus lacks inner coherence'; the result was, in the one case, a novel of 'astonishing quality', in the other, a drama that was,

20. See sections 3 and 4 below.

finally, 'more like a marionette show'.[21] Mason's second discussion of Sartre amplified the misgivings of its predecessor. He spoke now of 'the fashionable craze' for existentialism in France – *L'Etre et le Néant* is by all accounts a long and difficult work: its role in the fashionable world seems analogous to that played by *Das Kapital* when Marxism was a literary fashion.' His analysis of *L'Age de raison* and *Le Sursis* followed that of *Les Mouches* in tracing the negative effects of an 'arbitrary philosophical paradigm', in this case 'the notion of liberty': 'even the existentialist who is convinced of the internal coherence of the system should feel unhappy about the internal coherence of the novels.' Mason admitted to knowing 'next to nothing' about Sartre's philosophy, and conceded, referring to the short 'manifesto', *L'Existentialisme est un humanisme*, that 'there is a strenuous ethical side to his thought which so far has not been embodied either in a treatise or a literary work'. But his expectations were not, apparently, high. Invoking the declaration of the latter work together with the notorious 'atmosphere' of the literary productions, he concluded: 'there is an active "fifth column" in the most sanguine humanist who must acknowledge the existence on a wide scale of debased living, crude relationships, lack of roots etc. Yet the notion of what fine living, human relationships, continuity might be, the ideal of a civilization is not lost.' However, ' "l'existentialisme", as a fundamental attitude in the works under review, "n'est pas un humanisme".'[22]

Camus's writings were more sympathetically received. Although 'not apparently cogent as "pure philosophy" ', Mason wrote, they represented 'an attitude towards life and death shared by many people in our times'. In Meursault, the protagonist of *L'Etranger*, Camus presented nothing less than 'the collapse of European civilization'. Yet – and in this he stood in notable contrast to Sartre – 'latent in the style' of his work were 'qualities of austerity and restraint which suggest that there is at least a *struggle* towards health and sanity'. The novel's achievement was based on 'drastic limitation and simplification', and fell short of the 'heroic and tragic' values of its author's declared 'philosophical attitude'; but 'to judge it unsatisfactory is not to deny its promise'. Mason discerned a similar promise in the *Lettres à un ami allemand* which, although flawed by rhetoric and sentimen-

21. 'Existentialism and Literature: A Letter from Switzerland,' xiii, 2 (September '45), pp. 82–98.   22. 'Les Chemins de la liberté,' xiv, 1 (Summer '46), pp. 2–15.

tality, seemed to him to imply an 'element of *active revolt*' that was absent from *L'Etranger*. 'It may be that M. Camus will now be able to present a man with these qualities, a hero who is capable of doing as well as suffering.'[23] Mason's hopes were quickened by the appearance of *La Peste*.[24] Pronouncing the new novel 'heartening', he described it as 'enacting' the 'statements' of the *Lettres*. However, he went on to distinguish between 'the novel proper' and 'the moralized fable', with critical intent. The 'myth' of *La Peste* had 'no poetic life, no richness and density, but just sufficient concreteness to carry the reflections on experience and the philosophical attitude'. In its movement towards certain positive values, the novel marked an advance from *L'Etranger*, but it was nevertheless a kind of 'handbook' suited more to 'the political leader' than to those who valued 'the novel proper'. Perhaps, Mason suggested, '*La Peste* is once again merely a *part* of M. Camus's experience?' At any rate, the case of Camus was left open – as it turned out, *sine die*.

Mason's second major theme was 'the state of literary criticism in France'; and his general estimate, like Turnell's ten years earlier, was somewhat uncertain, poised between respect for the productivity and self-possession of French literary intellectuals and dismay at the dearth of what he considered 'strict literary criticism'.[25] The outstanding general trait of French critical culture, in his view, was a fascination with ideas. Thus, 'the Marxist debate which occupied and exhausted the English literary world in the pre-war years [was] still being fought out in French periodicals', and thus too there was now an 'invasion' of the novel and drama by philosophers, and of criticism by philosophers and sociologists alike.[26] The consequence of this critical intellectualism was that 'the distracting power of . . . philosophic bias' was unharnessed, leading criticism into mistaken analytic approaches and hindering the formation of consensual judgment on the major literary figures of the present and recent past, while manifest deficiencies of 'sensibility' went unmarked and uncorrected.[27] One of the most distinguished representatives of this culture was

23. 'M. Camus and the Tragic Hero,' xiv, 2 (December '46), pp. 82–9.
24. 'Albert Camus: Difficult Hope,' xiv, 4 (September '47), pp. 306–12.
25. 'André Malraux and His Critics,' xiv, 3 (Spring '47), p. 162.
26. Ibid., p. 163; 'A Note on Contemporary "Philosophical" Literary Criticism in France,' xvi, 1 (March '49), pp. 54–60.
27. 'A Note . . .'; see also Henri Peyre's objections to 'André Malraux . . .' and

Critique, the monthly review founded at the end of the war by Georges Bataille; the achievements of its first two years formed the subject of one of Mason's last reports.[28] Mason praised *Critique* for its vigour and versatility, for its avoidance of intellectual schematism and for a breadth of international coverage that made it 'one of the most open-minded and least parochial of French periodicals': it seemed to him 'totally preoccupied with setting in motion a vigorous current of ideas and [exhibited] remarkable powers of intellectual assimilation'. And yet 'of literary criticism as practised in *Scrutiny* there is not a trace'. Value-judgments appeared as if pre-formed, and were simply asserted; reduction of literature to its constituent 'ideas' was common; close analysis of texts was almost entirely lacking; and 'more than this, a glaring failure in sensibility does not appear to disqualify a reviewer'. Accordingly, even at this peak of approbation, Mason's conclusions were ambivalent: 'I shall be satisfied if this report ... serves to arouse interest in a remarkable review – remarkable in the sense that it really fulfils the claims made in the preface to the first number. At the same time I trust I have to some extent substantiated the remarks made on various occasions in this journal concerning the difficulty of finding common ground between English and French critical journals.'[29]

Scrutiny's representation of contemporary French culture may have been ambivalent, but the relationship that underpinned it was simple: a one-way communication from elsewhere addressed to a relatively homogeneous audience whose imputed stance was that of the author, this relationship was precisely what *Scrutiny* called it, one of 'report'. The case of the United States was inevitably more complex. Here, the underlying relationship was reciprocal and two-fold: *Scrutiny* was now beginning to be known and discussed in the US, and in some quarters to be actively sponsored, so that its appreciation of American culture would henceforth have to take note of its own reception there; and just as the growth of a transatlantic reputation

Mason's rejoinder ('Contemporary French Criticism,' xv, 1, December '47, pp. 19–23).

28. ' "Critique": The First Two Years,' xv, 2 (Spring '48), pp. 137–47.

29. Ibid., p. 147.

posed the question of an American role for *Scrutiny*, so it also attracted American collaborators who, in return, would have a distinctive role to play in a circle that had previously been almost exclusively English. At the same time, the larger Anglo-American relationship that formed the context of these specialized exchanges was itself changing. The presence of 'the Columbia contingent' at Cambridge and in *Scrutiny*, at once testifying to the unspent historic prestige of English culture and signalling the rise towards effective dominance of its American counterpart, marked just one cross-current in the new North Atlantic politics and culture then emerging.[30]

The first of *Scrutiny*'s post-war Anglo-American exchanges was initiated by a notice of Knights's *Explorations* published in the *Kenyon Review* in the autumn of 1946. The occasion of Knights's book had been used for some general observations on *Scrutiny*, and it was on these that Leavis commented in a note published several months later. The *Kenyon* was 'the best of those American reviews which, published from universities, give American criticism so marked an advantage over British', Leavis wrote. And now, in the person of Eric Bentley, it had '[handed] *Scrutiny* a handsome bouquet', praising it as 'one of the best literary journals of today', ranking its literary criticism above that of Richards, Brooks, Burke or Ransom, and commenting: 'what a pity so many Americans think that the best British literary journal is *Horizon*.' However, Bentley had gone on then to criticize what he saw as the limitations of the journal. 'Of course *Scrutiny* differs as widely from *Horizon* in its intentions as [the *Kenyon Review*] does from *Partisan Review*. Indeed *Scrutiny* is the most special and specialized journal of the four. Its offering of creative literature is negligible. Its coverage of foreign literature and of non-literary matters is haphazard and of uneven quality. The number of contributors to the magazine is very small, and of the happy few only three or four seem to have a character of their own; the others use the ideas of the editors as mechanical formulas.' If none of these generalizations was flawless, all had some basis in fact. *Scrutiny*'s 'offering of creative literature' was by this time not even 'negligible'; and confinement to the

30. 'The Columbia contingent' is Richard Poirier's phrase, from a letter to the author, March 3, 1976. For the reflections of one of its members on *Scrutiny* and Cambridge after the war, and on Anglo-American cultural relations at that time, see Norman Podhoretz, *Making It*, London 1968, ch. 3. and especially pp. 76–80, 86–92.

criticism of English and American literature, organizational shrinkage and epigonism were, if not established features, among the main emergent tendencies of the journal. That Leavis was at least partly aware of these tendencies was evident in the terms of his reply. He rejected Bentley's strictures on the journal's 'non-literary' record, citing Wilfrid Mellers's music criticism in its defence, and insisted that its coverage of foreign literatures was 'less inadequate' than Bentley suggested. He returned his critic's comment on the brevity of the contributing list with the observation that 'the maintenance of any serious standards means, surely, that one can't even suppose – whatever one's illusions about oneself – that there are many possible contributors to choose from'. And to the most cutting charge of all, that of epigonism, he replied with a general defence of *Scrutiny* and its circle. The charge 'appears to us unjust, and to be based on a misconception, one encouraged by the account sedulously propaganded by our academic detractors'. In reality, '*Scrutiny* has no orthodoxy and no system to which it expects its contributors to subscribe. But its contributors do, for all the variety represented by their own positions, share a common conception of the kind of discipline of intelligence literary criticism should be, a measure of agreement about the kind of relation literary criticism should bear to "non-literary matters", and, further, a common conception of the function of a non-specialist intellectual review in contemporary England. They are, in fact, collaborators (and unpaid). Here is the explanation of the survival of *Scrutiny* for fifteen years, and (if we may say so) of the influence it has, in spite of the fierce and mean hostility of the "official" literary and academic worlds. If *Scrutiny* had had behind it nothing more positive than the idea of running a high-brow review (and our criticism of the *Kenyon* . . . is that we have been able to discern nothing more positive behind [it]), then there would have been neither influence nor survival.'[31]

Leavis's observations were followed some eighteen months later by

31. ' "The Kenyon Review" and "Scrutiny",' xiv, 2 (December '46), pp. 134–6. Bentley edited an anthology entitled *The Importance of 'Scrutiny': Selections from 'Scrutiny: A Quarterly Review', 1932–48* (New York 1948). *Horizon* (1940–49), which was edited by Cyril Connolly with the assistance of Stephen Spender, was in its last years actually dependent on US sales for its survival, and was for a time the British distributor of *Partisan Review* (see Ian Hamilton, *The Little Magazines*, London 1976, pp. 142–5).

Mason's 'Note on Intellectual Life in the USA'. This article opened in a critical key, citing a recent report by Simone de Beauvoir on the air of negativity and exasperation that seemed pervasive in New York's left-intellectual milieux, and James T. Farrell's *The Fate of Writing in America*, which complained of the progressive concentration of US publishing and the consequent elimination of small, independent enterprises.[32] However, the greater part of it was taken up by an admiring account of the new-style *Partisan Review*, which was now available in England through the agency of *Horizon*. Availing himself of the categories set out in a recent PR essay on American intellectuals, Mason defined the journal as part of the 'true' intelligentsia of university teachers and independent writers – a part which, moreover, had proved itself capable of addressing contemporary issues while avoiding the modishness and perverse oppositionism to which the 'bohemian' intelligentsia was constitutionally prone.[33] The standards maintained by the journal gave grounds for optimism, in Mason's view. For there was a 'fundamental similarity' between the predicament of the US intelligentsia and that of its English counterpart. The PR commentator had characterized 'true intellectuals' as an 'elite proletariat'; and, 'without wishing to make too much of the analogy,' Mason added, 'there does seem to be ground for desiderating among these proletarian groups, if not world-wide, at least civilization-wide unity. PR already has its contacts with Europe and within Europe with England through Mr Koestler's "London Letter". Now that a "British edition" is available we have every reason to welcome a review which, besides keeping us informed about intellectual life in the USA, in the state of abnormal poverty from which we suffer as regards literary journals, sets a standard well above the *Horizon* level.'

Mason's arguments were promptly taken up by one of *Scrutiny*'s new-found American associates, Seymour Betsky. Betsky's opinion was that *Scrutiny*'s coverage of US culture had been unrivalled in England, but that if there was to be serious exploration of the possible 'common ground' between English and American intellectuals, it

32. xv, 3 (Summer '48), pp. 222–6. De Beauvoir's account had appeared in *Les Temps Modernes*, December '47.

33. The other categories were (i) newspaper journalists and other writers for mass-circulation organs, and (ii) orthodox Communist writers such as the *New Masses* circle.

would have to improve. Its basic defect was 'a curious absence of the habit of extensive and thoroughgoing *comparison* with the English scene point for point'; and if this was to be remedied, English intellectuals would have to cultivate 'at least a modicum of the peculiar American self-consciousness, "the work of self-understanding that America seems (unlike England) to undertake with a certain verve", as Mr Mason himself once put it' – in his 1938 essay on the *New Republic*. Betsky paid tribute to 'the consistency and focused intelligence' of *Scrutiny's* 'constant attempt to fix social and cultural disintegration in England', but repeated that still more might be accomplished if, instead of using the USA as a 'symbol of all that is reprehensible in contemporary life', the journal were to undertake a serious comparative study of the two countries. America's problems were England's also, and in some areas at least, American intellectuals had been more energetic than their English counterparts in analysing them; to overlook this was to succumb to Anglocentric prejudice. At the same time, Betsky was confident that *Scrutiny's* role in American culture was potentially a major one. Its conception of 'the organic community of England's past' might stimulate America's chronically 'rootless' intellectuals to 're-read their own history with a different intent, with an added dimension, and might offer new possibilities to be explored'. In a school system where 'almost nothing at all' had yet been done to devise practical correctives to 'the commercialization of culture', the work done in English grammar schools by 'Downing trained men' would be an important source of inspiration. *Scrutiny's* conception of 'the English School' and of the 'integrating' function of the university would greatly assist students in higher education. And the instability of 'standards' in American culture could be remedied if the American critic's unmatched skill in 'technical, intellectual and social *exegesis*' were to be regulated by the discipline of evaluation – the 'collaborative standards' and agreed valuations through which the Leavis circle had 'established the critical terms and the critical climate in which fruitful discussion can take place'. Betsky was, then, convinced of the benefits of Anglo-American rapprochement on the ground of Arnoldian criticism, and suggested that 'with the increased recognition that *Scrutiny* has received in America, one might hope for livelier exchanges in the future'. Yet his parting note was one of apprehension: it might be, he feared, that both *Scrutiny* and its American counterparts were now so settled in the habit of rejection as to be disabled from cooperation.[34]

The imputation of 'complacency' came as a 'disagreeable shock' to Mason, and in his reply, he attempted to allay the misgivings that had caused Betsky to make it. He began by reminding Betsky that his original observations had been addressed to a *Scrutiny* audience, in whom a lucid recognition of the state of English literary culture could safely be assumed. He then went on to define the practical form and limits of fruitful international cultural communication in the existing state of 'civilization' and, given these limits, the particular benefits of communication with the United States. 'Our civilization', he suggested, was 'the area covered by the sales of the English, Italian, German and French language editions of *Reader's Digest*'; and within it, the system of 'interlocking directorates' that ruled English culture was dominant. The restrictions on serious and productive cultural exchange were correspondingly severe. However, 'what can still be done is, perhaps, to study the intellectual climate in the centres that characterize our civilization. The significant varieties which may be discovered not only enrich our sense of the values we strive to keep alive at home, but provide a measure by which we can see ourselves as more or less removed from an ideal "centre".' Among these centres, the most important for *Scrutiny* was the United States, which, even if it was not free of the characteristic deformities of modern literary life, had 'long since ceased to accept dictation of its values from a London group, however powerful the hold of such a group on the moulding of opinion in England'. Mason conceded that coverage of American literature had lapsed, in the unpropitious circumstances of the war and for want of suitable material, but he went on to affirm the journal's existing 'indebtedness, large and extensive', to 'the free, generous, disinterested spirit of inquiry exhibited by the best American writers', and to insist that fertile reciprocal contacts had already been established across the Atlantic. In conclusion, taking the point of Betsky's closing comment, he singled out one service that American collaborators might usefully perform. The standards of *Scrutiny*'s founding generation had been tempered by the 'shocks' of Eliot and Lawrence, and the productions of the thirties, tested against these,

34. 'Intellectual Life in the USA: Comment and Reply,' xv, 4 (December '48), pp. 278–88.

could only appear flaccid. However, 'the critical faculties are undoubtedly numbed by constant repudiation and there is a danger (which we can never safely ignore) that the emergence of genuine new talent might be overlooked. Again, the successful application of a critical method calls for increasing vigilance as the years pass. The capacity for self-criticism has its limits however resolutely practised. Why should the graftings and cross-fertilizations not come from the America one senses over the horizon?'[35]

Some of the interwoven themes and valuations of the Mason-Betsky exchange were developed in detail by *Scrutiny*'s leading American contributor, Marius Bewley. Bewley's main concern was to trace the line of 'tradition' in American culture, and the first of his 'Notes from America', published in mid-1948, was devoted to a writer whose titles to traditionality, although widely accepted, were false: H. L. Mencken. Bewley rejected Edmund Wilson's claim that Mencken embodied 'the civilized consciousness of modern America'. If 'civilized' implied a 'classical' belief in a common moral and social order and an emphasis not on society's 'lines of internal division' but on its 'organic unity', then Mencken was not 'civilized'. His criticism was, as Eliot had concluded, 'destructive and facile', and nowhere more so than in its persistent and indiscriminate campaign against the idea of 'the moral'. The vitiating effects of Mencken's amoralism were evident not only in his conceptions of art (which he described as 'beautiful balderdash') and of the cultural elite (an 'aristocracy' given over to aesthetic pleasure and 'quasi-mystical' contemplation of a meaningless universe) but even, Bewley argued, in his philology. His evaluation of idioms was morally 'anarchistic', guided only by the crude aestheticist yardstick of 'clang-tint' and characterized by an unshakeable belief in the vitality of American English. Bewley himself was repelled by the moral insensitivity of the local idioms exalted by Mencken, and rejected his attempts to rank them with those of seventeenth-century England: 'this is no fresh language, but a tired, thin-blooded language, deadly sophisticated in a popular way, and afraid to stop moving lest it should not easily get into motion again.'[36]

35. 'Measure for Measure: or Anglo-American Exchanges,' XVI, 1 (March '49), pp. 2–8.
36. 'Notes from America (I): Mencken and the American Language,' XV, 3 (Summer, '48), pp. 182–94.

Bewley returned to this theme some eighteen months later, this time in disagreement with *Scrutiny*'s first reporter of American culture, Henry Parkes, whose book, *The American People*, had just appeared. Although generally impressed by Parkes's account of his adopted culture, Bewley took issue with his idealization of eighteenth- and nineteenth-century agrarian America and his unbalanced treatment of 'the colloquial frontier heritage'. Against this, he stressed the brutalism of the old frontier society and the sadistic strain that had passed from it into the popular culture of the present. While repudiating 'a bloodless Genteel Traditionalism' as 'fatal', he doubted whether 'the main line of development' would 'stem from the frontier heritage': the valuable 'line' was the one that passed through Hawthorne, Melville and James. What Parkes revealed in his failure to appreciate Hawthorne was not traditionality of a positive kind but 'a strong prejudice in favour of a particular kind of aggressive Americanism developed in an agrarian society, and carrying on in somewhat less amiable forms today'.[37]

If Bewley was acutely aware of the contradictions of contemporary American culture, he was also confident of its overall superiority to that of England. His 1951 essay on 'Aspects of Modern American Poetry' was based on an emphatic contrast between an energetic, purposeful and optimistic America and the 'exhaustion', the 'extreme aridity and discouragement', the 'utter inanition' that prevailed in England; and his diagnosis of the English condition was more radical than any that *Scrutiny* had ever before attempted. 'The undeniable dessication of English poetry today, while it may partly spring from causes that appear remediable, is also part of a larger historical cycle. ... Trapped in their time, English poets have not been able to evolve new forms because the time has not yet provided a basis for new speech.' The terms of this explanation were nebulous, but it was clear that the causes of England's cultural predicament were to be sought in its own national history. What the pertinent aspects of that history might be, the contrasting fortunes of American culture made plain. The American poet's 'conviction of function, of important work to do, arises first of all from the material circumstances of American life, its overwhelming activity on every side, its mere physical appearance

---

37. 'The American People,' xvii, 1 (Spring '50), pp. 66–71.

of bustle and directed energy. Since the war there has been an intensification of the desire to explore and define American experience, not in itself only, but in its relations with the world. And the fact that the American poet, unlike the English poet, is not inclined to resent his present government, permits him to feel functionally associated with that experience.' This was the insistent theme of Bewley's essay, its occasional reservations notwithstanding: a Whitmanian affirmation of the American future, domestic and global. The energy of contemporary American poets was sustained by their 'relationship with a society that is in the process of undertaking new responsibilities that enlarge its historical consciousness and its sense of obligation': America's burgeoning culture was driven by its expanding political and economic power, and its success seemed no less assured.[38]

Of English literary culture itself, comparatively little was said in the later forties. *Horizon*, the leading literary journal of the day, was a regular target of critical asides, but nothing approaching the intensity of the pre-war polemics was ever directed at it, and *Scrutiny*'s amplest judgment on it, that of R. G. Cox, was also among the more lenient: 'a disappointingly unequal magazine which occasionally publishes an interesting article but which has no real policy or standards beyond fashionable eclecticism and a feeling that culture shouldn't be made to toe the party line.'[39] Leavis reported a marked improvement in the post-war *Times Literary Supplement*: he noted the 'disappearance of the anti-highbrow leaders' and commented, more generally, that although 'not all the reviews, of course are good, . . . enough of them are to make it plain that there is an intelligent and disinterested controlling purpose'.[40] This judgment was shared by Cox, but neither

38. XVII, 4 (March '51), pp. 334–52. Bewley believed that the positive momentum of American culture was strong enough to overcome its negative features. Norman Podhoretz's view was that in Lionel Trilling, America already possessed a critic wholly alive and committed to the problems of his culture: 'of *The Liberal Imagination* and of its author, it is possible to feel that they are doing for America, at least, the work Arnold himself might have done' ('The Arnoldian Function in American Criticism,' XVIII, 1, June '51, p. 65).

39. 'Mixed Currency,' XIV, 1 (Summer '46), pp. 59–60. Compare R. G. Lienhardt's comments on its editor ('From Playground to Grave,' XIII, 3, Autumn-Winter '45, pp. 224–9) and also Mason's ('Art: the Religion and the Saint,' XVI, 4, Winter '49, pp. 344–56).

40. 'The Times Literary Supplement,' XIV, 2 (December '46), pp. 133–4.

writer was disposed to impute any general significance to the improvement. Leavis still looked elsewhere, to America's university reviews and to the 'intelligently directed' Dublin monthly, *The Bell*, for exemplars of vigorous and 'disinterested' critical practice; and the moral of Cox's survey of English literary journalism since 1919 was the familiar one: 'the serious literary periodical today cannot hope for any great influence or authority and has for the most part a hard struggle to survive.'[41]

Scrutiny's enmity towards the official academic representatives of 'culture' remained undiminished, and was reinforced now by its comparable enmity towards the state-sponsored authorities who became prominent in the national culture after the war. Leavis's first anti-academic excursion after 1945 was against the English Association and its quarterly organ, *English*. Its mediocrity, he declared, furnished a retrospective vindication of Henry James, who, offered the chair of the Association in 1912, had declined it, giving as his reason a belief in 'absolutely independent, individual and lonely virtue, and in the serenely unsociable (or if need be at a pinch sulky and sullen) practice of the same . . .'.[42] James's precept was a fair description of *Scrutiny*'s actual situation – or, at least, so much could be inferred from the terms of the editors' attack on the Arts Council some three years later. The occasion of the attack was the announcement of a poetry competition to be organized as part of the forthcoming Festival of Britain; the particular object of *Scrutiny*'s disaffection was the adjudicating panel, which included such prestigious figures as Kenneth Clark, Maurice Bowra, David Cecil and Basil Willey. For one reason or another, the editors claimed, none of these nominees could be presumed fit to judge English poetry. But what other candidates were available? 'In fact, hasn't one to go back to the time of Leslie Stephen to find an England in which the qualified authorities could be counted on to be sufficiently known and respected?' Today, authentic standards were in abeyance. *Scrutiny* was systematically ignored. And yet, the editors insisted, in a curiously suspended concluding qualification, 'there is now a general recognition in all the literary centres

41. See F.R.L., 'An Irish Monthly,' and ' "The Kenyon Review" and "Scrutiny",' XIV, 2, pp. 134, 134–6; and Cox, 'The Critical Review Today: Prolegomena to a Historical Inquiry,' XIV, 4 (September '47), pp. 256–68, at p. 261.

42. 'Henry James and the English Association,' XIV, 2 (December '46), pp. 131–3.

I

of the English-speaking world, and wherever English literature is studied, that *Scrutiny*, whatever its faults and shortcomings, has for seventeen years maintained a strenuous and lonely pre-eminence in the language as representing the function of criticism.'[43]

The particular value of these scattered writings on politics, on education, on French, American and English culture, is that they revealed the general context of Scrutiny's last years of operation in a way that the more substantial specialized studies very often did not. The morality of the novel and of criticism, the character of the American 'tradition' and its affiliations with that of England: these were major themes of the novel criticism that now occupied the main tendency in the journal. The relation between morality and politics, between 'culture' and the modern State, were central to the work of a secondary tendency whose characteristic intellectual gesture was a new kind of historical retrospect. Of the general problems that shaped this work and determined the ambivalent perspective in which it was carried forward, some – like the changing patterns of Western, and especially English-speaking, culture – were obviously beyond *Scrutiny*'s capacity to control, or, without a firm purchase on contemporary politics, even to focus. Other, apparently more localized and amenable to determined action, were still more perplexing. Above all, there was the contradictory evidence of *Scrutiny*'s status in the national culture: rising sales combined with organizational depletion, peda-

43. 'Poetry Prizes for the Festival of Britain, 1951,' xvi, 4 (Winter '49), pp. 334–5. See also F. R. Leavis, 'Mr Pryce-Jones, The British Council and British Culture,' xviii, 3 (Winter '51–'52), pp. 224–8, in which Leavis rehearsed his general case against the English literary establishment. Behind this polemic lay another, never published except in a ten-page cyclostyled document prepared and privately circulated by Leavis, ' "Literary Periodicals" and the *Times Literary Supplement*'. In August 1950, the *TLS* had published a lengthy 'Critical and Descriptive Survey of Contemporary British Writing for Overseas Readers' which, in its section on 'Literary Periodicals', omitted to mention *Scrutiny* and in that on 'Literary Criticism' referred to it as advocating a 'scientific' criticism. Maurice Hussey's letter of protest was published by the *TLS* early in the next month, but Leavis's subsequent and much longer protest was not. There ensued a correspondence between Leavis and Alan Pryce-Jones, who was then editor of the *TLS*, in which the latter defended both the 'Survey' and his decision not to print the protest, all the while professing goodwill towards *Scrutiny*, and in the end dismissed the 'discussion' as 'silly'.

gogic influence that seemed only to redouble institutional isolation, a growing intellectual reputation in literary journals (and, as the editors for once admitted, in the universities) that had no observable effect on public life – in short, a victory that seemed, to those who had worked for it, more like defeat.

2

Culture and Civilization
(i): 'The Responsible Critic'

Scrutiny now became more than ever before a journal of literary criticism; and within this predominating interest, there occurred a further redistribution of attention. The defence of 'genuine' criticism remained a constant concern, and a sustained effort was made to deploy it in the one field where traditional scholarship was still dominant, that of medieval literature. Seventeenth-century English literature was represented almost exclusively by Shakespeare, who remained a central topic of critical discussion and was now more diversely treated than in the past; the literature of the eighteenth and nineteenth centuries, prose fiction apart, received very little attention, and that of the twentieth, not a great deal more. German literature continued to be discussed, but that of Italy disappeared from view, and only Mason's essays on Sartre and Camus counteracted the sharp decline in critical discussion of French literature brought about by Turnell's departure. However, this contraction of interest was only partly a result of the journal's organizational decline. It was also the result of a major redistribution of critical attention. In literary criticism as in other areas of interest, the displacements of the war years were confirmed, and now, in *Scrutiny*'s third and last phase, the proportions of the first were reversed: poetry, which before the war had claimed some fifty-eight per cent of all essays on literature, accounted for only ten per cent of those written after 1945, while the novel, over the same period,[1] increased its share from around eighteen to

1. These calculations are, as usual, per item. Taken in themselves, the novel's share increased by 239% from the first to the third period, while that of poetry declined by 82%.

sixty-one per cent of the whole. The great bulk of this critical activity was concentrated in one narrow band of English and American literary history: the nineteenth- and early-twentieth-century novel.

I

The precepts embodied in *Scrutiny*'s critical practice had as a rule been affirmed in polemical disagreement with two complementary deformations of 'genuine' literary criticism: one, the positivist concern with literary-historical 'fact', in which the question of value was either disregarded or spuriously deferred; the other, the imposition of aprioristic 'systems' of analysis and judgment whereby 'first-hand response' was stifled by 'abstraction'. This pattern of argument persisted into the later forties and early fifties, but with largely altered contents. The old antagonists of the thirties were no longer significant presences in English criticism: all but the most conservative exponents of traditional literary scholarship had reached some kind of accommodation with the 'critical revolution', which was now a full generation in the past; and interest in Marxist criticism was now confined to a dwindling and increasingly isolated minority of intellectuals. Their successors in the post-war period were the unwontedly technical forms of theory and 'explication' made current by the American New Critics, and the doctrinally-motivated criticism of Christian Discrimination.[2]

Discussion of *Scrutiny*'s studies in medieval literature and Shakespeare will be reserved for the next section, where the political and philosophical themes echoed in them are collocated.

Enright's main critical excursion in German literature was a four-part study of 'Goethe's "Faust" and the Written Word' (xiii, 1, Spring '45, pp. 11–37; 3, Autumn-Winter '45, pp. 188–99; 4, Spring '46, pp. 292–305; and xiv, 1, Summer '46, pp. 26–46). This was followed by 'Goethe's "Roman Elegies",' xv, 3 (Summer '48), pp. 174–82; 'The Case of Stefan George,' xv, 4 (December '48), pp. 242–53 – significantly more critical than its wartime predecessor – and 'The "Doctor Faustus" of Thomas Mann,' xvii, 2 (Summer '50), pp. 154–67.

2. 'The return of religion as a grouping-force of novelists and critics' was mentioned by a reviewer in the *Times Literary Supplement* as one of the defining features of English literary culture in the later forties; others were a retreat from politics and 'the assimilation and forgetting of Freud' ('Review of Reviews,' January 8, 1949, p. 32).

Scrutiny's opposition to the New Criticism was based on an unqualified refusal to countenance even the most tentative analytic distinction between 'fact' and 'value', or to recognize the legitimacy of any kind of theoretical discourse on literature, whether as part of a more elaborate social theory or in the form of a rigorously delimited and autonomous poetics. Thus, Bewley attacked Kenneth Burke's conceptual system as a 'well-oiled and metallic' apparatus built with a typically American 'flair . . . for the mechanical' from designs that owed much to Marxism and fuelled by 'a strong religious nostalgia'; even the relatively suggestive notion of literature as 'symbolic action' was suspect in its origins and useless for the purposes of evaluation; and as a prospective critical method, the system was simply self-defeating: 'any critical vocabulary so highly organized, no matter how desperately it may reach out towards flexibility, has misunderstood the nature of literature and rigidified the sensibility of the critic in certain set responses.'[3] Betsky went still further, in a scornful review of René Wellek and Austen Warren's *Theory of Literature*. It was, he said, an 'indispensable reference book for those students interested *not* in literary analysis, evaluation and tradition, but in literary "problems" '; but as a training in 'general approach and method' it was 'clearly a major catastrophe'. The essential basis of such a training was not 'profitless philosophical speculations' but 'the exacting task of first-hand judgment', of 'determining – demonstrating in particular, concrete acts of analysis and judgment – the degree of achieved realization of intention in the work of literature itself'. The *Theory of Literature* might legitimately be consulted by those 'who become interested, in the natural course of literary study, in peripheral problems,' Betsky conceded; but beyond this, it simply represented the emergence of a 'new antiquarianism' not significantly different from the old.[4] Betsky's preference was clearly for a criticism based on practical precedent – 'standards inevitably grow out of the continual effort to fix the degree of realization'. But in so far as the routine formulae in which he expressed himself suggested a codified practice, they misled; for as Robin Mayhead made plain in his comments on 'modern American critical method and opinion', there was equal

3. 'Notes from America (II): Kenneth Burke as Literary Critic,' XV, 4 (December '48), pp. 254–77.
4. 'The New Antiquarianism,' XVI, 3 (September '49), pp. 260–4.

hostility to *any* attempt to systematize a methodology of criticism. 'Although one may speak of critical "tactics" or "approach" to describe the extremely general means by which the critic goes about ordering his responses and making discriminations of relevance between them, there cannot be, properly speaking, any such thing as a *technique* of criticism.' The impression conveyed by the New Criticism, with its emphasis on 'form' and on critical 'technique', on explication and 'pattern-tracing' at the expense of value-judgment, was of 'a new academic spirit no less potent than the old, with seemingly infinite possibilities of a strangling proliferation as time goes on'.[5] Norman Podhoretz shared this estimate of the tendencies now dominant in American criticism, but was confident that in the work of Lionel Trilling, 'the Arnoldian function' was still performed for American society. 'Arnold exerted the most fertilizing kind of influence on his biographer,' he wrote. Trilling's relationship with 'his immediate cultural environment', as exemplified in *The Liberal Imagination*, was that of the 'properly Arnoldian critic'; and it was this that shaped his approach to literary criticism itself. In a situation where the once challenging New Criticism had become 'a New Academicism', Trilling was 'pretty much alone among American critics in reminding us that a return to the text must be followed by a fresh departure from the text if criticism is to come alive. And we all know where the departure leads – into society, and politics, and history.'[6]

If the characteristic defect of the New Criticism was a morally indifferent technicism, the cardinal error of Christian Discrimination and allied critical currents was to subordinate the processes of reading and judgment to a pre-formed *Weltanschauung* for which literature was of little more than instrumental value. To adopt such an approach, R. G. Cox argued, was to undermine the very possibility of criticism as *Scrutiny* understood it. Replying to S. L. Bethell's call for a literary criticism 'completed by explicit theological beliefs', he wrote: 'perhaps the real point at issue between Mr Bethell and the *Scrutiny* critics . . . is that (like the Marxists) he rejects the possibility of that working

5. 'American Criticism,' xix, 1 (October '52), pp. 65–78. The books under review included Reuben A. Brower, *The Fields of Light*, and Cléanth Brooks, *Modern Poetry and the Tradition*.

6. 'The Arnoldian Function in American Criticism,' xviii, 1 (June '51), pp. 59–65. Trilling's *Matthew Arnold* was reviewed by F. R. Leavis: see 'Arnold's Thought,' viii, 1 (June, '39), pp. 92–9.

measure of agreement about values which is implied in a living tradition, that cultural continuity which Dr Leavis has called preserving for the race "the ability to draw on its most significant experience".[7] However, this religiously-motivated criticism differed from its Marxist 'predecessor' in that it served not only to inspire partisan disruptions of 'the common pursuit' but to revitalize academic conservatism, not only to inflate the value of inferior literature but also, and more dangerously, to domesticate what was genuinely radical and new. It was the latter considerations that were uppermost in F. R. Leavis's first discussion of the subject, a review of an academic symposium on the writings of T. S. Eliot. His objections to the symposium were both historical and critical. In the first respect, it backdated Eliot's acceptance, edulcorating the true record of English literary culture in the twenties and early thirties (including the scandalizing impact of Leavis's 'pioneer book', *New Bearings*, in Cambridge) and obscuring the specific role of Eliot's 'association with religious orthodoxy' in his ascent to respectability; and in the second, its analyses were dominated by 'Anglo-Catholic' exegesis and New-Critical explication, at the expense of the evaluative process that was central to his own criticism. Taken as a whole, the symposium was an anodyne, seemingly 'calculated . . . to promote, not the impact of Eliot's genius – a disturbing force and therefore capable of ministering to life – but his establishment as a safe academic classic'. In opposition to this, Leavis reaffirmed the real originality and value of Eliot's contribution to English criticism: not the 'highly selective' and sometimes erroneous judgments of a working poet, and certainly not the pronouncements characteristic of his later work, but the lessons of *The Sacred Wood*. Recalling its formative influence in the early twenties, he wrote: '. . . if I had to characterize the nature of the debt briefly I should say that it was a matter of having had incisively demonstrated, for pattern and incitement, what the disinterested and effective application of intelligence to literature looks like, what is the nature of purity of interest, and what is meant by the principle (as Mr Eliot himself states it) that "when we are considering poetry we must consider it primarily as poetry and not as another thing".'[8]

7. 'Background and Doctrine,' xv, 3 (Summer '48), pp. 226–31.
8. 'Approaches to T. S. Eliot,' xv, 1 (December '47), pp. 56–67. The volume under review was B. Rajan (ed.), *T. S. Eliot: A Study of His Writings by Several Hands*; the

However, these lessons were lost on the practitioners of Christian Discrimination, which Leavis attacked, in a phrase borrowed from Eliot, as 'the most active and formidable of contemporary "gang-movements" '.[9] As he wrote of one of its leading propagandists, George Every: 'he shows no compelling interest in [literature], and no aptitude for its study.' Leavis listed the critical *bêtises* to which Every was led by his doctrinal commitment, and here again, one of his foremost concerns was to redeem Eliot from the stifling embrace of orthodoxy: 'to take, in any measure, what Mr Eliot's poetry has to give is to be educated into a new understanding of the nature of precision in thought, and at the same time to experience intimately an emotional and spiritual discipline. And this holds, irrespective of whether or not the reader subscribes to Christian doctrine.'[10] To put the matter in this way was to disqualify the particular claims of Christian Discrimination or any other heteronomous value-system in criticism: to recognize, as Leavis insisted in his concluding remarks on Every, that 'there can be no substitute for the scrupulous and disinterested approach of the literary critic'; that, in Cox's still more forthright affirmation – made in another context but equally apposite here – 'literary criticism is not just an alternative approach to literature, but the condition of discussing it relevantly at all.'[11]

II

Very little of *Scrutiny*'s critical energy was any longer expended on English poetry. Between 1945 and 1953, only four articles were devoted to the pre-twentieth-century corpus. The first of these, by Harding,

---

contributors included M. C. Bradbrook, Helen Gardner, Cléanth Brooks and Wolf Mankowitz.

9. 'The Logic of Christian Discrimination,' xvi, 4 (Winter '49), pp. 339–44.

10. Ibid., p. 334. This was a constant theme in *Scrutiny*'s discussions of Eliot's later poetry. See, for example, two reviews of Raymond Preston's *'Four Quartets' Rehearsed*: H. A. Mason's in *Scrutiny* ('Elucidating Eliot,' xiv, 1, Summer '46, pp. 67–71) and L. C. Knights's in *Humanitas*, a Catholic journal with which *Scrutiny* maintained cordial relations (i, 1, Summer '46, pp. 41–42). *Humanitas* (1946–48) was based at Manchester University. Among the other contributors common to the two journals were Every, Wilhelm Schenk, Maurice Hussey, F. N. Lees, J. L. Russell and Storm Jameson.

11. 'Auden as Critic and Poet,' xviii, 2 (Autumn '51), p. 159.

was an attempt to elucidate 'the rhythmic intention' of Wyatt's poetry: arguing against the dominant tradition of English prosodic analysis, whose norm was the iambic pentameter line, Harding proposed an alternative, psychologically-derived category, 'the rhythmic unit', which helped both to explain the apparent anomalies of Wyatt's textual revisions and to illuminate his relationship with the English tradition of 'pausing verse' whose pre-eminent exponents were Langland and the translators of the Psalms.[12] In the second, on 'the colloquial mode of Byron', Marius Bewley provided a kind of annex to *Revaluation*. Expanding one of the side-notes of Leavis's study, Bewley argued that Byron's colloquiality was not, as had conventionally been assumed, an Italianate feature, but rather the sign of his descent from 'certain Caroline poets', notably Sir Francis Kynaston. By this means, he suggested, 'it may just be possible to show that, after all, Byron *does* "belong" '.[13] The third, by F. N. Lees, was a practical criticism of *The Windhover*, and the last, a discussion of Crashaw by John Peter.[14]

Scrutiny's commentaries on post-war English poetry were sparse and dispirited. 'It may be obscurantist to say so,' went one reviewer's judgment on the current situation, 'but the distribution of faint praise to the innocuous doesn't do much good. And since producing poetry is such a routine job, reviewing it can't be any better.'[15] The mood conveyed here was fairly general. There was little to raise the journal's reviewing above the level of routine, except the occasional acknowledgement that this was indeed the case. Eliot's return to verse drama after the great moment of *Four Quartets* was noted and discussed, but without enthusiasm.[16] The career of Ronald Bottrall,

12. 'The Rhythmical Intention in Wyatt's Poetry,' xiv, 2 (December '46), pp. 90–102.

13. 'The Colloquial Mode of Byron,' xvi, 1 (March '49), pp. 8–23. See also Donald Davie's critical remarks on this essay, and Bewley's reply (xvi, 3, September '49, pp. 234–6, 236–41).

14. ' "The Windhover",' xvii, 1 (Spring '50), pp. 32–7; 'Crashaw and "The Weeper",' xix, 4 (October '53), pp. 258–73.

15. A. I. Doyle, 'Contemporary Verse,' xiii, 2 (September '45), p. 153. Compare Leavis's remark: 'there is a limit to profitable reiteration' ('The Progress of Poesy,' xv, 4, December '48, p. 310).

16. See John Peter, ' "The Family Reunion",' xvi, 3 (September '49), pp. 219–30; and idem, 'Sin and Soda,' xvii, 1 (Spring '50), pp. 61–6. See also Bewley's remarks on Christopher Fry ('The Verse of Christopher Fry,' xviii, 1, June '51, pp. 78–84).

it was now agreed, had not borne out its early promise.[17] Auden's 'development' was finally pronounced 'inverted', for reasons and with results that had first been identified long ago and were now simply harped upon, in one review after another.[18] The novelty provided by Dylan Thomas was of a purely negative kind: Wolf Mankowitz's review of *Deaths and Entrances* was among the most abusive ever printed in the journal, and its successors were scarcely more favourable.[19] Marius Bewley's appreciation of contemporary American poetry momentarily broadened *Scrutiny*'s range of reference and sounded a rare note of optimism, but its complement was an equally striking depiction of England's literary 'inanition'.[20]

The consuming critical interest of *Scrutiny*'s last years was prose fiction. Its twenty-six post-war issues contained no fewer than forty contributions in this field, the great majority of them devoted to the English and American novel; and of these, more than half were written by F. R. Leavis. The novel criticism of these eight years represented the most sustained and concentrated achievement of *Scrutiny*'s career, yielding two major full-length critical works and the core materials of a third.[21]

The most influential of these works, *The Great Tradition*, had been initiated in 1941 with a pair of essays on Conrad; it was resumed now, just as the war ended, with a series of four on George Eliot. Leavis concurred in the established view that 'major discriminations' were necessary in any overall judgment of Eliot's work, but rejected the assumptions on which these had commonly been made. He cited

17. H. A. Mason, 'Room For Doubt? Mr Bottrall's Selected Poems,' xiv, 3 (Spring '47), pp. 317–22; Peter Lienhardt, rev. Bottrall, *The Palisades of Fear*, xvii, 1 (Spring '50), pp. 81–3.

18. R. G. Lienhardt, 'Auden's Inverted Development,' xiii, 2 (September '45), pp. 138–42; H. A. Mason, 'Mr Auden's Quartet,' xv, 2 (Spring '48), pp. 155–60; F. R. Leavis, 'The Progress of Poesy'; Robin Mayhead, 'The Latest Auden,' xviii, 4 (June '52), pp. 315–9.

19. 'Dylan Thomas,' xiv, 1 (Summer '46), pp. 62–7. See also R. G. Cox, 'The Cult of Dylan Thomas,' xvi, 3 (September '49), pp. 247–50; and Robin Mayhead, 'Dylan Thomas,' xix, 2 (Winter '52–'53), pp. 142–7.

20. xvii, 4, pp. 334–52.

21. Respectively, *The Great Tradition* and Bewley's *The Complex Fate*, and *D. H. Lawrence: Novelist*. Leavis's essays on Lawrence are discussed in section 4 below.

James's opinion – that for Eliot the novel 'was not primarily a picture of life, capable of deriving a high value from its form, but a moralized fable, the last word of a philosophy endeavouring to teach by example' – and rejected it. 'Is there any great novelist whose pre-occupation with "form" is not a matter of his [*sic*] responsibility towards a rich human interest, or complexity of interests, profoundly realized? – a responsibility involving, of its very nature, imaginative sympathy, moral discrimination and judgment of relative human value?' This avowedly anti-Flaubertian conception was the major premiss of all Leavis's novel criticism, and, as he emphasized in this particular case, the key to a proper understanding of Eliot's 'great-ness'. Thus, while he acknowledged the presence of 'undigested' conceptual elements in certain parts of her work, his own critical stress fell on her *lapses* of 'intelligence', on 'the direct (and sometimes embarrassing) presence of personal need' in or alongside even her greatest achievements.[22] The 'great' George Eliot, he argued, was the artist in whom the sociological percipience of *The Mill on the Floss* and the 'profoundly and essentially moral imagination' of *Silas Marner* had developed towards the 'mature genius' exhibited in *Middlemarch*, where 'art' and 'intellect' came together to 'enact' a powerful, concrete analysis of the individual in society. But within this development there had persisted a psychological 'weakness', a propensity for romantic longing, of which the 'idealized' heroines of *The Mill on the Floss* and *Romola* were characteristic expressions. These two aspects of Eliot's character were deeply at odds, and their artistic results were incommensurable; but, Leavis argued, they had nevertheless been inseparable. They were responsible for the radical inequality of *Felix Holt*, and for the weaknesses of *Middlemarch*, in which the sociological intelligence that had already been evident in *The Mill on the Floss* coexisted with 'the old immaturity' that had found expression in Maggie Tulliver. And in the case of *Daniel Deronda*, this constitutional dialectic had reached its highest pitch of intensity, actually dividing the novel into two 'fairly neatly separable masses': one, 'Gwendolen Harleth', which Leavis hailed as a work of 'Tolstoyan depth and reality', representing Eliot's art 'at its maturest', and another, where her underlying emotional drive was given full and artistically negli-

22. 'Revaluations (xv): George Eliot (i),' XIII, 3 (Autumn-Winter '45), pp. 172, 173, 176; *The Great Tradition* [1948], ch. 2.

gible expression, of which he concluded: 'there is nothing to do but cut it away . . .'.[23] Leavis's drastic verdict on *Daniel Deronda* epitomized his overall judgment on its author. The Eliot canon was not simply given in one or another period of her career or even in a certain selection of individual works. It was necessary, rather, to establish it in a process of disengagement conducted as much within as among the separate constituents of her *œuvre*. The members of the canon were the sub-plot of *Felix Holt*, the greater part of *Middlemarch* and the 'novel' that constituted 'the good half' of *Daniel Deronda*. In these works, the antinomies that threatened Eliot's art were transcended: 'analysis' was wholly 'enacted' in concrete 'creation' and 'emotion' assumed its proper function as 'a disinterested response defined by its object, and hardly distinguishable from the play of the intelligence and self-knowledge that give it impersonality'.[24]

(Leavis punctuated his appreciation of Eliot with allusions to Flaubert, whom he saw as the incarnation of formalism and moral anomie in the modern novel.[25] Two essays by Martin Turnell, published in tandem with the first and second parts of 'George Eliot', corroborated his judgment from the other side. Flaubert was indeed 'a great writer', Turnell wrote, but one 'with whom there was something badly wrong'. Technically brilliant but 'undoubtedly defective' in 'sensibility', Flaubert had himself been unable to benefit from his own contribution to the modern novel. He had broken new ground in the novel of personal relationships, but *Madame Bovary* was a 'nihilistic' work. *L'Education sentimentale* might indeed depict the 'disillusion' of the nineteenth century, but its motive forces were 'the aberrations of the author's own personality'. *Un cœur simple*, in which he turned from the 'torrid sex-laden atmosphere' of these novels to consider 'normal and healthy' experience, was his 'only perfect work of art'. Turnell freely granted Flaubert's magisterial role in the history of

23. 'George Eliot (i),'; 'George Eliot (ii),' xiii, 4 (Spring '46), pp. 257–71; 'George Eliot (iii),' xiv, 1 (Summer '46), pp. 15–26; and 'George Eliot (iv): "Daniel Deronda" and "The Portrait of a Lady",' xiv, 2 (December '46), pp. 102–31 ('is' italicized in the original, p. 129). According to Ronald Hayman, Leavis was subsequently invited to 'extricate' and edit the quasi-novel *Gwendolen Harleth* for publication: he agreed, but the 'novel' never appeared (*Leavis*, London 1976, p. 76).

24. 'George Eliot (iii),' p. 26. The particular context of this formulation was the discussion of *Middlemarch*.

25. See, for example, 'George Eliot (i),' p. 173; 'George Eliot (iii),' p. 25.

the novel, and in particular his positive influence on the writers with whom Leavis was especially concerned – 'it is inconceivable,' he wrote, 'that [James and Conrad] could have produced the masterpieces they did without his example.' But the main effect of his literary-historical avowals, in the context of his general argument and still more in the setting provided by *Scrutiny*'s editors, was to confirm Flaubert as the symbolic antithesis of 'the great tradition'.[26])

'*Gwendolen Harleth*' was the bridge between George Eliot and Henry James. It had inspired *The Portrait of a Lady*, Leavis declared; and, as he went on to argue in an extended comparative analysis, was 'decidedly the greater' of the two.[27] However, within the Jamesian canon *The Portrait of a Lady* was pre-eminent; the main concern of Leavis's studies in James was to displace the late novels from the centre of critical attention, instead establishing this and the other works of the years around 1880 as the pinnacle of James's artistic achievement.[28] James was a 'poet-novelist', Leavis affirmed, but not in any aestheticist sense: the example of Austen and Eliot, qualified by that of his native forebear, Hawthorne, had enabled him to gauge the value of the French tradition and led him to an 'early and decisive' renunciation of it. As he had himself written in the preface to *The Golden Bowl*, 'the "taste" of the poet' was essentially 'his active sense of life'. His 'poetic' quality lay in the power of his 'controlling interests', in the moral depth from which he wrote and, in turn, elicited response. The primary focus of James's 'interests' was the relation between America and Europe. Already given in his early cultural formation, the complex 'interplay' of the two had formed the constant setting of his

26. 'Flaubert (I),' XIII, 3, pp. 200–18; 'Flaubert (II),' XIII, 4, pp. 272–91.

27. 'George Eliot (IV) . . .', p. 103.

28. Leavis's writings on James were less systematic than those on Conrad and Eliot. The second part of the chapter in *The Great Tradition*, 'The Later James,' first appeared as a review-essay on Blackmur's edition of the novelist's 'Critical Prefaces' ('Henry James,' V, 4, March '37, pp. 398–417); the first, '*To The Portrait of a Lady*,' was written directly for the book, drawing on various essays and reviews from *Scrutiny*, including: 'Henry James's First Novel,' XIV, 4 (September '47), pp. 295–301; 'Henry James and the Function of Criticism,' XV, 2 (Spring '48), pp. 98–104; 'The Novel as Dramatic Poem (III): "The Europeans",' XV, 3 (Summer '48), pp. 209–21; and ' "The Portrait of a Lady" Reprinted,' XV, 3, pp. 235–41. I have found it more convenient, in some cases, to refer to Leavis's arguments in the form in which he organized them in *The Great Tradition*.

life, and it was 'not surprising,' Leavis wrote, 'that, in the mind of a genius, the outcome should [have been] a bent for comparison, and a constant profound pondering of the nature of civilized society and of the possiblity of imagining a finer civilization than any he knew'.[29] Leavis explored the course of James's 'international theme' from *Roderick Hudson* through *The American* and *Daisy Miller*, *The Europeans* and *Washington Square*, plotting the changing values of 'America' and 'Europe' and their final resolution in 'an ideal positive' that was neither American nor European – the 'inclusive harmony' of *The Portrait of a Lady*.[30] After this novel and *The Bostonians* – 'the two most brilliant novels in the language' – James went into decline. His writing suffered a hypertrophy of 'artistry' and indirection; 'his moral taste' was let 'slip into abeyance'. The late style was not wholly infertile (it included such 'admirable successes' as *The Awkward Age* and *What Maisie Knew*) but its main products, *The Wings of the Dove, The Ambassadors* and *The Golden Bowl*, far from the great works that the James 'cult' revered them as being, were in Leavis's view radically defective – documents in the 'case' of a man who had become 'too much a professional novelist' and ceased to 'live enough'.[31]

James was more extensively discussed in *Scrutiny* than either Conrad or Eliot – more so, in fact, than both together – and unlike them, he was not the monopoly of a single critic. His stories, and the critical fortunes of his work in general, were discussed by Q. D. Leavis, in terms that reinforced the main themes of her partner's concurrent studies.[32] The intellectual sources and artistic functions of his symbolism were examined by Quentin Anderson.[33] And his place in the American tradition of the novel was the subject of *Scrutiny*'s most ambitious venture in this area, Bewley's series on 'James's Debt to Hawthorne'.

Bewley's purpose was to establish the artistic and moral continuities between Hawthorne and James, and so to confirm the latter's

29. *The Great Tradition*, London 1972, pp. 148–51.

30. Ibid., pp. 152–78.

31. Ibid., pp. 178–99, 188.

32. 'Henry James: The Stories,' xiv, 3 (Spring '47), pp. 223–9; rev. Philip Rahv (ed.), *The Great Short Novels of Henry James*, xiv, 4 (September '47), p. 305; and 'The Institution of Henry James,' xv, 1 (December '47), pp. 68–74.

33. 'Henry James, His Symbolism and His Critics,' xv, 1, pp. 2–19.

'essential Americanism'. His first essay undertook a detailed comparative analysis of *The Blithedale Romance* and *The Bostonians*, arguing that the earlier novel 'had laid down the suffragist vocabulary and the Transcendental speech rhythms authoritatively as far as literature was concerned' and that James, coming afterwards, 'had the advantage of all Hawthorne had already done – and not done'. It was 'an interesting comment on the important function of tradition in the creative act,' he concluded, 'that James's masterpiece among the American novels, should have had so conspicuous a precursor in American literature.'[34] The moral counterposition of America and Europe was the topic of Bewley's second essay. Here, he paired *The Marble Faun* and *The Wings of the Dove*, showing how the moral schema underlying Hawthorne's novel had been reproduced in James's, and establishing the symbolic kinship of their heroines – it was from *The Marble Faun*, he suggested, that James had learned how to 'canonize an American girl'.[35] However, in inheriting Hawthorne's moral Americanism, James also inherited its abiding problem: 'the American problem', to which Bewley devoted the last of these essays. The relation between America and Europe, as both novelists perceived it, was among other things a relation between the present and the past; 'for the American, Europe *is* the past in a symbolic way that it can never quite be for the European himself.' But if this was so, then America was not a fully-formed alternative to Europe and, *a fortiori*, could not meet the needs of a whole and undivided personal allegiance. Hawthorne never mastered this problem: deeply American and yet never completely reconciled to this commitment, he was subjected by it to 'a long and agonizing martyrdom' whose motif, repeated throughout his work, was solitude. However, with solitude came insight, and when James confronted 'the American problem', it was not only in less constricting circumstances but with the precedent of Hawthorne to learn from. Hawthorne's influence saved James from the ' "slightly disenchanted and casually disqualified" cosmopolite' which, like many of his own *dramatis personae*, he might have become, and made of him 'an American novelist' concerned

34. 'James's Debt to Hawthorne (I): "The Blithedale Romance" and "The Bostonians",' XVI, 3 (September '49), pp. 185, 195.

35. 'James's Debt . . . (II): "The Marble Faun" and "The Wings of the Dove",' XVI, 4 (Winter '49), pp. 301–17, at p. 310.

'at a serious moral level with certain national and social problems'.[36]

Bewley's 'revaluation' of James Fenimore Cooper took the pursuit of the American James a stage further. Cooper was 'an important American novelist', he maintained, not because of outstanding artistic success ('although he has given us one or two masterpieces of a high order') but because he had been an early practitioner of a new kind of novel. In the best of his very uneven *œuvre*, 'an action is the intensified motion of life in which the spiritual and moral faculties of men are no less engaged than their physical selves'. For this conception, he was indebted to Jane Austen – his first novel, *Precaution*, was in fact an imitation of *Persuasion*. However, it was only when he moved 'onto his own territory, which was not the English drawing-room', that he was able to exploit the most fundamental of Austen's novelistic resources: the 'ability to confer a moral dimension on an action, and to make that dimension the bright, bracing air in which the novel lived and found its form'. It was, then, of no account that his narratives dealt in large-scale and often violent actions: 'the scope, the glory, and the danger of an action are only deceptively played out on an external stage. Their significance for art, as for the human being, is enacted on the interior stage of self-awareness and knowledge.' Bewley cited Cooper's Revolutionary novels, *Lionel Lincoln* and *Wyandotté*, as examples of an art whose main formal structure was 'a personally felt moral dilemma or problem'; and in the actual substance of these dilemmas and problems, he saw 'the American sensibility in the process of formulating one of its most characteristic expressions': the dialectic of cultural anomaly that was to reach its highest pitch half a century later in the novels of Henry James. Bewley went on then to trace the continuities of perspective and cultural characterology from Cooper to James. The 'divided loyalties' of the Revolutionary novels, he argued, presaged 'the international novel' whose 'essential note' was 'that it provides a stage on which the American and European cultures dramatically encounter, criticize, and possibly supplement each other'. In *The Travelling Bachelor*, he identified the forerunners of James's cultivated expatriates, and in the hero of Cooper's 'great masterpiece', *The Deerslayer*, the original of his ideal American. 'Without even suggesting the question of

36. 'James's Debt . . . (III): The American Problem,' XVII, 1 (Spring '50), pp. 14–31, at pp. 24, 30–31.

"influence",' he concluded, 'and speaking only in the broadest of generalities, one might say that Natty Bumppo dramatically struck the American imagination and tradition at one of its moments of sophisticated, self-justifying awareness, and Strether or Adam Verver was the reflex.'[37]

Bewley's approach was tendentially divergent from Leavis's, in that it situated James in the general cultural history of America, while the latter enshrined him in a 'tradition' that pertained primarily to a trans-historical moral order and only secondarily, if not contingently, to the particular histories of England and America. However, this divergence became a matter of open controversy on only one occasion, and even then, little attempt was made to clarify its extent, much less to correct it. The dispute was instigated by Bewley's reflections on 'appearance and reality in Henry James'. American culture was inordinately dependent on ideals, Bewley argued, and in consequence of this was distinguished by a perplexed awareness of the relation between 'appearance' and 'reality'. This problem had been prominent in Hawthorne's work, and was still more so in James's – in *The Golden Bowl*, for example, where the conventional sense of 'reality' was capsized and exposed as 'the world's artificial system'. The novelistic strategies to which this preoccupation led were intrinsically perilous, he continued. For the novel was constitutionally dependent on a certain minimum of stability in social and moral surfaces, and too radical a disturbance of these was liable to result in an interminable series of displacements in which the intelligibility of 'moral action' was lost. *The Turn of the Screw* had risked this chaotic outcome, he wrote; but in *What Maise Knew*, the strategy had been successful, producing a fiction in which the relationship between 'appearance' and 'reality' was explored without loss of poise.[38] Leavis responded immediately. He was not, he conceded, 'much interested' in *The Turn of the Screw*, which seemed to him 'a triumph, conceived in a spirit that Poe might have applauded, of calculating contrivance . . .' What he was concerned to query was the misrepresentation of *What Maisie Knew* to which Bewley had been led in the interests of 'the famous thriller'. Rejecting his collaborator's account, he insisted that the

37. 'Revaluations (XVI): James Fenimore Cooper,' XIX, 2 (Winter '52–'53), pp. 98–125.

38. XVII, 2 (Summer '50), pp. 90–114.

novella was properly to be seen as the record of its heroine's education, that her development was towards a 'surer and surer judgment of personality' – in other words, he implied, towards moral truth.[39] The exchange proved infertile. Bewley replied, defending the purpose of his essay, and justly observing that Leavis appeared uninterested in it; the difference between them, he believed, was at bottom one of moral outlook. Leavis in turn restated his objections, conceding nothing. 'Mr Bewley and I have not shaken one another,' he concluded. 'We must submit the case to others.'[40]

It is not feasible here to explore fully the issues raised in the dispute between Bewley and Leavis. However, it might be suggested that their differences were at once larger than either really acknowledged, and yet less divisive than this observation, in its turn, might be taken to imply. The dispute was to a significant extent one between an American and an English critic. If Bewley tended to set 'the tradition' in the main course of social history in a way that Leavis did not, it was perhaps because of a sense of national confidence that was certainly not echoed in Leavis's vision of modern England.[41] On the other hand, Bewley's critical categories did not differ significantly from Leavis's: the novel as 'moral action' and the idea of 'tradition' were central to both. Moreover, the traditions constructed by them were anything but antithetical. Bewley's 'Americanism' seems to have been of the same stamp as James's: for him too, Europe was not merely another place, but an inseparable element in the American past. Accordingly, his 'tradition' was not autarkic. Beginning with Cooper, portrayed here as the disciple of Austen, and culminating in Henry James, it was a loop-circuit through which the main current of 'the great tradition' also flowed.

Leavis's post-war criticism did not differ in principle or in method from his earlier studies in the novel. However, as it increased in volume, its distinctive procedures and themes were consolidated and

39. XVII, 2, pp. 115–27.
40. 'Maisie, Miles and Flora, the Jamesian Innocents: A Rejoinder,' with an afternote by Leavis, XVII, 3 (Autumn '50), pp. 255–63.
41. See Chapter Two, section 4, above, for the general considerations implicit here.

in some cases clarified. The critique of George Eliot furnished a remarkable practical demonstration of the chief methodological feature of Leavisian criticism: the dualism of 'recognition' and 'explanation'.[42] Leavis drew a line through Eliot's work, separating her 'mature', 'concrete' art from the 'immature' wish-fulfilments that coexisted with it, 'recognizing' and affirming the one and 'diagnosing' the other in a vein of psychological suggestion that was itself motivated as much by moral distaste as by 'disinterested' theoretically grounded examination. If *Daniel Deronda* constituted the extreme case of Eliot's artistic predicament, Leavis's readiness to dismember the novel was the logical terminus of his own methodological dualism.

The object of critical recognition was now named. The novel was a species of 'dramatic poem' whose 'essential' principle of order was moral. There was also the more specialized case of the 'moral fable' – *Silas Marner* or *The Europeans* – which Leavis was particularly concerned to defend against those who expected 'a loosely generous provision of incident and scene' but were 'innocent of any adult criterion of point and relevance in art'.[43] However, if Leavis constantly distinguished the two, it was not, as has been implied, because they were contraries – the first work to be analysed under the rubric of 'the novel as dramatic poem' was precisely a 'moral fable', *Hard Times*.[44] The actual relation between them was suggested in his chapter on James: '. . . though *The Portrait of a Lady* is on so much larger a scale than *The Europeans*, and because of its complexity doesn't invite the description of "moral fable", it is similarly organized: it is all intensely significant. It offers no largesse of irrelevant "life"; its vitality is wholly that of art.'[45] Thus, the 'moral fable' was certainly not antithetical to 'the novel as dramatic poem'; nor, at the same time, was it merely a sub-set of the larger category. It was, if anything, its *epitome*: the novel brought to the ultimate pitch of moral concentration.

The purport of the novel was knowledge; in particular, 'sociological' knowledge of an order that no other mode of exploration

42. Again, see Chapter Two, section 4.

43. *The Great Tradition*, p. 164.

44. See Michael Tanner, 'Literature and Philosophy,' *New Universities Quarterly*, xxx, 1 (Winter '75), p. 57, where this is suggested. For *Hard Times*, see xiv, 3 (Spring '47), pp. 185–203. This was the one Dickens novel that Leavis was prepared, at this time, to admit to 'the great tradition'.

45. *The Great Tradition*, p. 176.

could attain. The central achievement of *Middlemarch* was its analysis of the individual in society, which Leavis championed as 'real knowledge; that is, knowledge alive with understanding'. The same heuristic powers were manifest in James, who, as Leavis argued, possessed 'in an exceptionally high degree, the kind of knowledge of individual humans and concrete societies that we expect of a great novelist – knowledge that doesn't favour enthusiasm for such constructions as the [Comtean] religion of humanity'.[46] The essential truth embodied in the novel was the sociality of the individual. 'It is only here and there, in the individual focus, that consciousness exists,' Leavis wrote, 'and yet, as the experience of great literature brings home to us very forcibly, and the more forcibly the more we ponder it, that is not the last word: the individual focus of consciousness is not an insulated unit, whose relations with others are merely external and susceptible of statement in Benthamite terms.'[47] However, the nature of the knowledge governed the form of its accessibility. It was not simply to be read off, as from a statistical table or work of sociological inquiry. This knowledge was available only – or, at least, above all – in 'the experience of great literature', and then, only to those whose intellectual disposition was adequate to the experience. Fundamental to any sociology or politics, the knowledge of human sociality, of the 'community of consciousness', could nevertheless be elicited only in the act of critical recognition. Literary criticism was culture's gift of wisdom to a blinded civilization.

46. *The Great Tradition*, p. 157.
47. 'Henry James and the Function of Criticism,' p. 100. This commendation did not, of course, include the later James, of whom Leavis wrote: '[he] paid the penalty of living too much as a novelist, and not richly enough as a man. He paid the price, too, of his upbringing – of never having been allowed to take root in any community, so that, for all his intense critical interest in civilization, he never developed any sense of society as a system of functions and responsibilities' – 'Henry James and the Function of Criticism' (p. 102).

3

Culture and Civilization
(ii): Lost Hierarchies, Lost Wholes

This was the dominant tendency in the post-war *Scrutiny*. Its orientation was, broadly speaking, liberal and modern, and the novel criticism in which it mainly expressed itself was socially committed in a sense that had been established in more than a decade of argument. As such, it represented both the perfection of the project and its involution. For the process of displacement that underlay this novel criticism was to all appearances a process of withdrawal from the large contemporary issues that had once been objects of direct and sustained concern. The more 'genuine literary criticism' came into its own, the more simply specialist it appeared to be. If *The Great Tradition* was energized by a powerful conviction of social responsibility, it did not, on that account, seem so much the less a study of certain English-language novelists by a literary academic from Cambridge.

There was, however, a second tendency which grew in strength in the later forties and which not only recovered but extended the thematic range of the early *Scrutiny*. Here, questions of political history and theory, of social structures and the meaning of their transformation, of the theory and practice of education, were discussed in their own right and more systematically than ever before. Yet the condition of this synoptic coverage was an involution no less grave than that of the dominant tendency and exactly complementary in its effects. Whereas the latter was basically liberal and modern in outlook but increasingly restricted in scope, its counterpart achieved its much greater discursive range at the cost of deepening conservatism and fixated retrospection. The problems that agitated the writers of this secondary tendency lay in the present, but their area of reference was almost invariably an historical field that extended backwards from the English Restoration into an unrecorded folk past; the basis of their universalism was very often religious; their gestures ranged from the contrastive, through the contemplative, to the militantly reactionary; the leitmotiv of their writings was *loss*: the loss of order, wholeness and certainty in every cell of modern English society.

I

The strategic prospectus of the war years had come to nothing. However widely Leavis's conception of critical collaboration between 'culture' and the State had been admired, the institutional proposals that followed from it had been disregarded. Outside the circle of his pupils and followers, the English School, the 'humane centre' that would 'check and control' public policy, remained a 'sketch'. The residual outcome of this prospectus was, of course, the 'Downing school' in which Leavis was to propound his views for a generation to come. Within *Scrutiny* itself, however, and in particular within this secondary tendency, another kind of response was soon evident. Blocked by contemporary historical conditions from realizing their central strategic goal, a number of writers turned back into the past in search of images, both critical and consolatory, of the unity of politics and 'culture'.

The first of these initiatives – paradoxically – was L. C. Knights's essay on Clarendon's *History of the Rebellion*. The contemporary relevance of this work, Knights argued, lay not in its analysis of the English Revolution (it lacked all appreciation of the socio-economic bases of the Revolution and of the mass opposition to Royalism) but in the opportunity it gave for considering 'the relation of "politics" and "culture" '. Its real greatness lay in the unity of moral and political wisdom that it exemplified, in its 'constant reference beyond politics – beyond, that is, the conflict of forces – to the human ground', and ultimately, in its author's formative milieu: a society in which there existed 'a highly developed sense of the person, ... for which personal and moral issues mattered, and which possessed a language in which these issues could be intelligently discussed'.[1]

1. 'Reflections on Clarendon's History of the Rebellion,' xv, 2 (Spring '48), pp. 105–16, at pp. 111, 112.

Knights attempted to fix the peculiar quality of Clarendon's work by setting it beside Trotsky's 'very different but in some ways comparable' *History of the Russian Revolution*. The latter, he argued, was 'clearly the product of an age dominated by the idea of scientific law'. Here, Clarendon's sensitivity (often admittedly excessive) to personal motivation had been replaced by a mind that thought exclusively in terms of 'masses and social forces'. Among the dominant impressions left by the book was that of 'the absence of the personal – especially of the irrational, or non-rational – motives that certainly played a part in the actions he describes. Nor is there a single person – not even Lenin – who appears in the book as anything more than a bloodless embodiment of political will or of some social category.' For all its apparent phenomenological richness, 'the total effect [of the trilogy] is of something abstract and schematized. One cannot resist the conclusion that the pattern, so vigorously asserted in its complex detail, is to a large extent imposed.'[2] However, Knights was not primarily concerned to adjudicate between competing methodologies. The more pertinent contrast, he believed, was between their different attitudes to politics and its relations with 'that wider human life, which only from one angle appears as political life'. He criticized what he termed the 'scientific bluff' and 'sleights' of Trotsky's history, explaining them as signs of a 'blindness to everything in life but some schematized abstractions', symptoms of 'the disease of a mind that thinks solely in terms of power'. Trotsky, he alleged, was 'the embodiment of political will masquerading as destiny or impersonal law'. Clarendon, on the other hand, did not reduce politics to this level. His particular political allegiance notwithstanding, he practised a mode of political writing that helped to sustain 'attitudes and habits of mind that are, in the long run, more important than any programme'. His adherence to 'certain intellectual and moral principles, "and integrity above all" ', made him 'a source of political wisdom of a kind not easily come by'. In this sense, Knights reiterated, his substantive political judgments were not important. 'What matters is that we should be aware of the qualities – inherent in the handling of his material – that were to contribute to the more lasting achievements of civilization long after the political cause that he supported was lost. To be responsive to such qualities, and ourselves to foster

2. Ibid., p. 114.

such qualities, in our political thinking, offers the only alternative to a progressive deterioration of public life to which those who are concerned for personal values cannot afford to be indifferent.'[3]

In Knights's essay, present and past were held in a precarious balance. If he found his model of political virtue in seventeenth-century England, it was with contemporary practice emphatically in view. His conclusions were correspondingly irresolute: Clarendon, for all his great wisdom, had been mistaken, both politically and historically, in his judgment of the Revolution. No such inhibition was present in T. A. Birrell's study of Roger North, in which the historic dissociation of politics and 'culture' was attributed directly to the Revolution and its aftermath. In the early Stuart period, Birrell argued, it had never been assumed that 'politics was of necessity an amoral activity'. Caroline England had always had a place for 'disinterested political service from the man of culture and sensibility – the number of poets who were engaged in political service under the early Stuarts is not without relevance.' However, the ethos of the poet-statesman had not survived the collapse of the *ancien régime*: indeed, Birrell maintained, 'the growth of democratic ideas (to use Whig terminology) was achieved by the un-moralization of political life.' Birrell traced the dissociation to the period of the Popish Plot and in particular, to the intrigues of the Earl of Shaftesbury. This conjuncture marked 'the disappearance of the traditional concept of politics as represented by Clarendon. – With Shaftesbury, politics did not consist in the application of moral principles and values to events, nor were integrity and maturity any longer the criteria of political judgment. Shaftesbury turned politics into the business of creating and moulding public opinion in the interests of immediate expediency.' The spirit of resistance to the new politics was Roger North, parliamentarian and sometime Attorney General. Birrell gave an account of North's anti-Lockean politics – his unflagging allegiance to 'traditional values' against the probabilism and scepticism that furnished philosophical sanction for rule by expediency – and his firm belief in the Common Law, which he conceived as embodying invariable norms of natural justice and equity, and which, although guaranteed primarily by the monarchy, was in no sense a system of 'coercive legal machinery' but an expression of 'the medieval *liber et*

3. Ibid., p. 116.

legalis homo'. He went on then to recount North's sharpening awareness that 'the cultural elite, the administrative and executive class, was losing its place in society'. For North and his peers, he wrote, the moral strains of Restoration politics were too much to bear; they retired 'into activities which were far less obviously of social "usefulness" '. North's withdrawal from public life, his rejection, 'deliberate, conscious and . . . painful', of the traditional social role of his class, was the direct result of the Restoration's expulsion of 'moral obligation' from political life. For Birrell, the contemporary moral was plain: 'the outlook that must belong to an intellectual elite worthy of the name, an outlook derived from personal integrity, mature awareness, and humane sensitivity, is the very outlook that it is impossible to maintain in political life – and political life is, or should be, *par excellence* the sphere of the social activity of the elite. The values of humanism, qualified by whatever adjectives you like, are not only at a discount in modern society, they are virtually inhibitive to what goes by the name of responsible social activity. The case of North shows that the fault does not lie with the humanist, and that in answer to the familiar question, the modern Bezonian is quite justified in refusing *either* to speak *or* die.'[4]

Knights had looked back to the mid-seventeenth century for a moral example to guide the political thinking of the twentieth. Birrell returned to the Revolution itself, to analyse the destruction of the moral State, the consequent exile of the humanist elite and the onset of an epoch of pragmatism in which, even now, the only justifiable posture was one of aristocratic refusal.[5] In the third of these essays, Wilhelm Schenk went back still further, to dwell on the wisdom of the medieval polity.[6] The core of Schenk's essay was a sharply

4. 'Roger North and Political Morality in the Later Stuart Period,' XVII, 4 (March '51), pp. 282–98.

5. Compare Martin Turnell's words: 'Now that an egalitarian society is becoming a reality and levelling down has been elevated into a political first principle, we are more conscious of what was valuable in the aristocratic societies of the past' ('Proust and His Critics,' XVI, 3, September '49, p. 267). Turnell elaborated this theme very explicitly during these years, though not in *Scrutiny*: see 'The Patrician in Politics: Some Reflections on Re-reading Baudelaire,' *The Cornhill Magazine*, vol. 162 (Autumn '46), pp. 128–37; 'An Intellectual Looks at the Crisis,' *The Nineteenth Century and After* CXLIII (January '48), pp. 21–7 (and also 'John Donne and the Quest for Unity,' *The Nineteenth Century and After* CXLVII, 1950, pp. 262–74).

6. The 'last', that is, in logical sequence: it actually appeared mid-way between

critical discussion of Castiglione's *Libro de Cortegiano*. Contrary to prevailing opinion, he argued, the protagonists of this work had little in
common with the great *uomini universali* of the Italian Renaissance:
'Castiglione's courtier ... is the true precursor of a cultural type
well-known among the educated classes of our own day: the sophisticated dilettante constantly searching for amusement, as if to conceal
from himself and from the world his inner emptiness' – its title might
more pointedly be rendered, he suggested, as *The New Statesman*.
Schenk's main objection was to Pietro Bembo's treatise on language,
which opposed courtly to popular language and exhorted practitioners of literature to avoid the latter.[7] The English renaissance, he
maintained, was very different from the 'esoteric and precious' culture
epitomized in Bembo's argument. Whereas the Italian was the preserve
of an exclusive, self-conscious nobility, the English was distinguished
by its 'many successful attempts ... to combine refinement with
genuinely popular culture; its greatest achievements, as well as many
of the minor ones, reflect the experiences and problems of a great
people with its roots in the remote past. Tradition was being challenged by a new spirit, but the response often combined elements of
both.' The distinctive quality of the English renaissance was best
embodied in Sir Thomas Elyot's *Book of the Governor*, whose fastidious
synthesis of Erasmian humanism and Christian piety was in turn
typified in the life and work of Elyot's friend, Thomas More. More
was 'a courtier certainly, and ... open to new influences', but he was
nonetheless 'firmly rooted in the popular culture of the Middle
Ages'. For if the examples of Petrarch and Castiglione were widely
imitated in the English court, there was also another, older world
that survived 'in the parish-communities all over the country, in
many a gentleman's household, in schools and vicarages, in guilds
and fraternities', a world where men continued to believe in 'a supernaturally sanctioned natural order which man could violate only at
the price of his own undoing'. Among the essential truths of this
world, in which so many of the great writers of the time were formed,
was the interdependence of hierarchy and equality: as the medieval

Knights's and Birrell's ('The "Cortegiano" and the Civilization of the Renaissance,' XVI, 2, June '49, pp. 93–103).

7. Pietro Bembo, born into a patrician family in Venice in the later fifteenth
century, was a diplomat and collector of works of art and learning. He figured
as a participant in the dialogues of *Il Cortegiano*.

commonplace had it, the human world was a social hierarchy of men equal in the sight of God. It was in this sense that the social criticism of More and his successors was to be understood: when they denounced contemporary abuses it was in the name of 'an underlying idea of equality which, in an important sense, outweigh[ed] all inequalities without obliterating them'. Hierarchy and equality, refinement and popularity were not mutually exclusive: indeed, Schenk concluded, 'it may well be that the vitality of a civilization depends on a certain balance between them'.

These three essays formed a definite logical series. Knights began by affirming the transcendent validity of the moral in relation to political history, citing Clarendon as an exemplary case. The symptomatic inhibition of his analysis – his inability to endorse Clarendon's particular historic allegiance – was removed by Birrell, who saw the disastrous rupture between politics and morality as the necessary concomitant of the Revolution, and upheld the Caroline governing elite as the embodiment of their pristine unity. With Schenk's meditations, the series reached its logical and historical terminus: politics was reduced to the moral administration of a social order designed by God and to be governed according to the highest ideals of Tudor statesmanship. The regressive tendency so clearly displayed here was, as has already been said, a secondary tendency in *Scrutiny*; but it was not fundamentally at odds with the dominant tendency. On the contrary, its effect was actually to illuminate the sense of their common project. In Birrell's essay, with its appeal to an historically continuous moral-cultural elite, and in Schenk's, with its evocation of a moral State based on natural hierarchy, the real historical pertinence of the journal's strategic conceptions was laid bare. The ideal for which it had struggled in the present – a homogeneous clerisy united with the common life in a relation of natural superordination and with the State in a relation of disinterested counsel – was none other than the 'reality' that was now contemplated in these aureate memories of late-feudal England.

Birrell's analysis of the Revolution was pressed further by Harold Wendell Smith in a series of four essays published between the autumn of 1951 and the spring of 1953. The scope of these essays was unprecedented in *Scrutiny*. Devoted successively to the role of 'right reason' in Restoration politics, 'the dissociation of sensibility', the social logic of 'nature, correctness and decorum', and the poetry of the later Metaphysicals, their intention was a comprehensive historical sociology of seventeenth-century culture.[8] They were also remarkable – in this context at least – for their emphasis on the historical centrality of class struggle. Politics, poetry and religion, the theatre, the coffee-house and the architecture of the countryside – all were referred by Smith to the commanding fact of class, and their individual histories, to the shifting terms of class relations across the century. Thus, he concurred in Tawney's analysis of 'religion and the rise of capitalism', and produced a parallel reading of seventeenth-century art and architecture, presenting Dryden as the avatar of the self-seeking bourgeois writer, the theatre as the appropriate diversion of a politically hollow monarchy and the great Palladian houses as the Royalists' symbolic recovery of the old order. An analysis so comprehensive as this could only lead to a judgment in which political, philosophical, religious and aesthetic considerations were equally and inseparably compounded; and Smith unhesitatingly gave it, in answer to the question that lay at the core of his inquiry: what was the essential human significance of the Revolution?

Smith adhered to modern political usage in designating the ensemble of anti-Royalist forces as 'progressive', but the thrust of his argument was to strip the term of all affirmative connotation. What the Revolution signified, in his estimation, was not merely the overthrow of a feudal order, but the destruction of Order itself. Its victory had confirmed the dissociative tendencies released by the Reformationary doctrine of *die zwei Reiche* and multiplied them on the widest imaginable scale: by the end of the century, society had been torn from nature, the individual from society, public appearance from private reality, form from substance, thought from emotion and both from language, and so on endlessly, in what amounted to a total schism of being.

The exemplary artist of the old order was Shakespeare. His age had

---

8. ' "Reason" and the Restoration Ethos,' xviii, 2 (Autumn '51), pp. 118–36; ' "The Dissociation of Sensibility",' xviii, 3 (Winter '51–'52), pp. 175–88; 'Nature, Correctness and Decorum,' xviii, 4 (June '52), pp. 287–314; and Cowley, Marvell and the Second Temple,' xix, 3 (Spring '53), pp. 184–205.

been distinguished by 'the integration, the philosophical duplication, of the social (political, economic, and religious) and the natural, so that they all appeared as reflections of one another and of a Divine order', and his art, accordingly, had been 'at the same time profoundly social and profoundly natural, both sensory and abstract, both individual and general, being simultaneously of man and of Nature, of human order and Divine, because interpenetrating all was the same firm and fixed structure, the conception of the social organism, in sickness or in health, in control, or unbalanced by excess'.[9] The artistic prototype of the new disorder was Dryden. By this time, 'the King had so cheapened himself, the Court had become so dependent on the City, and, in the absence of real solidity, manners and dress had become so much the determinant of position, that the way was open for the ascent of the type represented by Dryden, the ambitious compromise figure of the *bourgeois gentilhomme*.' In his hands, literature was denatured and turned to the purposes of worldly advancement. 'Its mind was no longer its own. It had become equivalent to the periwig, or the fashionable coat, or the "proper conversation", all simply current tender for social position.'[10]

Dryden's exaltation of 'versification and numbers' as 'the greatest pleasure of poetry' was in one respect the specifically literary instance of his general cultivation of 'manners'. However, it was also one of those 'manufactured and artificial versions of order which the chaos and progressive character of the age threw up to comfort and stabilize itself', and, in this respect, symptomatic of a graver condition: the pressure of a permanent human need which had been satisfied by the old regime but was now obliged to seek relief in man-made regularities.[11] It was in this sense that Smith interpreted Dryden's 'reactionary' counterpart, Cowley, and the politico-cultural tendency to which he belonged. The main object of Cowley's contemplation was 'Nature', a domain secluded from civil conflict and the vicissitudes of individual fortune. However, his interest in 'solitude, Nature and gardens' was not simply a proto-Romantic trait: it was 'a conservative move' with a precise historical meaning. 'The terms of his apostrophes to solitude are noteworthy', Smith observed: 'he refers it back . . . to

9. 'Nature, Correctness and Decorum,' pp. 287-8.
10. Ibid., p. 295.
11. Ibid., p. 300; cf. ' "The Dissociation of Sensibility",' p. 188.

the state of a pristine early world. . . . "Before the branchy head of number's tree/Sprang from the trunk of One". We need not doubt that he has in mind another world of England, not so long since past' – the natural 'social organism' of the *ancien régime*.[12] What Cowley sought in solitary communion with Nature, the defeated Royalist landowners reaffirmed in the manifest order of Palladian architecture. The values of the Palladian style – 'order, balance, regularity and harmony of parts' – constituted an implicit refusal of the urban-bourgeois ethos; 'for those who stood apart in defence against the unsettling activities of [the] progressive philistines, the Palladian country home with its natural grounds was a symbol of stable order, both bygone and desired.'[13] It was, of course, an 'artificial' order, and in this respect not substantially different in cultural effect from the 'manners' of Restoration London. The 'reactionary' neo-classicism of the countryside was only a memory, and its complaisant metro-politan counterpart a brittle semblance, of the substantive moral, social, natural order that had been destroyed by the Revolution.

Scrutiny's regressive secondary tendency was also represented in more strictly literary-critical activity. Here its characteristic occasions were Shakespeare and medieval poetry and drama.

It did not monopolize the journal's post-war Shakespeare studies, which indeed were more diverse now than formerly, but in the most substantial among them – those by Traversi and L. A. Cormican – its pressure was evident.[14] Traversi's central critical concern, as always, was with the conception of the drama as poem and with its gradual perfection across the span of Shakespeare's career, his wider, 'extra-critical' preoccupations remaining relatively unobtrusive. Yet the last and much the longest of his post-war essays was devoted to a

12. 'Cowley, Marvell and the Second Temple,' p. 188.

13. Ibid., p. 195. See Geoffrey Walton's criticism of Smith on this point and on the fourth essay generally (XIX, 4, October '53, pp. 328–30).

14. See, for example, James Smith, ' "Much Ado About Nothing",' XIII, 4 (Spring '46), pp. 242–57; J. C. Maxwell, ' "Timon of Athens",' XV, 3 (Summer '48), pp. 195–208; John F. Danby, 'The Shakespearean Dialectic: An Aspect of "Antony and Cleopatra",' XVI, 3 (September '49), pp. 196–213; L. C. Knights, 'On the Tragedy of Antony and Cleopatra,' XVI, 4 (Winter '49), pp. 274–300; and idem, ' "Troilus and Cressida" Again,' XVIII, 2 (Autumn '51), pp. 144–57.

'dramatic poem', *King Lear*, whose symbolic action was, precisely, the undoing of the 'natural order'.[15] In a painstaking analysis of the play, Traversi traced the chain-reaction that Lear's initial act of passion had detonated – the disruption of reason by calculation, of common custom by lawless egoism, of 'supernaturally sanctioned harmony' by 'uncontrolled instinct operating outside the balanced order of "nature" ' – in the family and in politics, through to the 'universal anarchy' of the heath and the comprehensive 'social and cosmic reversal of established values'. He then traced the counter-movement of *Lear*'s later acts, affirming the restoration of the filial bond and the reunification of the personal and the political in the 'natural', the 'old order of tradition'. The consonance of interest between Traversi and writers like Birrell or Smith seems relatively plain. Like them, though in a different and more oblique register – and like his old associate, Turnell – he was as if fixed in contemplation of the moment of rupture in which the anarchic desires of modernity were released. If his arguments remained within the idiom and thematic boundaries of literary criticism, it was – in part at least – because the representations of chaos that particularly concerned him were set in a larger symbolic organization whose sovereign motif was 'reconciliation', in the ultimate stability of Shakespeare's dramatic order.[16]

The cultural foundations of that order were analysed in their turn by L. A. Cormican, in a perspective that was unambiguously defined in the opening sentences of his study. 'It is just three hundred years since influential thinkers in England began to consider civilization as a process of liberation from medieval forces. Today, however, it is impossible to have the assurance, common even thirty years ago, that the Middle Ages were merely a prelude to our own nobler world. Such a shift in historical and cultural thinking is bound to have effects on literary criticism. In the following notes I wish to suggest that the new depth, pliability and range which Shakespeare's style achieves about 1600 results to a great extent from an increased power to make effective dramatic use of a number of medieval convictions

15. ' "King Lear," ' Parts 1, 2 and 3, xix, 1 (October '52), pp. 43–64; xix, 2 (Winter '52–'53), pp. 126–42; xix, 3 (Spring '53), pp. 206–30. In this period, Traversi also wrote on *Henry* iv, parts 1 and 2, xv, (1, December '47, pp. 24–35; xv, 2, Spring '48, pp. 117–27), and *The Tempest* (xvi, 3, June '49, pp. 127–57).

16. See ' "King Lear" (i),' p. 43; ' "King Lear" (iii),' p. 214; and cf. ' "The Tempest",' passim.

and attitudes.'[17] Cormican's central theme was the role of Catholic liturgy and medieval ethics in the formation of Shakespeare's tragic vision. From *Julius Caesar* onwards, he argued, Shakespeare's drama was rooted in spoken idiom and so, inevitably, in religion, which according to the 'medieval belief' still current, was 'co-terminous with life and conduct'. The outstanding distinction of this religious culture, compared with the Puritan innovations that were soon to follow, was the liturgy and the modes of apprehension associated with it. Through the liturgy, the Elizabethan age had direct access to Platonism, 'the philosophical basis for the employment of significant detail'. Mediated in this form, Platonism was not an abstract system but a spontaneous 'habit of mind' whose central 'human significance' was 'its power to direct the mind to the things of greatest importance and intensest interest to human beings, namely the inner workings of the mind and the dealings of man with an unseen world'. This was Shakespeare's patrimony. Drawing upon it, he was able to shape a tragic drama pervaded by a sense of 'mystery' in the universe, rich in 'dramatic suspense', and created in a language of 'enactment' whose cultural matrix was the sacramental practices of the *Book of Common Prayer*.[18] Shakespeare's debt to 'the medieval ethic' was equally great. His habit of extensive borrowing, which he shared with Dante and Aquinas, reflected the distinctively medieval assumption of community, 'the feeling of a spiritual community [which] was deeper between the tenth and the sixteenth centuries than ever before or since'; and his 'almost complete indifference to the contemporary forms which political, social and economic problems were then taking' was owing to a general 'insouciance about temporal and material things'. In these respects, Shakespeare reproduced the defining traits of medieval morality: its objectivity and its reference to a sovereign eternal order. He postulated a human nature created by a supernatural being and incapable of changing itself. If he amplified the role of subjective propensity and choice, it was without conceding anything to the notion of progress. Morality was legislated by the deity; the business of mankind was to abide by it. Cormican

17. 'Medieval Idiom in Shakespeare: (1) Shakespeare and the Liturgy,' xvii, 3 (Autumn '50), pp. 186–202, at p. 186.

18. Ibid., pp. 197, 199. Conversely, Cormican believed, 'the isolation of the Bible from its liturgical setting had unfortunate effects on popular habits of mind and on the writing of poetry' – as Milton was to show (p. 197).

K

characterized his study as a contribution to the ecology of drama: 'the whole justification for examining the medieval ethic is the hope of disentangling some of the elements which helped to make the great tragedies possible and to make them popular.' It appeared, however, that these 'elements', as he appraised them, were effectively the preconditions of 'great tragedy' *tout court*. He implicitly denied that 'communal or traditional beliefs' of a non-religious kind could sustain the highest forms of drama ('to take away all analogy between self-made suffering in this world and self-made suffering in eternity is to rob the dramatist's material of its richest meaning') and that the operations of supra-individual law in human existence might be amenable to non-transcendental explanation: 'neither Spencer's formula of "blood and soil", nor Shaw's version of Creative Evolution,' he declared, 'can supply as effective, as organizing a concept for tragedy as the medieval Providence.'[19]

The retrospective course of Cormican's analysis was continued in relay by John Speirs. Where the former had sought to establish the fundamental medievalism of Shakespearean drama, the latter set out to trace the origins of medieval literature back into an immemorial pagan past.[20] The conscious purpose of Speirs's essays was to extend the hegemony of 'literary criticism' into the domain of medieval studies;[21] their actual import was yet another elaboration of *Scrutiny*'s vision of Old England.

The first of this group of essays was a revaluation of *Sir Gawain and the Green Knight*. Dissenting from the prevailing scholarly approach to the poem, and in particular from learned attempts to derive it from the French romances, Speirs hailed *Gawain* as 'a great English poem' whose true setting was 'the first great creative moment of (I shall dare to say) *modern* English literature – the moment of the *Canterbury Tales* and *Piers Plowman*'. All three works, their great individuality notwith-

19. 'Medieval Idiom in Shakespeare: (II) Shakespeare and the Medieval Ethic,' XVII, 4 (March '51), pp. 298–317. Only the eighteenth century could rival the Middle Ages, Cormican maintained; yet the Augustan synthesis was exclusive, its unity won at the cost of universality (p. 301).

20. Cormican himself noted 'the unresolved residue of paganism' in the medieval ethos and in Shakespeare, but did not elaborate the point (ibid., p. 300).

21. See Speirs, rev. George Kane, *Middle English Literature*, XVIII, 2 (Autumn '51), pp. 161–4; and the exchange between John Gilliard Watson and Speirs (XVIII, 3, Winter '51–'52, pp. 191–6).

standing, came from 'the same English community' and were 'nourished' in 'a common English soil'. *Gawain* was a Christian poem, but its 'principle of life' was drawn from the far older sources of popular ritual. It was 'clearly a midwinter festival poem'; its basic rhythms were those of seasonal ritual; its world-view was that of Christianity 'in harmony with pre-Christian nature-belief'. The fact of its existence, Speirs continued, was further proof that 'there existed in England in the fourteenth century not only a vivid local life but . . . a higher degree of *civilization* than exists anywhere, perhaps, in the twentieth . . .'. It testified to 'the existence of a truly integrated public, trained to respond'; and today 'it should be as well known to us as Eliot's *Waste Land*: it equally belongs to the great English tradition.'[22]

Speirs's exploration of medieval literature and of the ageless 'English tradition' continued with a discussion of two fourteenth-century alliterative poems, *Winnere and Wastour* and *The Parlement of the Three Ages*. From the former work alone, he declared, it was possible to infer 'the existence not only of a whole social order with an individuality of its own, a unique human community at the back of it, but also a tradition of poetic and an audience trained to listen to poetry in that tradition'. It was, as all the poetry of that tradition was capable of being, 'both robustly regional in character and, at the same time, . . . national . . .'. And in addressing 'a delicate social and economic problem that was the concern and responsibility of the King himself', its author displayed an untroubled confidence in the weight of poetry in discussions of public policy. This 'non-Chaucerian' poetry was part of the central English tradition, Speirs insisted, and must at last be recognized as such: 'these alliterative poets were using essentially the same language as Shakespeare and in essentially the same way; and it seems that anyone prepared to deny the essential connection of these poems with the tradition of modern English poetry must be prepared to deny modern English poetry itself the characteristic qualities of English.'[23]

Speirs believed that *Winnere and Wastour* – 'if we respond to it' – was 'sufficient in itself to force us to revise our conventional notions of the civilization of medieval England'. Yet he also held that it was not

22. ' "Sir Gawain and the Green Knight",' xvi, 4 (Winter '49), pp. 274–300.
23. xvii, 3 (Autumn '50), pp. 221–52.

wholly of its time: it belonged to a 'dying culture' whose roots lay in pre-Christian myth and folk ritual. This eidetic image of a popular culture still older and more authentic than the medieval became most vivid in the last of this group of studies, on the Mystery Plays.[24] These play cycles did not share the didacticism of the Moralities, Speirs argued: their basic organization was ritual. Furthermore, their deepest source was not the liturgy of the dominant, Christian religion but the rites of the pagan past. They were in fact a kind of compensation – and sometimes very conspicuously so – for the repression of 'the Old Religion' and the dramatic rituals associated with it. Speirs proceeded to discuss a selection of Mysteries, analysing their structural dependence on the abiding patterns of mythic thought and comparing their main dramatic figures with those of extant popular games, in order to demonstrate the pressure of 'the other source of life which the Christian drama found when it passed out of the Church-buildings and among the people'.[25] The Mystery Cycles, with their ambiguous fusion of pagan and Christian dramatic ritual, constituted 'the only truly national (and communal) English drama before the Shakespearean . . .'; and it might well be, Speirs suggested, that their role in shaping Elizabethan drama was more fundamental than that of the Moralities or of fashionable Renaissance models. The matrix of Elizabethan drama was 'the traditional civilization of England as a whole', and the mainspring of that tradition was the unmediated spiritual wisdom of the people. The Mystery Cycles had been 'adopted by the townspeople and kept up by them for the same kinds of reason that old pagan ceremonies and dances continued to be kept up, in some cases almost desperately, in defiance of the prohibitions of the Church – because they were still, though perhaps obscurely, felt to be sacred and fundamental to life.'[26]

II

Images of public virtue, evocations of wholeness and order, explorations of a past within a past and of an ageless *Volksgeist* – what did

24. 'The Mystery Cycle: Some Townley Plays,' Parts 1 and 2, XVIII, 2 (Autumn '51), pp. 86–117, and XVIII, 4 (June '52), pp. 246–65.

25. XVIII, 2, p. 99.

26. XVIII, 4, pp. 264, 265.

these retrospective gestures mean for present policy? They did not imply an *alternative* to the 'Sketch for an English School': rather – or so I have suggested – they were consolatory responses to its apparent failure. However, they did have an important 'modern' counterpart in *Scrutiny*, and this precisely in the 'politically' central field of education. The dominant educational voice of the post-war *Scrutiny* was Geoffrey Bantock, and in his essays the latent ideological energies of the secondary tendency were concentrated and released: not in a new strategic vision of educational reform but in fierce anathemas on modern education and the society that had spawned it.

The temper of British educational thought just after the war was epitomized in the work of theorists like Frederick Clarke, who advocated a unified educational system adequate to the requirements of a 'much more thoroughly collectivist' society.[27] Bantock's response to this development, and to the social-democratic measures that had induced it, was one of conservative outrage. His opening broadside, 'The Cultural Implications of Planning and Popularization', was aimed at Karl Mannheim's *The Meaning of Planning in a Mass Society*. 'Certain intellectual circles are accepting the social conditions of planning and all that it entails without realizing that these changes may have repercussions that would be culturally unfortunate,' he wrote. 'It may be that in the conflict of loyalties "culture" will have to go by the board; but it is as well to realize something of what is likely to happen.' His objections to planning were threefold. First, all planning entailed the imposition of the *abstract* on the ultimately indefinable flux of the 'organic' human totality, of the *dead* on the 'living organism'. Furthermore, social planning reflected only the individual preferences of its originator – and who planned the planner? Doubly disabled – by the desires of the controlling individuals and, more radically, by 'human imperfection' – even the most ingenious plan was obliged to modify itself in keeping with the vagaries of

27. See Curtis and Boultwood, pp. 220–81, for inter- and post-war educational thought. Clarke, one of the earliest advocates of educational planning, was from 1937 Director of the University of London Institute of Education; his major work was *Freedom in the Educative Society* (1947).

the actual, and thus was bound to capsize into the liberal individualism that it claimed to overcome. Second: psychologically, planning represented an attempt to escape the insecurity that had resulted from three centuries of 'individual assertion', into the anonymity of an automatistic, heteronomous social mechanism. Third, Bantock charged, 'what society lacks in depth it is to make up in movement'. Mannheim's vision of a 'dynamic society' presupposed a rejection of tradition – 'the wisdom of the race' – which alone could guide fruitful social change. It betokened a 'lack of being' and a consequent cult of 'becoming' that complemented the futile desire to harness the future. The true exemplar of modern man was Macbeth Repentant: sundered from the community and so from his moral being, he took refuge in mere chronological seriality.

Bantock then turned to Mannheim's conception of popularization, which he attacked as a simplistic Baconian-Cartesian essentialism, the product of the limited scientific reason of the post-medieval world. It was not, strictly speaking, possible to reformulate any thought, he argued, much less to abstract its simple essentials for 'creative diffusion'. The proposal to do so was at bottom the product of changed political conditions: 'it is hard to avoid the conclusion that Professor Mannheim is subconsciously rationalizing a state of affairs that, once political power has been placed in the hands of those not conspicuously capable of undertaking the responsibility, as it now has, can only be made endurable by sentimentalizing the nature of the forces faced with the necessity of achieving some sort of order in the present chaos. [His] views are in fact symptomatic of a period that has sought relief from the complexity of living and from the tensions of the age by the creation of new, simplified *social* mythologies; the nineteenth-century myth of the noble savage has been replaced by the myth of the noble scion of the masses who is to provide us with those expressions of genuineness, spontaneity, dynamism, creativity, originality and all those other qualities which the superficial taste of our age finds so desirable.'[28]

As this contemptuous inventory suggests, Bantock was no more

28. xiv, 3 (Spring '47), pp. 171–84. Mannheim, sometime Professor of Sociology at Frankfurt-am-Main and an associate of the Institute for Social Research, came to Britain in the thirties. After a brief association with the LSE, he became Professor of Education at London University. He died shortly before the publication of Bantock's essay.

sympathetic to libertarian conceptions in educational theory. The essay on Mannheim was followed, a year later, by another on the 'cultural implications of freedom in education', in which he attacked the cultivation of 'shallow pragmatism' at the expense of 'more transcendental values'.[29] The logical accompaniment of the prevailing political reliance on 'mechanical' planning, he argued, was an increasing educational emphasis on individual will: these twin errors, the consequence of the changed 'balance of political authority and the growing intellectual impoverishment of our political and social life', were the torn halves of a vanished whole, the pre-modern 'community'. If Mannheim's concept of order was inadequate, so too were current notions of 'freedom' and 'self-expression'.

The principal 'evidence of our deterioration' was the preoccupation with experiment in education and the 'general adoption of the standards of youth'. The former was an attempt to compensate for a 'basic uncertainty', to 'cover insufficiency by surface agitation'. The idealization of youth was even more indicative of inner emptiness: the redemption of social 'being' was entrusted to those who were still 'becoming', the adults of tomorrow. But 'only a civilization in decline, wishing to surrender that which constitutes civilization, could wish to avoid its responsibilities by projecting its hopes on to a future generation.' Education was properly a 'stabilizing process', whose purpose was the 'encouragement, not of what its object already superabundantly possesses, but of other aspects that it can only attain by a growing into'. It injected 'being' into what was otherwise 'a meaningless becoming'. The child-centred schemes espoused by the 'offshoots of the Rousseau-Froebel-Pestalozzi line of educational thought' were in direct contradiction with this ideal. In mistaking the raw material of the educational process for its objective, such theorists merely furnished excuses for 'the abeyance or the depreciation of attempts at rational forethought and control' and compromised 'all possibility of cultural coherence'. The teacher's abdication from his or her responsibilities was 'merely another aspect of the general abandonment of intellectual and moral leadership in our society'.

If education had become almost systematically aimless, Bantock

29. 'Some Cultural Implications of Freedom in Education,' xv, 2 (Spring '48), pp. 82–97.

continued, it was because of a general reluctance – or inability – to define objectively desirable aims. Transcendental values had been sacrificed to political expediency: 'it is realized that, now that for the first time in human history a whole population is being educated, and thus clamours for attention, a vast majority can find no place in the traditional educational system, for their mental abilities are inadequate to the discipline exacted.' Now that 'the mediocre must have their chance', those values had been discarded, with consequences that posed mortal dangers to 'our civilization'. If modifications of the educational system were sometimes necessary, it was not because values did not exist objectively, but because complete apprehension of them was beyond the power of an imperfect humanity. Nevertheless, they remained the guiding star from which educational practice could not on any account be distracted by the pull of political demands. The 'standards of maturity' could safely be reconciled with 'the requirements of the many' only if it was accepted that educational policy must be differential, in conformity with the varying capacities of different social classes. No merely individual or social 'need' could outweigh the timeless authority of 'the highest truths known to man'.[30]

At this point, Boris Ford intervened to challenge Bantock's theses. Arguing from his own practical experience, he affirmed the active and experimental nature of the learning process and insisted that constant attention to method was one of the hallmarks of any conscientious teacher. He criticized Bantock's rigid counterposition of authority, tradition and objective values to freedom, experiment and personal taste, and denied that objective values, in education or in literary criticism, were ultimately demonstrable. He defended experimentation as an honest response to uncertain conditions, and pointed out that the value of freedom and spontaneity as pedagogic principles was dependent on the social framework within which they were applied. His own experience of a *kibbutz* school whose maintenance was the collective responsibility of its pupils suggested that 'freedom' was not synonymous with 'purposelessness' and that chaos was not

30. Ibid., pp. 83, 84, 94, 95, 96.

the inexorable alternative to the authoritarian imposition of values.[31]

Replying, Bantock attempted to dissociate himself from the authoritarianism with which Ford had charged him. Given the 'deleterious' nature of contemporary civilization, he argued, the spontaneous development of the child would in most cases lead to the assimilation of inferior values. The role of teachers, who constituted 'one of the few organized civilizing influences', must therefore be active and normative. Further, the authority of the teacher derived from that of the subject taught and the unchanging value of the truths that it encompassed. Here Bantock accused Ford of relativism: he was 'at one with the age' in his uneasy attitude to the notions of authority and of objective values. 'The modern idea that the acceptance of or respect for value goes no further than the individual's capacity for rational comprehension' was typical of 'an era which makes man the measure of all things. . . . One at least of the advantages of living in a religious age was that the ultimate standard became what was by definition the Incomprehensible.' It was precisely because the child could not know 'by the light of nature' what it wanted or did not want that authority was legitimate, and even indispensable, in education. Bantock went on to assert that the freedom represented by Zionist settlement schools of the kind commended by Ford was in reality illusory. It signified a degree of 'social integration' that actually hobbled human potential: 'for as the social is only one aspect of man, the child is in fact being confined to what amounts to a very limited range of human possibilities, and can become "free" only within those very restricting limits.' The 'culture' to which Bantock gave allegiance recognized both social relationships and the existence of a realm that transcended them. 'True social integration,' he asserted, 'can only be the by-product of the pursuit of some end which is not itself. To make social integration consciously the aim of human endeavour' was to elevate 'something which is essentially human and imperfect' to the status of an ideal. The logical terminus of 'man-made social plans' was the concentration camp.[32]

---

31. 'Freedom in Education: Thoughts Provoked by Mr Bantock,' xv, 3 (Summer '48), pp. 162–73.
32. 'Authority and Method in Education: Some Reflections on Mr Ford's Rejoinder,' xv, 4 (December '48), pp. 289–309, at pp. 290–92, 294.

In his next major contribution to *Scrutiny*, Bantock moved towards a positive formulation of the views implied in these polemics. 'Mr Eliot and Education' was a discussion of *Notes Towards a Definition of Culture*, in which it had been asserted that the maintenance of a 'high state of culture' required the combined presence in society of stratification and intercommunication and that culture could never become a mere objective for its participants, but was either unself-consciously lived, or was abstract and dead.[33] These beliefs, Bantock observed, led Eliot to 'question one of the most cherished assumptions of modern educational policy – the idea of equality of opportunity' – which, if enforced, would create excessive social 'fluidity', to the detriment of 'cohesion' and 'continuity'. Bantock welcomed this line of argument (which was obviously akin to his own concern with 'being' and 'becoming') as a challenge to the 'unthinking acceptance of the superficial social catch-phrases of the day . . .'. With obvious approval, he contrasted Eliot's 'organic' conception of culture with the abstractive tendencies of Arnold's thought, exemplified in such terms as 'equality', 'reason', 'the best self' and the like, and indicating an unresolved liberal belief in the 'application of abstract notions . . . to concrete realities'.[34] It was no longer possible to sustain that untroubled optimism, he wrote: the discovery of 'the subconscious depths of the human mind' had done much to undermine 'the "belief that nothing but benefit can come from making enquiry self-conscious".' However, while concurring in Eliot's suspicion of 'self-conscious rationalism' and sharing his doubts about 'the effectiveness of conscious cultivation', Bantock nevertheless felt constrained to qualify his insistence on the organic nature of culture. Cultural development was not so plant-like a process that all attempts at conscious design were superfluous or impotent. It was still necessary to adjudicate the merits of different educational strategies. Today, because of the effects of the extended division of labour and of uni-

33. xvi, 1 (March '49), pp. 64–70. The book was also discussed by Cormican ('Mr Eliot and Social Biology,' xvii, 1, Spring '50, pp. 2–13) and D. F. Pocock ('Symposium on Mr Eliot's "Notes",' xvii, 4, Autum '50, pp. 273–6). Cormican was much more critical of Eliot, complaining of his over-general arguments, paucity and imprecision of historical reference and aloofness from practicality, among other things. Imprecision and a decline into 'Swiftian' negativity were the main charges of Pocock's contribution.

34. See further Bantock's last essay in *Scrutiny*, 'Matthew Arnold, HMI,' xviii, 1 (June '51), pp. 32–44.

versal suffrage, the ideally 'unified educational process of home, social environment and school' had been disrupted. Abstract political conceptions – the voter, the citizen – had created the need for an 'abstract' educational system that occluded the differences among human beings, in the name of 'an abstract uniformity which such ideas as "parity of esteem" have brought about'. In opposition to this, Bantock urged a fully elaborated cultural corporatism. 'Is there any *necessary* distinction,' he asked, rebuking an egalitarian educationist, 'between fulfilling the functions of a housewife and being a citizen with a proper sense of values'? One 'possible approach to the question of what to do with the less self-conscious classes', while preserving the integrity of culture, was to encourage more specialization at every level, so that people could live more fully, and therefore more exclusively, within their own social group or class, thus eliminating the need for an 'imposed generalized notion of culture that serves to relieve, at present, the tedium of leisure'.

The charge laid by Ford – that Bantock had exploited certain devices of 'phraseology' and reference to produce a spurious correspondence between *Scrutiny*'s positions and his own anti-liberal, un-Arnoldian attitudes – is impossible to sustain, as Bantock himself was confidently aware.[35] The quasi-medieval corporatism that pervaded his essays paralleled the political and social themes of the studies on Clarendon, North and Castiglione, and the associated regressive tendencies displayed in the writings of Smith, Cormican and Speirs, and brought them to a contemporary polemical point. If this idiom was unusually philosophical, invested with a metaphysical pathos that had hitherto been absent from the journal, the conceptions so formalized were nonetheless recognizably those of 'literary criticism' itself: his distinction between 'being' and 'becoming' distilled the essence of the more familiar distinction between 'tradition' and 'history'; and in postulating the existence of 'the Incomprehensible', of indefinable but authoritative things-in-themselves, he extracted the irrationalist kernel of Leavisian 'analysis and judgment'.[36] Anything but an

35. See 'Freedom in Education . . .,' pp. 162–3, and 'Authority and Method . . .,' pp. 289–90.

36. For an especially clear formulation of the notion of the *Ding-an-Sich*, see

ideological interloper, Bantock simply generalized the themes of *Scutiny*'s two tendencies to a level where their substantial unity became apparent. He was remarkable for the candour and consistency with which he railed against social democracy, but his polemics were not, in strict logic, anomalous. They were rather the forthright response of a 'modern Bezonian' who, for once accepting the notorious challenge, resolved to 'speak'.

Bantock, rev. Hans J. Morgenthau, *Scientific Man versus Power Politics*, xv, 4 (December '48), pp. 331–5.

Leavis and Lawrence

F. R. Leavis's affinities were clearly with the first rather than the second of *Scrutiny*'s complementary tendencies, even if, as chief editor, he bore equal responsibility for both. However, his contributions to the last volumes of the journal suggest that as a writer too he was not simply assimilable to one or the other. For in these essays, exceptionally, *Scrutiny*'s 'political' ambition persisted in all its original force and scope. This was evident, for example, in his Preface to *Mill on Bentham and Coleridge*, which appeared first as an essay in the number for June 1949.[1] In this essay, Leavis ranged widely across the cultural history of nineteenth- and early-twentieth-century England, discoursing not only on these titular subjects but also on Beatrice Webb and George Eliot, Dickens, Arnold and I. A. Richards. He analysed the political role of Philosophic Radicalism and appraised the social rationale and moral limitations of the utilitarian tradition as a whole; he discussed the purpose and manner of Mill's essays and contrasted them with the reversed priorities of Richards's neo-Benthamite approach to Coleridge; he compared Webb with Eliot and contrasted Mill's systematic rigour with 'the flexibility, the sensitiveness, the constant delicacy of touch for the concrete in its complexity', that constituted Arnold's 'essential strength'. Leavis's purpose here was to further his conception of 'the English school': to introduce certain key texts in a programme of 'liberal education' and, through reflection on these, to illustrate the central concerns and procedures of such an education. The guiding conviction of the Preface was that

1. 'Mill, Beatrice Webb and the "English School",' xvi, 2, pp. 104–26 (F. R. Leavis, introd., *Mill on Bentham and Coleridge*, London 1950).

of his major wartime essays: that 'a serious study of literature inevitably leads outwards into other studies and disciplines, into fields not primarily literary...'; that the duties of 'criticism', in its fullest, Arnoldian signification, pertained not only – or even predominantly – to the proper conduct of literary analysis but to 'the general function of critical intelligence in a civilized community'.[2]

This was the spirit that had animated *The Great Tradition* and which was now to achieve full incarnation in the essays on D. H. Lawrence. The course of Leavis's reflection on Lawrence after the Minority pamphlet of 1930 is only sparsely recorded. Three years later, reprinting the pamphlet in *For Continuity*, he alluded only to certain minor changes of 'stress', not sufficiently important, apparently, to warrant any revision of the text: '... if I were to rewrite the long essay on [Lawrence] it would certainly be different. But I shall never again, I suppose, be able to give the body of his works the prolonged and intensive frequentation that went to the preparing of that essay, whatever its crudities.'[3] Lawrence occupied a symbolic role in Leavis's writing, as a counterpoint to T. S. Eliot. But although this symbolic opposition became gradually more vivid and insistent, there was no sign that the prospect of 1933 had been revised, or of how sweeping the revaluation of Lawrence's novels was to be. Leavis began in spring 1950 with a discussion of *St Mawr* and continued with long studies of *Women in Love* and *The Rainbow*, and a final essay on *The Captain's Doll* – all in critical celebration of a novelist whom he now regarded as 'our last great writer' and 'still the great writer of our own phase of civilization'.[4]

Leavis's purpose in this series was threefold. First, he demanded that Lawrence's novels be recognized as objects for *literary criticism*. Repudiating the attempt, which he particularly associated with Middleton

2. Ibid., pp. 34–5, 126.

3. *For Continuity*, p. 2. See pp. 34–5 above.

4. *St Mawr*: XVII, 1, pp. 38–53. The three-part essay on *Women in Love* appeared in XVII, 3 (Autumn '50), pp. 203–20; XVII, 4 (March '51), pp. 318–30; and XVIII, 1 (June '51), pp. 18–31. That on *The Rainbow*, also in three parts, appeared in XVIII, 3 (Winter '51–'52), pp. 197–210; XVIII, 4 (June '52), pp. 273–87; and XIX, 1 (October '52), pp. 15–30. *The Captain's Doll* was analysed in XIX, 4 (October '53), pp. 273–96. All but the last appeared under the rubric, 'The Novel as Dramatic Poem'. The quoted phrases come from *D. H. Lawrence: Novelist* (London 1955, p. 9), the greater part of which consisted of these essays from *Scrutiny*.

Murry's *Son of Woman*, to read them as documents of a psychological case-history, he insisted on the 'impersonality' of Lawrence's greatest work and the labour of 'creative intelligence' that had gone into its production.[5] Second, and again with particular reference to Murry, he defended Lawrence's novelistic organization against strictures on its distinctive modes of characterization. Such strictures were not only ill-founded in their own terms, he replied; they threatened to obscure the 'deep informing themes' of a novel like *Women in Love*, a 'dramatic poem' whose 'significances' were not reducible to a drama of 'character'.[6] Leavis's third and most pressing purpose was expressed in the essay on *St Mawr*: '. . . creative genius (and can it ever be other than intelligent?) manifests itself as supreme intelligence in Lawrence. . . . What is it but intelligence that we have in that deep insight into human nature; that clairvoyant understanding of so wide a range of types and of social milieux; that generalizing power which never leaves the concrete – the power of exposing the movement of civilization in the malady of the individual psyche?' Leavis reiterated this conviction again and again in the essays that followed. In *The Daughters of the Vicar*, 'the supreme qualifications of a great novelist for the work of a social historian' were made manifest, he wrote; *Women in Love* 'analysed' the England of 1914 with 'astonishing comprehensiveness'; and in *The Rainbow*, 'in the significantly different histories of his three generations', Lawrence recorded 'an essential part of the history of civilization in England'.[7] The faculty that produced these 'dramatic poems', not the 'doctrinal' element in Lawrence but his 'creative intelligence' as such, was a peerless instrument of psychological and social *knowledge*.[8]

Much of Leavis's criticism was taken up with the elaboration of this 'knowledge' and of the ethical imperatives derived from it. Here as never before, the works under discussion functioned, so to say, as *pre*-texts for a generalizing discourse on human existence in the modern world. 'Criticism' led constantly 'outwards into other studies', becoming psychology, sociology, ethics and, at the limit, ontology.

The central category of Lawrence's discourse was 'spontaneous-

5. See '. . . "Women in Love" (I),' pp. 203–5; '. . . "The Rainbow" (III),' p. 19.

6. '. . . "Women in Love" (III),' pp. 18–31.

7. See respectively XVII, 1, p. 47; XVIII, 3, pp. 205–6; XIX, 1, p. 30; and XVIII, 4, p. 283. See also 'Mill, Beatrice Webb and the "English School",' pp. 117–19.

8. '. . . "Women in Love" (II),' pp. 326–8.

creative fullness of being'.[9] Leavis took immense pains to dissociate this and the other ideas clustered around it from irrationalism, primitivism or any other cult of 'the dark gods'. Such velleities, he insisted, were in reality the offspring of 'industrial civilization', which with its pervasive 'mechanism', its exaltation of 'will and idea' and concomitant desiccation of the somatic springs of life, reproduced them as its other face.[10] Lawrence's purpose – and, by extension, his own – was not to aggravate this dissociation of being but to restore it to wholeness.

The principal focus of his analysis and advocacy was the individual: 'no one could have been more profoundly possessed by the perception that life is a matter of individual lives, and that except in individual lives there is no life to be interested in or reverent about.' This 'intense preoccupation' was not, however, in any sense individualist: as *St Mawr* and *Women in Love* made plain, Lawrence was wholly aware of the social conditioning of the psyche; and conversely, his moral insistence 'on the individual, or "fulfilment" in the individual, as the essential manifestation of life carries with it a corollary; one that points to the specific vocation of novelist (rather than, what is so often proposed to us as Lawrence's, the lyric poet's) more unmistakeably: it is only by way of the most delicate and complex responsive relations with others that the individual can achieve fulfilment.'[11]

Yet here too, the individual, and therefore the moral, remained uppermost; for as Leavis affirmed, 'except between "fulfilled" individuals – individuals, that is, who are really themselves, recognizing their separateness or otherness, and accepting the responsibility of that – there can be no personal relations that are lasting and satisfactory.'[12] The key-note of this theme was 'otherness'. Among the

9. '. . . "The Rainbow" (ii),' p. 278. The phrase was Lawrence's own.

10. '. . . "Women in Love" (ii),' pp. 219–20; '. . . "St Mawr",' pp. 43, 44, 46. This insistence was standard in *Scrutiny*: see also H. A. Mason, 'The English Kafka,' xiv, 2 (December '46), p. 158 (which also called for a 'revaluation' of Lawrence); F.R.L., 'D. H. Lawrence Placed,' xvi, 1 (March '49), pp. 44–7, introducing a letter from H. Coombes; and the exchange between Robert D. Wagner and Leavis on this point ('Correspondence: Lawrence and Eliot,' xviii, 2, Autumn '51, pp. 136–43).

11. '. . . "The Rainbow" (i),' pp. 202, 203; '. . . "St Mawr",' p. 47; '. . . "Women in Love" (i),' pp. 205–6, 208, 213.

12. '. . . "The Rainbow" (i),' p. 203.

most notable modalities of the dominion of 'will and idea', Leavis argued, analysing *The Captain's Doll*, was 'an essential possessiveness, and, inseparably from that, a denial of the living reality (which is unpossessable) of the possessed'. This proclivity, whether in the form of Mrs Hepburn's wish to domesticate her husband's 'dark, masterful force' or in the form of Hannele's initially abstractive perception of it, entailed the suppression of 'the fact of *otherness*: we cannot possess one another,' Leavis insisted, 'and the possibility of valid intimate relations . . . depends on an acceptance of this truth.' What appeared 'negative' in Lawrence's captain – his 'repudiation of "love" and his "meaninglessness" ' – was essentially *positive*: his attitude was one of 'insistence on reality, and the insistence, negative as it may have seemed to Hannele, the "idea"-bound, expresses an ultimate – an unsentimental and unideal – vital faith, a profound assertion of life and wholeness.'[13]

The notion of 'otherness' was also the key to the precise bearing of the Lawrentian critique of 'industrial civilization': in what it originated, what it envisaged and what it most emphatically did not. If Lawrence perceived 'mechanism' as a social condition, it was not in order to formulate proposals for political reform. 'No one could have been more incapable than he in any mood of finding any felicity of meaning in "the greatest good of the greatest number" ', Leavis declared; and when, as in *The Daughters of the Vicar*, he explored the 'life'-denying effects of 'class', it was 'in no democratic spirit' – excessive subjective immersion in one's class was inimical to 'life', but class as such was not.[14] The 'political' cognate of 'otherness' was rather the notion of 'disquality', which functioned in *Women in Love* as a critique of 'equality' and associated manifestations of the democratic-utilitarian ethos, and beyond that, signified Lawrence's transcendence of all discourse that assigned primary human significance to political and social calculus.[15] The source of his insight into the fact of 'disquality' was rather 'a kind of steady religious passion', a belief in 'the oneness of life', 'the separateness and irreducible otherness of lives', 'the supreme importance of "fulfilment" in the individual' and, above all, in the ultimate sovereignty of something 'beyond'. The 'religious' in

13. XIX, 4, pp. 284, 287, 291. Compare '. . . "The Rainbow" (I),' p. 202.
14. '. . . "The Rainbow" (I),' pp. 202, 205–6.
15. '. . . "Women in Love" (I),' pp. 217–18.

Lawrence was 'the intensity with which his men and women, hearkening to their deepest needs and promptings as they seek "fulfilment" in marriage, know that they "do not belong to themselves", but are responsible to something that, in transcending the individual, transcends love and sex too'.[16] What the 'beyond' actually 'points to', Leavis wrote, 'is what all the varied resources of Lawrence's dramatic poem [here, *The Rainbow*] are devoted to defining'. Like the captain's 'force', as Hannele sensed it, it was 'the more real because indefinable'. Its symbolic attributes were equally the light of the rainbow or the captain's 'darkness'. 'Enacted' or sensed, resplendent or obscure, it was ineffable.[17]

If any initiative can be said to have fused *Scrutiny*'s twin tendencies, it was Leavis's study of Lawrence. These essays were in one respect the 'ideal' achievement of the journal's novel criticism. Pronouncing freely on marriage and on politics, on the course of English history and on the conditions of human existence, they represented the practice of 'the responsible critic' at the furthest limit of its cultural ambition. Yet their thematic affinities with the work of the 'regressive' tendency were unmistakeable. It was not only that Leavis repeatedly associated Lawrence's art with that of Shakespeare, or that certain passages in *The Rainbow* reminded him of the England of *Sir Gawain*, with its substratum of pagan belief.[18] His meditation on 'disquality' was a distant but recognizable echo of Bantock's animadversions on social democracy. His attacks on the dominion of 'will and idea' reinforced Bantock's campaign against planning. And in the notion of an indefinable 'beyond', Bantock's 'Incomprehensible' was confirmed as the true goal and authoritative arbiter of human effort.

Where Leavis apparently differed from Bantock and the other representatives of the 'regressive' tendency was in his belief that existential 'wholeness' was still in some sense attainable. His warrant was Lawrence: '. . . when I think of the career that started in the ugly mining village in the spoilt Midlands, amidst all those apparent disadvantages, it seems to me that, even in these days, it should give us

16. '. . . "The Rainbow" (I),' pp. 202, 210.
17. '. . . "The Rainbow" (II),' p. 278; ' "The Captain's Doll",' p. 279, 296.
18. See for example '. . . "The Rainbow" (II),' p. 273f; for *Gawain*, see '. . . "The Rainbow" (III),' p. 22.

faith in the creative human spirit and its power to ensue [*sic*] fulness of life.'[19] Lawrence fortified Leavis in his opposition to 'industrial civilization' and, at the same time, in his conviction that 'the human spirit' remained undefeated. More particularly, by his rejection of Moore and Keynes, he underwrote his champion's oppositional stance in Cambridge.[20] And above all, his novels provided 'literary criticism' with its justifying occasion. The relationship of 'vindication' between Leavisian criticism and Lawrence's art was reciprocal. Both rejected 'abstraction' in the name of the 'particularity' and 'concreteness' of 'life'. Lawrence denounced the rule of 'will and idea' for its repression of spontaneity and 'otherness'; Leavis attacked its literary-critical counterparts as enemies of 'unprompted first-hand response': the captain's doll, symbolizing both personal and intellectual possessiveness, was as potent an image for criticism as for ethics. Their common counter-gesture was 'recognition' (the metaphor of 'pointing' was a recurrent one in Leavis's essays, and was itself 'enacted' by them in their characteristic procedures); their highest attitude, 'reverence' before an indefinable but compelling 'reality'. The encounter between them, then, was almost perfect in its mutuality, the discourses of critic and novelist validating each other in an endless exchange of 'recognition'. The extraordinary intensity of Leavis's essays on Lawrence – their energy of affirmation and raptness of attention – was that of a criticism in communion with its 'ideal' object.[21]

Yet it was just at this moment of critical fulfilment that Leavis and *Scrutiny* were most disturbingly challenged. 1951 had seen the founding of *Essays in Criticism*, a quarterly journal of literary studies edited from Oxford by Leavis's old antagonist, F. W. Bateson. The new journal was not conceived as an alternative to *Scrutiny* – Bateson's admiration for the latter was explicit – but its main objective was to transcend

19. 'Mr Eliot and Lawrence,' xviii, 1 (June '51), p. 73. 'Ensure' seems more appropriate here, though 'ensue' makes sense and also gives a meaning consistent with Leavis's position. This sentence was reproduced in *D. H. Lawrence : Novelist* without alteration (p. 15).

20. See 'Keynes, Lawrence and Cambridge,' xvi, 3 (September '49), pp. 242–6.

21. This is not to claim that Leavis was wholly uncritical of Lawrence's works. These remarks refer to his dealings with what he considered the canonical works and to the general tenor of his study.

what its editor had long regarded as the chief limitation of *Scrutiny* criticism: a lack of scholarship. Two years later, Bateson published his methodological programme, illustrating his arguments with (among other things) a passage from *Revaluation*. It was this that instigated the new round of polemic.

Bateson's solution to the problems of criticism as he perceived them was 'a discipline of contextual reading'. Through painstaking examination of economic, political, literary and other cultural evidence, the analyst was to reconstruct the original context of the work in question, and so to achieve an 'objective', because historically pertinent, determination of its meaning and relative value. Bateson's main motive was the desire to open a critical path to 'correct' reading, to the literary 'object as in itself it really is'; the second was to establish literary criticism as a socially responsible pursuit, practised and publicly respected as such. 'Contextual reading' was in this respect a means of infusing 'social issues, in the widest sense of the term, into purely literary criticism', to produce a 'discipline' which, in return, could claim special heuristic efficacy across the entire range of social life. 'If it is true,' he reasoned, 'that a work of literature cannot be properly understood or appreciated except in terms of the social context in which it originated, the skilled reader will tend, by the nature of his skill, to understand and appreciate contemporary social processes better than his neighbours.' Thus, the 'discipline of contextual reading' to which *Essays in Criticism* committed itself was more than a matter of procedural adjustment: it was an avowedly Arnoldian cultural strategy designed to secure 'the function of criticism at the present time'.[22]

According to Leavis, however, it was more accurately seen as 'the progeny and the destined progenitor of confusion and misconception'. In a rejoinder published a few months later, Leavis launched a frontal attack on Bateson's programme, challenging his critical qualifications and pouring scorn on his claims to social responsibility. Rejecting the notion of pure scholarship, he denied that 'accuracy' could have any validity except as a subordinate function of critical 'relevance': cognition and judgment were inseparable. Furthermore, he argued, neither criterion could be satisfied by the 'contextual'

22. 'The Function of Criticism at the Present Time,' *Essays in Criticism*, III, 1 (January '53), pp. 1–27.

method. Whereas the work to be analysed was a determinate entity, tangibly 'there', its ascribed 'context' was an arbitrary construction which, however insistently posited, could never be re-created at an equivalent order of actuality. And in so far as knowledge of the social context was deemed necessary, it would not be imported from else-where: 'it is to creative literature, read *as* creative literature, that we must look for our main insights into those characteristics of the "social context" ... that matter most to the critic – to the reader of poetry.' Impotent as a guarantor of 'accuracy', contextual reading was also incapable of establishing any sure norm of evaluation: judg-ment, if it was to be 'relevant' at all, could only issue from 'one's personal living (which inevitably is in the twentieth century)'.[23] Bateson's claims for the social efficacy of criticism were no less mis-conceived, Leavis continued. The function of criticism was to assist in the formation of 'the contemporary sensibility', to ensure that creative literature was 'read, understood and duly valued, and has the influence it should have ...'. Its *social* function, more mediate than Bateson allowed, was to create and sustain an 'intelligently responsive and decisively influential' educated public. 'It is through such a public, and through the conditions of general education implied in the existence of such a public, that literature, as the critic is concerned with it, can reasonably be thought of as influencing con-temporary affairs and telling in realms in which literary critics are not commonly supposed to count for much.' The self-proclaimed posture of *Essays in Criticism* was, therefore, both self-deluding and inadequate. For at the same time as it affirmed the special sociological competence of 'the skilled reader', it appeared complacent about the 'social pro-cesses' which should be the special concern of the critic: those which had 'virtually brought the function of criticism in this country into abeyance'. Did Bateson believe, Leavis demanded, as certain of his contributors appeared to believe, 'that it doesn't matter what the reviewing in the weeklies or the Sunday papers is like; or how the BBC uses its immense resources, and its formidable powers of literary influence; or what the British Council does with its prestige, its authority and the public funds; and that it doesn't matter if all these are shown ... to work together in a system that brings in also the

23. 'The Responsible Critic: or The Function of Criticism at Any Time,' XIX, 3 (Spring '53), pp. 162–83, at pp. 162, 163, 174, 176.

universities, and if the system imposes the valuations and the ethos of the Sunday reviewing?' And did he really imagine that the existence of *Essays in Criticism* at Oxford and the survival of *Scrutiny* at Cambridge could suffice to maintain 'the function of criticism' in England? If so, Leavis concluded, 'I cannot take seriously his idea of the function of literature, or his interest in literature, or his conception of its importance – and a peculiarly ironical light is thrown on his own view that the "skilled reader" may be counted on to contribute to the community . . . a superior insight into "contemporary social processes".'[24]

The debate was continued in a second exchange, but without resolution. Bateson, while pressing his objections to Leavis's 'insistence on reading everything written in English as though it was written yesterday', emphasized his admiration for *Scrutiny* and renewed his plea for cooperation between the two journals in the interests of their shared commitment to literature. Leavis remained obdurate. He reiterated his criticisms of Bateson, asserting that the latter's rejoinder had justified them 'with a completeness that the most sanguine controversialist can seldom, in his dreams, have hoped for . . .', and returned then to his attack on 'the system', the network of universities, journals, broadcasting and other public cultural institutions whose operations, he believed, now threatened to bring about 'the death of literature'. 'That this is fact no one has seriously attempted to deny. It *is* fact; it is new; and it must be appalling to all who really believe that literature matters', he concluded. 'To make a show of energizing on behalf of the function of criticism while ignoring this situation is to be worse than futile.'[25]

What was the significance of the Leavis-Bateson exchange? The main methodological issue and the theoretical problems underlying it remain, in very different intellectual settings, as pressing today as they were in 1953. The question of *Scrutiny*'s want of scholarship is one

24. See ibid., pp. 176–80. Leavis's particular reference was to Martin Jarrett-Kerr, 'The Literary Criticism of F. R. Leavis,' *Essays in Criticism*, II, 4 (October '52), pp. 351–68. See also Leavis's reply and the ensuing exchange in *Essays in Criticism*: 'The State of Criticism: Representations to Fr Martin Jarrett-Kerr,' III, 2 (April '53), pp. 215–33; Leavis, Jarrett-Kerr and Patrick Cruttwell, 'The State of Criticism,' III, 3 (July '53), pp. 363–7; and F. W. Bateson, 'Editorial Commentary,' III, 4 (October '53), pp. 478–81.

25. 'The Responsible Critic,' XIX, 4 (October '53), pp. 317–21, 321–8.

that might be debated, essay by essay, at considerable length. What is primarily interesting for present purposes is Bateson's tacit 'contextual reading' of his own critical and editorial project, in relation to that of *Scrutiny*. Leavis's Cambridge was the repository of an inherited cultural potential and – in so far as the powers there had not wholly dissipated that potential – a base from which to prepare and lead a general cultural struggle; Bateson's Oxford was an academic workplace. Leavis saw his journal as an instrument of struggle; Bateson's was conceived out of a desire 'to provide Oxford with a journal that might perform a complementary function in that university to the one performed so brilliantly by *Scrutiny* at Cambridge'. In what Leavis upheld as a 'discipline of intelligence' that performed an indispensable social function by virtue of its intrinsic capacities, Bateson saw 'purely literary criticism', an ahistorical and tendentially subjectivist academic specialism that could become 'relevant' only through methodological reform. In sum, while duplicating every major coordinate of *Scrutiny*'s activity – its institutional form and attachments, the intellectual appeal to Arnold and the goal of a socially responsible and effectual criticism – Bateson's programme entailed a systematic 'misrecognition' of its self-understood character and purposes. His appeal for cooperation was consequently predestined to frustration, for it came from outside that community of recognition which constituted the element of *Scrutiny*'s existence and whose matrix was the maximum programme of 'the critical revolution'.

This alone would account for the embattled acerbity of Leavis's response. However, there was a further aggravating circumstance, on which by this time Leavis had decided to act. *Essays in Criticism*, just beginning its career, was apparently confident and secure; *Scrutiny*, after twenty years, was nearing exhaustion. The prominence of Bateson's journal in Leavis's calculations is a matter for speculation; at any rate, the issue that carried the second round of the exchange was *Scrutiny*'s last. 'Only narrowly evaded a number of times before,' Leavis wrote in his 'valedictory' statement, the decision to close had now been taken. The reason was one of organization. The war had dispersed the original 'connection' and, although new contributors had been found in subsequent years, 'never again was it possible to form anything like an adequate nucleus of steady collaborators'.[26]

26. 'Valedictory,' xix, 4 (October '53), p. 254.

Behind this organizational predicament lay the frustration of his hopes for Cambridge. The 'Valedictory' was reticent on this point, but Leavis's private opinion was emphatic. *Scrutiny* had closed, he confided to Storm Jameson, 'because I am beaten. . . . The immediate cause of death is the impossibility of holding anything like an adequate collaborating team in the field. But the radical cause is my utter defeat at Cambridge. To run a review and a one-man "English School" (the two going essentially together) in ostracism – no, it couldn't be done forever. People flatter me about my "influence", but it has failed to get me a glimmer of recognition at the place where above all it matters. How could *Scrutiny* be made a permanency, except from a continuing centre of intellectual life at an ancient university?' The local effect of *Education and the University* had been entirely negative, sealing his 'life-long' exclusion from the deliberations of the English Faculty. 'When I am retired . . . all that I have worked for at Cambridge peters out.'[27]

Nothing of this sense of personal defeat appeared in Leavis's public statement. He recounted *Scrutiny*'s career, defending the course that it had chosen and affirming the value of what it had achieved. He insisted that its influence had been 'decisive', and that only pusillanimity, self-interest and malice obscured this fact from general recognition. Moreover, he refused to accept that its demise had been pre-ordained. 'Disinterested and grounded judgment, unequivocally expressed, will tell, however resented and penalized – will tell, if only a *pied-à-terre* can be established from which to put it into currency: that is the moral.' Where such a '*pied-à-terre*' might now be found, he did not say. It was, he observed, surveying the universities and 'culture-bearing' journalism of the day, 'a disturbing question'. Yet he did not relinquish the old perspective. Coming to his 'parting salute', he quoted Clough's famous first line – 'Say not, the struggle naught availeth' – and commented: 'the recall of following lines will halt itself at a proper point.'[28] Even now, as the community of 'culture' was dispersed, its organ closed down and its base declared lost, his spontaneous appeal was to those who 'knew already'.

27. From a personal letter, reproduced in Jameson, *Journey from the North*, vol. 2, p. 298. Jameson added: 'in this letter, and one he wrote a month later, he spoke of his wife's bitter sense that both their lives had been sacrificed "for nothing".'

28. 'Valedictory,' pp. 255–7.

Five

'Scrutiny' in Retrospect

A quarter-century has passed since Leavis's 'parting salute'. In that time, *Scrutiny* has grown in prominence, and become an ineffaceable image in the memory of the national culture. Its nineteen volumes have been reprinted by one of the most venerable publishing houses in the land, and given still wider currency in a two-volume anthology published soon afterwards.[1] It has been extensively discussed, by champions and critics alike, and obsessively referred to, on a thousand academic and journalistic occasions. For all but a year of that quarter-century, its chief editor persevered in the campaigns that he had initiated in the early thirties, attracting widespread partisanship and, on at least one notorious occasion, inciting England's intellectuals to polemical acts of rare extremism.[2] The response to his death, in the spring of 1978, showed that here at least, the due course of probate was neither possible nor even much desired. It is as if *Scrutiny*'s career was not simply an episode, an 'origin' to which certain phenomena can retrospectively be ascribed, but, as Walter Benjamin might have said, an *Ursprung*, an irruption never 'ended', into a cultural order perpetually vulnerable to its impact.[3]

1. The journal was reissued, with a twentieth volume containing an index and F. R. Leavis's *'Scrutiny': A Retrospect*, by the Cambridge University Press in 1963. The two-volumed *Selections from 'Scrutiny'*, compiled by Leavis, appeared under the same imprint five years later.

2. This was 'the Leavis-Snow controversy' of 1962. The main texts are: C. P. Snow, *The Two Cultures* (the Rede Lecture, 1959); F. R. Leavis, *Two Cultures? The Significance of C. P. Snow* (the Richmond Lecture, 1962), first published in the *Spectator*, March 9, 1962. The ensuing outrage flooded the intellectual weekly press, most notably the *Spectator* and the *Times Literary Supplement*.

3. *The Origin of German Tragic Drama*, London 1977.

So, the moment of *Scrutiny* persists – and with it, the complex of claim and counter-claim, of memories and forgettings, insistences and repressions, that obscure the real history of the journal and its place in the history of mid-century England, thwarting attempts at systematic analysis. This study has attempted to specify the conditions of emergence of *Scrutiny*, to elucidate the workings of its discourse and to plot the elaboration and modification of this discourse in the changing conditions of the journal's twenty-year-long itinerary. Certain further questions should now be put, and at least provisionally answered. How should this discourse be characterized and situated? What were its cultural functions? What do these, in their turn, reveal about the career and fate of the journal? And what, finally, were its cultural effects?

Scrutiny's affiliations with the major English tradition of social criticism have been widely discussed, most commandingly in the study that has given the tradition its common name, Raymond Williams's *Culture and Society*.[4] In attacking industrialism and commerce, the historic destruction of an older order and the despoliation of its natural setting, the now pervasive spirit of 'mechanism' and calculative rationality, the progressive atrophy of organic wholeness in individuals and in society, the *Scrutiny* group continued a line that included Cobbett and Shelley, Carlyle and Lawrence. In propounding the idea of a disinterested clerisy centred on literature and capable of guiding the moral life of an aberrant society, they resumed an argument initiated by Coleridge and brought to classical maturity by Arnold. Driven by a cultural discontent whose first cause was the bourgeois revolution, and profoundly at odds with the Marxist and social-democratic 'jacobins' of their own time, they were tied by a double bond to Edmund Burke.

Genealogical considerations of this kind are pertinent, but their efficacy is limited. They are of course essential in arguments directed towards the elaboration of 'traditions', as Williams has shown; and in analyses whose objectives are more strictly historiographical, they can often illuminate the sense of the object in relation to which they are cited. But what they cannot establish, except in a purely differen-

4. London 1958. See especially III, 4, ii, on F. R. Leavis.

tial way, is the specificity of their primary object and its place in the ensemble to which it historically belongs. Very commonly, they result in a slack and conventional enumeration of more or less verifiable 'influences'; in more exacting studies, the context that is said to unite the members of the 'line' becomes generic, stretched into a continuous 'background' that no longer determines, except at the most abstract level, and, at worst, merely reproduces the perceptual field of the discourses under analysis. So, while *Scrutiny*'s native lineage should not be discounted, it may be more pertinent to consider the journal and its discourse in a comparative, broadly 'synchronic' perspective – not as a point in the 'time' of a national cultural history but as an occupant of the wider cultural 'space' of European thought around and after the turn of the century.

For the themes cited just now, far from distinctively English, are equally familiar in that international context: they are in fact the common currency of what Stuart Hughes has described as 'the revolt against positivism', the principal action in a broader 'reorientation of European social thought 1890–1930'.[5] Hughes's description is not definitive, either in its substantive characterization or in its chronological delimitation of the phenomenon; yet there is no doubt of the reality and historic significance of the cultural catena that he seeks to identify – nor, I would argue, of *Scrutiny*'s role within it. In its strict circumscription of positivist reason, *Scrutiny* echoed a theme that was stated in countless variations, from Freud's scientifically-inspired exploration of the unconscious to Bergson's irrationalist celebration of intuition and the *élan vital*.[6] The Leavisian epistemological themes of 'recognition' and 'inwardness', of cultural knowledge as 're-creation', as the identity of knower and known, belong to that tradition of *Verstehen* (sympathetic understanding) whose representatives include the Germans Dilthey and Rickert, the Italian Croce – and, in another, very different variant, Max Weber. *Scrutiny*'s defence and

5. H. Stuart Hughes, *Consciousness and Society* [1958], St Alban's 1974, pp. 33–67 and passim. See Göran Therborn, *Science, Class and Society*, London 1976, pp. 187–8, where the difficulties of Hughes's thesis are emphasized.

6. Freud was by vocation a *scientist*, and made no concessions to 'the unknowable'; but he was no more privileged than any other scientist in respect of the bourgeois civilization in which he was formed and carried on his work. For an analysis of the pre- and anti-scientific strains in his cultural formation, see Sebastiano Timpanaro, *The Freudian Slip*, London 1976, pp. 175–206.

programmatic sponsorship of 'the minority' can be placed in a band of thought that included both Julien Benda, with his unworldly attachment to an historically continuous humanist clerisy, and the mordant political 'realism' of elite theorists such as Mosca or Pareto. And in its insistence on the social centrality of 'community' (whether the 'organic' order of old England or the universal 'third realm' of Leavis's late writings), the *Scrutiny* group recovered a theme that preoccupied thinkers as diverse as the left-republican sociologist Durkheim and Arthur Möller, the conservative-romantic author of *Das Dritte Reich*.[7]

Scrutiny's place in this cultural ensemble seems evident but also indefinite. To begin with, the variety of the ensemble was reproduced inside the journal itself. The accelerated professional development and wide cultural diffusion of psychology were registered in Harding's work and in the 'diagnostic' tropes of F. R. Leavis's essays on Auden and George Eliot; the impact of sociology, in the writings of Q. D. Leavis and Knights. Croce's aesthetics was expounded in an early number of the journal, and Bergson's metaphysics was sympathetically assessed by Parkes.[8] The critique of historical decline was stated in religious and in humanist, in Right- and Left-inclined versions, and the case for an elite in forms that ranged from Q. D. Leavis's radical-meritocratic polemics through the nostalgic aristocratism of a Birrell or a Turnell to the blatant and contemptuous corporatist diatribes of Geoffrey Bantock. Furthermore, it is possible also to relate *Scrutiny* to the other components of the ensemble in a series of *contrasts*. However insistent its affirmations of 'the inherited wisdom of the race', however compulsive its regressive search for the undifferentiated and

7. For the *verstehende* tradition in German thought, see Hughes, ch. 6, and Therborn, pp. 278–95; for Croce, Hughes, pp. 200–29; for sociological elite theory, Therborn, pp. 186–206, and for Durkheim, ibid., pp. 240–70. An extended account of Arthur Möller van den Bruck and the tradition of reactionary 'cultural criticism' in Germany is given in Fritz Stern, *The Politics of Cultural Despair*, Berkeley and Los Angeles 1961. *Das Dritte Reich* (not to be assimilated to the movement that later installed the regime of that name) appeared in 1922.

8. James Smith, 'Evaluations (II): Croce,' II, 1 (June '33), pp. 28–44; H. B. Parkes, 'The Tendencies of Bergsonism,' IV, 4 (March '36), pp. 407–24 (see also idem, 'Nietzsche,' X, 1, June '41, pp. 51–60). Herbert Agar suggested, in the course of a hostile notice of *New Bearings* ('Literary Notes,' *English Review*, June '32, p. 679), that Leavis had taken over – and debased – certain Crocean theses. A direct connection between Leavis's and Croce's aesthetics seems improbable, but it is interesting that Agar should have thought to suggest one.

unmediated spirit of the English 'community', the 'culture' to which it adhered was always in some sense trans-national, and its attitude to the national *State*, in the international crises of the thirties and during the war, was firmly anti-chauvinist. If Leavis's critical epistemology moved within the boundaries of *Verstehen*, he was also obdurate in his repudiation of the relativism so closely associated with neo-idealist history.[9] In these respects, *Scrutiny* was more akin to Benda than to Möller or Dilthey. Yet Benda's angular rationalism was probably much less sympathetic than the vitalism of Bergson, his long-time adversary. And neither thinker sorted readily with the 'sociological' element in *Scrutiny*'s vocation.

Before *Scrutiny* can be assigned its proper place in this web of associations, it will be necessary to determine what was fundamental in its own categorial ensemble: what it was that organized these separate and potentially discrepant themes into a stable discursive unity. The category in question was that of *community*. It was the posited historic fact of community that authorized and equipped the 'cultural' critique of industrial-commercial 'civilization'. It was the abiding fact of *human* community that called forth a 'minority' as homogeneous and compact as the most hermetic elite and yet firmly opposed to any form of preciosity, parasitism or pharisaic arrogance in its relations with society. It was the 'human norm' incarnated in 'community' that dictated the goal of an integrated perception of things, neither rationalist nor simply vitalist, beyond 'the dissociation of sensibility'; and that too which made it possible to espouse a *verstehende* epistemology quite free of relativist implications. In *Scrutiny*'s discourse on the modern crisis, 'community' was, in one form or another, the premiss of analysis, the remedial means and the ultimate goal.

Within the broad cultural field referred to here, two types of discourse are therefore of special comparative importance. The first and much the earlier is the romantic exploration of 'national culture' (*Volksgeist*); the second is classical sociology: in both, the central

9. A constitutional problem of this tradition was that the methodological ideal of 'sympathetic understanding' led simultaneously to relativism and to its antithesis: the assumption of a constant or absolute reality that could found the possibility of understanding (see Hughes, pp. 190–91ff). Croce's dictum, 'every true history is contemporary history,' could be used to underwrite both Bateson's historicism and Leavis's critique of it.

310

object of attention was the community of customs, values and beliefs that was taken to form the essential unifying principle of society.[10] The complex relations of continuity and rupture between these two discourses can only be acknowledged here (the most important single difference is that whereas the *Volksgeist* could only be intuited, the 'ideological community' of sociology was amenable to systematic investigation and even, in certain respects, to regulation).[11] What is more important, for present purposes, is to draw attention to certain parallelisms in their categorial structures. Both discourses were premissed on the conviction that rationalist systems were unable to explain – or, *a fortiori*, to enhance – human solidarity, in individual nations or society in general: Von Savigny, the leader of the Historical School of Law, was 'an incisive critic of natural law and social contract theories, of voluntarist legislation and ambitious constitution-making'; Durkheim's starting-point was a critique of liberal economics.[12] Both were drawn, accordingly, to *binary* accounts of society in which positivist or naturalist conceptions of the economy were braided with idealist conceptions of the 'community' that enveloped it.[13] From these it was deduced, in an enigmatic but logical development of argument, that the ultimate foundations of social order were *spiritual* in nature – the 'national spirit' of Romantic thought or Durkheim's 'collective representations'. And in both cases, there was a strong tendency to relegate, if not to dissolve, the *political*: 'both Herder and the Romantics tended towards a cultural sublimation of politics,' Therborn observes; and he has also shown how Durkheim, accepting the basic structures of the Third Republic, was led to propose *moral* solutions to its problems.[14]

These were also the main structures of *Scrutiny*'s discourse. The first principle and polemical leitmotiv of *Scrutiny*'s argument was that utilitarianism, be it in social science or in Ricardian aesthetics, was blind and actively inimical to the central human fact of 'community'. In elucidating the nature of community and the conditions and forms of its maintenance in the modern world, the journal elaborated a

10. I am especially indebted, in what follows, to Göran Therborn (pp. 178–86, 240f).
11. Ibid., pp. 182–3. The quoted phrase is Therborn's.
12. Ibid., pp. 180, 245–7, 252f.
13. Ibid., p. 182, 254–9.
14. Ibid., p. 182, 262–70.

binary discourse that united a technicist conception of 'civilization' (the domain of quantities and means) with a complementarily idealist conception of 'culture' (the domain of qualities, values and ends). The 'community' so affirmed was a spiritual entity, incarnated not in social structures but in 'tradition'. And the principal effect of this discourse, manifest equally in its utterances and its practical policy, was a categorial dissolution of politics.

It is not possible to assimilate *Scrutiny* wholly to either of these types of discourse on 'community'. The Romantic moment so clearly marked in the writings of, say, Speirs, must be set beside the socio-logical inclinations of Knights, whose debt to Tawney was consider-able and avowed, and Q. D. Leavis, 'cultural anthropologist' and admirer of Veblen. If its anti-scientific rhetoric and fascination with the national past were strongly redolent of Romanticism, *Scrutiny* was nonetheless aware of its relationship with sociology,[15] and its field of action was, unalterably, that of the classical sociologists: 'the epoch of wars and revolutions'. The value of this double comparison is that it illuminates the *specificity* of this late and marginal English contribution to 'the reorientation of European social thought' in the first half of the twentieth century. England's major sociological effort – Spencer's *System* – had been worn out by the domestic and overseas trials of late-Victorian imperialism, and was succeeded only by the reformist calculus of the Webbs. In the space so created, there appeared a distinctive local mutation, a 'Romantic' abroad in the age of soci-ology, *Scrutiny*'s post-dogmatic but non-scientific discourse on 'the ideological community'.

This was not *Scrutiny*'s most striking comparative distinction, however. For uniquely among its European siblings, the name and self-proclaimed nature of this English discourse on community was 'literary criticism'. Art was certainly not excluded from the cultural field mapped by Hughes – Croce produced an aesthetics, Bergson contributed a theory of the comic, Freud wrote several major papers on individual artists, and the lesser representatives of this culture included novelists and poets – but none of its major figures was primarily concerned with aesthetic questions, and nowhere else was

15. See F. R. Leavis, *Education and the University*, p. 31.

L

it ever imagined that the privileged occasion of a discourse on 'community' might be the 'analysis and judgment' of literature. Furthermore, *Scrutiny*'s adherents were self-consciously (and notoriously) a *militant* cultural current, intellectually compact and, by the late forties, represented at every level of the national educational system, from professorial chairs to the class-rooms of unnumbered secondary schools. Why should such a discourse have emerged in this cultural sector and taken this particular form?

Some elements of an explanation have already been suggested. The end of the First World War saw the onset of a comprehensive crisis of British society, marked economically by a complex interlacing of obsolescence and innovation, stagnation and growth, and politically by a halting and protracted recomposition of the old forms of representation. One prominent effect of this crisis was a loosening of the national cultural ensemble, new and taxing problems appearing to challenge it while the accumulated resources of its inherited discourses were depreciated or written off. There ensued a period of pronounced cultural 'competition'. Psychology, anthropology and Marxism struggled for rights to synoptic explanation in the domain that had formerly been monopolized by religion, systematic philosophy, liberal economics and sociology; and in other quarters, the Arnoldian programme was revitalized.

This disturbance of the discursive universe was redoubled by the quickening *social* recomposition of the intelligentsia that inhabited it. The aggregate effect of the changing occupational structure of the economy, the long process of reform and expansion in education, and the economic and political crises of the inter-war period, was to weaken the old intellectual bloc, whose inner cohesion and general authority had rested on its ties of kinship and privileged social intercourse with a confident ruling class. The inter-war intelligentsia was, by contrast, divided by social origin and occupational position, by political and cultural allegiance – deprived, in every salient respect, of security.

The multiple relations between these two orders of contradiction were central to the whole cultural history of inter-war Britain; Cambridge was in no sense unique. But in the unusual institutional conditions that prevailed there in the early twenties, they interacted with explosive force, producing a 'critical revolution', and so were *fused* by a new and pressing material interest: the need to defend a young and vulnerable 'discipline', against an haut-bourgeois belle-lettrism that hindered it from the rear and, on another front, against the steady, pre-emptive advance of a broadly 'social-scientific' culture which, by its very existence, proclaimed the obsolescence of the Arnoldian programme and threatened to relegate its partisans to the status of *ci-devant* amateurs. This was the magnitude of the historical charge borne by the idea of 'vindication' which, as term and still more as gesture, was so central a motif in the discourse of *Scrutiny*. 'Vindication': of the moral potency of literary studies, of the insistence that careers and status be governed always and only by talent, of the objective social importance and responsibility of those who practised and taught an indispensable 'discipline of intelligence' – in this one word were condensed the cultural and social drives that sustained a uniquely ambitious and militant 'literary criticism' for more than a quarter of a century and made it the dominant discourse of a whole profession.[16]

It may be possible, in the light of the conclusions ventured here, to decipher two of the most stubborn enigmas of *Scrutiny*'s career. The first concerns its role as cultural 'outlaw'. F. R. Leavis in particular always maintained – and he is followed in this by those who uphold his standard today – that *Scrutiny*'s campaign for critical integrity was met with harassment and victimization, misrepresentation and outright suppression, the reflexive gestures of a 'system' based on vested social and professional interest and encompassing the literary organs of the capital, the broadcasting and other cultural agencies of the State, and the universities. How can these charges be reconciled with the measurable evidence of *Scrutiny*'s public renown and influence, and – to state the problem at its paradoxical extreme – with the vast, almost folkloric dissemination that they themselves have received? The second question, equally enigmatic, is related to the first. Why

16. One further line of analysis is necessary before the above explanation of this discursive 'substitution' (literary criticism for a 'classical' sociology) can be judged complete: that is, an examination of the historical constitution of 'English' as a school and university discipline, comparing the process with its equivalents abroad. Such an analysis was, regrettably, not possible here.

was it that *Scrutiny* dwindled and closed at the very time that Leavis's influence as a critic and teacher was nearing its zenith?

'As for the literary world,' Leavis averred in his valedictory statement, 'a rich subject awaits some (probably American) researcher: the discrepancy between the official or conventionally agreed valuation of *Scrutiny* and the evidence of a decisive influence exerted.'[17] The charge implied in this statement has been repeated many times since. It is now common knowledge and is widely accepted as valid. It is by no means a groundless charge – *Scrutiny* and its contributors provoked hostility and derision in many quarters of English cultural life and continue to do so today; and, although the evidence in the matter is not and may never become available in its entirety, there seems little doubt that the Leavises (particularly Q. D. Leavis) suffered real and now irreparable injustice in their professional lives. Yet it must also be said – the more flatly for these qualifications – that the charge as stated constitutes a profound misrepresentation of the reception accorded to *Scrutiny*. Research into such matters can never be presumed complete, nor is it practical here to record its findings in detail. All that is offered is some indicative data and a general conclusion.[18]

The suggestion that *Scrutiny* and its leading contributors were ignored by the main reviewing organs of their time, or that they were systematically attacked, misrepresented or depreciated in them, is incorrect. If the journal was facetiously handled in the *London Mercury*, it was greeted with enthusiasm by the *Bookman*, to which Leavis himself contributed, and by the *Highway*, the organ of the Workers' Educational Association. Between June 1932 and the end of 1937, eighteen of *Scrutiny*'s twenty-two published issues received individual notices in the classified periodicals review of the *Times Literary Supplement*; the

17. XIX, 4 (October '53), p. 255. The continuing operations of the 'system' in the late seventies have recently been denounced in one of the most polemical works ever produced by *Scrutiny* or its intellectual descendants: Garry Watson's *The Leavises, the 'Social,' and the Left*, Swansea 1977.

18. The documentary evidence for what follows – some one hundred notices and reviews concerning the career, closure and reissue of *Scrutiny* or works by its main contributors produced between 1930 and 1953 – is grouped in the Select Bibliography below (II.1.i–iii). It will not be noted here except where specific reference is made to particular items.

content of these notices was, naturally, varied, but none of them was hostile and the majority were favourable. *Scrutiny* was very seldom mentioned in the relatively unsystematic and more foreign-oriented coverage to which this regular review gave way in the late thirties; but the TLS maintained its practice of reviewing the individual productions of the Leavis circle. *New Bearings, Fiction and the Reading Public, Culture and Environment, For Continuity* and *Revaluation* were all reviewed as they appeared, never less than respectfully and sometimes in highly commendatory terms. Knights's *Drama and Society in the Age of Jonson* was accorded a long and favourable front-page review; *Education and the University* was welcomed in an editorial statement; and the reviewer of *The Great Tradition* applauded Leavis as having 'thrown more light upon the aims and methods of the novel than any previous critic'.[19] It was not until the early fifties, and the appearance of *The Common Pursuit* and the second edition of *New Bearings*, that the tone of the TLS turned cold. Elsewhere, these books met with a more mixed but still, on balance, favourable reception. The notices of *New Bearings* printed in the *English Review*, the *Fortnightly Review* and the *Observer* were hostile, and in the latter two cases, demonstratively philistine; but the book was commended in the *New Statesman* and *Spectator*, the *Highway* and, above all, in the *Bookman*, where it was repeatedly praised by the editor, Hugh Ross Williamson, and acclaimed by Geoffrey Grigson as 'a book of great criticism'.[20] *Fiction and the Reading Public* was attacked in the *Observer* and the *New Statesman*, criticized in the *English Review* and patronized in the *Listener*, but praised in the *Sunday Times*, the *Spectator* and, especially, the *Bookman*. The response to *Culture and Environment* included a mixed review in *Life and Letters* and a more positive one in the *New Statesman*, two enthusiastic notices in the *Highway*, one of them by Storm Jameson, and a commendatory editorial in the *Listener*. The appearance of *Revaluation* was the occasion of Stephen Spender's attack on Leavis in the *Criterion*.[21] The book was grudgingly received by Bonamy Dobrée in the *Spectator*, in a mercurial review whose every compliment was shot through with ironic counter-suggestion. *The Great Tradition* was similarly greeted by Dobrée, again in the *Spectator*, but amidst all the ambiguity, it was still commended as 'one of the

19. 'Intelligence and Imagination,' February 12, 1949, p. 104.
20. LXXXII, 487 (April '32), pp. 41–2.
21. XVI, lxiii (January '37), pp. 350–53.

best and most stimulating books on the English novel that has yet been written'.[22]

The first implication of this sample is that, except in the most mindlessly gourmet or philistine milieux, and with all critical qualifications made, the *Scrutiny* circle were recognized from the outset as literary and cultural critics of high calibre, as major exponents of the new poetry and criticism and trenchant commentators on cultural and social problems – the state of reviewing, for example, or the phenomenon of 'standardization' – that were then causing widespread anxiety. However, there is a second, which balance-sheets of 'favourable' and 'unfavourable' reviews can only obscure: an almost universal resistance, varying in degree from the most genial complacency to the most outspoken aggression and expressed in every conceivable register, in the face of *Scrutiny*'s critical *style*, the values it embodied and the cultural duties that it sought to impose. It was not the substantive judgments or analytic procedures of *New Bearings* that provoked unease, but their 'narrowness' and rigour, the unaccommodating, 'puritan' tenor of the exposition. *Fiction and the Reading Public* was criticized less often for its historical analysis than for its activist conclusions. 'My first comment on this admirably argued and scholarly work must be in praise of its passionate sincerity,' wrote J. D. Beresford in the *Sunday Times*. However, it lacked 'sympathy and understanding' and was marred by a 'schoolmistress's impatience'. The serious and intelligent minority was as numerous as ever; it was merely that the literate but stupid had proliferated to form an entirely new 'class'.[23] The TLS hailed Leavis as a 'pioneer' but appeared unconcerned about the stratification of the reading public, concluding that 'from [her] masterly marshalling of evidence, historical and critical, it is possible, without undue optimism, to draw a very different set of inferences'.[24] The *Spectator*'s reviewer, meanwhile, found her diagnosis exact but 'unduly discouraged', and her programmatic suggestions 'a Utopian dream' – 'but one never knows. The old parable still holds good and the age of miracles is never really past.'[25] Widespread from the outset, such qualifications became increasingly marked in *Scru-*

22. 'The Aeolian Harp,' October 23, 1936, p. 694; and 'The Importance of Fiction,' December 3, 1948, pp. 736–7.

23. 'Reading for Pleasure,' April 17, 1932.

24. 'The Reader of Fiction,' April 28, 1932.

25. Arthur Waugh, 'Fiction and Its Readers,' April 16, 1932.

tiny's reception. The editor of the *Bookman*, who had hailed the emergence of this 'compact and militant body of criticism' as 'the most
important thing in the literary world of 1932', was by 1934 beginning
'to understand *leavisphobia* at last'.[26] Over the next twenty years, what
Ross Williamson had praised as 'militancy' (and the *Observer* derided
as 'high priori' minoritarian arrogance) was depicted variously as
quasi-religious fanaticism or psychological aberration, consigned to
the realm of literary folklore (F. R. Leavis 'is the Bandersnatch of
criticism, whom ... it is wiser to shun than to seek', wrote a TLS
reviewer in 1952) or simply deplored as perverse incivility. By the
time of the *Scrutiny* reissue in 1963, the master-pattern of majority
literary-critical opinion had been fixed. Leavis was a fine, a remarkable,
even a great critic, with eccentric, or unfortunate, if not unconscion-
able polemical manners – and, as Graham Hough described it, 'a
fervent sense of mission whose precise direction is now not easy to
discern'.[27] 'Demolition Squad at Work' was the title of Anthony
Quinton's *Sunday Telegraph* review, 'Roundheads and Cavaliers' that of
John Bayley's in the *Sunday Times*. At least three reviewers alluded to
the practices of Stalinism in discussing the style of the journal and its
chief editor;[28] C. B. Cox complained of its propensity for 'personal
abuse' and warned that 'this tone ought never to be heard again in
literary dispute'; and even Seymour Betsky spoke of the 'world of
vexatious charge and counter-charge' that Leavis's absolutism had
helped to create.[29] The loyalist riposte was entitled *Dr F. R. Leavis: The
Ogre of Downing Castle and Other Stories*.[30]

This second sample is no more complete than the first; and neither
is comprehensive in its range or in its account of the items that it
selects. Nevertheless, they are representative; and together, they
reveal the basic, constant pattern of *Scrutiny*'s reception in the dominant culture. A majority of writers, academic and 'metropolitan',
was from the outset prepared to accord the *Scrutiny* circle a more or

26. 'The Renaissance of Criticism,' LXXXIII, 495 (December '32), pp. 143–5.
27. 'Scrutineers, O Scrutineers!', LXXXVI, 511 (April '34), p. 2.
28. See J. G. Weightman, 'The Passion of "Scrutiny",' *The Nation*, December 7,
1963, pp. 393–4; Bayley, 'Roundheads and Cavaliers,' *Sunday Times*, and John Wain,
'Twenty-one Years with Dr Leavis,' *Observer*, both October 27, 1963.
29. Respectively, ' "Scrutiny": A Revaluation,' *Spectator*, October 25, 1963, p. 531;
and 'Scrutiny Rescrutinized,' *Universities Quarterly*, XVIII, 1 (December '63), pp. 82–91.
30. John Heilpern (ed.), Howard Jacobson *et al.*, Oxford 1963.

less prominent place within a pluralist literary-critical culture; with the passage of time, the majority grew steadily larger, and the proffered place more prominent. But virtually no one was prepared to accept that the condition of English culture as *Scrutiny* perceived it was new or alarming, that counter-measures were necessary and possible and that the ethics and tactics of *Scrutiny* were the appropriate ones. It was not that there was widespread disagreement with *Scrutiny*'s analysis: fundamental and comprehensive challenges to its central aesthetic, cultural and social presuppositions were and still are exceedingly rare. It was that very few were prepared, in principle and in practice, to answer its *call to struggle* – or, as the decades passed, able even to recognize that such a struggle existed, unless as the construction of a tormented and tyrannical psyche. But in rejecting this, the dominant culture rejected everything, including the 'actual literary criticism' – the 'rigour', the 'insight', the 'taste' – which, with this or that reservation made, was so widely held to compensate for the ill-effects of a disagreeable cultural episode. For what it rejected, and increasingly was unable even to focus, was the strategic objective that would make the discourse on community more than a contemplative pastime, that would fulfil the demand for *carrières ouvertes aux talents*, that, in sum, would 'vindicate' a life's commitment to the 'analysis and judgment' of literary texts: the formation of a homogeneous, institutionalized but non-'academic', socially 'disinterested' but militant clerisy.

How is *Scrutiny*'s reception to be explained? In order to answer this question, it is necessary to consider its role in the cultural history of the mid-century. *Scrutiny*'s objective cultural function was twofold: to mediate the establishment of a new, professionally chartered discourse on literature in the national culture; and, in the same process, to mediate the large-scale entry of a new social layer into the national intelligentsia. These were the source of its dynamism and appeal, and its real historic achievements. But they were also the cause of its Passion.

The early reaction to *Scrutiny*'s militancy was on the whole a rearguard phenomenon, composed equally of cultural obscurantism and social presumption. Attacks on 'the preferences of a rather pharisaical minority', reviews snidely entitled 'First Class Passengers Only' and facetious references to 'the storm troops of Discrimination' were the natural reflexes of a consumerist literary culture whose latitudinarian 'taste' was less democratic than patronizing, and formed by the same complacent social expectations that supported the more subtle pleasures of belles lettres and 'scholarship for its own sake'.[31] However, by the end of the war, *Scrutiny's* 'vanguard' campaign against the old regime had succeeded; within a further few years, the rebellious ideas of the thirties had become dominant in the teaching of English. The literary canons established by Leavis became highly influential, his critical methods even more so; and the broad cultural themes of his journal became commonplaces of secondary education. Many accepted them literally and in their entirety; reformed or diluted, debased or syncretized, they became the faith of a whole profession, an inclusive vision of things that no other school subject and few university disciplines even attempted to match. Yet, by the same token, this could not be a militant faith, and as it spread, *Scrutiny* itself was once again isolated. To the extent that the new 'English' gained in security and general educational prestige, the old militancy seemed unnecessary and even insupportable, and those who persisted in it, merely petulant, 'over-sensitive' or 'paranoid'. The rigours of Leavisian 'collaboration' were ultimately irreconcilable with the etiquette of workaday professional intercourse. The institutionalization of post-war 'English' was thus a contradictory process, in which *Scrutiny* simultaneously won and lost; and although these contradictions were duly negotiated, they could never be quite suppressed. The myth of literature's lonely integrity, of criticism as witness to the authentic and opponent of the prevailing order of things, became endemic in a large and respectable profession whose cultural hubris was in reality all too widely indulged, and the 'ostracism' of *Scrutiny* became the open secret of the culture.

The enigmas of *Scrutiny's* institutional success were further deepened

31. See respectively, Michael Sadleir, 'Best-Sellers: A Massacre,' *New Statesman,* April 30, 1932, pp. 559–60; anon., reviewing *New Bearings* in the same journal, February 27, 1932, pp. 266–8; and anon., 'Getting Together,' *Life and Letters* x, 56 (August '34), pp. 624–7. See also the terms of Arthur Calder Marshall's attack on F. R. Leavis and Knights as epigones of Eliot, Richards and Empson: 'the emotions of the dining-room grow big in the servants' hall. Whom the master dislikes, the housemaid hates' ('One Must Have Standards,' *New Statesman,* June 1933, p. 739).

by the social thrust of its campaign, which was to mediate the introduction of a new, mainly petit bourgeois and self-consciously 'provincial' social layer into the national intelligentsia. The long sequence of educational reform that culminated in the Act of 1944 created the material conditions for a relative equalization of access to intellectual careers. But the immediate effect of this process was to intensify social antagonisms within the intelligentsia, creating a kind of caste system that organized every aspect of intellectual life from academic appointments to the minutiae of personal manner.[32] Before the neophyte social layers could become fully a part of the intelligentsia, certain alterations were necessary: in the manifest social commitments of the dominant culture, in its occupational traditions, in the whole impalpable system of connotation that had been organized in the culture by more than a century of haut-bourgeois predominance. It was here that *Scrutiny* played a crucial role. This aspect of the journal's campaign was lucidly perceived by some at least of its leading figures – Q. D. Leavis's assaults on Woolf, Sayers and Gordon were outstanding cases in point – and was often discussed in the decade after its closure, especially among younger intellectuals who were and openly proclaimed themselves its beneficiaries. Malcolm Bradbury, writing in 1956 on 'the rise of the provincials' in English culture, testified to the moral power exercised by Leavis over young intellectuals like himself who had 'been brought up in lower middle-class households where this kind of nonconformist strenuousness is to be found, where moral issues are pressing'. Educational and other cultural opportunities had only recently come to 'the children of these homes', he continued, and 'to people of this background, dilettantism and the "amused superiority" of the sophisticated may well be repugnant'. They were very often graduates of the nineteenth-century provincial universities whose ruling virtues were 'good hard work, keeping decent and getting on'. It was to this generation, in these social and cultural circumstances, that *Scrutiny* spoke most directly; for 'the training in taste' that it had adumbrated was qualitatively different from 'that Good Taste that one associates with the dons of Oxford colleges, with

32. For discussions of the social dynamics of English culture in the mid-century, see Edward Shils, 'The Intellectuals (I): Great Britain,' *Encounter* IV, 4 (April '55), pp. 5–16; and A. H. Halsey, 'British Universities and Intellectual Life' [1958], in Halsey *et al.* (ed.), *Education, Economy and Society*, London 1965, pp. 502–12.

Virginia Woolf or E. M. Forster – it is far less dilettante and elite, involving rather a rigorous training in discrimination.' Bradbury went on then to trace the rapidly spreading influence of *Scrutiny* and, finally, to evoke the social timbre of the culture now emerging: '... already certain common references, attitudes of mind, traits of style, even, suggest the nature of the change. And certainly the rebellion of the middle-brows has not been without its victories, and there have come into the literary scene new tones and manners, a new provincialism in the better sense of the word, a stringency not at all urbane, beating out the meaning of good taste on its own pulse.'[33]

Awareness of this change was pervasive in English cultural discussion in the fifties. In 1953, some three years before the appearance of Bradbury's essay, Stephen Spender had spoken out against what he saw as 'a rebellion of the Lower Middle Brows', 'an uprising against the intellectual trends of Oxford, Cambridge, and London, and the influence on literary figures of Paris and Berlin', a 'new provincial puritanism' that dealt with literature in the spirit of 'sanitary engineering'.[34] Three years after 'The Rise of the Provincials', one ex-pupil of Leavis's, Martin Green, was announcing his vision of a new cultural 'hegemony' in which the trophies of aristocracy and Empire would at long last be displaced by the values of little-British 'decency'.[35] Assessments of the new post-war sensibility were as various as their authors, but on one issue there was broad agreement: a decisive shift had occurred in the social equilibrium of English culture, most markedly in the literary sector, and its leading intellectual agency had been *Scrutiny*.

For *Scrutiny* itself, this social shift, like the discursive shift associated with it, was both a victory and a defeat. For it was not only that the

33. *Antioch Review* XVI, 4 (December '56), pp. 469–77, esp. pp. 471, 475, 477 – see also K. W. Gransden's claim that 'Leavis is the master (not always acknowledged) of a whole generation of the new articulate, the intelligent outsiders who have made their way without influence, just using their literary wits' (*Encounter* XII, 6, June '59, pp. 89–90). Bradbury's commendatory use of the term 'middle-brow' may seem absurd in this connection, but the values that it connoted here were those of *Scrutiny*, as qualified by the greater national provinciality of post-war English culture. It should be noted that Spender, speaking for the cosmopolitan 'highbrows' of the inter-war period, used the same term, in a negative sense, to describe *Scrutiny*'s offspring. See also Martin Green, n.35 below.
34. 'Comment: On Literary Movements,' *Encounter* I, 2 (November '53), pp. 66–8.
35. The 'heroes' of this petit-bourgeois 'hegemony' were to be D. H. Lawrence, George Orwell, F. R. Leavis and Kingsley Amis. In Green's eyes, Leavis represented

militancy of the early days became progressively less necessary and desirable; what was more important was that the objective limits of *Scrutiny*'s revolt had now been reached. It had been a quintessentially *petit bourgeois* revolt, directed against a cultural order that it could not fundamentally alter or replace.[36] *Scrutiny*'s oppressor was the *pays légal* of British history and culture, the educational system, the temporal Cambridge, the coteries, metropolitan journalism and academic criticism; all it could invoke against it was the *pays réel* of 'English tradition', 'culture', 'education', the 'essential Cambridge', the minority, a 'higher journalism' and 'genuine literary criticism' – so many idealized versions of what actually existed, differentiated and ratified only by reference to a recessive past. It was, accordingly, a *moralistic* revolt from within the given culture: bearer not of an alternative order but of the insistence that the existing order should live by its word, and this by permitting the optimum organization of its best human resources, the disinterested minority who expected nothing but the due recognition of talent and dedication. By the same token, however, the cogency of the programme was in direct proportion to the level of the inner-cultural social antagonisms to which the 'vindication' of 'the minority' seemed the appropriate solution; as these subsided, palliated by material reform, the dwindling world role of the imperial ruling class and the rise of a new plainness in the national culture, the perceptible discrepancy between the *pays légal* and the *pays réel* was greatly diminished, and those who insisted on the need to abolish it were isolated as incorrigible sectarians and purists. As Bradbury observed, perhaps over-neatly, 'the end of

---

'sanity and vigour and masculinity and Britishness'. More than this, 'he was intensely and integrally British. Not Europeanized, not of the intelligentsia, not of the upper classes, not of Bloomsbury, not of any group or set. . . . [He] comes to us from generations of decency and conscience and reasonableness and separateness, of private houses hidden behind hedges, along the road from Matthew Arnold and John Stuart Mill. . . . Alone in all Cambridge his voice has echoes of the best things in my parents' England, makes connections between all the parts of my experience' ('British Decency,' *Kenyon Review* xxi, 4, Autumn '59, pp. 505–32). Leavis deserved better from his admirers than this phantasmagoria. Still, such were the fantasies that he unlocked in sections of the intelligentsia. See now Green's *Children of the Sun* (London 1977), which narrates the doings of England's unmanly, irresponsible, cosmopolitan haut-bourgeois intelligentsia after 1918, but also qualifies its author's earlier allegiance to 'British decency', and endorses a higher dandyism whose inspiration is the novels of Vladimir Nabokov.

36. The term 'petit bourgeois' is not entirely satisfactory here, in part because

[Scrutiny] itself seemed the turning point in the growth of its reputation'.[37] The diffusion of Scrutiny's cultural themes, and their practical
'vindication' in the profane form of a self-confident and upwardly
mobile profession, rendered its organized combativity obsolete, if not
superfluous. It had been an inspirational enterprise, effectively the
forcing-house of a new discipline, its legitimating ideology and its
characteristic sensibility, but it was now de trop. Increasingly, as the
culture changed around it, Scrutiny summoned its readers to yesterday's struggles, exhorted them to what came naturally, menaced them
with revelations of the obvious. By the mid-fifties, there was only its
chief editor, supported by a lesser 'minority' phenomenon, 'the
Leavisites', bent still on a passionate, unending perturbation of the
status quo.

These were the twin cultural movements, discursive and social, that
brought Scrutiny into being and carried it away, that closed it down and
made it, quite literally, a living legend. Both were of relatively long
duration, extending from the early twenties into the late fifties, and
neither can be precisely periodized without more thorough analysis
than is feasible here. However, it seems clear that the decade after
the Second World War was decisive for their development. 1945 was
not only the year in which Butler's meritocratic educational reforms
began to take effect; it also saw the emergence of the first whole
generation of specialist teachers of English trained in the spirit of 'the

---

of the relative theoretical indeterminacy into which it has fallen. It is not that
Scrutiny 'reflected' the state or 'expressed' the interests of the English petit bourgeoisie as a whole, with all its historically constituted peculiarities and propensities, or even that its adherents were invariably of petit bourgeois origin (though
many of them, including the most important, were drawn from this social layer).
But it must be recognized that the profession 'represented' by the journal was and
is, on any acceptable definition, part of the petit bourgeoisie, and that its members – in modern England at least – have typically been of uncertain status in
relation both to the other professions and to the rest of the intelligentsia. Göran
Therborn has remarked of the sociological exponents of 'community' that they
were typically 'tinged by aristocratic attachments and traditions or . . . related
to the petty or lower bourgeoisie' – 'subaltern' fractions for whom capitalism
was an 'unnatural' society (p. 421). These class ascriptions require more thorough
historical and theoretical analysis than either Therborn's book or this more
limited study provides, but the existing evidence gives no reason to think them
perverse.
37. 'The Rise of the Provincials,' p. 475.

critical revolution' – a generation deeply influenced by Richards and Leavis but relatively lacking in the inter-disciplinary competence that had produced their innovations and sustained them in practical form.[38] 1949 saw the closure of *Horizon*, the last influential literary organ of extra-academic provenance to be conducted in England. Then, just over twelve months later, in the New Year of 1951, *Essays in Criticism* was founded: fusing the innovations of the inter-war period with an older tradition of academic philology – each being said to correct and complete the other – Bateson's journal marked the 'settlement' after the excesses of the 'revolution', the symbolic initiation of the reformed academic discipline of English.[39]

There was a further historical shift, broader than and independent of this national-cultural sequence, which also intervened, as it had done in the past, to alter the fortunes of the journal: that of politics. *Scrutiny*'s discourse was at once compatible and at odds with the emergent cultural formations of the Cold War in the West. It was evidently anti-Communist; but in its most rigorous and militant post-war expressions, it was also opposed to the prevailing order in the West. Always sceptical of contemporary versions of 'progress', *Scrutiny* in its last days was becoming demonstratively hostile to the entire political and social universe of post-war Britain – to all those tokens of freedom and prosperity on which the ideological defence of the West was now coming to depend. By 1953, the newly-founded monthly, *Encounter*, was calling anti-Communist intellectuals to a cultural campaign of a much less ambiguous kind. Yet here again the general rule of *Scrutiny*'s history was obeyed, and the outcome was at once a failure and a success. For while *Scrutiny* militant was too mani-

38. The transition to the new specialism was visible in the history of *Scrutiny* itself. The high period of the journal was that commanded by F. R. Leavis and the early graduates of Cambridge English, Harding, Knights, Q. D. Leavis and Thompson – five authors who, in aggregate, wrote on virtually every topic that *Scrutiny* ever discussed. The second *Scrutiny* generation, led by Cox and Ford, was markedly more restricted in range. Among the succeeding generations of regular contributors, the broad cultural themes of the early years were more often than not reduced to conventional tropes in the discourse of specialized appraisers of English literature.

39. See, in this context, Bateson's essay on the *Review of English Studies*, the 'critical' counterpart of his 'scholarly' dissent from *Scrutiny* ('Organs of Critical Opinion: I. The *Review of English Studies*,' *Essays in Criticism* VI, 2, April '56, pp. 190–201).

festly reactionary, too 'totalitarian' in style to be really viable in Cold War conditions,[40] the less exacting, more diffuse variants of its cultural meta-politics created a certain discretionary space for intellectuals who felt uneasy in the simple role of watchdogs of the West, and, more important still, offered an element of real 'neutrality', a power of 'disinterested' moral radiation that the harbingers of 'the end of ideology' could never command. Hence, while the journal itself was gradually starved of active collaboration, its moral 'politics' became widely diffused in an intelligentsia already suspected of 'neutralist' proclivities, at a time when the ionization of politics was virtually complete.[41]

In this way, cultural and political change combined to seal the fate of *Scrutiny* and its posthumous fortune. If by the mid-fifties it was 'histoire terminée', every circumstance conspired to ensure that it would also remain 'histoire interminable'.[42]

What was *Scrutiny*'s legacy to English culture, and how is it to be regarded by socialists today? Most obviously, of course, there have been the subsequent activities of its editors and contributors, and their self-proclaimed descendants. The many books written by the Leavises, Knights, Harding, Mellers, Traversi and others, the National Association of Teachers of English, founded by Thompson and Ford, and its organ *The Use of English*, the seven volumes of the Pelican *Guide to English Literature*, devised by Ford and largely written by *Scrutiny* contributors and their immediate posterity, are among the most conspicuous monuments to the cultural triumphs of the journal.

40. The recurrence of Cold War imagery in discussions of the 1963 reissue is noteworthy in this regard. Fritz Stern's study (see n. 7 above), written towards the end of the Cold War, was avowedly concerned with 'the *pathology* of cultural criticism', with 'the *dangers* and *dilemmas* of a particular type of cultural despair' (p. xi, my emphases) and repeatedly stressed the role of *Zeitkritik* in the cultural pre-history of National Socialism (pp. xi–xxx, 289–98).

41. For British intellectual 'neutralism' and the creation of *Encounter* as an antidote to it, see Christopher Lasch, 'The Cultural Cold War: A Short History of the Congress for Cultural Freedom,' in his *The Agony of the American Left*, London 1973, pp. 70–71.

42. 'Histoire terminée, histoire interminable' is the title of Louis Althusser's Preface to Dominique Lecourt, *Lyssenko*, Paris 1976 (translated into English as *Proletarian Science? The Case of Lysenko*, London 1977). No analogy between the two cases is intended here.

There have also been various attempts to resume the 'critical function in new or longer-lived journals. *The Human World* (1970–74) provided temporary accommodation for a gathering of Right-wing Leavisites and other species of cultural reactionary; it won a number of contributions from Leavis, but was eventually disowned by him. A more specialist, and revisionist, continuation of Leavisian criticism exists in the *Cambridge Quarterly*, which was founded in 1965 under the editorship of H. A. Mason and, again, was before long repudliated by Leavis. And the notion of a 'humane centre' has recently been revived in the liberal *New Universities Quarterly* (edited by Ford), in which some of Leavis's last writings were published.[43] These and related post-*Scrutiny* developments are a study in themselves. For present purposes, it is more pertinent to consider the after-life of *Scrutiny* in the general culture, in its three distinguishable aspects: its style of cultural practice; the aesthetic and critical canons that it propagated; and, underlying these, its discourse on 'community'.

Scrutiny's style is less a legacy than an unhappy memory. It was from the beginning the main ground of hostility to the journal, and the passage of nearly fifty years has done little to make it any more acceptable to the dominant culture. There was, and still is, good reason for this virtually uniform reaction. For what that style embodied – what its exponents avowedly sought – was an intellectual formation of a type virtually unknown in and deeply alien to English bourgeois culture: an 'intelligentsia' in the classic sense of the term, a body of intellectuals dissociated from every established social interest, pointed in its subordination of amenity to principle, united only by its chosen cultural commitments. This was the spectre that induced the self-consoling scorn of the *Observer* in the early thirties, that caused one reviewer after another to reach for epithets like 'prim', 'narrow', 'priggish' and 'puritan', and whose presence, much faded now but still resistant to exorcism, can be discerned in even the calmest 'establishment' criticism of the most clockwork among

43. For Leavis's public comments on *The Human World*, see his letter to the *Listener*, January 18, 1973 (*Letters in Criticism*, p. 151) and on the *Cambridge Quarterly*, his letters to the *Oxford Review* (another neo-Leavisian venture), the TLS, February 17, 1966, and the *Spectator*, November 4, 1972 (*Letters . . .*, pp. 119–24, 125 and 159 respectively). *Universities Quarterly* acquired its new name and an expanded editorial board at the end of 1975, when it published a symposium to mark Leavis's eightieth birthday (xxx, 1, Winter).

Leavis's latter-day epigones. The idea of a pure, 'free-floating' intelligentsia was always a myth, albeit one of the more noble of bourgeois myths; and by the end of the war, the tension in *Scrutiny*'s posture between 'vanguard' and 'elite' had been largely resolved in favour of the latter.[44] None the less it is wholly appropriate that the two most penetrating critiques of *Scrutiny* yet written in England – by Marxists: Anderson and Eagleton – should both have emphasized and paid tribute to this dimension of its work.[45] As Eagleton wrote, 'no more militant, courageous and consistent project is to be found in the history of English criticism'. Indeed, a larger and more precise claim should be made. *No* sector of English culture in the present century – Right or Left, literary or other – has produced anything comparable to *Scrutiny*, or a writer who surpassed F. R. Leavis in this respect. Genuinely militant writing does not consist in partisanship clamantly asserted (though this may on occasion play a necessary part). Its fundamental precondition is an analysis and a perspective capable of determining the meaning and potential of particular conjunctures and so, the character of the interventions to be made in them. This precondition was met in *Scrutiny* and, with special completeness and consciousness, in the writings of F. R. Leavis – it might be said indeed that his early polemical collection, *For Continuity*, was a more militant cultural intervention than either of the comparable Marxist productions of the same decade, Caudwell's *Studies in a Dying Culture* or Day Lewis's symposium, *The Mind in Chains*. The polemical practices of *Scrutiny* and its chief editor were by no means above all reproach. But the excesses and aberrations of Leavis's later years (not to speak of the routine demonstrations of the epigones) have too often been presented as the essential features of his journal's cultural style – erroneously, and for reasons that are at least equally questionable.

44. These terms are Terry Eagleton's (*Criticism and Ideology*, London 1976, pp. 14–15). Eagleton correctly relates this aspect of *Scrutiny* to the petit bourgeois character of the enterprise. It should be added, however, that this was also a constitutional trait of romantic 'cultural criticism', which the poet Von Hofmannsthal described, in an almost cognate paradox, as a 'conservative revolution' (cit. Stern, p. xv).

45. In 'Components of the National Culture,' *New Left Review* 50 (May-June 1968), and *Criticism and Ideology*, pp. 12–16, respectively. Raymond Williams was perhaps the first of *Scrutiny*'s critics to commend this quality in the journal: see 'Our Debt to Dr Leavis,' *Critical Quarterly* I, 3 (Autumn '59), pp. 245–7; and his article on the reissue ('Scrutiny,' *Guardian*, October 25, 1963).

M

This militant, committed, interventionist cultural practice must be seen and judged at its best and in all its real historical significance. It was *Scrutiny*'s least welcome 'contribution' to England's dominant culture; today, among socialists at least, it should be defended and honoured.

If the style of *Scrutiny*'s campaign is an unhappy memory, its substance is more like a mortmain. This component of the legacy was most obviously a literary one, itself comprising three elements: a critical-historical canon defining the major 'traditions' of English literature; a loosely formulated methodology of critical practice; and a cluster of ideas concerning the nature of literature and its place in social life. How have these been received by its posterity? It might be said, somewhat schematically, that the first was extremely influential, winning widespread assent in the fifties, and, in spite of multiplying disagreement over specific judgments, has remained the one ineluctable point of reference in English literary-critical discussion ever since. The second, in company with Ricardian 'practical criticism' and the methods of the New Critics, was more or less naturalized as the technically necessary approach to literary language, and has only recently begun to be challenged by alternative methodologies, derived largely from French and Russian semiotics. And the third, commingled with kindred conceptions of a dilute romantic character, has become part of the spontaneous ideology of academic literary criticism and of English teaching at every level of education. These generalizations may be charged with obscuring the real variety of literary criticism in contemporary England; but they are supported by a further generalization which the diversifying trends of the last decade have yet to invalidate. Many critics have argued, more or less successfully, against one or another or Leavis's particular judgments; some have challenged one or another of his general assumptions or procedures; whole books exist whose very structure 'enacts' an overthrow of his criticism; but *none* of these writers has produced anything even resembling an integrated account and assessment of his aesthetic and critical position. Forty years have passed since Wellek asked Leavis to furnish a systematic defence of his criticism, and twenty-five since Bateson demonstrated its innate subjectivism. In that time, Leavis's manifestly evasive rejoinders have become famous, while his challengers have gone unanswered, neither rebutted nor reinforced. It is this circumstance rather than the prevailing level of acceptance of *The Great Tradition* that suggests the persistent strength of *Scrutiny*'s hegemony in English criticism. Marxist critics have been considerably more synoptic and probing in their analyses of Leavis and *Scrutiny*, but none of them has focussed centrally and in detail on this dimension of their subject.[46] Their studies are the groundwork for the systematic and exhaustive Marxist critique of Leavisian aesthetics and criticism that must one day be written.

The persistence of this aesthetics and criticism is the main index of *Scrutiny*'s cultural power. But the most pervasive and damaging effects of that power are generated at another level, in that complex of ideas that invests the apparently specialist procedures of 'literary criticism', in the discourse on 'community'. This was the source of *Scrutiny*'s profound appeal in education: in English, where it furnished literary studies with an enviable social warrant and directly legitimated the expansion of criticism into new territories of study (journalism and advertising above all), and, to a lesser extent, in the 'humane' disciplines as a whole, where it underwrote the privileged status of education as a site of corrective social criticism. It has also been the source of *Scrutiny*'s quite constant appeal for the Left, over nearly fifty years.[47] The reasons for this are not difficult to find. At the most practical and pertinent level, it was evident that *Scrutiny* had opened up an educational space within which the cultural institutions of bourgeois-democratic capitalism could be subjected to critical analysis – a space which was to be utilized to remarkable effect, most notably by Raymond Williams and the Centre for Contemporary Cultural Studies founded by Richard Hoggart at Birmingham University. And more

46. Anderson's essay discusses Leavis's epistemology but not his aesthetic categories. Eagleton's miniature likewise omits discussion of them. Williams's *Marxism and Literature* includes a radical critique of the whole macro-historical cultural formation known as 'literary criticism', but in a context of general argument from which such particular considerations are excluded (London 1977, esp. pp. 45–54).

47. This is another history for another occasion, but a short-list of sources may help to substantiate the point: A. L. Morton, 'Culture and Leisure,' *Scrutiny* I, 4 (March '33), pp. 324–6; John Drummond, 'Culture,' *Cambridge Left* I, 2 (Winter '33–'34), pp. 46–8; the journals *Politics and Letters* (1947–48) and *The Critic* (1947); Richard Hoggart, *The Uses of Literacy*, London 1957; Raymond Williams, *Culture and Society 1780–1950*, London 1958; Richard Collins, 'Revaluations,' *Screen Education* 22 (Spring 1977), pp. 31–7.

generally, *Scrutiny* seemed in some obvious respects a 'natural' ally of the Left: not socialist perhaps, but including socialists among its followers, and in any case resolutely opposed to a 'civilization' which was, in truth, that of capitalism. The privilege of hindsight is all too easily abused. But it should always have been apparent to socialists – or at least much more so than it was – that the educational themes and practices handed down by *Scrutiny*, seen as the elements of a *strategy*, were never more than a radical-romantic counterpoint to the conventional wisdom of liberal-Fabian educational policy, a latter-day variation on the romantic/utilitarian antinomy that constitutes one of the abiding structures of industrial-capitalist culture in general and, very conspicuously, that of modern Britain. And it should certainly be clear today that these themes, where they are more than so much sedimented common sense, have lost whatever element of radicalism they once possessed: their most energetic continuators today, at the level of public debate, are not the analysts of 'popular culture' and teachers of 'media studies' (who have re-worked their 'heritage' to a point where it is merely sentimental to speak of origins) or the liberal-humanist theorists of education (whose conceptions, long since irreversibly hybridized, are now falling into official disfavour) but the *Black Papers*, the leading intellectual agency of the meritocratic counter-revolution. Furthermore – and this is the crucial consideration – there was always an element of a grave error in the supposition that *Scrutiny*'s critical discourse on 'community' could in any significant sense assist the cause of socialism or even be tapped for that purpose. It is not that *Scrutiny* was 'Luddite' – this charge was always either uncomprehending or confusionist, and scarcely deserves even the meagre dignity of a debating point – nor merely that it idealized the past and saw only what was meretricious in the present – there is truth in this, but the problem was never one of 'balance'. It is essentially that the basic and constant discursive organization of the journal, the matrix of its literary and cultural criticism and of its educational policies, of its radical and conservative manifestations alike, was one defined by a dialectic of 'culture' and 'civilization' whose *main* and *logically necessary effect* was a *depreciation*, a *repression* and, at the limit, a *categorial dissolution* of *politics as such*. Nothing could be more disorienting for socialist cultural theory than the ingestion of a discourse whose main effect is to undo the intelligibility of its ultimate concern:

political mobilization against the existing structures of society and State.

So, to say that criticism of this kind should be identified and contested in all its unnumbered variations is not only to register the evident need for a comprehensive theoretical critique of its assumptions, mechanisms and effects. What is in question is not simply another set of 'bourgeois ideas', or even a set of ideas which Marxists of a certain cultural formation must take special pains to understand. For if 'literary criticism' is certainly not a 'natural' articulation of 'response' to literary art, neither is it simply an ideological mode of reading to which a scientific alternative must be posed by Marxists specializing in aesthetics – and it is not because they are relatively underdeveloped that such Marxists quite consistently receive much more hostile treatment at the hands of academic reviewers than do their fellow-Marxists in economics, sociology or philosophy. 'Literary criticism' as it is mainly practised in England is in reality the focal activity of a discourse whose foremost general cultural function is the repression of politics. This discourse had done much to shape, and still sustains, England's cultivated, politically philistine (and so, conformist) intelligentsia; it is reproduced daily, with countless particular inflections, by the entire national educational system: it is a key element in the 'cultural formula' of bourgeois Britain, part of an ensemble of cultural *domination*. What is required, then, is a vigorous contestation not only of 'ideas' but of the institutions and practices that sustain them, in journalism, in education and elsewhere – a concerted cultural struggle for which the only modern precedent in England is *Scrutiny*. Other models will be cited and new ones imagined, but one way or another, something of that peerless militancy will have to be discovered by the Left before the moment of *Scrutiny* can at last be ended.

Select Bibliography

I. PRIMARY SOURCES

1. *Scrutiny: A Quarterly Review*, 19 volumes, Cambridge, May 1932–October 1953.
2. *Writings by 'Scrutiny' editors and contributors published elsewhere.*
Bantock, Geoffrey Herbert, 'Literature and the Social Sciences,' *Critical Quarterly* XVII, 2 (Summer 1975).
Bewley, Marius, *The Complex Fate*, with an introduction and two interpolations by F. R. Leavis, London 1952.
Ford, Boris, 'The First Scrutineers,' *Comment*, February 5, 1977.
Harding, Denys W., 'Some Social Implications of Industrial Psychology,' *Highway* XXV (March 1933).
——, *The Impulse to Dominate*, London 1941.
Jameson, Storm, 'Fighting the Foes of Civilization: the Writer's Place in the Defence Line,' TLS, October 7, 1939.
——, *Journey From the North*, 2 volumes, London 1969, 1970.
Klingopulos, G. D., 'D. H. Lawrence – Novelist,' *Universities Quarterly* X, 2 (February 1956).
Knights, Lionel Charles, 'Four Quartets Rehearsed,' *Humanitas* I, 1 (Summer 1946).
——, *Drama and Society in the Age of Jonson*, London 1937.
——, *Explorations: Mainly on the Literature of the Seventeenth Century*, London 1946.
Leavis, Frank Raymond, 'T. S. Eliot: A Reply to the Condescending,' *Cambridge Review*, February 8, 1929.
——, 'Cambridge Poetry,' *Cambridge Review*, March 1, 1929.
——, *Mass Civilization and Minority Culture*, Cambridge 1930.

334

Leavis, Frank Raymond, 'On D. H. Lawrence,' *Cambridge Review*, June 13, 1930.

——, *D. H. Lawrence*, Cambridge 1930.

——, 'Empson's Criticism,' *Cambridge Review*, January 16, 1931.

——, 'Criticism of the Year,' *Bookman* LXXXI, 483 (December 1931).

——, *New Bearings in English Poetry*, London 1932 (with Retrospect 1950, London 1950).

——, *How to Teach Reading: A Primer for Ezra Pound*, Cambridge 1932.

——, 'Poetry in an Age of Science,' *Bookman* LXXXII, 487 (April 1932).

——, 'Poetry-Lovers, Prosody and Poetry,' *Spectator*, May 14, 1932.

——, 'This Age in Literary Criticism,' *Bookman* LXXXIII, 493 (October 1932).

——, and Denys Thompson, *Culture and Environment*, London 1933.

——, ed. and introd., *Towards Standards of Criticism: Selections from 'The Calendar of Modern Letters' 1925–7*, London 1933 (reprint with new Introduction, London 1976).

——, *For Continuity*, Cambridge 1933.

——, ed. and introd., *Determinations. Critical Essays*, London 1934.

——, 'Shelley's Imagery,' *Bookman* LXXXVI, 516 (September 1934).

——, *Revaluation: Tradition and Development in English Poetry*, London 1936.

——, *Education and the University: A Sketch for an 'English School'*, London 1943 (second, expanded ed., London 1948).

——, 'Literary Criticism and Politics,' *Politics and Letters* I, 2–3 (Winter-Spring 1947–8).

——, *The Great Tradition: George Eliot, Henry James, Joseph Conrad*, London 1948.

——, 'The State of Criticism: Representations to Fr. Martin Jarrett-Kerr,' *Essays in Criticism* III, 2 (April 1953).

——, Reply to L. D. Lerner (q.v.), *The London Magazine* II, 3 (March 1955).

——, *D. H. Lawrence: Novelist*, London 1955.

——, 'Literary Studies: A Reply [to W. W. Robson, q.v.],' *Universities Quarterly* XI, 1 (November 1956).

——, *'Scrutiny': A Retrospect*, Cambridge 1963.

——, *'Anna Karenina' and Other Essays*, London 1967.

——, *English Literature in Our Time and The University*, London 1969.

——, and Q. D. Leavis, *Lectures in America*, London 1969.

——, and Q. D. Leavis, *Dickens: the Novelist*, London 1970.

——, *Nor Shall My Sword*, London 1972.

——, *The Living Principle*, London 1975.

——, *Thought, Words and Creativity*, London 1976.

Leavis, Queenie Dorothy, *Fiction and the Reading Public*, London 1932.

Mason, H. A., 'F. R. Leavis and *Scrutiny*,' *The Critic* I, 2 (Autumn 1947).

Parkes, Henry Bamford, *Marxism: A Post-Mortem*, London 1940.

Podhoretz, Norman, *Making It*, London 1968.

Schenk, Wilhelm, 'Social Radicalism Past and Present,' *Humanitas* I, 2 (Autumn 1946).

Tomlin, E. W. F., 'The Bankruptcy of Political Thought,' *Arena* I, 2 (July 1937).

——, 'Marxist Economics,' *Arena* I, 3 (October-December 1937).

Traversi, Derek, 'Marxism and English Poetry,' *Arena* I, 3 (October-December 1937).

T[urnell], G. M[artin], rev. *Scrutiny* and *Determinations*, *Colosseum* II, 5 (March 1935).

——, 'The Function of a Catholic Critic,' *Colosseum* II, 8 (December 1935).

——, 'The Criticism of Mr F. R. Leavis,' *Colosseum* III, 12 (December 1936).

——, 'The Patrician in Politics: Some Reflections on Re-reading Baudelaire,' *Cornhill Magazine* 162 (Autumn 1946).

——, *The Classical Moment*, London 1947.

——, 'An Intellectual Looks at the Crisis,' *The Nineteenth Century and After* CXLIII (January 1948).

——, 'John Donne and the Quest for Unity,' *The Nineteenth Century and After* CXLVII (1950).

Winkler, R. O. C., 'The Critic and Leviathan,' *Politics and Letters* I, 1 (Summer 1947).

II. SECONDARY SOURCES

1. *The Response to 'Scrutiny'*
(i) 1932–53

Agar, Herbert, 'Humanism Inside Out,' *English Review*, June 1932.

Anon., 'Poetry Today,' *Sunday Times*, March 13, 1932.

——, rev. *New Bearings in English Poetry*, *The Highway* XXIV (April 1932).

336

Anon., 'A Critical Quarterly,' *The Highway* XXV (January 1933).

——, rev. *Culture and Environment, Life and Letters* IX (March 1933).

——, 'Taste Without Tears,' *Life and Letters* X (May 1934).

——, 'Getting Together,' *Life and Letters* X (August 1934).

——, 'First-Class Passengers Only,' *New Statesman*, February 27, 1932.

——, rev. *Culture and Environment, New Statesman*, February 18, 1933.

Armitage, Gilbert, 'Criticism of the Year,' *Bookman* LXXXIII, 495 (December 1932).

Beresford, J. D., 'Reading for Pleasure,' *Sunday Times*, April 17, 1932.

Brown, Ivor, 'A Purge for Poetry,' *Observer*, November 11, 1932.

Browne, Wynyard, 'The Culture-Brokers,' *London Mercury*, XXVIII, 167 (September 1933).

Calder Marshall, Arthur, 'One Must Have Standards,' *New Statesman*, June 3, 1933.

Church, Richard, 'The Labyrinthine Way,' *Spectator*, March 26, 1932.

Dobrée, Bonamy, ' "So Circumspect and Right",' *Spectator*, June 29, 1934.

——, 'The Aeolian Harp,' *Spectator*, October 23, 1936.

——, 'The Importance of Fiction,' *Spectator*, December 3, 1948.

Drummond, John, 'Culture,' *Cambridge Left* I, 2 (Winter 1933–4).

Dupee, F. W., 'British Periodicals,' *Partisan Review* V, 1 (June 1938).

Editorial, 'Real v. Substitute Living,' *Listener*, February 15, 1933.

Eliot, T. S., 'A Commentary,' *Criterion* XI, xlv (July 1932).

Grigson, Geoffrey, 'A Book of Great Criticism,' *Bookman* LXXXII, 487 (April 1932).

Hussey, Maurice, Letter to the Editor, TLS, September 1, 1950.

Jameson, Storm, 'The Cultivation of Values,' *Highway* XXV (March 1933).

Kingsmill, Hugh, '1932 and the Victorians,' *English Review*, June 1932.

Linnell, John, rev. *New Bearings in English Poetry, Fortnightly Review*, April 1932.

Partridge, Eric, 'Fiction and the Public,' *English Review*, July 1932.

Quennell, Peter, 'A Chronicle of Recent Books,' *Life and Letters* VIII (June 1932).

Sackville-West, V., rev. *Fiction and the Reading Public, Listener*, May 25, 1932.

Sadleir, Michael, 'Best-Sellers: A Massacre,' *New Statesman*, April 30, 1932.

Spender, Stephen, rev. *Revaluation, Criterion* XVI, lxiii (January 1937).

Squire, J. C., 'Shakespeare as a Dramatist: Remarkable New Essay,' *Sunday Times*, April 24, 1932.

Stonier, G. W., 'The Big Bad Wolf,' *New Statesman*, November 24, 1934 (and ensuing correspondence: H. Sydney Pickering, December 1; Geoffrey Grigson, and also Edith Sitwell and Stonier, December 8; Grigson, John Sparrow, the Editor, December 15; Sitwell again, December 22).

Strong, L. A. G., 'Criticism and Reviewing,' *Spectator*, August 20, 1932.

Turner, W. J., 'Education and Music,' *New Statesman*, December 3, 1932.

Waugh, Arthur, 'Fiction and Its Readers,' *Spectator*, April 16, 1932.

Williams, W. E., 'Notes and Comments,' *Highway* XXV (March 1933).

Williamson, Hugh Ross, 'Notes at Random,' *Bookman* LXXXI, 486 (March 1932); LXXXII, 488 (May 1932); LXXXIII, 495 (December 1932); LXXXIV, 499 (April 1933); LXXXVI, 511 (April 1934); LXXXVI, 514 (July 1934).

Walpole, Hugh, 'Some Books I Have Enjoyed in 1933,' *Bookman* LXXXV, 507 (December 1933).

Wolfe, Humbert, 'Three Critics,' *Observer*, May 8, 1932.

TLS, 'New Bearings,' April 21, 1932.

——, 'The Reader of Fiction,' April 28, 1932.

——, 'Culture and Environment,' March 16, 1933.

——, rev. *How to Teach Reading*, March 23, 1933.

——, rev. *For Continuity*, May 3, 1934.

——, 'Critical Essays,' August 16, 1934.

——, 'The Norm of English Poetry: Intelligence and Sincerity in Unity,' October 17, 1936.

——, 'Ben Jonson: Poet (The Social Background of the Plays),' June 5, 1937.

——, 'How Russia Killed Marxism,' August 10, 1940.

——, rev. *The Impulse to Dominate*, December 27, 1941.

—— (editorial), 'Readers and Citizens,' January 15, 1944.

——, 'Review of Reviews,' January 8, 1949.

——, 'Intelligence and Imagination,' February 12, 1949.

——, 'Three Political Philosophers,' December 29, 1950.

——, 'Pursuit of True Judgment,' February 29, 1952.

——, notices of *Scrutiny*: June 16, 1932; September 22, 1932; January 12,

1933; April 27, 1933; June 29, 1933; September 28, 1933; February 1, 1934; March 22, 1934; August 9, 1934; November 8, 1934; June 27, 1935; February 8, 1936; September 12, 1936; January 16, 1937; March 20, 1937; August 7, 1937; September 18, 1937; December 25, 1937.

(ii) Closure

Anon., 'The Younger Critics,' TLS, August 29, 1952.

——, 'Scrutiny 1932–1953,' *Poetry* (Chicago) 84, 1 (April 1954).

Daiches, David, 'Two Decades of Hard Knocks and High Standards; End of "Scrutiny" the Immitigable,' *Guardian*, December 9, 1953 (correspondence: F. R. Leavis, December 15; Paul Reed, December 16; Daiches, December 18; F. R. Leavis, December 23; P. Mansell Jones, December 24).

James, C. L. R., 'Britain's New Monthlies,' *Saturday Review*, May 22, 1954.

Jameson, Storm, 'Scrutiny,' *Time and Tide* XXXV, 5 (January 30, 1954).

Lerner, L. D., 'The Life and Death of *Scrutiny*,' *London Magazine* II, 1 (January 1955).

Nury, Daniel, 'Scrutiny: A Quarterly Review 1932–53,' *Etudes anglaises*, année 9, no. 4 (oct.-déc. 1956).

Spender, Stephen, 'Comment: On Literary Movements,' *Encounter* I, 2 (November 1953).

Williams, Raymond, 'Editorial Commentary,' *Essays in Criticism* IV, 3 (October 1954).

(iii) The Reissue (1963)

Anon., 'Vindication: "Yes, But —",' TLS, November 1, 1963.

Bamborough, J. B., 'The Influence of F. R. Leavis,' *Spectator*, October 25, 1963.

Bateson, F. W., 'The Alternative to *Scrutiny*,' *Essays in Criticism* XIV, 1 (January 1964).

Bayley, John, 'Roundheads and Cavaliers,' *Sunday Times*, October 27, 1963.

Betsky, Seymour, 'Scrutiny Rescrutinized,' *Universities Quarterly* XVIII, 1 (December 1963).

Black, Michael, 'The Third Realm: An Expository Essay on "Scrutiny",' *The Use of English* XV, 4 (Summer 1964); and XVI, 1 (Autumn 1964).

Bradbury, Malcolm, 'Looking Back at "Scrutiny",' *Birmingham Post*, October 29, 1963.

Brower, Reuben A., 'Scrutiny: A Revolution from Within,' *Partisan Review* XXXXI, 2 (Spring 1964).

Cox, C. B., ' "Scrutiny": A Revaluation,' *Spectator*, October 25, 1963.

Daiches, David, 'How Many Children Had Lady Macbeth?' *New York Times Book Review*, November 10, 1963.

Dawson, S. W., '*Scrutiny* and the Idea of a University,' *Essays in Criticism* XIV, 1 (January 1964).

Gottlieb, Robert, 'Scrutiny Bound,' *New Republic*, December 7, 1963.

Heilpern, John, ed., *Dr F. R. Leavis: The Ogre of Downing Castle and Other Stories*, Oxford 1963.

Hough, Graham, 'We *Were* Cambridge,' *Listener*, November 7, 1963.

Jacobson, Dan, 'Scrutiny in Retrospect,' *New Statesman*, October 25, 1963 (see Kermode *infra*).

Janssens, G. A. M., 'The *Scrutiny* Reprint – An Interim Assessment,' *English Studies* XLV, 1 (February 1964).

Kermode, Frank, 'Some Reservations,' *New Statesman*, October 25, 1963 (see Jacobson *supra*).

Knight, G. Wilson, '*Scrutiny* and Criticism,' *Essays in Criticism* XIV, 1 (January 1964).

Quinton, Anthony, 'Demolition Squad At Work,' *Sunday Telegraph*, October 27, 1963.

Tomlinson, Charles, 'Scrutiny Ten Years After,' *Hudson Review* XVII, 2 (Summer 1964).

Trodd, Kenneth, 'Report From the Younger Generation,' *Essays in Criticism* XIV, 1 (January 1964).

Vaizey, John, '*Scrutiny* and Education,' *Essays in Criticism* XIV, 1 (January 1964).

Wain, John, 'Twenty-One Years with Dr Leavis,' *Observer*, October 27, 1963.

Weightman, J. G., 'The Passion of "Scrutiny",' *The Nation*, December 7, 1963.

Williams, Raymond, 'Scrutiny,' *Guardian*, October 25, 1963.

(iv) Other Writings on *Scrutiny* and its Contributors

Bamborough, Renford, 'Literature and Philosophy,' in idem (ed.), *Wisdom: Twelve Essays*, London 1974.

Bateson, F. W., 'Contributions to a Dictionary of Critical Terms: II. Dissociation of Sensibility,' *Essays in Criticism* I, 3 (July 1951).

——, 'Second Thoughts: II. L. C. Knights and Restoration Comedy,' *Essays in Criticism* VII, 1 (January 1957).

Bilan, R. P., 'The Basic Concepts and Criteria of F. R. Leavis's Novel Criticism,' *Novel* IX, 3 (Spring 1976).

Black, Michael, 'A Kind of Valediction: Leavis on Eliot, 1929–75,' *New Universities Quarterly* XXX, 1 (Winter 1975).

Bradbury, Malcolm, 'The Rise of the Provincials,' *Antioch Review* XVI, 4 (December 1956).

Brittain, Victoria, 'F. R. Leavis: Half a Century of Arousing Academic Enmity,' *Times*, February 17, 1975.

Buckley, Vincent, *Poetry and Morality*, London, 1959.

——, 'Leavis and His "Line",' *Melbourne Critical Review* 8 (1965).

Casey, John, *The Language of Criticism*, London 1966.

Collins, Richard, 'Revaluations,' *Screen Education* 22 (Spring 1977).

Coulson, Peter, 'The Attack on Leavis,' *Essays in Criticism* XIII, 1 (January 1963).

Cronin, Anthony, 'A Massacre of Authors,' *Encounter* VI, 4 (April 1956).

Davie, Donald, 'Second Thoughts: III. F. R. Leavis's "How to Teach Reading",' *Essays in Criticism* VII, 3 (July 1957).

Eagleton, Terry, *Criticism and Ideology*, London 1976.

Fraser, John, 'A Tribute to Dr F. R. Leavis,' *Western Review* XXXIII, 2 (Winter 1959).

——, 'Leavis, Winters, and "Tradition",' *Southern Review*, N.S., 7, 4 (Autumn 1971).

——, 'Leavis and Winters: A Question of Reputation,' *Western Humanities Review* XXVI, 1 (Winter 1972).

Gomme, Andor, 'Why Literary Criticism Matters in a Technologico-Benthamite Age,' *New Universities Quarterly* XXX, 1 (Winter 1975).

——, *Attitudes to Criticism*, Carbondale 1966.

Gransden, K. W., Letter to the Editor, *Encounter* XII, 6 (June 1959). (See Grigson *infra*).

Green, Martin, 'British Decency,' *Kenyon Review* XXI, 4 (Autumn 1959).

——, *Children of the Sun*, London 1977.

Greenberg, Martin, 'The Influence of Mr Leavis,' *Partisan Review* XVI, 8 (August 1949).

Gregor, Ian, 'The Criticism of F. R. Leavis,' *Dublin Review* 226, 457 (1952).

Grigson, Geoffrey, 'Leavis Against Eliot,' *Encounter* XII, 4 (April 1959).

Hayman, Ronald, *Leavis*, London 1976.

Heyl, Bernard, 'The Absolutism of F. R. Leavis,' *Journal of Aesthetics and Art Criticism* XIII, 2 (December 1954).

Holbrook, David, 'F. R. Leavis and "Creativity",' *New Universities Quarterly* XXX, 1 (Winter 1975).

Holloway, John, 'The New "Establishment" in Criticism,' in idem, *The Charted Mirror*, London 1960.

Inglis, Fred, 'Attention to Education: Leavis and the Leavisites,' *New Universities Quarterly* XXX, 1 (Winter 1975).

Jarrett-Kerr, Martin, 'The Literary Criticism of F. R. Leavis,' *Essays in Criticism* II, 4 (October 1952).

Jones, Alun, 'F. R. Leavis and After,' *Critical Quarterly* I, 3 (Autumn 1959).

Kaufman, R. J., 'F. R. Leavis: The Morality of Mind,' *Critical Quarterly* I, 3 (Autumn 1959).

McCormick, John, 'London Letter: Some New Figures,' *Poetry* (Chicago), 83, 5 (February 1954).

McLuhan, H. M., 'Poetic vs. Rhetorical Exegesis: The Case for Leavis against Richards and Empson,' *Sewanee Review* LII, (April 1944).

Mayo, Robert D., *The English Novel in the Magazines 1740–1815*, Evanston 1962.

Moody, A. D., 'Retreating from Literature: Scholarism and Ideology,' *Melbourne Critical Review* 6 (1963).

Ricks, Christopher, ' "Fiction and the Reading Public",' *Listener*, June 2, 1966.

Rillie, John A. M., 'Orange or Grid: A New Model for Critics,' *Twentieth Century* CLXV, 985 (March 1959).

Robson, W. W., 'Literary Studies,' *Universities Quarterly* X, 2 (February 1956).

——, 'Mr Leavis on Literary Studies,' *Universities Quarterly* XI, 2 (February 1957).

Singh, G. S., 'Better History and Better Criticism: the Significance of F. R. Leavis,' *English Miscellany* 16 (1965).

Stein, Walter, 'Christianity and the Common Pursuit,' *The Northern Miscellany of Literary Criticism* 1 (Autumn 1953).

342

Steiner, George, 'F. R. Leavis,' *Encounter* XVIII, 5 (May 1962).

Tanner, Michael, 'Literature and Philosophy,' *New Universities Quarterly* XXX, 1 (Winter 1975).

Trilling, Lionel, 'Dr Leavis and the Moral Tradition,' in idem, *A Gathering of Fugitives*, London 1957.

Trodd, Kenneth, ' "Scrutiny" in the Thirties,' *The Review* 11–12 (1964).

Walsh, William, *A Human Idiom: Literature and Humanity*, London 1964.

Wandor, Micheline, 'F. R. Leavis and "The Living Principle",' *Marxism Today* 21, 1 (January 1977).

Watson, Garry, *The Leavises, the 'Social', and the Left*, Swansea 1977.

Williams, Raymond, 'Our Debt to Dr Leavis,' *Critical Quarterly* I, 3 (Autumn 1959).

Wright, Iain, 'On the Social Responsibility of Literature,' *Times Higher Educational Supplement*, November 12, 1976.

2. *Historical and General*

Addison, Paul, *The Road to 1945*, London 1975.

Adorno, Theodor, W., *Prisms*, London 1967.

Alvarez, A., *Beyond all This Fiddle*, New York 1969.

Anderson, Perry, 'Components of the National Culture,' *New Left Review* 50 (May-June 1968).

Annan, Noel Gilroy, *Leslie Stephen: His Thought and Character in Relation to His Time*, London 1951.

——, 'The Intellectual Aristocracy,' in J. H. Plumb (ed.), *Studies in Social History*, London 1955.

Ayer, A. J., *et al.*, *The Revolution in Philosophy*, London 1956.

Bateson, F. W., 'Organs of Critical Opinion: I., *The Review of English Studies*,' *Essays in Criticism* VI, 2 (April 1956).

——, 'Organs of Critical Opinion: IV. *The Times Literary Supplement*,' *Essays in Criticism* VII, 4 (October 1957).

Bradbury, Malcolm, *The Social Context of Modern English Literature*, Oxford 1971.

Braithwaite, R. B., 'Philosophy,' in Harold Wright (ed.), *University Studies: Cambridge 1933*.

Bronowski, Jacob, 'Recollections of Humphrey Jennings,' *Twentieth Century* CLXV, 983 (January 1959).

Brower, Reuben, Helen Vendler and John Hollander (ed.), *I. A. Richards: Essays in His Honor*, New York 1973.

Connolly, Cyril, *Enemies of Promise*, London 1938.

Cox, C. B., and A. E. Dyson (ed.), *The Twentieth-Century Mind*, 3 volumes, Oxford 1972.

Dangerfield, George, *The Strange Death of Liberal England*, London 1936.

Day Lewis, Cecil, *The Buried Day*, London 1948.

Dodsworth, Martin, 'Empson at Cambridge,' *The Review* 6–7 (June 1963).

Eliot, T. S., 'The Idea of a Literary Review,' *(New) Criterion* IV, i (January 1926).

——, *The Sacred Wood*, London 1920.

Febvre, Lucien, 'History and Psychology' and 'Sensibility and History', in Peter Burke (ed.), *A New Kind of History: From the Writings of Febvre*, London 1973.

Gill, Roma (ed.), *William Empson: The Man and His Work*, London 1974.

Grigson, Geoffrey, *The Crest on the Silver*, London 1950.

Gross, John, *The Rise and Fall of the Man of Letters*, London 1969.

Halsey, A. H., 'British Universities and Intellectual Life,' in idem, Jean Floud and C. Arnold Anderson (ed.), *Education, Economy and Society*, London 1965.

Hamilton, Ian, *The Little Magazines: A Study of Six Editors*, London 1976.

Heath, Frederick, 'The Disease of Criticism,' *English Review*, April 1932.

Hexter, J. D., 'The Education of the Aristocracy in the Renaissance,' in idem, *Reappraisals in History*, London 1961.

Hobsbawm, Eric, *Industry and Empire*, London 1969.

Homberger, Eric, William Janeway and Simon Schama (ed.), *The Cambridge Mind: Ninety Years of 'The Cambridge Review' 1879–1969*, London 1970.

Hughes, H. Stuart, *Consciousness and Society: The Reorientation of European Social Thought 1890–1930*, London 1959.

Jameson, Storm, 'The Dangers of Fiction,' *Highway* XXV (November 1932).

Kearney, Hugh, *Scholars and Gentlemen: Universities and Society in Pre-industrial Britain 1500–1700*, London 1970.

Kermode, Frank, *Romantic Image*, London 1957.

Liddell Hart, Basil, 'The Second World War,' in C. L. Mowat (ed.), *The Shifting Balance of World Forces 1898–1945*, New Cambridge Modern History, vol. XII (second, revised ed.), Cambridge 1968.

Lovell, Alan, and Jim Hillier, *Studies in Documentary*, London 1972.

Lucas, F. L., 'English Literature,' in Harold Wright (ed.), *University Studies: Cambridge 1933*.

Lynd, Robert S., and Helen Merrell Lynd, *Middletown: A Study in American Culture*, New York 1929.

Mackerness, E. D., 'George Sturt and the English Humanitarian Tradition,' *Essays and Studies 1969*, XXII N.S.

Mirsky, Dmitri, S., *The Intelligentsia of Great Britain*, London 1935.

Morris, Margaret, *The General Strike*, London 1976.

Mowat, Charles Loch, *Britain Between the Wars 1918–1940*, London 1969.

Orwell, George, *Collected Essays, Journalism and Letters*, 4 volumes, London 1970.

Pollard, Sidney, *The Development of the British Economy 1914–1967*, London 1969.

Potter, Stephen, *The Muse in Chains*, London 1937.

Putt, S. Gorley, 'Technique and Culture: Three Cambridge Portraits,' *Essays and Studies 1961*, XIV N.S.

Quiller-Couch, A. T., *Memories and Opinions: An Unfinished Autobiography*, Cambridge 1944.

Read, Herbert, *Julien Benda and the New Humanism*, Seattle 1930.

Richards, I. A., *Principles of Literary Criticism*, London 1924.

——, *Science and Poetry*, Psyche Miniatures 1, London 1926.

——, *Practical Criticism*, London 1929.

Richter, Melvin, *The Politics of Conscience: T. H. Green and His Age*, London 1964.

Roberts, R. Ellis, 'An Open Letter to Frank Swinnerton,' *New Statesman*, March 26, 1932.

Santayana, George, *Soliloquies in England and Later Soliloquies*, London 1922.

Spender, Stephen, *World within World*, London 1951.

Stern, Fritz, *The Politics of Cultural Despair: A Study in the Rise of the Germanic Ideology*, Berkeley and Los Angeles 1961.

Sturt/'Bourne', George, *Change in the Village* [1912], introd. Geoffrey Grigson, London 1955.

——, *The Journals of George Sturt 1890–1927*, 2 volumes, E. D. Mackerness (ed.), Cambridge 1967.

Taylor, A. J. P., *The Origins of the Second World War*, London 1961.

——, *English History 1914–1945*, Oxford 1965.

Therborn, Göran, *Science, Class and Society*, NLB 1976.

Thomson, Robert, *The Pelican History of Psychology*, London 1968.

Tillyard, E. M. W., *The Muse Unchained: An Intimate Account of the Revolution in English Studies at Cambridge*, London 1958.

Trotsky, Leon, *Literature and Revolution*, Michigan 1960.

Warmington, Eric, 'Society and Education in Cambridge 1902–22,' *New Universities Quarterly* XXX, 1 (Winter 1975).

Watson, George, *Politics and Literature in Modern Britain*, London 1977.

West, Alick, 'Mirsky's One-Sided Picture,' *Left Review* I, 9 (May 1935).

Willey, Basil, *Cambridge and Other Memories 1920–53*, London 1968.

Williams, Raymond, *Culture and Society 1780–1950*, London 1958.

——, *The Long Revolution*, London 1961.

——, *The Country and the City*, London 1973.

——, *Keywords: A Vocabulary of Culture and Society*, London 1976.

Woodhouse, Michael, and Brian Pearce, *Essays on the History of Communism in Britain*, London 1975.

Young, Alan, and Michael Schmidt, 'A Conversation with Edgell Rickword,' *Poetry Nation* 1 (1973).

3. Periodicals Surveyed

Arena; Calendar of Modern Letters; Cambridge Journal; Colosseum; Criterion; The Critic; English in Schools; Humanitas; Left Review; New Writing; Folios of New Writing; New Statesman; Life and Letters; Politics and Letters; Times Literary Supplement.

Index

348